Removing Tax Barriers to China's Belt and Road Initiative

Removing Tax Barriers to China's Belt and Road Initiative

Edited by

Michael Lang

Jeffrey Owens

Published by:
Kluwer Law International B.V.
PO Box 316
2400 AH Alphen aan den Rijn
The Netherlands
E-mail: international-sales@wolterskluwer.com
Website: lrus.wolterskluwer.com

Sold and distributed in North, Central and South America by:
Wolters Kluwer Legal & Regulatory U.S.
7201 McKinney Circle
Frederick, MD 21704
United States of America
Email: customer.service@wolterskluwer.com

Sold and distributed in all other countries by:
Air Business Subscriptions
Rockwood House
Haywards Heath
West Sussex
RH16 3DH
United Kingdom
Email: international-customerservice@wolterskluwer.com

Printed on acid-free paper.

ISBN 978-94-035-0120-8

e-Book: ISBN 978-94-035-0121-5
web-PDF: ISBN 978-94-035-0122-2

© 2019 Michael Lang & Jeffrey Owens

All rights reserved. No part of this publication may be reproduced, stored in a retrieval system, or transmitted in any form or by any means, electronic, mechanical, photocopying, recording, or otherwise, without written permission from the publisher.

Permission to use this content must be obtained from the copyright owner. More information can be found at: lrus.wolterskluwer.com/policies/permissions-reprints-and-licensing

Printed in the United Kingdom.

Editors

Prof. Dr DDr. h.c. Michael Lang is Vice Rector Human Resources of WU, Head of the Institute for Austrian and International Tax Law of WU (Vienna University of Economics and Business) and Academic Director of both the LLM Programme in International Tax Law and the doctoral programme in international business taxation (DIBT) of this university. He is President of the Austrian Branch of the International Fiscal Association (IFA).

Prof. Dr Jeffrey Owens completed his doctoral work at Cambridge University in the United Kingdom in 1973. In addition to his economic degrees, he is a qualified accountant. He continued an academic career (visiting professor at the American University of Paris, Bocconi University, Italy and Queen Mary's College, London) with his career as an international civil servant. He has focused his attention on questions of tax policy and tax administration, with particular emphasis on international taxation and related domestic issues. He established a major taxation programme at the OECD and extensively developed OECD contacts with non-member countries. His earlier work dealt with the development of international currency markets and the implications for monetary policies. He has made numerous contributions to professional journals, has published a number of books and has been the author of many OECD publications on taxation. His position at the OECD and his frequent participation at international conferences have provided him with a unique international perspective on tax policy.

Contributors

Prof. Dr Mingxing Cao (Bristar) holds a PhD in Tax Law from the Peking University Law School, China, as well as both lawyer and accountant qualifications and licenses. He is currently the director of the China International Tax Center and the deputy dean of the China Center for Fiscal Development at the Central University of Finance and Economics, China. Bristar has been nominated as the Secretary General of the Chinese branch of the International Fiscal Association and is organizing the first pilot master's and doctorate international tax programme in China. Bristar's areas of expertise include economics law, tax policy and law, and international tax law. He authored the book *A Dialectic Analysis of the Evolution of the Modern Tax Law: A Counter-Polar Analysis of the United States and China* and launched the serial book project on Chinese International Tax Innovation at the China Tax Publishing House. He is the chief editor of both the *OBOR International Taxation Monitor* (published by the China Financial Publishing House) and the *China International Tax Review* (published by China Law Press).

Prof. Dr Xiaojing Cui is Professor of Law and Doctoral Supervisor at Wuhan University, China, and serves as the vice president of the Fiscal and Tax Law Research Association of the Hubei Law Society. She has been a Fulbright senior visiting scholar at Georgetown University in the United States, a visiting scholar at Paris I University (Panthéon Sorbonne) and a post-doctoral fellow at University of Paris XI, France. Professor Cui is mainly engaged in the research of basic theory and frontier issues of international taxation law. She has managed and completed the National Social Science Fund Major Project and Youth Project, Humanities and Social Sciences Youth Project and Major Project of the Ministry of Education, as well as further projects entrusted by the Ministry of Finance and the State Administration of Taxation. She has published more than thirty academic articles in Chinese and English in authoritative and high-profile journals, such as the *Chinese Journal of Law*, *China Legal Science*, *Peking University Law Journal*, *ZUEL Law Journal*, *Modern Law Science*, *Law Review and Law Science*. Several of these contributions have been republished in journals including *Xinhua Digest*, *Chinese Social Science Digest* and *Duplicated Materials of People's*

University. A number of her monographs have also appeared in works issued by an authoritative publishing house.

Prof. Dr Yang He is the vice dean of Beijing School of Public Finance and Taxation at the University of Finance and Economics, China. She received her doctoral degree in Economics in 2010 and was a visiting scholar at the School of Public and Environmental Affairs (Indiana University, United States) from 2007 to 2009. Her research interests include international taxation and local public finance.

Master Lai Hongyu holds a Bachelor's degree in Economics. She is a graduate of the School of Public Finance and Taxation at Beijing Central University of Finance and Economics and is in a master's-doctorate combined programme at the School of Data Science of Fudan University, China. Her research focuses on the statistics of international taxation and econometrics.

Dr Jasmin Kollmann holds a Master's degree in Laws from the University of Vienna. She completed her PhD in the field of tax law at the Institute for Austrian and International Tax Law, WU (Vienna University of Economics and Business). Currently, she works as a senior consultant at EY in Munich.

Jie Lei is a PhD student of World Economics, Institute of Finance and Economics Research, Central University of Finance and Economics, Beijing, China.

Liu Qichao, MPA, holds a Master's degree in Public Administration from Beijing Normal University, China. He works as an associate researcher at the China International Tax Center, focusing on customs law and international tax law.

Dr Alicja Majdanska completed her PhD in Tax Law at the Institute for Austrian and International Tax Law, WU (Vienna University of Economics and Business). She is a Polish tax advisor and worked for a few years in Polish tax law firms where she advised in Polish and international tax cases. Currently, she works as a tax manager in a multinational enterprise.

Sathi Meyer-Nandi, LLM, was a guest researcher at the Institute for Austrian and International Tax Law, WU (Vienna University of Economics and Business), currently working for GIZ, the German Development Agency for International Cooperation. Before joining the Institute, she worked in practice, first as legal counsel at a bank and then as an international tax advisor at one of the Big Four in Zurich. She also advised the Swiss Development Agency on diverse issues such as tax treaty policy with developing countries, BEPS and AEOI.

David Orzechowski, LLM, BSc (WU), was a research and teaching assistant at the Institute for Austrian and International Tax Law, WU (Vienna University of Economics and Business). He is currently a PhD candidate and lecturer at the same institute.

Contributors

Prof. Dr Jeffrey Owens completed his doctoral work at Cambridge University in the United Kingdom in 1973. In addition to his economic degrees, he is a qualified accountant. He continued an academic career (visiting professor at the American University of Paris, Bocconi University, Italy and Queen Mary's College, London) with his career as an international civil servant. He has focused his attention on questions of tax policy and tax administration, with particular emphasis on international taxation and related domestic issues. He established a major taxation programme at the OECD and extensively developed OECD contacts with non-member countries. His earlier work dealt with the development of international currency markets and the implications for monetary policies. He has made numerous contributions to professional journals, has published a number of books and has been the author of many OECD publications on taxation. His position at the OECD and his frequent participation at international conferences have provided him with a unique international perspective on tax policy.

Jonathan Leigh Pemberton is the Project Director of Cooperative Compliance at the WU (Vienna University of Economics and Business) Global Tax Policy Center. In addition to this role, he is an independent advisor, drawing on a strong background in tax administration and policy development, as well as considerable experience working in an international environment. As a member of the UK senior civil service for fourteen years, he demonstrated an ability to identify and implement major improvements to the tax system, employing a mix of policy changes and operational improvements. At the OECD, he built on this experience, working in an international context for the benefit of both more advanced tax administrations and developing countries that participate in the OECD's global relations programme. He is an international fellow of the Tax Administration Research Centre (TARC) at Exeter University, United Kingdom.

Xue Peng, LLM is a research and teaching assistant and PhD candidate in the field of transfer pricing at the Institute for Austrian and International Tax Law, WU (Vienna University of Economics and Business).

Dr Raffaele Petruzzi, LLM, is the managing director of the WU Transfer Pricing Center at the Institute for Austrian and International Tax Law at WU (Vienna University of Economics and Business) and an international tax advisor specializing in international corporate taxation and transfer pricing at L&P – Ludovici Piccone & Partners, Milan, Italy, as well as providing transfer pricing advisory at L&P Global, Vienna, Austria. Since 2007, Raffaele has gained extensive experience in dealing with topics related to international corporate taxation and transfer pricing from both a practical perspective (by working in different countries within international advisory firms and in the tax department of a multinational) and an academic perspective.

Mag. Norbert Roller is an independent consultant for international tax law, his clients are both international organizations as well as law firms. Before he worked for the Austrian Ministry of Finance from 2009 to 2016. He was responsible for the supervision of mutual agreement procedures and tax rulings. He was also part of OECD Working

Groups 6 (Transfer Pricing) and 11 (Aggressive Tax Planning), as well as of the EU Joint Transfer Pricing Forum. He is also a lecturer at the University of Applied Sciences Vienna (FH Campus Wien) and has lectured at OECD seminars.

Mirna Solange Screpante, LLM, graduated in Accounting from Universidad de Buenos Aires, holds a Master's in Tax Law from Universidad Austral, Argentina and holds an LLM in Corporate and International Taxation from Universität zu Köln, Germany. She served as a Teaching Assistant at Universidad de Buenos Aires and Universidad Austral. She has been Visiting Scholar at Max Planck Institute and IBFD. Currently, she is Research and Lecturer Fellow at the Institute for Austrian and International Tax Law, WU Vienna and Visiting Professor at Universidad Austral in the Master in Tax Law. She is member of the Argentine Association of Fiscal Studies (AAEF). She has participated in conferences in Argentina and abroad and is the author of several articles published in Argentina and in international journals in English, German and Spanish.

Yuliya Shved, LLM, holds a Master of Laws (LLM) in Business Law from the Belarusian State University and a Master of Laws (LLM) in Advanced Studies in International Tax Law from ITC Leiden, Leiden University (the Netherlands). While working in the corporation, she managed various investment projects. Since 2010 she also delivers lectures in the Belarusian State University in the area of tax (financial) law. Currently, she offers her services to companies from Europe, China, Russia and UAE on matters concerning investments and international transactions.

Dr Karoline Spies is a post-doctoral research and teaching assistant at the Institute for Austrian and International Tax Law, WU (Vienna University of Economics and Business).

Dr Romero J.S. Tavares is a researcher and lecturer at the Global Tax Policy Center and Transfer Pricing Center of the Institute for Austrian and International Tax Law, WU (Vienna University of Economics and Business), where he earned his PhD/DIBT with honours in 2018. He is an International Tax Partner with PwC focused on Global Structuring and Value Chain Transformation, with a career spanning twenty-five years in the US, Europe and Brazil. The author can be contacted at romero.tavares@wu.ac.at.

Yaqiong Tian is a PhD student of world economics, Institute of Finance and Economics Research, Central University of Finance and Economics.

Prof. Dr Tong Wei is a professor at the Institute for Finance and Economics of Beijing Central University of Finance and Economics, as well as a professor at Beijing Research Base for Finance and Economics. She is also the director of the Research Center of Russia, Eastern Europe and Central Asia. Tong Wei is an evaluation expert for the China Development Bank and an evaluation expert on budget performance at the Ministry of Finance as well as several international financial organizations. She is on the list of 'New Century Excellent Talents' of the Ministry of Education. She was a visiting scholar at Financial University under the government of the Russian Federation and Kyiv National Economic University. Her research fields cover public finance, government budgets, financial investment and financing, expenditure performance evaluation, and finance and economics of Russia, Eastern Europe and Central Asia. Tong Wei is the author of more than twenty academic monographs, including 'China's Local Budget Reform', 'Government Budget System of Russia', 'Legal Framework and Budget System of Russia', 'Comparative Research on Sino-Russian Budget Reform'. She has published more than sixty articles on domestic and overseas economic core topics in periodicals, including *Reform*, *Finance and Economics*, *Taxation Research*, *Public Finance Research*, *Russian, Eastern Europe and Central Asian Studies* and *Finance* (Финансы). Many of her papers were fully reprinted in 'Copied Newspapers and Periodicals of Renmin University'. Tong Wei has overseen over more than thirty projects at home and abroad.

Vladimir Tyutyuryukov, PhD, obtained his doctoral degree in Economic Policy and Administration at Masaryk University, Czech Republic, for his thesis *Tax Systems in the EAEU Region: Tax Harmonisation, Tax Competition?* Currently he is an Associate Professor at National Research University Higher School of Economics, Moscow, Russia. His experience includes tax accounting, tax consulting, international tax planning, audit of tax accounting, tax policy research and advice to governmental bodies and NGOs in Russia and in Kazakhstan, and teaching tax and accounting courses at university.

Prof. Dr Wang Wenjing holds a Doctoral degree in Economics. She is the head of the Department of International Taxation at the School of Public Finance and Taxation at Beijing Central University of Finance and Economics. Her research focuses on international taxation matters related to Belt & Road issues.

Ying Shaokai holds a Bachelor's degree in Economics. He is a graduate of School of Public Finance and Taxation at Central University of Finance and Economics, Beijing, China. His researches focus on the international taxation.

Summary of Contents

Editors	v
Contributors	vii
Preface	xxv

CHAPTER 1
The Belt and Road Initiative: Will Tax Be a Facilitator or a Barrier?
Jeffrey Owens   3

CHAPTER 2
Neo-BEPS: China's Proposal for International Tax Reform from the Perspective of the Belt and Road Initiative
Cao Mingxing (Bristar)   35

CHAPTER 3
Research on the International Taxation Issues under the Belt and Road Initiative: Comparison of Corporate Income Tax Laws and Tax Treaties
Wenjing Wang   39

CHAPTER 4
Comparison of Tax Issues in the Main Belt and Road Countries and Industries of Chinese Outbound Foreign Direct Investment
Yang He & Ying Shaokai   49

CHAPTER 5
Preferential Treatment under Chinese Tax Treaties with Belt and Road Countries and Disputes Regarding Their Application
Cui Xiaojing   55

Summary of Contents

CHAPTER 6
Going-Global Enterprises: Tax Planning for Cross-Border Earnings in Belt and Road Countries
Cao Mingxing & Liu Qichao — 83

CHAPTER 7
International Tax Coordination under the Belt and Road Initiative
Wenjing Wang & Hongyu Lai — 105

CHAPTER 8
Analysis of Financial and Tax Operations in Five Central Asian Countries
Wei Tong, Jie Lei & Yaqiong Tian — 115

CHAPTER 9
The Role of Border Crossing Procedures in the Transportation of Goods along the New Silk Road: The Impact of Technical and Administrative Requirements
Jasmin Kollmann — 137

CHAPTER 10
Transfer Pricing Issues Related to the One-Belt-One-Road Project
Raffaele Petruzzi, Mirna Solange Screpante, Claire (Xue) Peng, Norbert Roller & Vladimir Tyutyuryukov — 169

CHAPTER 11
Tax Treaties Between Belt and Road Countries
Sathi Meyer-Nandi, David Orzechowski & Vladimir Tyutyuryukov — 197

CHAPTER 12
VAT Challenges in the Belt and Road Initiative
Yuliya Shved & Karoline Spies — 259

CHAPTER 13
Asia: Global Tax Policy Post-BEPS and the Perils of the Silk Road
Romero J.S. Tavares & Jeffrey Owens — 285

CHAPTER 14
Creating a Positive Tax Climate for Complex Multijurisdictional Investment Projects
Jonathan Leigh Pemberton & Alicja Majdanska — 307

Index — 319

Table of Contents

Editors	v
Contributors	vii
Preface	xxv

CHAPTER 1
The Belt and Road Initiative: Will Tax Be a Facilitator or a Barrier?
Jeffrey Owens   3

1	Introduction	3
2	The Belt and Road: The Tax Dimension	4
3	Tax Levels, Structures and Tax Administrations Diverge	5
4	The Role of Tax Certainty in Promoting FDI along the BRI	5
5	Multilateral Cooperative Compliance: Relevance for BRI	7
6	Potential Tax Barriers and Suggested Approaches	8
7	Conclusion	18
Appendix I: A Multilateral Tax Treaty for the Belt and Road Initiative (BRI)		19

CHAPTER 2
Neo-BEPS: China's Proposal for International Tax Reform from the Perspective of the Belt and Road Initiative
Cao Mingxing (Bristar)   35

1	Introduction	35
2	BEPS: Financial and Fiscal Crisis, Predicament of Globalization and the Advancement and Limitations of the Policy Response of International Taxation	36
3	Neo-BEPS: The Belt and Road Initiative, Neo-Globalization, Policy Response of International Taxation, China's Version 2.0 and Its Forecasting	37

Table of Contents

CHAPTER 3
Research on the International Taxation Issues under the Belt and Road
Initiative: Comparison of Corporate Income Tax Laws and Tax Treaties
Wenjing Wang 39

1	Introduction		40
2	Basic Situations of Countries along the Belt and Road		40
3	Comparison of Corporate Income Tax Laws of Countries along the Belt and Road		42
	3.1	Nominal Corporate Income Tax Rates	42
	3.2	Anti-Avoidance Provisions in Corporate Income Tax Laws	43
4	Comparison of Chinese Bilateral Tax Treaties with Countries along the Belt and Road		44
	4.1	Permanent Establishments	44
	4.2	Limited Tax Rates for Passive Income	45
		4.2.1 Limited Tax Rates for Dividends	45
		4.2.2 Limited Tax Rates for Interest	45
		4.2.3 Limited Tax Rates for Royalties	45
	4.3	Tax Sparing Provisions	46
5	International Tax Challenges under the Belt and Road Initiative		46
	5.1	Conflicts under the Three Legal Systems	46
	5.2	Different Coordination Objectives under the Silk Road Economic Belt and the 21st Century Maritime Silk Road	47
	5.3	Cooperation under the BEPS Initiative	47

CHAPTER 4
Comparison of Tax Issues in the Main Belt and Road Countries and
Industries of Chinese Outbound Foreign Direct Investment
Yang He & Ying Shaokai 49

1	Introduction	49
2	Economic Development and Industry Structure in the Main Belt and Road Countries	50
3	Tax Policies in the Main Belt and Road Countries	51
4	Conclusion	53
References		53

CHAPTER 5
Preferential Treatment under Chinese Tax Treaties with Belt and Road
Countries and Disputes Regarding Their Application
Cui Xiaojing 55

1	Introduction		56
2	Preferential Treatment under Tax Treaties		56
	2.1	Interest Article in Tax Treaties	58

	2.2	Dividends Article in Tax Treaties	59
	2.3	Royalties Article in Tax Treaties	61
3	Impact of the OECD/G20 BEPS Project on the Application of Preferential Treatment under Tax Treaties		62
	3.1	Provisions on Treaty Shopping under BEPS Action 6	63
	3.2	The Connotation and Application Requirements of the LOB Rules	64
	3.3	Connotation and Application Requirements of the PPT Rules	65
	3.4	Suggestions for Balancing Compliance with the BEPS Project and Access to Treaty Benefits	66
4	Empirical Analysis of the Preferential Tax Treaties Used by Chinese Going-Global Enterprises		69
	4.1	Case of Chinese Unicom Red Chip Company: Dividend Discount	69
		4.1.1 Facts of the Case	69
		4.1.2 Analysis of the Legal Issues	70
	4.2	Case of Huaxin Cement Limited Company	71
		4.2.1 Facts of the Case	71
		4.2.2 Analysis of the Legal Problems Involved	72
	4.3	Case of Jerry Petroleum Company	74
		4.3.1 Facts of the Case	74
		4.3.2 Analysis of the Legal Issues Involved	75
5	Solution to Address Disputes Regarding Tax Treaties Benefits		75
	5.1	Local Relief in the Host Country as the Main Solution	76
	5.2	Diplomatic Protection as Auxiliary Solution	76
	5.3	MAP Between Contracting Countries	77
6	Conclusion		80

CHAPTER 6
Going-Global Enterprises: Tax Planning for Cross-Border Earnings in Belt and Road Countries
Cao Mingxing & Liu Qichao   83

1	Introduction		84
2	The New Opportunity for Chinese Going-Global Enterprises to Invest Abroad Against the Background of the Belt and Road Initiative		84
	2.1	General Performance of Chinese Going-Global Investment	84
	2.2	Major Investment Destinations and Industrial Models of Going-Global Enterprises along the Belt and Road	85
3	Comparison of the Tax Rates in Key Destinations for Investment by Going-Global Enterprises along the Belt and Road		88
	3.1	Comparison of Corporate Income Tax Rates	88
	3.2	Comparison of Tax Rates in Chinese Tax Treaties with Key Investment Destinations	89

Table of Contents

4		Three Tax Planning Approaches for Going Global Enterprises Regarding Cross-Border Earnings Against the Background of the Belt and Road Initiative		90
	4.1	The Legal Issues of International Tax Planning for Cross-Border Income		90
	4.2	Three Tax Planning Approaches for Going Global Enterprises in Terms of Cross-Border Earnings		92
		4.2.1	Active Income from Foreign Operations: General Contracting and Sub-Contracting of Construction Projects	93
		4.2.2	Passive Income from Foreign Investment in High-, Medium- and Low-Tax Jurisdictions	95
		4.2.3	Passive Income from Foreign Investment: Intangible Assets	98
			4.2.3.1 Software Sales and Licensing	99
			4.2.3.2 Setting up Foreign Subsidiaries for Intangible Assets	101
5	Conclusion			102

CHAPTER 7
International Tax Coordination under the Belt and Road Initiative
Wenjing Wang & Hongyu Lai 105

1	Introduction		106
2	Basic Economic Circumstances of Countries along the Belt and Road		106
	2.1	Population Density	107
	2.2	Economy Level	108
	2.3	International Trade and Investment	109
	2.4	Comparison of Economic Factors along the Belt and the Road	109
3	Chinese Bilateral Tax Treaties with Countries along the Belt and Road		110
4	International Tax Proposals to Boost Implementation of the Belt and Road Initiative		111
	4.1	International Tax Rules Should Be Top-Level Designed under the Belt and Road Initiative	111
	4.2	The Tax Treaty Network Should Be Improved on a Timely Basis	111
	4.3	Tax Policies for Outward-Oriented Economic Development Should Be Implemented in China	112
	4.4	A Tax Coordination Mechanism for the Cross-Border Economic Cooperation Zone Should Be Explored	113

Table of Contents

CHAPTER 8
Analysis of Financial and Tax Operations in Five Central Asian Countries
Wei Tong, Jie Lei & Yaqiong Tian 115

1	The Reform of Public Finance Systems and Policy Changes of the Five Central Asian Countries		116
	1.1	Kazakhstan	116
	1.2	Uzbekistan	117
	1.3	Kyrgyzstan	117
	1.4	Tajikistan	118
	1.5	Turkmenistan	119
2	Financial State of the Five Central Asian Countries		119
	2.1	Kazakhstan	120
	2.2	Uzbekistan	121
	2.3	Kyrgyzstan	124
	2.4	Tajikistan	126
	2.5	Turkmenistan	129
3	Fiscal Comparison Between the Five Central Asian Countries and Major Economies of the World		131
	3.1	The Size of Fiscal Revenue and Expenditure	131
	3.2	The Proportion of Fiscal Revenue and Expenditure in GDP	132
	3.3	Comparison of Per Capita Fiscal Revenue and Expenditure	134
References			135

CHAPTER 9
The Role of Border Crossing Procedures in the Transportation of Goods along the New Silk Road: The Impact of Technical and Administrative Requirements
Jasmin Kollmann 137

1	Introduction		138
2	One Belt One Road Initiative: Transport Aspects		139
	2.1	The Silk Road Economic Belt: The Initiative	139
	2.2	Transport by Road	140
3	International Organizations Promoting Road Transport along the Silk Road		142
	3.1	International Road Transport Union	143
	3.2	The UN Economic and Social Commission for Asia and the Pacific	146
	3.3	The UN Economic Commission for Europe	148
	3.4	Central Asia Regional Economic Cooperation Programme	151
4	Cross-Border Trade and Customs Issues along the Silk Road		152
	4.1	Trade Facilitation Agreements	153
		4.1.1 Shanghai Cooperation Organization Agreement on Facilitation of International Road Transport	153

		4.1.2	Basic Multilateral Agreement on International Transport for the Development of the Transport Corridor Europe-Caucasus-Asia	154
	4.2	Customs Agreements		155
		4.2.1	TIR Convention	155
		4.2.2	Economic Cooperation Organization Transit Transport Framework Agreement	157
		4.2.3	Eurasian Economic Union	159
	4.3	Convention on the Contract for the International Carriage of Goods by Road		160
	4.4	Bilateral Agreements Facilitating International Trade and Customs along the Silk Road		161
5	Tackling Bottlenecks along the Silk Road			162
	5.1	Current Status of Border Crossings Efficiency		162
	5.2	Recommendations for Trade Facilitation		165
6	Conclusion			166

CHAPTER 10
Transfer Pricing Issues Related to the One-Belt-One-Road Project
Raffaele Petruzzi, Mirna Solange Screpante, Claire (Xue) Peng, Norbert Roller & Vladimir Tyutyuryukov   169

1	Introduction		169
2	Relevant Areas of Study		172
	2.1	Manufacturing Activities	172
	2.2	Services and Financial Transactions	175
	2.3	Intangible Property	178
	2.4	Cost Contribution Arrangements	180
	2.5	Documentation	184
	2.6	Advance Pricing Arrangements	187
3	Conclusion and Proposals		191

CHAPTER 11
Tax Treaties Between Belt and Road Countries
Sathi Meyer-Nandi, David Orzechowski & Vladimir Tyutyuryukov   197

1	Introduction		199
2	Residency: Article 4 of the OECD and UN Models		201
	2.1	General Residency Criteria	201
	2.2	Tiebreaker: Individuals	203
	2.3	Tiebreaker: Persons Other than Individuals	203
3	Permanent Establishment: Article 5 of the OECD and UN Models		205
	3.1	Fixed Place of Business Permanent Establishment	205
	3.2	Specific Activity Exemptions	208
	3.3	Agency PE	209

	3.4	Insurance Undertakings	210
	3.5	Independent Agent	211
	3.6	Separate Entity	211
4	Transportation: Article 8 of the OECD and UN Models		212
	4.1	General Approach	212
	4.2	Taxation of the Leasing of Vessels, Vehicles and Containers	213
	4.3	Land Traffic	213
	4.4	Further Modifications Found in Article 8 of Chinese Treaties with Belt and Road Countries	218
5	Dividends: Article 10 of the OECD and UN Models		218
	5.1	General Taxing Rights	218
	5.2	Definition of Dividends	220
	5.3	PE Provision	220
	5.4	Further Modifications Found in Article 10 of Chinese Treaties with Belt and Road Countries	221
	5.5	Non-Tax BRI Treaties	221
6	Interest: Article 11 of the OECD and UN Models		222
	6.1	General Taxing Rights	222
	6.2	Definition of Interest	223
	6.3	PE Provision	223
	6.4	Determining the Source	223
	6.5	Arm's Length Interest Rate	224
	6.6	Further Modifications Found in Article 11 of Chinese Treaties with Belt and Road Countries	225
7	Royalties: Article 12 of the OECD and UN Models		226
	7.1	General Taxing Rights	226
	7.2	Mutual Agreement on Application	227
	7.3	Definition of Royalties	227
	7.4	PE Provision	228
	7.5	Determining the Source	228
	7.6	Arm's Length Royalties Rate	229
	7.7	Further Modifications Found in Article 12 of Chinese Treaties with Belt and Road Countries	229
8	Capital Gains: Article 13 of the OECD and UN Models		229
	8.1	General Taxing Rights	229
	8.2	Taxing the Alienation of PE Property	230
	8.3	Taxing the Alienation of Vessels and Vehicles	230
	8.4	Taxing the Alienation of Shares	230
	8.5	Taxing Rights in Other Cases	232
9	Income from Employment: Article 15 of the OECD and UN Models		232
	9.1	Article 15 of the OECD and UN Models	232
	9.2	Article 15(1) and (2) of Chinese Tax Treaties	232
	9.3	Article 15(3) of Chinese Tax Treaties with Belt and Road Countries	233
10	Directors' Fees: Article 16 of the OECD and UN Models		234

Table of Contents

11		Method Articles: Article 23 of the OECD and UN Models	235
	11.1	Article 23A and 23B of the OECD and UN Models	235
	11.2	Application of the Method Articles in China	235
	11.3	Taxes Payable under Chinese Tax Treaties	237
	11.4	Indirect Tax Credit	237
12		Conclusion	254
	12.1	Tax Treaty Design Questions	254
	12.2	Suggestions	255
	12.3	Harmonization of Construction PE Timeframe	255
	12.4	Inclusion of Deemed PE for Insurance Undertakings	256
	12.5	Treatment of Oil and Gas Transportation by Pipeline	257
	12.6	Special Provision on Interest Income	257
	12.7	A Common Approach to Anti-Treaty Shopping	257

CHAPTER 12
VAT Challenges in the Belt and Road Initiative
Yuliya Shved & Karoline Spies 259

1		VAT as a 'Good Tax'		260
	1.1	The Character and Importance of VAT		260
	1.2	Neutrality		262
	1.3	Implementing the Destination Principle		263
2		The Belt and Road Initiative and VAT		264
	2.1	VAT in the Belt and Road Countries		264
	2.2	VAT Transactions in the Belt and Road Initiative		265
	2.3	VAT Challenges in the Belt and Road Initiative and Solutions Thereto		265
		2.3.1	Double Taxation (or Non-Taxation)	266
		2.3.2	Lack of Dispute Resolution Mechanism	267
		2.3.3	Disproportional Documentary Requirements	268
		2.3.4	Irrecoverable Input VAT	268
3		Existing Harmonization: The EAEU Treaty		270
	3.1	Historical Background		270
	3.2	The EAEU and VAT		273
	3.3	Scope		273
	3.4	Supply of Goods		274
		3.4.1	Place of Taxation	274
		3.4.2	Export of Goods	274
		3.4.3	Import of Goods	275
		3.4.4	Practice	277
	3.5	Supply of Services and Works		279
		3.5.1	Place of Taxation	279
		3.5.2	Documentary Requirements	280
		3.5.3	Practice	281
	3.6	Conclusion		282

| 4 | A Comprehensive Multilateral Treaty for VAT? Or Mere Soft Law Instruments? | 282 |

CHAPTER 13
Asia: Global Tax Policy Post-BEPS and the Perils of the Silk Road
Romero J.S. Tavares & Jeffrey Owens 285

1	Putting Asia and BEPS in Perspective			286
	1.1	Investment Climate		286
	1.2	Consequences of BEPS Measures		287
2	Navigating Asia Through BEPS Minimum Standards and Recommendations			293
	2.1	Policy Choices Underlying Joint Enforcement of BEPS Actions: Digital Economy Ring-Fencing Versus Permanent Establishment and Transfer Pricing Reforms		293
		2.1.1	A New Nexus in the Form of a Significant Economic Presence	297
		2.1.2	A Withholding Tax on Certain Types of Digital Transactions	297
		2.1.3	An 'Equalization Levy'	297
	2.2	The Effectiveness of New Standards for Interest Deductibility and Hybrid Mismatches		300
3	Equity Considerations			304
4	Conclusion			305

CHAPTER 14
Creating a Positive Tax Climate for Complex Multijurisdictional Investment Projects
Jonathan Leigh Pemberton & Alicja Majdanska 307

1	Introduction		307
2	Cooperative Compliance as a Way to Improve Tax Compliance and Business Confidence Domestically		309
	2.1	The Concept of Cooperative Compliance	309
	2.2	Essential Features of Cooperative Compliance	310
3	Multilateral Cooperative Compliance: From Domestic Relationship to Cross-Border Cooperation		313
4	A Potential of Multilateral Cooperative Compliance for the OBOR Initiative		314
5	JITSIC as a Model?		316
6	Conclusion		317

Index 319

Preface

In 2013, the President of the People's Republic of China, Xi Jinping, announced the Belt and Road Initiative (BRI). The project, also known as the New Silk Road, has the potential to become a remarkable step in establishing and strengthening multinational trade corridors and may turn out to be the most significant macroeconomic undertaking in the world by 2020, with an estimated USD 350 billion committed to BRI projects by China.

Through a massive investment in infrastructure, the initiative aims to improve interconnection with neighbouring countries. More specifically, the Silk Road Economic Belt and the 21st Century Maritime Silk Road will improve the inter-connectivity between countries along the route and will open up new opportunities for investment and cooperation in the areas of infrastructure, energy, transportation and agriculture. By 2025, it is expected to see the BRI spreading substantially into other sectors such as technology, manufacturing, real estate, logistics and warehousing, as well as information and communications.

The Belt is a land corridor that passes through Central Asia before reaching Europe and connects two of the world's largest economies, China and Europe. The route will emerge as a major logistics corridor. The Maritime Road is a densely populated consumer and industrial opportunity that connects China and Europe. The Road passes through Southeast Asia, South Asia, the Middle East and East Africa. The project involves regions that are home to 69% of the world's population and 51% of its GDP.

Since the announcement of the initiative, it has gradually gained international attention related to the wide range of policies and issues that need to be addressed during implementation. All the priorities assumed under the BRI entail tax consequences, as the BRI will accelerate the globalization of Chinese firms; create world-class multinationals and supply chains; and open up new opportunities for companies in Belt and Road countries.

Tax has the capacity to undermine these ambitions. The tax environment varies widely from country to country along the Belt and Road. The administrative capacity of

Preface

tax administrations is not well engineered. Tax transparency is not ensured, interpretation of international tax rules varies between countries and dispute resolution mechanisms are weak. At the same time, the improvement of tax policies related to China's going-global strategy and the strengthening of tax administration cooperation with other Belt and Road countries are crucial.

In order to analyse potential tax barriers to the BRI, the Global Tax Policy Center at Vienna University for Economics and Business (WU) created the International Tax Policy Forum on the Belt and Road Initiative, with the first meeting being held on 12-13 June 2017 in Beijing, jointly organized with Peking University Tax Law Center and the Central University of Finance and Economics (CUFE). Researchers from the Vienna University of Economics and Business, together with several Chinese universities, tax practitioners, businesses and members of tax administrations from around the world, participated in this symposium. In the presence of Zhang Zhiyong, former SAT Deputy Commissioner, and Mr Tizhong Liao, Deputy Director of the SAT International Department, the speakers presented their findings, including determinations as to whether potential tax barriers for investment may arise in the Belt and Road region and how to remove them. The research papers presented at this meeting were revised to take account of the input received during the symposium. These papers form the chapters of this book.

The second meeting of the Forum was held in Vienna on 17 April 2018, and the outcomes of this meeting formed the basis for the discussion at The Belt and Road Initiative Tax Cooperation Conference (BRITCC), held in Astana on 14-16 May 2018. This is a significant ongoing activity of the WU Global Tax Policy Center, in cooperation with leading Chinese research institutes, the State Administration of Taxation of the People's Republic of China, State Revenue Committee of the Republic of Kazakhstan, the IBFD and MNEs that operate along the Belt and Road.

The editors would like to thank Renée Pestuka David Orzechowski and Melody Ishin Hsiao, who were mainly responsible for organizing the symposium and making essential contributions to the preparation and publication of this book. The editors would also like to thank all the authors who have patiently revised their contributions in order to enhance the quality of this book, and Constance McCarthy, who contributed greatly by linguistically editing the authors' texts.

Michael Lang,
Jeffrey Owens

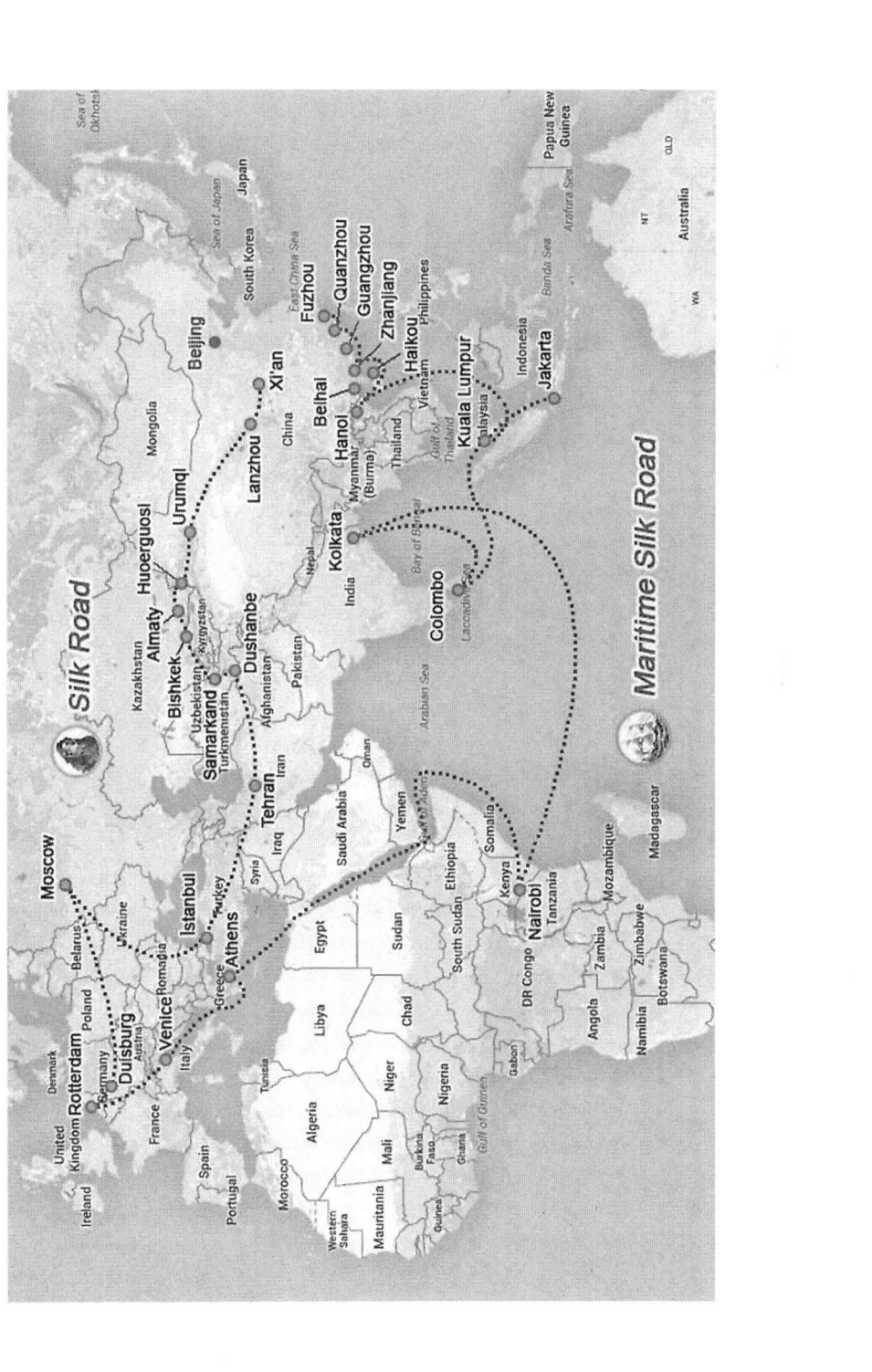

CHAPTER 1

The Belt and Road Initiative: Will Tax Be a Facilitator or a Barrier?*

Jeffrey Owens

1 Introduction
2 The Belt and Road: The Tax Dimension
3 Tax Levels, Structures and Tax Administrations Diverge
4 The Role of Tax Certainty in Promoting FDI along the BRI
5 Multilateral Cooperative Compliance: Relevance for BRI
6 Potential Tax Barriers and Suggested Approaches
7 Conclusion
Appendix I: A Multilateral Tax Treaty for the Belt and Road Initiative (BRI)

1 INTRODUCTION

More than two millennia ago, Eurasian countries opened their trade routes linking Asia, Europe and Africa. The Silk Road symbolized the spirit of a shared cultural heritage. Today, that heritage is being re-launched by China, with its 'Belt and Road' initiative. The aim is to develop new overland and maritime links, which will once again bring together China, Central Asia, Russia, Africa and Europe and link these countries to both the Indian Ocean and the Mediterranean Sea. The implementation of the 'Belt and Road' initiative (BRI) will focus on improving the inter-connectivity between the countries along the route and will open up new opportunities for

---

* This paper is part of a broader WU GTPC Project on International Tax Policy Forum on the Belt and Road Initiative, which has been led by Professor Jeffrey Owens, WU GTPC, with input from Researchers at the WU Institute: Laura Turcan, Sriram Govind, Raffaele Petruzzi, Nathalie Bravo, Jasmin Kollmann, Sathi Meyer-Nandi, David Orzechowski, Karol Adam Dziwinski, Alicja Majdanska; Caroline Heber, Romero Tavares and Karolina Spies.

investment in communication links (road, rail and shipping) and new opportunities for cooperation in the areas of energy, transportation, agriculture and manufacturing.

The emphasis will be to develop an open, inclusive relationship between countries recognizing that civilization thrives when trade growths. The Belt and Road summit for international cooperation (BRF) held in Beijing on 14–15 May 2017 brought together over 100 participants and emphasized that promoting trade, FDI and innovation will be three of pillars of this initiative, which is also seen as supporting the 2030 agenda for sustainable development.

At a time when the world is experiencing political and economic uncertainty and when the US is withdrawing from a multilateral and interconnected world, the hope is that by bringing countries together this initiative will encourage mutual respect, harmony and will provide a much-needed boost to global growth and inclusive development.

Achieving this vision will require billions of dollars of investment in infrastructure and the development of new manufacturing centres. The need for such investment was one of the reasons that led the Chinese government to create the Asian Infrastructure Investment Bank (AIIB), one of whose first actions was to set up 'The Silk Road Infrastructure Fund'. International and regional organizations support this initiative.

This note explores the question of whether tax, broadly defined, will be a facilitator or a barrier to the development of the Belt and Road initiative, and explores how think tanks and academic institutions, both in China and elsewhere, can contribute to developing proposals to remove these potential tax barriers and to ensure that the benefits of the BRI are fairly shared between the participating countries. The note first sets out the background to this initiative and then examines the relevance of tax certainty and how it could be achieved. It goes on to discuss the potential tax barriers and solutions and concludes with some broader policy questions.

In 2017, the GTPC of Vienna University of Economics and Business, working closely with the SAT and a number of Chinese research institutes,[1] created a 'BRI Tax Forum' which brings together governments, business, international organizations and research institutes along the route to explore these tax issues and to provide policy-makers with a solid array of policy-relevant research. This group has met in Vienna and Beijing in 2017, with the latest meeting being in April 2018 at WU Institute. This note draws upon these discussions. (www.wu.ac.at/taxlaw/institute/gtpc/)

2 THE BELT AND ROAD: THE TAX DIMENSION

The countries along the BRI have diverse taxes and all of these taxes – whether on profits, income, consumption, capital, financial transactions or property – will

---

1. Shanghai Lixin University of Commerce, Center for International Tax Law and Comparative Taxation (CITACT), Xiamen University, Central University of Finance and Economics (CUFE), Center for International Tax Law at East China University of Political Science and Law (ECUPL), Wuhan University.

potentially impact on the decisions of both the public and private sector to undertake the long-term investments required to achieve the goals set for the BRI.

One of the key issues is: how will these different national taxes interact? Will this interaction create uncertainty and lead to double taxation and cross-border tax disputes? Or will the interaction lead to a tax environment which provides the certainty, predictability and consistency which business need to undertake these investments.

3 TAX LEVELS, STRUCTURES AND TAX ADMINISTRATIONS DIVERGE

Comprehensive data does not exist, but information provided by the IMF[2] suggests that in many of the BRI countries, tax levels are on average are less than 25% of GDP, with some countries raising less than 15% and others more than 30%. The main sources of revenues are derived from the extractive sector and VAT; profit taxes; taxes on immovable property, and payroll taxes, while personal income taxes tend to be low. The tax administrations in many of these countries are weak, and many lack the basic skills necessary to apply complex international tax rules (*see* Annex II).

4 THE ROLE OF TAX CERTAINTY IN PROMOTING FDI ALONG THE BRI

Tax certainty is a key component to provide a tax environment which is conducive to FDI in the BRI and in the long term it is in the interest of both government and business to minimize as far as possible tax uncertainty.

Tax certainty can be defined as the capacity to make an accurate assessment of the tax and compliance costs associated with an investment or a continuation of an investment in a country over the lifecycle of the investment/company, which requires the right balance between facilitating compliance and identifying and curbing aggressive tax planning. Achieving tax certainty will be difficult in a BRI context which encompasses countries with different legislation, varying tax cultures and tax capacity and MNEs with complex business operations.

Some of the fundamental requirements for tax certainty are:

(a) At the level of tax policy:
 - The legislation is unambiguous and clear, leaving no or little room for unintended misinterpretation.
 - The legislation realizes the policy aims determined by the government.
 - The law is designed to minimize administrative costs, striking the right balance between tax compliance and the burden on taxpayers.
 - The legislation will be as much as possible in line with international standards and best practices, both in terms of content and administrative practice (this includes avoidance of double taxation, not

---

2. *See* IMF government finance statistics (GFS), 2015.

imposing unnecessary compliance costs on cross-border activities, and preventing harmful tax competition).
- Legalization needs to be based upon a 'principle' based approach.

In the context of the BRI it is particularly important that tax incentives be designed in ways which minimize tax uncertainty by avoiding discretionary incentives, ensuring any incentives are under the control of the Ministries of Finance and are subject to regular evaluation and transparency:

(b) At the level of tax administration:
- Incentivized and capable to apply the tax legislation in accordance with the letter and spirit of the law.
- Supported by efficient and effective administrative and IT platforms.
- Social skills and tools to ensure compliant taxpayers are served as efficiently as possible by providing clarity on the taxation positions in as early as possible a stage.
- Guidelines, safeguards, tools and skills to ensure that non-compliant taxpayers are identified and appropriately curbed.
- The response of the tax administration should be proportional to the behaviour of the taxpayers.
- Checks and balances should be in place to ensure that the elements above are continuously guaranteed, including through the availability of mediation processes and well-functioning administrative and judicial appeal procedures.
- Establish metrics for evaluating measures of success in achieving high compliance that go beyond simple revenue yield measure.

BRI taxpayers also have a role to play in creating tax certainty, in part by introducing a well-functioning tax control framework, which links business reality with tax compliance, ensuring the availability of the right information at the right time, abiding by the spirit and letter of the law and ensuring that taxes are paid at the right time and in the right place.

What measures can BRI governments take to improve tax certainty?

The following paragraphs set out some proposals that BRI countries may wish to consider:

(a) *At the level of policy and implementation:*
- Engage business and other stakeholders both in policy formulation and drafting of legislation.
- Ensure tax policy makers and tax administrations are working together to formulate new policies.
- Establish transparent and open consultation processes.

- Issue white papers that enable input from a wide variety of stakeholders before legislation is finalized.
(b) *At the level of legislation:*
- Draft legislations in clear and unambiguous ways.
- All legislation should be first issued in a draft format and go through a process of consultation.
- Ensure the purpose of specific sections of the law are clearly stated so that taxpayers and the courts have a clear basis for interpreting the more detailed and technical provisions (principles-based legislation).
(c) *Other measures can include:*
- Issuing clarifications and public rulings that are binding on the tax administration.
- Avoiding as far as possible retroactive legislation.
- Centralizing all large business cases into a large business unit so as to achieve a consistent application of the rules.
- Issuing clear guidance to regional tax offices on how they can apply legislation and tax treaties and regularly monitor that this guidance is followed.Exploring all the options to resolve issues and questions prior to the submission of tax return or an audit.
- Using a variety of methods to increase the awareness of tax officials on the way business models are evolving and the speed of change. This could take the form of regular meetings between business and tax officials and briefings by business to senior executives in the tax administration.

5 MULTILATERAL COOPERATIVE COMPLIANCE: RELEVANCE FOR BRI[3]

One particularly effective way to reduce tax uncertainty is to introduce a cooperative compliance model, which represents a shift from a retrospective and primarily repressive control to a cooperative relationship between tax administration and taxpayers that is much more likely to involve a discussion of tax treatment in real-time or even prospectively. It is intended to deliver quality compliance, which means payment of taxes due on time in an effective and efficient manner. At the heart of the concept is a simple exchange of transparency for certainty. The taxpayer undertakes to be wholly transparent about the tax positions that it has taken in its return and the transactions that are likely to give rise to a tax risk. The taxpayer does not limit this disclosure to the information required by the administrative provisions of tax law and does not seek to invoke legal privilege to prevent access to documents that could be relevant to the determination of tax liability. In return, the tax administration agrees to offer the taxpayer early certainty about the tax treatment of the taxpayer's business

---

3. The text is an extract from a chapter in: A. Majdanska & J. L. Pemberton, Creating a positive tax climate for complex multijurisdictional investment projects, in Lang/Owens (eds.), Removing Tax Barriers to the Belt and Road Initiative, Kluwer Law International 2018, forthcoming.

transactions. Experience shows that this is often easiest to achieve this if the discussion takes place as close as possible to the time when those transactions take place, which is why the cooperative model often encourages the parties to discuss issues before a tax return is even filed, or, in certain circumstances, before a transaction takes place.

The OECD's 2013 report spelled out the core features of the concept: justified or demonstrable trust; transparency; cooperation; collaboration; voluntary disclosure; timely advice on significant positions; and early legal certainty.[4] The cooperative compliance model works on the basis that if a taxpayer is voluntarily and fully transparent, and able to show 'how it does that', the tax administration should provide early tax certainty and do so in advance, where appropriate. Cooperative compliance is traditionally unilateral, but a number of countries are now exploring an approach which could be of interest for groups of BRI countries, perhaps combined with a focus on specific sectors.

Most of the investments in the BRI initiative will involve operations in more than one country. This will entail reviewing businesses' value chain, how tax risks are managed and what drives customer and shareholder value. Multilateral cooperative compliance could be a way of addressing any potentially contentious tax issues in advance, providing early tax certainty to participants in the BRI initiative. It could help significantly reduce tax costs of handling the tax assessment of taxpayers that operate cross-border and avoid long and costly tax disputes that may emerge once the BRI initiative unfolds.

6 POTENTIAL TAX BARRIERS[5] AND SUGGESTED APPROACHES

This section identifies potential tax barriers to the BRI and provides suggestions on how these may be addressed at the level of either individual countries or groups of countries which are engaged in specific BRI projects or sectors. Wherever possible these suggestions build on existing international best practices, but in some cases it is proposed to tailor the approach to the specific needs of the BRI.

(a) VAT Systems Deviate from the International Norm

Issues:

With the notable exceptions of Russia and China, which completed its transformation to a proper VAT system in 2017, most of the emerging and developing countries on the

---

4. OECD, Cooperative Compliance: A Framework – From Enhanced Relationship to Cooperative Compliance (OECD Publishing 2013).
5. For an analysis of relevant treaty policy in China's tax treaties *see* 'Tax Treaties between the Belt and Road Countries', Sathi Meyer-Nandi, David Orzechowski, Vladimir Tyutyuryukov, Vienna, in Lang/Owens (eds.), Removing Tax Barriers to the Belt and Road Initiative, Kluwer Law International 2018, forthcoming.

BRI do not operate standard VAT systems.[6] VAT refunds are paid, if at all, after long delays; services are given a broad exemption. In many cases, VAT operates more like a tax on imports and exports.

The Belt, Road Initiative project will involve VAT issues triggered by the non-harmonized national VAT rules, the lack of a comprehensive knowledge of VAT systems and the lack of qualified staff and human resources at the tax administrations. There are four main potential obstacles to cross-border transactions in the Belt, Road Initiative in the area of VAT: double taxation or non-taxation, dispute resolution, documentary requirements and irrecoverable input VAT.

The first issue, double taxation or non-taxation, follows from a lack of harmonization of taxation principles and the place of supply rules between states along the Belt, Road Initiative. Some of these states may follow the destination principle; others may favour the origin principle. Even if the countries were able to agree on these basic principles, they would need to decide on the same proxies and their interpretation to identify where the supply of goods or services should be taxed. Similarly, non-harmonized VAT rules may also lead to non-taxation, if both states allocate the taxing right to the other jurisdiction. Non-taxation has distortive effects on the competition and economy.

Recommendations:

The OECD International VAT/GST Guidelines may help to prevent double as well as non-taxation in some scenarios. These guidelines are, however, very broad and thus not every double or non-taxation case may be addressed. To make the Belt, Road Initiative a success, a dedicated BRI agreement may need to be found on how the standard supplies of goods and services should be taxed along the road.

Where there is a VAT dispute between states (or between a non-resident taxpayer and the tax administrations), there is no international legal framework to resolve the conflict. One approach is to examine the applicability of dispute resolution or arbitration rules of other treaties for VAT (double taxation treaties, investment treaties, WTO law). However, these treaties may not be sufficient help. Most importantly, dispute resolution for double taxation issues requires a legal basis to rely on and, hence, a binding bi- or multilateral VAT treaty with place-of-taxation rules in the first place. As long as there is no such bi- or multilateral treaty in place, dispute resolution for double taxation issues may be difficult. If, however, the states can agree on common VAT-principle, a dispute resolution mechanism could be implemented.

Another problem businesses have to face along the Belt, Road Initiative is the irrecoverable input VAT. VAT should not be a tax on businesses. However, many BRI states immediately use the input VAT to finance current public spending and thus may have problems to refund the input VAT. To ensure the neutrality of VAT, a mechanism needs to be found that safeguards the capability of states to refund input VAT, perhaps by developing a set of good practices.

---

6. For a full analysis of VAT systems *see* 'VAT Challenges in the Belt and Road Initiative', Caroline Heber, in Lang/Owens.

Even if states follow the destination principle and apply similar place-of-taxation rules and proxies, they still also might ask for different and very burdensome documentary requirements to benefit from zero-rating, input VAT refund or other benefits.

One approach which could address many of the issues discusses above would be a general zero-rating between the entities building the infrastructure for the Belt, Road Initiative and the ones using the infrastructure for passing-through goods. In these cases, the goods and services are supplied to businesses, and thus VAT should not burden any of these transactions. Simplification can be achieved by not levying the VAT on the transaction and refund it later on. If the supplies were zero-rated, there would not be any problem with refunding the input VAT. To make the zero-rating system working, unique VAT-ID numbers needs to be issued which identify the entities engaged in building and using the Belt, Road Initiative. Only if these specific VAT-ID numbers are used, the zero-rating mechanism could be applied. If the states were able to agree on to whom a BRI-VAT-ID number should be issued, this would help resolve the place of supply rules. If the transactions are zero-rated, it does not matter where the transaction should be taxed.

(b) The Network of Bilateral Tax Treaties is Incomplete

Issues:

While China and Russia have a broad network of treaties, most of the BRI emerging and developing countries have very limited treaty networks which do not always reflect best practices (*see* Annexes I and II for details). Even where treaties are in place, they do not always reflect current economic trading patterns. There is a need for an up to date analysis of the existing BRI tax treaty network, which would identify which provisions require modification to facilitate trade and investment.[7] Countries may wish to consider developing a multilateral instrument to coordinate provisions, thereby facilitating a closer economic integration. Particular attention should be paid to the mechanisms found in treaties to minimize and resolve cross-border tax disputes, and there may be a case for initiating a BRI dispute resolution platform (*see* (e) below).

Some of the potential problems include:

(1) Incoherent and fragmented treaty wording: When looking at China's tax treaties with BRI countries, there is no consistent approach in the wording of provisions. The majority of provisions found in China's treaties with BRI countries follow the wording of either the OECD or UN Models. However, next to the variations resulting from the different versions of the Models, in multiple treaties there are further deviations from the Models, resulting in uncertainty and complexity for doing business in the region. Especially differences in the PE definition (construction and service PE in particular)

---

7. *See* 'Tax Treaties between the Belt and Road Countries', Sathi Meyer-Nandi, David Orzechowski, Vladimir Tyutyuryukov, in Lang/Owens (eds.), Removing Tax Barriers to the Belt and Road Initiative, Kluwer Law International 2018, forthcoming. This analysis is limited to Chinese treaties with BRI countries.

increase the administrative burden of companies. A project with the same characteristics may constitute a PE in one BRI country (and entail tax and compliance issues) but not in another BRI country. These variations in the PE thresholds, together with the extreme differences in withholding tax rates, further create the potential for tax competition between BRI countries. Due to the weak anti-avoidance rules, there is also an open pathway for tax abuse by businesses.

Additionally, the special provision on interest income, which limits source country withholding taxes when the recipient of the interest income is a financial institution connected to the government of the other state, is of relevance for the BRI. Since infrastructure investments are generally highly geared and much of the debt funding will be provided via public financiers, such clause encourages infrastructure investment. However, currently, only approximately two-thirds of China's treaties with BRI countries include such provision and depending on the time of implementation, the wording of these provisions vary in their scope of application. Due to the relevance of this provision, such deviation is problematic. Additionally, BRI countries could consider broadening such clause also to capture debt provided by private financier for BRI infrastructure investment.

(2) No clear treaty policy aligned with the objectives of the BRI: It appears that China's later tax treaties with the BRI countries have a tendency to shift more towards the wording of the OECD Model, meaning being less source country friendly. Since the BRI countries will mainly constitute net capital importing countries, with the capital streaming predominantly from China into their economy, and capital income flowing the other way around, the treaties with China will most likely have an asymmetric nature. Hence, when not neutralized through sufficient gains from increased FDI, the shift in taxing powers from the source country to the residence country induced by the tax treaty, might not be sustainable in the long-term, when development of the whole region is one of the objectives.

Recommendations:

(1) Harmonization of key provisions through cooperation: The standardization of certain key provision – e.g., PE definition, the special provision on interest income and anti-avoidance rules – could improve certainty and reduce the level of complexity currently present when doing cross-border business in the BRI region. Ideally BRI countries could create a BRI Model Tax Treaty, which should be drafted in a dialogue between the key BRI countries, e.g., through the inauguration of a BRI tax treaty forum. One could also explore a process for a simplified multilateral instrument, which enables a rapid update of the most relevant key provisions in existing treaties.

(2) Agreement on specific tax treaty policy: The BRI countries together with China could try to agree on a specific BRI tax treaty policy which heeds the

asymmetric relationship of the capital flows between China and the BRI countries. The policy should be aligned with the development objectives of the region, which presupposes sufficient tax revenues generate by all participating countries.

(3) Identify ways to update and expand the BRI treaty network: Appendix I provides some suggestions for a multilateral approach to updating treaties. One way to extend the treaty network would be for countries which have very limited networks to engage in multilateral negotiations which lead to bilateral signing of treaties. The proposed BRI Tax Academy could play a role here.

(c) Transfer Pricing Practices Need to Be Simplified

Issues:

Many of the BRI emerging and developing countries along the BRI have rudimentary transfer pricing rules. Frequently, the legislation is unclear, the information requirements are inconsistent and the experience of tax administrations in applying the rules is at a very early stage. To achieve the goals of the BRI will require greater coordination of the valuation rules of intra-multinational transactions and greater consistency of the valuations used for VAT, customs and transfer pricing purposes.

The Transfer Pricing issues in the BRI can generally be divided into six categories relating to specific areas such as manufacturing activities, service and financial transactions, intangible properties, cost contribution arrangements, documentation and advance pricing agreements.

In the case of manufacturing activities, two major problems pertain to constant lack of comparable data in many BRI countries as well as to the allocation of location savings. A number of BRI countries face a shortage of publicly available commercial databases and do not have appropriate financial registries where companies record their corporate financial information. This leads in many cases to tax authorities using secret comparables which as a consequence puts taxpayers without the access to such data at a disadvantage and may cause infringing secrecy of the data used for assessment purposes. The location saving issue is strongly related to the access to data as many BRI countries tend to (over)use foreign data due to the insufficient availability of local comparables. In relation to this issue, a potential misuse of foreign comparables in practice arises as another problem.

When it comes to services and financial transactions in BRI countries, the topic seems to have significant importance with numerous countries implementing their own rules in this regard or at least having certain practices and recommendations. Those countries include, among others, China, Singapore, Russia, Vietnam, Indonesia and Hungary. Even though some of these countries try to follow OECD respective guidance, there still might arise a problem regarding diverging legal provisions and rules binding in different BRI jurisdictions.

Further, it should be noted that there exist many issues of potentially major significance related to transactions involving intangible properties. BRI countries in general follow OECD TPG in this regard but to different extents. Nevertheless, the general rules according to which the returns derived from the exploitation of intangibles are divided, is usually accepted. It has to be underlined, however, that certain countries either do not have specific legislation in this regard or do not follow OECD TPG, which might be detrimental to the development of the initiative. In addition, overly narrow or too broad definitions of intangibles in domestic laws of respective countries.

Another transfer pricing issue which needs to be given certain attention are the cost contribution agreements. The biggest problem in this regard for the BRI initiative comes from different approaches taken by tax authorities of diverse countries. Starting from non-acceptance of CCAs among former USSR states through missing any rules or treating CCAs as intra-group services (diverse countries in different regions) to general and formalized acceptance of CCAs (EU countries), the situation indicated generally limited proliferation of proper legislation in this regard. This further results in lack of expertise among tax authorities. In addition, CCAs raise certain doubts and suspicion among tax officers as it happens that the benefits stemming from this kind of arrangement are not explicit at first sight.

Another major transfer pricing issue is documentation. The legislation and practice of BRI countries varies greatly, reflecting different levels of transfer pricing experience of respective countries, their approach towards international developments as well as the capacity of tax administrations. However, clear trends of implementation of transfer pricing documentation can be observed in the last years, accelerated particularly by the developments of BEPS Action 13 as well as other international projects like the UN Transfer Pricing Manual. Other problems in this area include limited treaty networks in many BRI jurisdictions, which hinder the exchange of information as well as the common problem of processing transfer pricing documentation in English in certain countries.

The last potential problematic area among BRI countries is the implementation and the application of advance pricing agreements. There are various reasons why countries are cautious in this regard. Among the most important are a lack of transfer pricing experience and knowledge, lack of capacity (where tax officers are directed primarily to tax audits) and lack of trust in a cooperative character of procedure such as APA (tax authorities are reluctant towards cooperation intensively involving taxpayers).

Recommendations:

BRI countries may wish to consider the following actions:

- putting on equal footing transfer pricing rules understanding among BRI countries to build a bridge between jurisdictions with transfer pricing rules and jurisdictions without transfer pricing rules by the implementation of a commonly agreed set of guidelines among the BRI countries;
- focus further actions on development and promotion in the BRI countries of two key aspects, namely the improvement of guidance and the dissemination of the experience among the various stakeholders, e.g., by using the proposed BRI Tax Academy to develop training programmes for the target countries;

- commissioning policy-relevant research from academic institutions;
- considering the establishment of a BRI Transfer Pricing Forum (e.g., on a similar setting as the EU JTPF) of experts from both governmental institutions and private practice that regularly meets and analyses various pre-defined transfer pricing topics, in order to produce guidance that could constitute a useful practical tool to solve specific issues.

Regarding the issues related to manufacturing activities, in particular to lack of comparables and the allocation of location savings, the following actions might be considered:

- development of a network of multilateral safe harbours among groups of countries which could enhance the solution of issues related to lack of comparables data and allocation of location savings properly addressing at the same time all the numerous areas of concern;
- the development of a database including financial data of MNEs operating in the BRI countries.

As far as issues related to services and financial transactions are concerned, countries may wish to consider:

- the guidelines provided by international organizations might constitute a good source of reference for tax administrations and taxpayers, as well as practical tools for capability building in transfer pricing matters;
- the development of a network of multilateral safe harbours among the BRI countries for low value adding services (as well as for some types of financial transactions) and the development of a database including data on services and financial transactions in the BRI countries could be beneficial solutions.

Further, with reference to the issues concerning IPs, the following solutions could be explored:

- following the OECD/UN approach, the location of DEMPE functions should be considered as a key factor in the BRI countries when undertaking transfer pricing law modifications regarding IPs;
- the legal framework for IP protection, which is very well developed in the region (including copyright law, patent law, trademark law and the laws against unfair competition), should be also carefully considered;
- as regards the definition of IP, the first action that BRI countries could take is to align the definition of intangibles with the one suggested by the OECD/UN approach.

When it comes to CCAs-related issue, it would be desirable to update local legislation to allow CCAs following the efforts of OECD and UN in promoting uniform rules on CCA, especially considering the fact that the concept is new for many BRI countries and they will probably 'borrow' the regulations from the international bodies.

With regard to transfer pricing documentation issues, the BRI countries could consider the following actions:

- standardizing documentation requirements;
- balancing the tax administrations need for data with taxpayer's administrative burden and costs;
- requiring taxpayers to submit their transfer pricing documentation automatically in a timely manner.

Finally, the following solutions could be considered to make the application of APAs in the BRI countries more robust:

- introducing a multilateral APA programme in the BRI region (e.g., along BRI global value chains) could give businesses an opportunity to reach an agreement with the tax authorities in combination with other tax authorities on the future application of transfer pricing rules to their related party transactions;
- establishing specialized transfer pricing units separated into functional units within the same tax authority where each of those special units could work along the same special units of the other tax authorities' jurisdictions;
- determining the 'critical assumptions' in which the MAPAs are underpinned, so that if circumstances materially change on which the MAPA was agreed, parties will no longer be bounded by the MAPA;
- taxpayers should be required to lodge a brief annual report, which evidences their compliance with the agreed MAPA terms and conditions.

(d) Will Tax Incentives and Special Economic Zones Lead to a Race to the 'Bottom'?

Issues:

Governments along the BRI already make use of tax incentives to encourage FDI and an increasing number are also putting in place free trade zones. While there may be legitimate arguments in favour of these measures, they do run the risk of opening up new avenues for aggressive tax planning and undermining the tax base. They also raise the broader issue that sustainable investment should not be driven by tax considerations. BRI need to avoid a race to the bottom which could seriously undermine the tax base.

Recommendations:

BRI countries need to have a rigorous process in place to evaluate the risks and benefits of any tax incentive. This process should go through five stages:

(1) Setting out what is the longer term rationale of a policy of subsidizing investment.

(2) Agreeing on the amount of resources that should be devoted to achieving this objective.
(3) Deciding on what is the best policy instrument to achieve the goal: tax incentives, direct subsidies, regulatory measures, the government undertaking the investment itself.
(4) Determining the framework to analyse the cost and impact of the incentives and what will be the approach to accountability.
(5) Agreeing that only the Ministry of Finance can grant tax incentives.

The BRI countries could adopt a BRI Code of Conduct which could draw upon the work of the OECD, EU and regional bodies such as SADIC. Any tax incentive or Special Economic Zone should be well designed so that they target sustainable and real activities which do not distort investment decisions or encourage Base erosion.

(e) More Effective Mechanisms are Required to Minimize and Resolve BRI Tax Disputes

Issues:

The countries along the Road have diverse taxes and all of these taxes – whether on profits, income, consumption, capital or property – will potentially impact the decisions of both the public and the private sector to undertake the long-term investments required to achieve the goals set for the BRI. One of the key questions is how these different national taxes will interact. Will they create uncertainty and be applied in ways which lead to double taxation? Or will their interaction lead to a tax environment which provides the certainty, predictability and consistency which business needs? Inevitably, due to the interaction of the different tax systems, cross-border tax disputes will arise and this will require more effective dispute resolution mechanisms.

Recommendations:

The various measures to resolve disputes can be classified in two categories: domestic or international. BRI countries will have to address domestic tax administration structures and mechanisms to resolve or minimize tax disputes, as well as dispute resolution mechanisms at the international level.

Domestic:

Apart from the measures suggested in section 4 on tax certainty above these could include:

- Non-binding mediation and use of experts.
- Administrative tribunals which are independent of the tax administrations.
- Creating a Tax Ombudsman.
- Providing training for Judges on complex tax issues.

International:

- MAP: implementing the four minimum standards in BEPS Action 14, which have now been endorsed by many of the BRI countries and also looking at whether in the context of the BRI some of the best practice in Action 14 could also be endorsed.
- Using the upcoming UN Handbook on MAP as a basis for discussions between BRI countries and putting in place training programs for competent authorities based upon the Handbook. This could be carried out by the proposed BRI Tax Academy.
- Putting in place multilateral framework agreements between BRI competent authorities.

Apart from these specific measures, BRI countries or groups of countries may wish to establish dedicated technical platforms which would facilitate contacts between CA, assisting in documentation and filing requirements, improve communication with taxpayers on the progress of their case and help build up a picture of the main types of disputes on the BRI.

In the medium term there may also be a case to establish a BRI dispute resolution panel which countries would be able to consult to resolve cross-border disputes between groupings of BRI countries.

(f) Excises and Tariffs Need to Be Harmonized

Issues:

In many of the countries along the overland route, tariffs and excises are relatively low, except for agricultural goods. Exports and imports between these countries remain limited (less than 1% of China exports and imports go into countries in the Eurasian region). The exception is the inter-regional trade in the areas of natural resources, reflecting the construction of a number of regional distribution networks over the last ten years. Despite the low rates of these excises, there remains scope for greater coordination between countries in the design and implementation of these duties and to eliminate non-tariff barriers.

Recommendations:

The BRI countries should accelerate their cooperation with the WCO to minimize customs duties and to remove non-tariff barriers, identifying best practices. There is also scope for exploring how Blockchain technology can be used to simplify custom procedures drawing upon some of the pilot studies that the WCO, IBM and a number of shipping companies (e.g., Maersk) have recently carried out. The BRI countries could also look at the experience of other economic blocks such as the EU and the EEC.

(g) The Network of Bilateral Investment Treaties is Incomplete

Issues:

The network of BITs is incomplete between the Central Asian countries, although China and Russia do have extensive networks. There is considerable divergence in the BIT norms, although all provide for investor-to-state dispute resolution mechanisms, and in the vast majority of countries, tax is not explicitly excluded from the BITs.

Recommendations:

It would be desirable to explore the development of a BRI model BIT agreement, perhaps based upon some of the recent proposals put out by UNCTAD.[8] It may also be helpful to examine the interaction between BITs and Tax Treaties and to achieve a more consistent treatment of tax issues in BIT.

7 CONCLUSION

The investment in infrastructure required to complete the BRI will run into many billions of dollars. This investment will be undertaken by a mix of the public sector, state owned businesses, private/public partnerships and the private sector acting on its own. One of the main defining characteristics of this investment is that it will require a long-term commitment and involves projects which cross many frontiers. If we are to avoid that tax acts as a barrier, the countries along the route need to engage in a collective reflection on the following issues:

- Are the current tax rules facilitating the financial intermediation, which would be required to finance these projects?
- What can be done to achieve greater consistency in the design and application of VAT systems and tariffs and excises?
- Can a code of good conduct on the use of tax incentives and special economic zones be agreed upon?
- Can we develop Multilateral APA and rulings and develop a framework within which joint audits can be carried out and is there scope to develop a BRI database on comparables?
- Do provisions incorporated into tax treaties either hinder or encourage such investment and provide the certainty that investors seek?
- Are dispute mechanisms in these instruments effective?
- More generally, how can BRI governments, working with business, achieve greater tax certainty and will taxpayers' rights be respected in countries which have very different approaches to dealing with taxpayers?
- How can the proposed BRI Tax Academy assist in capacity building in BRI tax administrations?

---

8. Refer to the UNCTAD World Investment Report, 2015.

This is a very ambitious tax agenda but unless these issues are addressed, the risk is that tax will end up by being more of a barrier than a facilitator of the development of the BRI.

APPENDIX I: A MULTILATERAL TAX TREATY FOR THE BELT AND ROAD INITIATIVE (BRI)[9]

This appendix develops the concept of a multilateral tax treaty for the Belt and Road Initiative (BRI) inspired by the OECD's Multilateral Instrument. The object and purpose of a potential multilateral tax treaty between the countries participating in the BRI would be to swiftly update their tax treaties to avoid cases of double taxation that may discourage trade. Attention is particularly paid to the mechanisms that can be implemented in multilateral treaties in order to provide parties with the flexibility needed to achieve a wide participation.

The Multilateral Convention to Implement Tax Treaty Related Measures to Prevent BEPS: A Summary

The Multilateral Instrument proves that in international taxation a common goal may result in the successful conclusion of a multilateral treaty. As of 22 March 2018, seventy-eight States and non-States jurisdictions have signed the Multilateral Instrument and six other States have shown interest in signing it. Moreover, as the number of ratifications required for its entry into force has been reached, the Multilateral Instrument will enter into force on the 1 July 2018 and will start producing effects as from the 1 January 2019.

The object and purpose of the Multilateral Instrument are to swiftly incorporate into the tax treaty network the treaty changes proposed in the course of the OECD/G20 BEPS Project. As of today, the Multilateral Instrument may modify up to 1,122 tax treaties. This number may increase if more States join the Multilateral Instrument or new tax treaties are notified as Covered Tax Agreements that will be modified through the Multilateral Instrument. According to Article 2(1)(a) of the Multilateral Instrument, a Covered Tax Agreement is a treaty for the avoidance of double taxation with respect to taxes on income in force between two or more parties to the Multilateral Instrument as long as each of the parties has notified it as a treaty covered by the Multilateral Instrument.

Although the Multilateral Instrument is the result of multilateral negotiations, it will produce effects only on a bilateral basis. In this sense, the Multilateral Instrument will not terminate or replace the Covered Tax Agreements, instead it will apply alongside the Covered Tax Agreements in order to modify them. That is, the Multilateral Instrument and the Covered Tax Agreements must be interpreted

---

9. This appendix draws extensively on the work of Nathalie Bravo, LLM in International Taxation, PhD candidate Doctoral Programme in International Business Taxation (DIBT) and Recipient of the DOC Fellowship of the Austrian Academy of Sciences at the Institute for Austrian and International Tax Law, WU (Wirtschaftsuniversität Wien).

side-by-side[10] every time an interpreter determines which State has the right to tax a certain item of income. As a consequence, if a tax treaty does not exist between a pair or group of States, the Multilateral Instrument will not produce any effects between them.

The Multilateral Instrument provides parties with a high level of flexibility allowing them to shape their commitments differently. Flexibility was important for the conclusion of the Multilateral Instrument because flexibility facilities universal participation. The treaty makers of the Multilateral

Instrument tried to attain universal participation because, in their view, BEPS is 'a pressing issue not only for industrialized countries but also for emerging economies and developing countries'.[11] The Multilateral Instrument provides flexibilities to its parties by combining the use of the following mechanisms:

- A positive listing approach of the Covered Tax Agreements, which means that not all the tax treaties of the parties will be modified through the Multilateral Instrument. Only the tax treaties that parties effectively list as covered by the Multilateral Instrument will be considered Covered Tax Agreements – as long as all the parties to the respective tax treaty notify it as such.
- Opting-in mechanisms in the form of unilateral declarations. Parties to the Multilateral Instrument may opt into the application of additional provisions. Those additional provisions are binding only if parties expressly agree to their application. In most of the cases, the Multilateral Instrument establishes that if a party opts into an optional provision it must fulfil the additional commitment only in connection to other parties that have opted into the same additional commitment.
- Alternative provisions. Parties to the Multilateral Instrument may choose to apply one or none alternative provisions. Alternative provisions are established in the Multilateral Instrument because a BEPS concern may be tackled in different ways and all of them were accepted as valid outputs of the BEPS Project. Alternative provisions are binding only if parties expressly agree to their application. In some cases, the Multilateral Instrument allows that the party that opted into an alternative provision applies such a provision even if the other party or parties to a Covered Tax Agreement did not opt into the same alternative provision.
- Opting-out mechanisms in the form of reservations. Most of the provisions of the Multilateral Instrument are binding on all the parties unless the parties expressly opt out of them by making a reservation. Parties are allowed to make reservations to all the provisions of the Multilateral Instrument but are limited to the list of authorized reservations expressly defined in the Multilateral

---

10. Avery Jones, *Treaty Interpretation* (updated in 2017), in *Global Tax Treaty Commentaries* (2014), section 5.3.1.
11. Preamble of the Multilateral Instrument.

Instrument. The only exceptions to this rule are the reservations related to the scope of cases subject to mandatory binding arbitration since parties are free to decide on the scope of such cases.

The advantage of providing for a high level of flexibility in the Multilateral Instrument is that all the States interested in fighting BEPS may join the treaty despite their different tax policies and economic interests. Interestingly, although many States have availed of the flexibility provided by the Multilateral Instrument, all of them have accepted the implementation of the minimum standards related to treaty abuse and making dispute resolution mechanisms more effective. On the other hand, the disadvantage of providing for a high level of flexibility in the Multilateral Instrument is that harmonization of tax treaty provisions is not achieved. Thus, cases of double taxation or double non-taxation might still arise.

A multilateral tax treaty in the context of the BRI

Countries participating in the BRI can align their tax treaty provisions to avoid cases of double taxation and incentivize trade. For this purpose, a multilateral tax treaty inspired by the Multilateral Instrument may be implemented. The benefit derived from following an approach similar to the one of the Multilateral Instrument is that the existing tax treaties between the countries participating in the BRI will not be replaced. They will only be modified. Thus, the existing tax treaties and the new multilateral tax treaty between the countries participating in the BRI will coexist. The Multilateral Instrument has proven that such an approach can be successful even if States have different tax policies and different economic interests. This is the case because the States share a common goal and do not need to modify all their tax treaty provisions. Through the Multilateral Instrument, States will only modify the tax treaty provisions that create BEPS opportunities. Under a potential multilateral tax treaty between the countries participating in the BRI, the participating States will only need to modify the tax treaty provisions that may disincentivize investment and trade between them.

Moreover, a multilateral tax treaty between the countries participating in the BRI will swiftly update their tax treaties since a unique negotiation process, and a unique ratification process will be required. As proven by the Multilateral Instrument, although reaching agreement between a large number of participating States may be complex, such an agreement can be promptly reached if political willingness exists. Since countries participating in the BRI will most probably increase trade from and to other BRI countries, thereby strengthening their economy and increasing their tax revenues, it is likely that political willingness to avoid double taxation of trade operations between BRI countries will exist.

Under a potential multilateral tax treaty between the countries participating in the BRI, achieving a uniform application of tax treaty provisions may be more important than under the Multilateral Instrument. Nonetheless, if countries participating in the BRI do not agree on the substance of all the treaty provisions, mechanisms to provide flexibility could be implemented in the potential multilateral tax treaty, similarly to the mechanisms used in the Multilateral Instrument, e.g., opting-in mechanisms, alternative provisions and opting-out mechanisms in the form of reservations. Moreover, if certain provisions are considered to be essential for the operation of the potential multilateral tax treaty, the use of mechanisms to provide flexibility for those provisions could be limited, as it is the case with the provisions that set out the minimum standards in the Multilateral Instrument.

Many countries participating in the BRI do not have an extensive tax treaty network. If a country participating in the BRI does not have a tax treaty with another country participating in the BRI, the potential multilateral tax treaty, in principle, will not produce any effects. The potential multilateral tax treaty between the countries participating in the BRI, however, could deviate from the approach adopted in the Multilateral Instrument in this respect. Indeed, the potential multilateral tax treaty could establish stand-alone provisions that would fill tax treaty gaps between the countries participating in the BRI in order to avoid cases of double taxation. In other words, the potential multilateral tax treaty between the countries participating in the BRI could establish new rules to avoid cases of double taxation where a tax treaty does not yet exist between certain countries. If necessary, it could be agreed that those provisions of the potential multilateral tax treaty would apply only as long as parties do not conclude a tax treaty dealing with the same subject matter.

Finally, as the potential multilateral tax treaty between the countries participating in the BRI would most probably deal with matters that are not BEPS-related, such a multilateral tax treaty may coexist not only with the existing tax treaties but also with the Multilateral Instrument. The relationship between the potential multilateral tax treaty between the countries participating in the BRI and the Multilateral Instrument could be addressed through compatibility clauses. Compatibility clauses are provisions that regulate the relation between the provisions of a treaty and between those provisions and the provisions of other treaties dealing with the same or related matters.[12] Moreover, if a potential conflict of treaties could arise between the multilateral tax treaty between the countries participating in the BRI and the Multilateral Instrument, the compatibility clauses could determine which treaty should be applicable with preference by the parties to both treaties.

Annex I: Some Background Information

1. Growth of China's outward investment

In 2015, for the first time, China's ODI (overseas direct investment, USD 145.6 billion) surpassed the FDI (foreign direct investment, USD 135.6 billion).

---

12. ILC, *Draft articles on the law of treaties with commentaries, Documents of the seventeenth session and of the eighteenth session including the reports of the Commission to the General Assembly*, Yearbook of the ILC Vol. II (1966), at 214.

Chapter 1: Removing Tax Barriers to China's BRI

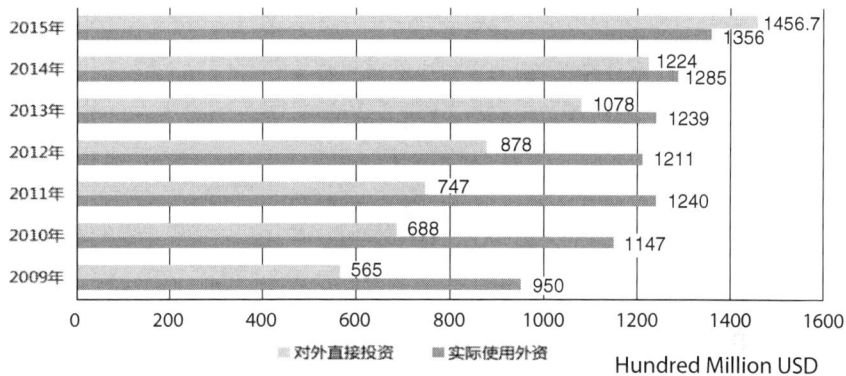

2. *China's accumulated direct investment in BRI*

As of 2015, China's accumulated direct investment in BRI countries was USD 115.68 billion, in relation to leasing and commercial services, manufacturing, construction, energy, mining, financial services, etc.

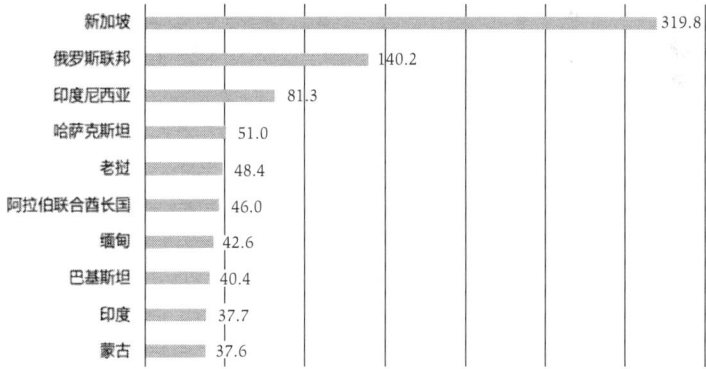

Hundred Million USD

3. *BRI Initiative Achievements*

By Year 2017: Chinese entities in BRI countries

- OETCA **75**
- Investment **$ 27 billion**
- Local taxes **$ 2.2 billion**
- Jobs **210,000**

Year 2017: Chinese entities in BRI countries

- Direct investment **$ 14.4 billion**
- M&A **62**
- Construction contracts **$ 144.3 billion**
- Trade **$ 1.1 trillion**

Data source: Ministry of Commerce of P.R. China

4. China's Tax Treaties with BRI Countries

4.1 Expanding Treaty Network

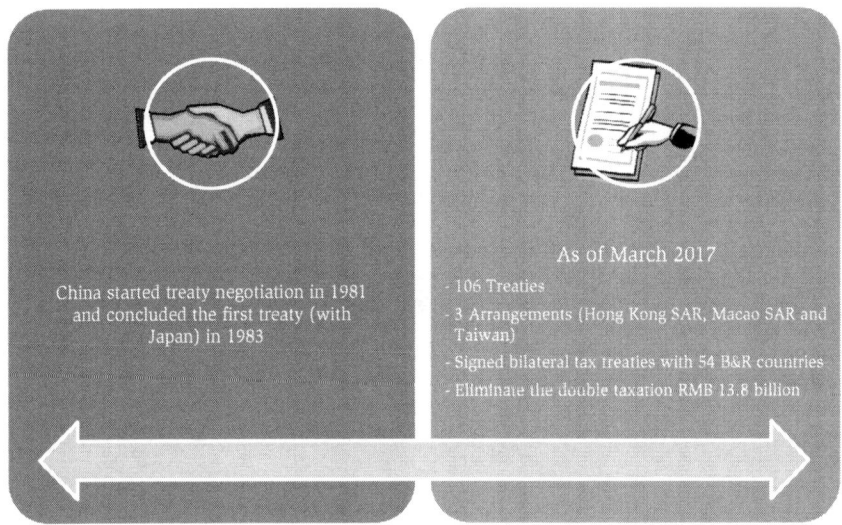

China started treaty negotiation in 1981 and concluded the first treaty (with Japan) in 1983

As of March 2017
- 106 Treaties
- 3 Arrangements (Hong Kong SAR, Macao SAR and Taiwan)
- Signed bilateral tax treaties with 54 B&R countries
- Eliminate the double taxation RMB 13.8 billion

Data source: State Administration of Taxation, P.R. China.

4.2 Model Tax Convention

- OECD Model: Residence regime
- UN Model: Territorial regime, extend the source jurisdictions of taxation
- China's tax treaties with BRI countries are mainly based on UN Model.

	OECD Model	UN Model
PE	A building site or construction or installation lasts more than 12 months	A building site or construction or installation lasts more than 6 months

	OECD Model	UN Model
Dividends	Hold at least 25% shares, taxes charged should not exceed 5%; In other cases taxes charged should not exceed 15%	Hold at least 10% shares, no requirements on the tax rates
Interests	Not exceed 10%	None
Royalties	Should only be taxed in the state of the beneficial owner of the payments	Can be taxed in both contracting states

4.3 Permanent Establishment

Construction PE
- Time threshold:
- More than 6 months: 17 countries, such as Singapore, Malaysia, etc.
- More than 12 months: 24 countries, such Kazakhstan, etc.
- More than 18 months: Mongolia, Russia, Belarus and Ukraine
- More than 24 months: The United Arab Emirates

Service PE
- Time threshold:
- aggregating more than 6 months in 12-month period: 20 countries, such as Singapore, etc.
- More than 24 months: The United Arab Emirates
- No Service PE: 15 countries, such as Uzbek, etc.

Agent
- All 54 countries

Insurance
- Indonesia, Thailand, Brunei, Vietnam, Nepal, Pakistan, Sri Lanka and Egypt.

4.4 Dividends

Tax rate	Percentage of holding shares	Countries
5%	None	Mongolia, Laos, Brunei, Kuwait, Saudi Arabia, Oman, Croatia, Macedonia, Montenegro, Serbia and Slovenia
7%		The United Arab Emirates
8%		Egypt

Tax rate	Percentage of holding shares	Countries
10%		Malaysia, Indonesia, Vietnam, Kampuchea, Kazakhstan, Kyrgyz, Uzbek, Belarus, Azerbaijan, Iran, Turkey, Israel, Qatar, Bahrain, India, Nepal, Pakistan, Sri Lanka, Bangladesh, Poland, Hungary, Albania, Bosnia and Bulgaria, and Bulgaria, Slovakia
5%/10%	25%	Singapore, Tajik, Turkmenistan, Ukraine, Moldova, Armenia, Syria, Czech, Estonia, Lithuania, Latvia and Russia (the total amount is at least 80,000 Euro)
15%/20%		Thailand
10%/15%	10%	The Philippines
0/3%	50%	Romania
0/5%/10%	50%, and the total amount is at least €2 million; 10%, and the total amount is at least €10 thousand;	Georgia

4.5 Interests

Withholding tax rate	Countries
0%	Russia
3%	Romania
5%	Kuwait
7%	Singapore, Israel, the United Arab Emirates
7.50%	Czech
8%	Tajikistan
10%	Other 46 countries, Kazakhstan, etc.

4.6 Royalties

Withholding tax rate	Countries
3%	Romania
5%	Georgia
6%	Russia
7%	Latvia

Chapter 1: Removing Tax Barriers to China's BRI

Withholding tax rate	Countries
3%	Romania
7.5%	Czech
8%	Egypt, Tajikistan
10%	45 countries, Kazakhstan, etc.
12.50%	Pakistan
10%/15%	Malaysia, Philippines
15%	Thailand, Nepal

4.7 Tax Sparing

Type		Countries
Bilateral	No effective term	Vietnam, Macedonia, Nepal, Oman, India, Kuwait, Pakistan, Bulgaria, Bosnia and Herzegovina, Thailand, Malaysia, Heishan and Serbia.
	10-year effective term	Brunei, Sri Lanka, Saudi Arabia (Expired) Cambodia (effective)
Unilateral		Singapore, the United Arab Emirates
None		35 countries, such as Kazakhstan

5. Singapore's tax treaties with BRI countries

- signed tax treaties with 82 countries, and 42 of them are BRI countries
- signed few tax treaties with Middle Asia and East Europe
- Mainly based on OECD Model

Dividends	• 0-25%
	• Most set threshold on shareholding ratios, preferential tax rate 0/5%;
	• high tax rates with Southeast Asia, 0 with Middle East
Interests	• 0-15%, mainly 5%
Royalties	• 0-25%, mainly 5%-10%

6. Features of China's tax treaties with BRI countries

Compared with Singapore, withholding tax rates are relatively high in China's tax treaties:

	China	*Vs.*	*Singapore*
Dividends	5%-10%		0-5%
Interests	Mainly 10%		Mainly 5%
Royalties	Mainly 10%		5%-10%

1. Higher shareholding ratios threshold	China-Russia: Hold at least 25% shares, tax rate 5% Singapore-Russia: Hold at least 15% shares, tax rate 5%
2. Few bilateral tax sparing provisions	Only 17 countries
3. No tax treaties with 10 countries	Burma, East Timor, Bhutan, Maldives, Afghanistan, Iraq, Jordan, Palestine, Yemen and Lebanon

7. Solving Tax-Related Disputes

Since 2008, more and more taxpayers resorted to SAT assistance in relation to tax-related disputes under Mutual Agreement Procedure (MAP). To streamline MAP mechanism, SAT issued Bulletin No. 56 in 2015 to deal with treaty-related MAP cases and Bulletin No. 6 in 2017 to deal with TP-related MAP cases:

- The Bulletin on Administrative Measures for Treaty-related Mutual Agreement Procedure (SAT Bulletin [2015] No. 56)
- The Bulletin on Administrative Measures for Special Tax Investigations and Adjustments and the Mutual Agreement Procedure (SAT Bulletin [2017] No. 6)

SAT actively applies MAP to address cross-border tax disputes for multinational enterprises.

	Bilateral APA Concluded	TP Corresponding Adjustments Concluded	Treaty MAP Concluded	Mutual Negotiation Meetings Conducted	Cases Involved	Double Taxation Eliminated (RMB)
2014	6	9	11	35	51	1.84 billion
2015	6	5	7	26	52	6.37 billion
2016	6	6	2	28	78	4.97 billion
Total	18	20	20	89	–	13.18 billion

Annex II: Recent Initiatives Related to BRI by the Chinese SAT

1. Issuing Tax Residency Certificate

With the "going global" strategy, the BRI Initiative in particular, an increasing number of enterprises and individuals began to apply for Chinese Tax Residency Certificate (TRC) to enjoy benefits of the tax treaty overseas investment or operations.

SAT issued *The Bulletin on the Issuance of Chinese Tax Residency Certificate (SAT Bulletin [2016] No. 40)* to simplify the application process, clarify the materials requested and time limit set, and optimizing relevant services.

2. Conducting Country-Specific Taxation Research

When going global, many enterprises have insufficient understanding of the tax systems and policies in investment destinations, failing to rationally identify relevant tax risks.

SAT has expanded the coverage of country-specific taxation research to all BRI and other main investment destinations for "going global" as well, including 95 countries and regions in total.

As of now, SAT has issued 59 country-specific tax guidelines based on above-mentioned research, many of which are in relation to RBI countries, to introduce the business environment, tax systems, tax treaties of relevant countries for "going global" enterprises.

3. Launching Tax Service Webpage

A tax service webpage for the Belt and Road Initiative has been launched on the SAT's website to provide:

- OBOR updates;
- Presentations of tax policies on outward investments;
- Interpretation to relevant cases;
- Country-specific tax guidelines;
- Media viewpoints;

4. Launching 12366 Shanghai (International) Tax Service Centre

In 2016, a Shanghai-based tax consultation platform, the SAT 12366 Shanghai (International) Tax Service Center, has been set up to address the policy consultation for enterprises that go global and respond to their demands.

- 12366 bilingual webpage to provide tax guidance
- 12366 bilingual hotline to address inquiries from taxpayers

5. Comprehensive Campaigns

- Workshops on relevant tax policies;
- Field visits to more than 800 enterprises;
- Online interviews to collect views and requests.

6. Capacity Building Assistance to Developing Countries

1. Joint-effort with Canada in leading the FTA Capacity Building Project
   In March 2015, the FTA Bureau consented an initiative proposed by the Commissioners of Canada and China on tax capacity building, with a key project aimed at assisting developing countries' capacity building as part of its 2015-2016 work programme.
2. Regular tax training programs for Asian and African tax officials as well as experience sharing activities.
   a) In 2016, 7 events took place in the OECD-SAT Multilateral Taxation Centre in Yanghzou, and around 80 tax officials from 13 developing countries joined.
   b) SAT conducted two seminars for 137 tax officials from over 40 developing countries.

Annex III: Overall Trends in Tax Structures and Levels[13]

1. Change in Government Revenue Share of GDP

Over the last four years advanced economy governments increased revenues to reduce deficits, but emerging markets suffered a big drop in revenues & now saddled with large budget deficits.

---

13. This information was taken from Jeffrey Owens's presentation: *Economic and Tax Policy Trends Around the World: Impacts on Tax Reform in China* (14 Jun. 2017).

Chapter 1: Removing Tax Barriers to China's BRI

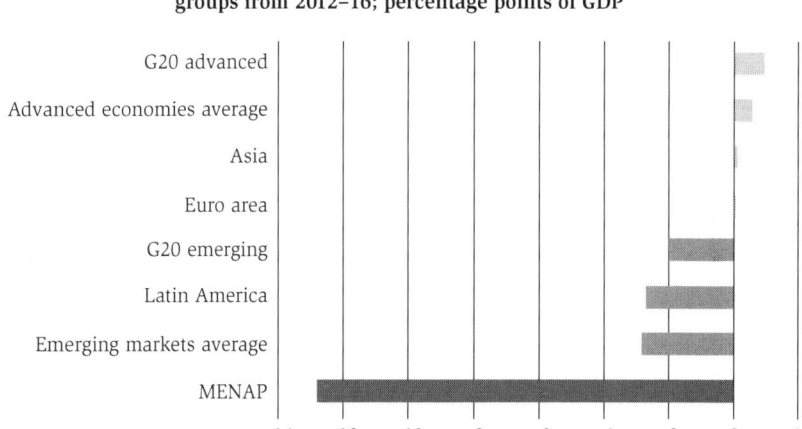

2. Government Budget Deficit

Budget deficits have come down but most major advanced economies still in deficit, sustaining pressure on tax administrations to maximize return as 'austerity fatigue' sets in.

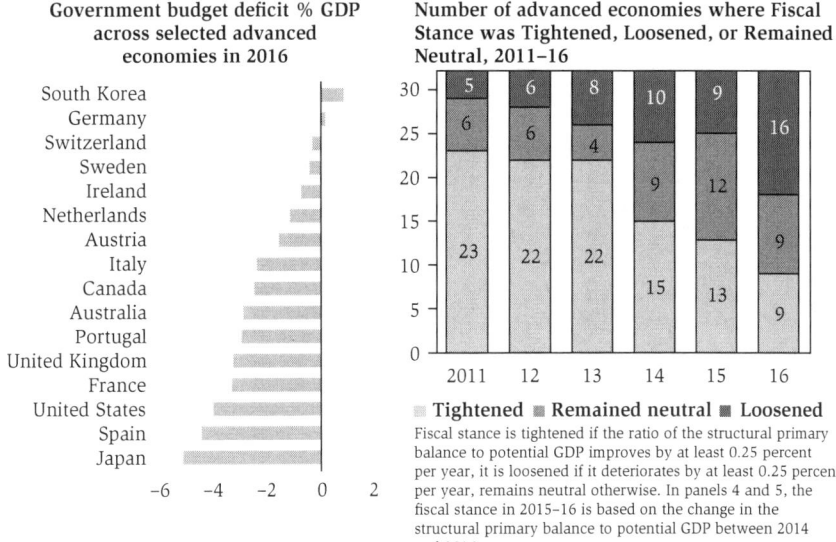

Source: IMF Fiscal Monitor data; October 2016.

3. Change in Government Revenue

Governments will be looking to raise revenues over the coming four years – emerging markets especially.

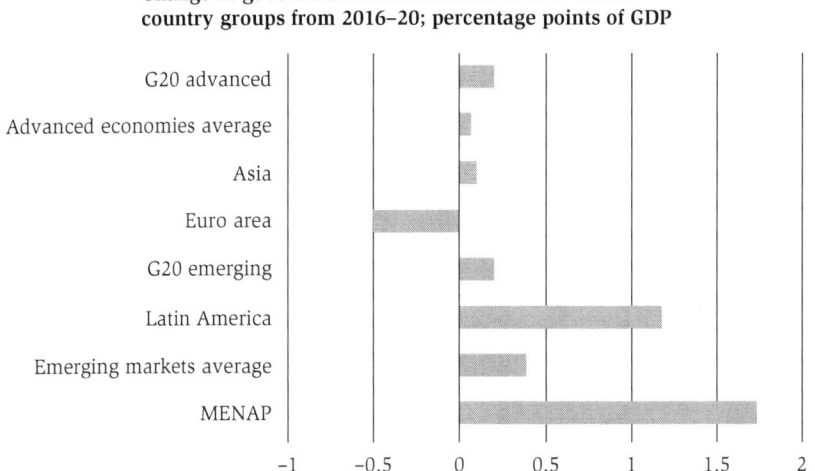

4. Percentage Point Change in Corporate Tax Revenue

Hence the relative contribution of corporate tax revenues to overall tax revenue has declined over the last decade

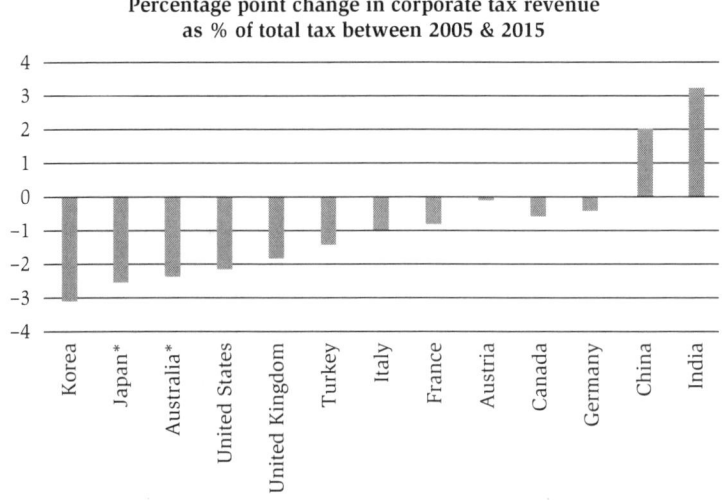

Chapter 1: Removing Tax Barriers to China's BRI

5. *Change in Tax Share of GDP Across G20*

In general, tax burdens have been increasing across the global economy post financial crisis

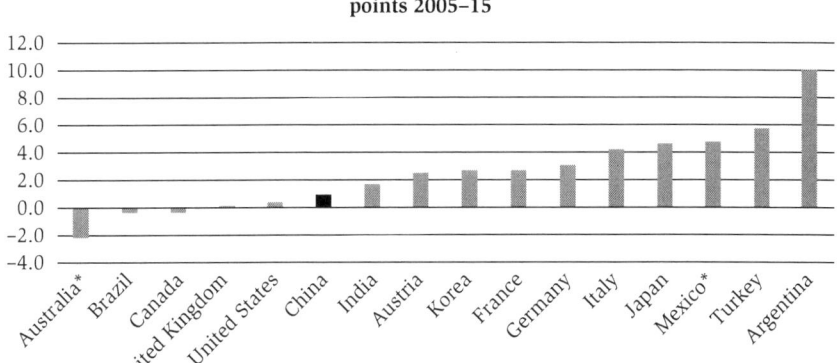

Change in tax share of GDP across G20; percentage points 2005–15

Source: EY Knowledge analysis of OECD date.

* Data until 2014.

CHAPTER 2

Neo-BEPS: China's Proposal for International Tax Reform from the Perspective of the Belt and Road Initiative

*Cao Mingxing (Bristar)**

1   Introduction
2   BEPS: Financial and Fiscal Crisis, Predicament of Globalization and the Advancement and Limitations of the Policy Response of International Taxation
3   Neo-BEPS: The Belt and Road Initiative, Neo-Globalization, Policy Response of International Taxation, China's Version 2.0 and Its Forecasting

1   INTRODUCTION

The Belt and Road Initiative is a major national policy that attempts to help Chinese enterprises to go global, build a new landscape of holistic opening up and integrate deeply into the world's economic system. The Belt and Road Initiative undertakes three historic missions, namely exploring new paths for economic growth, rebalancing globalization and creating new means of regional cooperation. Currently, it has been agreed that public finance is the cornerstone of national governance, and taxation is the hub to connect countries and communities; a well-designed public finance system is the institutional guarantee to optimize resource allocation, maintain market unity, promote social equity and achieve long-term stability. In the international arena, a fair order of international taxation has become a 'much-needed good' of the Belt and Road countries. It is imperative to identify and design an appropriate international taxation

---

*   For the unabridged version of this chapter, *see* China Taxation News, B1 (11 May 2017).

scheme so that China's overseas investment and cooperation with other Belt and Road countries can be given a boost to address the predicament in regional development and globalization.

2 BEPS: FINANCIAL AND FISCAL CRISIS, PREDICAMENT OF GLOBALIZATION AND THE ADVANCEMENT AND LIMITATIONS OF THE POLICY RESPONSE OF INTERNATIONAL TAXATION

In the wake of 2008, the worldwide financial crisis, the OECD/G20 Base Erosion and Profit Shifting (BEPS) initiative came into being with the aim to restructure the order for international taxation and the economy, as well as to tackle the governments' imbalance of payment. The BEPS initiative aims to build a fair and modern international tax system, and its basic framework includes ongoing cooperation to combat BEPS, tax information exchange and the use of a multilateral instrument for tax treaties. These approaches can help to increase taxation certainty and ensure fiscal security. For instance, as regards international transfer pricing, the reform scheme of the BEPS initiative has proposed the theory of value creation based on the notion that 'the outcome of transfer pricing should be consistent with value creation'. This theory represents a major advancement in the history of taxation. Transfer pricing files and country reports help to enhance global cooperation in tax administration, achieving unity and consistency in tax laws and norms. This is of major significance to the formal justice and procedural value in the international tax order.

However, strategy of the BEPS initiative still insists on the arm's length principle, recognizing the transactional profit split method only on a conditional basis, and emphasizes the distribution right of residual profit for capital/intangible assets, all of which exposes the limitations of the initiative. A typical case is as follows: In August 2016, the European Commission ruled that the transfer pricing agreed between the Irish government and Apple had violated EU law prohibiting 'government subsidy', and demanded that the Irish government levy the delinquent tax of EUR 13 billion against Apple. This ruling triggered asymmetric retaliation by the United States (US), which imposed USD 14 billion of penalties against Deutsche Bank. Complex cases like this show that the features of formality in the modern international taxation order are taking shape through the rules created under the mechanism of the BEPS initiative consisting of a unified transfer pricing system, automatic information exchange and a multilateral instrument to revise tax treaties. However, in circumstances where the unequal and non-independent exchange of value is commonplace, the mechanism of the BEPS initiative limits itself to the competition and allocation of stock value in the world economy and builds a relatively passive order which prioritizes anti-tax avoidance and closed-door competition for tax revenue.

Therefore, although the BEPS Action Plan provides a fine model for a joint response to international tax challenges, it still retains the drawbacks of a neo-liberalist mindset; the framework of the BEPS Action Plan is a crisis response system that focuses on cracking down on tax havens, but it has yet to rid itself of the conventional state-centric mentality. As a result, it cannot fundamentally retune the unequal distribution of international tax interests. Indeed, the BEPS mechanism fails to attach enough significance to helping developing countries and less-developed countries to consolidate fiscal governance, a key approach to improving global economic governance. Therefore, it is not capable of promoting a balanced development of the global economy.

3 NEO-BEPS: THE BELT AND ROAD INITIATIVE, NEO-GLOBALIZATION, POLICY RESPONSE OF INTERNATIONAL TAXATION, CHINA'S VERSION 2.0 AND ITS FORECASTING

To some extent, the Belt and Road Initiative is the product in response to the global economic crisis triggered by the financial crisis. Along the Belt and Road, China and the Silk Road countries share high-quality industrial capacity, discuss project investment, co-build infrastructure, co-share outcomes of cooperation, communicate policies, connect facilities, open trade, access capita and build people-to-people friendships. Ultimately, countries work together to build a community of interests, of a shared future and responsibility featuring political mutual trust, economic integration and cultural inclusion. Therefore, it becomes clear that Belt and Road Initiative not only blazes the path for Chinese enterprises to go global but also builds a new model for regional and global resource allocation, namely the new globalization model for the world's economy and society.

If the BEPS initiative prioritizes sharing benefits in a positive way, seeking a form of equity in the competition for stock value of business, then the Belt and Road Initiative is keen on consultation, co-establishment and co-sharing, seeking to expand the benefits through the consolidation of resources, and seeking to share growth through cooperation. As a result, neo-BEPS has emerged. Needless to say, neo-BEPS embodies the Belt and Road principles of consultation, co-establishment and co-sharing in international taxation, and ultimately develops itself into China's version 2.0 of the BEPS response mechanism. Supported by the idea of inclusive growth in the Belt and Road Initiative, neo-BEPS builds a more proactive order featuring going global, growth and co-sharing, which can be made possible by proactive fiscal policies embraced by the market-boosting and active governments. Only by doing so, can an innovative international tax system be built among the regions consisting of fair profit (share) principle, formulary allocation method, distribution right of region-specific advantages, tax safe harbours in industries and special tax administration regions. An international tax system characterized by streamlined processes, certainty, efficiency and equity can help to build the new order of co-creating the tax base, co-sharing profit, economic development and substantive social justice and fairness.

The neo-BEPS scheme demonstrates that the predicament of economic globalization is pushing forward the upgrading and modernization of the international tax order. As the governance in developed countries has been modernized from formal justice to substantive justice, from passive right/order to proactive right/order, the predicament of globalization will give rise to an in-depth change in modernizing the international taxation order. This will include the BEPS reform scheme characterized by limited intervention, passive rights and formal justice proposed by developed countries, and the neo-BEPS reform plan featuring proactive order and substantive justice proposed by emerging markets (represented by China). A progressive and systematic restructuring of the international tax order further indicates that taxation should not only be the target for competition but should also be a catalyst for cooperation. Globalization should not and will not stagnate; rather it will unfold through a brand new and more rational order.

CHAPTER 3

Research on the International Taxation Issues under the Belt and Road Initiative: Comparison of Corporate Income Tax Laws and Tax Treaties

Wenjing Wang*

1	Introduction
2	Basic Situations of Countries along the Belt and Road
3	Comparison of Corporate Income Tax Laws of Countries along the Belt and Road
	3.1 Nominal Corporate Income Tax Rates
	3.2 Anti-Avoidance Provisions in Corporate Income Tax Laws
4	Comparison of Chinese Bilateral Tax Treaties with Countries along the Belt and Road
	4.1 Permanent Establishments
	4.2 Limited Tax Rates for Passive Income
	4.2.1 Limited Tax Rates for Dividends
	4.2.2 Limited Tax Rates for Interest
	4.2.3 Limited Tax Rates for Royalties
	4.3 Tax Sparing Provisions
5	International Tax Challenges under the Belt and Road Initiative
	5.1 Conflicts under the Three Legal Systems

---

* The author can be reached at wwj@cufe.edu.cn. This chapter is translated and modified based on the author's article published in the *Journal of Law and Economy* (in Chinese), with some amendments and deletions.

> 5.2 Different Coordination Objectives under the Silk Road Economic Belt and the 21st Century Maritime Silk Road
> 5.3 Cooperation under the BEPS Initiative

1 INTRODUCTION

The 'Decision of the Central Committee of the Communist Party of China on Some Major Issues Concerning Comprehensively Deepening the Reform' put forward the proposal of 'promoting the construction of the Silk Road Economic Belt and the Maritime Silk Road and forming a new pattern of opening up in all directions' in 2013. China promulgated the 'Vision and Actions on Jointly Building the Silk Road Economic Belt and 21st Century Maritime Silk Road' in 2015. The Belt and Road Initiative has received many positive responses from countries around the world. The intention of multilateral cooperation in the region around the Silk Road Economic Belt and the 21st Century Maritime Silk Road is gradually achieving a consensus on more in-depth and comprehensive development. Meanwhile, the tax issues arising from cross-border economic activities is a critical topic that governments and corporations cannot avoid. It not only relates to the country's tax jurisdiction, but also affects corporations' decisions regarding whether or how to go global. Thus, this chapter emphasizes a comparison and analysis of corporate income tax laws and international tax treaties of countries along the Belt and Road, so as to discuss the international tax issues under the Belt and Road Initiative.

2 BASIC SITUATIONS OF COUNTRIES ALONG THE BELT AND ROAD

The Belt and Road Initiative has the features of wide geographic coverage; a diversified economic and social environment; and win-win cooperation. As the Initiative has not yet fixed on any specific areas and has a wide economic scope, the classification or grouping of countries along the Belt and Road has been the subject of much research. Current research on the classification is mainly based on spatial geography or characteristics of politics and economics, and no final conclusion has yet been reached. For example, Gong et al.[1] and Zou et al.[2] asserted six areas based on geographic location, including Mongolia and Russia, Central Asia, Southeast Asia, South Asia, Central and Eastern Europe, West Asia and the Middle East. Focused on the Silk Road Economic Belt, He and Zhang[3] asserted five categories based on regions, including East Asia, Central Asia, West Asia, Middle and Eastern Europe and Western Europe.

---

1. Gong Piping, Song Zhouying & Liu Weidong, *Commodity Patterns of China's Trade with Countries along The Belt and Road Initiatives*, Geographical Science Development 5, at 571–580 (2015).
2. Zou Jialing, Liu Chunla, Yin Guoqing & Tang Zhipeng, *China's Trade Patterns with Countries along the Belt and Road and Its Economic Contribution*, Geographical Science Development 5, at 598–605 (2015).
3. He Maochun & Zhang Jibing, *National Initiative Analysis of New Silk Road Economic Belt: Historical Opportunities, Potential Challenges and Countermeasures in China*, The People's Forum – Academic Frontiers 12, at 6–13 (2013).

Based on the above classifications, for purposes of this chapter, the author chose sixty-four countries along the Belt and Road as a research sample and further classified these countries into six categories:

- the eleven countries of Southeast Asia (Brunei, Cambodia, Indonesia, Laos, Malaysia, Myanmar, the Philippines, Singapore, Thailand, Timor-Leste and Vietnam);
- the eight countries of South Asia (Afghanistan, Bangladesh, Bhutan, India, Maldives, Nepal, Pakistan and Sri Lanka);
- the sixteen countries of West Asia and North Africa (Bahrain, Egypt, Iran, Iraq, Israel, Jordan, Kuwait, Lebanon, Oman, Palestine, Qatar, Saudi Arabia, Syria, Turkey, the United Arab Emirates and Yemen);
- the five countries of Middle Asia (Kazakhstan, Kyrgyzstan, Tajikistan, Turkmenistan and Uzbekistan);
- the eight countries of the Commonwealth of Independence States and related countries (Armenia, Azerbaijan, Belarus, Georgia, Moldova, Mongolia, Russia and Ukraine); and
- the sixteen countries of Middle and East Europe (Albania, Bosnia and Herzegovina, Bulgaria, Croatia, Czech Republic, Estonia, Hungary, Latvia, Lithuania, Macedonia, Montenegro, Poland, Romania, Serbia, Slovakia and Slovenia).

Using the above classification, this chapter compares the tax systems of countries along the Belt and Road from the perspectives of corporate income tax law and international tax treaties, in order to explain the essential international tax issues.

The economic development gaps among the sixty-four countries have been large. This includes not only countries at a high economic level (such as India and Russia), but also countries at a low economic level (such as Bhutan and Palestine). These sixty-four countries includes not only high national income countries (such as Poland and Singapore), but also lower national income countries (such as Afghanistan, Cambodia and Nepal). Nearly one-third of countries are similar to China, which belongs to middle-income countries according to the identification standards of the World Bank.[4] Furthermore, Afghanistan, Bangladesh, Bhutan, Cambodia, East Timor, Laos, Myanmar, Nepal and Yemen are the least developed countries under the identification framework of United Nations.

From the perspective of economic structure, there are also major differences among the countries along the Belt and Road. This includes not only the countries that have the most concentrated oil exportation but also those countries having a single economic structure and those countries that are rich in resources in Middle-Asia. Countries in South Asia and Southeast Asia have many intimate economic relations with China, and their economic development mainly depends on outward trade. These different types of economic structures have created space for multi-dimensional cooperation between China and countries along the Belt and Road.

---

4. *See* https://data.worldbank.org/.

From the perspective of legal characteristics, countries along the Belt and Road contain three types of typical legal systems, namely the civil law system, the Anglo-American legal system and the Islamic legal system. There are also some differences among the countries with an Islamic legal system along the Belt and Road, including not only the countries with a unification of state and church (such as Iran, Oman, Saudi Arabia and the United Arab Emirates), but also those countries with some extent of modernization (such as Afghanistan, Egypt, Jordan, Lebanon, Syria and Turkey).[5]

3 COMPARISON OF CORPORATE INCOME TAX LAWS OF COUNTRIES ALONG THE BELT AND ROAD[6]

As mentioned, countries along the Belt and Road feature three types of legal systems, namely the civil law system, the Anglo-American legal system and the Islamic legal system. Against the background of each country's legal system, the tax rules must be different from each other. The corporate income tax laws are closely related to the Belt and Road Initiative and significantly affect Chinese 'going global' enterprises. Therefore, it is necessary to summarize and compare the corporate income tax laws of the sixty-four countries, and then find commonalities and differences.

3.1 Nominal Corporate Income Tax Rates

The tax burden is an important factor influencing international commerce and investment. Comparing the nominal corporate income tax rates of Belt and Road countries in 2015, almost half of the countries' standard tax rates are below 20%.

First, from the perspective of the types of tax rates, only seven countries (Egypt, Hungary, India, Mongolia, Palestine, Syria and the United Arab Emirates) apply progressive tax rates. Among them, India uses a total progressive tax rate, while the other six countries use an excess progressive tax rate. The other fifty-seven countries use a proportional tax rate. The similar consistency of China and Belt and Road countries offers convenient cooperation for bilateral and multilateral international tax coordination to some extent in the implementation process of the Belt and Road Initiative.

Second, the arithmetic mean and median values of nominal tax rates in the 64 Belt and Road countries are 19.26% and 19%, respectively, which are both below the Chinese nominal rate (25%). In the fifty-seven countries with a proportionate tax rate,

---

5. Ma Mingxian, *Modern Islamic Law Research*, Xi'an: Northwestern University, World History Doctoral Dissertation (2005).
6. Referenced original materials sources: (1) The Chinese Certified Tax Agents Concentric Service Group. *Overview of the Tax Issues Concerning the Development of the Belt and Road Initiative* (China Tax Press 2015); (2) https://www.ibfd.org/; (3) websites of tax administrations in countries along the Belt and Road.

Chapter 3: International Taxation Coordination under the New Silk Road

only seven (Bahrain, Bangladesh, Bhutan, Israel, Pakistan, the Philippines and Sri Lanka) have a higher tax rate, and these countries are mainly located in South Asia. Five countries, including Indonesia, Iran, Malaysia, Myanmar and Nepal, have the same tax rate as China. All of the other forty-five countries have lower rates.

Third, the average tax rates in countries along the twenty-first Century Maritime Silk Road are less than that in countries along the Silk Road Economic Belt. Sorting the country groups from high to low, the arithmetic average of the nominal corporate income tax rates are the eight countries of South Asia; the eleven countries of East and South Asia; the eight countries of the Commonwealth of Independence States and related countries; the sixteen countries of Eastern Europe; and the five countries of Central Asia.

3.2 Anti-Avoidance Provisions in Corporate Income Tax Laws

Those responsible for the cross-border investment and business activities of enterprises always pay attention to international tax planning arrangements. Therefore, anti-avoidance provisions under domestic tax laws will also greatly affect the cross-border economic activities of enterprises. Among the sixty-four Belt and Road countries, less than one-third has a general anti-avoidance clause in the domestic tax law system. These countries are mainly located in Central and Eastern Europe, with some others mainly located in West Asia and North Africa.

Regarding special anti-tax avoidance legislation, most countries along the Belt and Road include the transfer pricing rules, intending to prevent enterprises from engaging in tax evasion and avoidance.

With regard to thin capitalization rules, countries along the Belt and Road pay less attention to this issue than to transfer pricing legislation. In those countries without thin capitalization rules, there may exist excessive securitization capital structures or excessive debt-based tax planning. As a whole, the tax law of Central and Eastern European countries generally includes thin capitalization rules, and the debt-to-equity ratio is usually set at 3:1 or 4:1.

Regarding controlled foreign company rules, the number of countries along the Belt and Road that have enacted such legislation is significantly less than the number of countries with transfer pricing and thin capitalization provisions. The reason why many countries lack such rules could be related to the direction of their capital flows. For net capital-importing countries, the tax authorities may not pay particular attention to the tax administration of overseas profits of controlled foreign companies.

On the whole, the anti-avoidance provisions in the corporate income tax laws of countries along the Belt and Road are not very perfect. In contrast, Central and Northern European countries generally have relatively tighter rules than other countries along the Belt and Road.

4 COMPARISON OF CHINESE BILATERAL TAX TREATIES WITH COUNTRIES ALONG THE BELT AND ROAD[7]

There are still ten countries among the sixty-four along the Belt and Road discussed in this chapter that had not signed bilateral tax treaties with China as at November 2017, namely Afghanistan, Bhutan, East Timor, Iraq, Jordan, Lebanon, Maldives, Myanmar, Palestine and Yemen. Although bilateral tax treaties have not been signed, the Chinese air or sea transport agreements with Lebanon and the Maldives contain tax exemption provisions in order to eliminate double taxation.

4.1 Permanent Establishments

The identification of a permanent establishment is an essential issue in the field of international taxation, and it is also a significant aspect of bilateral tax treaties. As described in the Chinese tax treaty with Singapore,[8] the term 'permanent establishment' specifically includes: (i) a place of management, (ii) a branch, (iii) an office, (iv) a factory, (v) a workshop and (vi) a mine, an oil or gas well, a quarry or any other place of extraction of natural resources. This treaty also lists the following exemptions from classification as a permanent establishment.

Comparing the article on permanent establishments in the Chinese tax treaties with fifty-four countries along the Belt and Road, the author finds that these fifty-four include provisions from both the United Nations Model Convention (e.g., the construction-project-type and labour-type permanent establishments are included), as well as provisions from the OECD Model Convention (e.g., the delivery function is contained in the list of exemptions from permanent establishment status). The significant differences between the provisions on permanent establishments under these fifty-four different treaties are the time criteria for the construction-project-type and labour-type permanent establishments. For example, the shortest criterion for construction-project-type permanent establishments is one hundred and eighty-three days or six months, while the longest is twenty-four months, and most treaties take the criterion of twelve months. And not all of these treaties contain provisions regarding labour-type permanent establishments. However, the Chinese treaties with South Asian and Southeast Asian countries usually contain provisions on labour-type permanent establishments, and the time criterion for construction-project-type permanent establishments is usually relatively short.

These articles on permanent establishments affect both international business and tax planning for multinational enterprises. Especially for those enterprises from countries the corporate income tax rate of which is less than that in China, they may pay more attention to the article on permanent establishment in order to avoid taxation

---

7. Treaties sources: http://www.chinatax.gov.cn/n810341/n810770/index.html.
8. This treaty is relatively significant because the State Administration of Taxation in China promulgated a special tax regulation (Document 75 in 2010) to explain the treaty's articles in order to set an example for the correct use of other bilateral tax treaties signed by China.

in China. The differences among bilateral treaties and domestic tax laws along the Belt and Road will have particular influences on the process of the initiative.

4.2 Limited Tax Rates for Passive Income

The tax rates for passive income under treaties are generally no more than the non-resident tax rates established under domestic tax law. Therefore, a brief comparison is made of the limited tax rates for dividends, interest and royalties in the Chinese treaties with countries along the Belt and Road.

4.2.1 Limited Tax Rates for Dividends

The prevailing tax rate applicable to the beneficial owner of dividends in most treaties is 10%. In the Chinese treaties with Bahrain, Brunei, Croatia, Kuwait, Laos, Macedonia, Mongolia, Oman, Saudi Arabia, Serbia and Montenegro and Slovenia, the rate is 5%. In the treaty with the United Arab Emirates, the rate is 7%; with Egypt, 8%. Countries such as Armenia, the Czech Republic, Estonia, Georgia, Latvia, Lithuania, Moldova, the Philippines, Singapore, Syria, Tajikistan, Thailand, Turkmenistan and Ukraine grant a lower limited tax rate to the beneficial owners of dividends when they meet certain shareholding requirements.

4.2.2 Limited Tax Rates for Interest

The limited tax rate applicable to the beneficial owner of interest in most treaties is also 10%. The rate is 5% in the Chinese treaty with Kuwait, and 7% in the treaty with the United Arab Emirates. The Chinese treaties with other countries such as the Czech Republic, Israel, Laos, Singapore, Sri Lanka, Syria, Tajikistan, Thailand, Turkey, Turkmenistan, Ukraine, Uzbekistan and Vietnam, have other preferential provisions for interest in addition to the limited tax rates, above. For example, the tax-exempt clause will apply to the specific interest income derived from the government or relevant government authorities of the other contracting state.

4.2.3 Limited Tax Rates for Royalties

The limited tax rate applicable to the beneficial owner of royalties in most treaties is also 10%. In the Chinese treaty with Georgia, the rate is 5%; with Romania, 7%; with Egypt and Tajikistan, 8%; and with Pakistan, 12.5%. For the Chinese treaties with, for example, Bulgaria, Israel, Laos, Malaysia, the Philippines and Poland, the tax rates depend on the type of royalties. In particular, in the Chinese treaties with Nepal and Thailand, the rate is 15% – which is relatively high.

In general, the limited tax rates in Chinese bilateral tax treaties with countries along the Belt and Road basically reflect the tax concession purpose – something to which 'go global' enterprises should pay more attention. Enterprises should make full use of the preferential provisions in existing bilateral tax treaties in order to avoid unnecessary international tax burdens.

4.3 Tax Sparing Provisions

Due to the effect of tax credit limitation and the fact that the corporate income tax rate in China is generally higher than in most countries along the Belt and Road, whether the preferential tax policies of the countries along the Belt and Road can attract Chinese capital effectively is affected to some extent by the tax sparing provisions in treaties. Comparing Chinese bilateral tax treaties with countries along the Belt and Road, most do not contain tax sparing provisions. The treaties with Bosnia and Herzegovina, Brunei, Bulgaria, India, Kuwait, Macedonia, Malaysia, Montenegro, Oman, Pakistan, Serbia, Slovakia, Sri Lanka, Thailand and Vietnam have a tax sparing provision with China mutually, which will stimulate bilateral investments to some extent.

5 INTERNATIONAL TAX CHALLENGES UNDER THE BELT AND ROAD INITIATIVE

With the development of the Belt and Road Initiative, the interaction between China and countries along the Belt and Road will be even more profound and broad. Under current domestic tax laws and tax treaties along the Belt and Road, cross-border taxation issues may arise and affect bilateral and multilateral cooperation.

5.1 Conflicts under the Three Legal Systems

The Belt and Road Initiative focuses not only on the relations between China and the countries along the Belt and Road. In the long run, this initiative may foster multinational economic cooperation. Therefore, differences under the Anglo-American legal system, the civil law system and the Islamic legal system as regards corporate income tax laws will inevitably lead to cross-border tax coordination issues. The problems stem from the internal differences among these legal systems. For example, the lack of anti-avoidance provisions in corporate income tax laws in many Southeast Asia countries will increase the systematic gaps of anti-tax avoidance cooperation between these countries with China and with other countries along the Belt and Road. In addition, the implementation of a single territorial jurisdiction or both territorial and residence-based jurisdiction will also give rise to unavoidable international tax coordination issues.

The fundamental principle to deal with these issues may rely on the coordination mechanisms under the Belt and Road Initiative. In the bilateral context, this issue can be resolved through consultations at the national level. However, if placed in the multilateral framework of the Belt and Road Initiative, it is necessary to establish a

Chapter 3: International Taxation Coordination under the New Silk Road

multilateral tax cooperation mechanism that will not only provide a communication platform for all countries, but also enhance multilateral tax collection and administration cooperation.

5.2 Different Coordination Objectives under the Silk Road Economic Belt and the 21st Century Maritime Silk Road

Based on this chapter's comparative analysis of corporate income tax laws, one can see that there are many differences in the corporate income tax laws between the countries along the Silk Road Economic Belt and the countries along the 21st Century Maritime Silk Road. On the one hand, this is related to the differences among the legal systems, while on the other hand, it is related to many factors such as geographic location, resources, economic structure and population density.

This chapter suggests that China should take a differentiated approach to cross-border tax coordination, considering the differences between the Belt and the Road. In future, when China will share and coordinate tax benefits brought by the cross-border economy with countries along the Belt and Road, it should make effective decisions according to the separate economic, social and tax characteristics.

5.3 Cooperation under the BEPS Initiative

In 2015, the OECD and G20 issued final reports on the Actions of the BEPS initiative that include not only many changes to existing international tax rules, but also means of deterring multinationals from evading global tax obligations and eroding national tax bases. These final reports indicate one path towards international tax coordination and management for China during the implementation of the Belt and Road Initiative, especially in the field of international anti-avoidance cooperation. However, considering the economic situations and tax collection and management abilities of countries along the Belt and Road, it may not be easy to achieve an effective international tax coordination mechanism in a short time. At present, a more feasible idea would be to promote the establishment of a bilateral, jointly functioning mechanism in the process of implementing the Belt and Road Initiative through various memorandums, dialogue mechanisms and other flexible means.

CHAPTER 4

Comparison of Tax Issues in the Main Belt and Road Countries and Industries of Chinese Outbound Foreign Direct Investment

Yang He & Ying Shaokai

1 Introduction
2 Economic Development and Industry Structure in the Main Belt and Road Countries
3 Tax Policies in the Main Belt and Road Countries
4 Conclusion
References

1 INTRODUCTION

Outbound foreign direct investment (OFDI) from China to Belt and Road countries reached 11.1% of total foreign direct investment in 2014, which continued to increase in the following years.[1] According to statistics of the Minister of Commerce, in 2016, Chinese enterprises made OFDI into fifty-three countries along the Belt and Road with a total amount of USD 14.53 billion. However, most of this OFDI flowed to several countries and industries, because of the economic diversity of Belt and Road countries. Some Belt and Road countries are less developed and lack the necessary infrastructure for further investment. It is useful to analyse tax issues in those countries and industries that have attracted the most foreign direct investment. This comparison is

---

1. CN: Ministry of Commerce, http://fec.mofcom.gov.cn/article/tjsj/tjgb/201512/20151201223579.shtml.

important for foreign investors in Belt and Road countries, and their experience is also helpful for other less attractive countries to improve their investment environment.

2 ECONOMIC DEVELOPMENT AND INDUSTRY STRUCTURE IN THE MAIN BELT AND ROAD COUNTRIES

The sizes of the economies in Belt and Road countries vary considerably. For example, the GDP of Russia accounts for 15.73% of total GDP in Belt and Road countries, while the GDP of Moldova accounts for only 0.06% of total GDP in Belt and Road countries. From the perspective of income per capita, there are eighteen developed economies (such as Czech Republic, Estonia, Israel, Latvia, Singapore, Slovakia and Slovenia), twenty-one middle-income countries and twenty-three low-income countries.

Regarding economic structure, there are countries with a diversity of industries, and some countries rely heavily on oil or other energy resources. The authors have chosen countries near the median gross domestic income per capita to evaluate their industry structure, including Bulgaria, India, Mongolia, the Philippines and Turkey.

Table 4.1 Industry Structure of Middle-Income Belt and Road Countries

	Agriculture GDP (%)	Industry GDP (%)	Services GDP (%)	Significant Industries
Bulgaria	5	24.8	70.2	Tourism, shipbuilding, food processing, medicine, agriculture, forestry
India	13.9	26.2	59.9	Agriculture, industry, services, textiles, medicine
Mongolia	16.5	40.4	43.1	Farming, agriculture, processing, construction, tourism, communications
Philippines	11.21	30.93	57.85	Agriculture, service outsourcing, tourism, manufacture, coal and transportation, communications, warehousing
Turkey	8.9	27.3	63.8	Textiles, automobiles, agriculture, tourism

Data source: Country Guidelines for OFDI 2014, Chinese Ministry of Commerce.

Table 4.1 indicates that the share of agriculture within GDP in Mongolia is the highest at 16.5%, while the share of services within GDP in Bulgaria is highest at 70.2%. The significance of services in Bulgaria, India, the Philippines and Turkey is more than 50% of GDP. In other words, the economic structure in Southeast Asia countries still relies on agriculture, while Middle Eastern and West Asia countries are more developed in services sector.

Chapter 4: Tax Issues in the Main Belt & Road Countries and Industries

3 TAX POLICIES IN THE MAIN BELT AND ROAD COUNTRIES

In the Belt and Road countries, the top ten countries that attract OFDI from China are by investment magnitude, Singapore, Indonesia, Russia, Kazakhstan, Laos, Turkey, Thailand, Malaysia, Cambodia and Vietnam. In 2013, the OFDI in these countries reached USD 8.45 billion and the number increased to USD 8.81 billion in 2015[2] The tax structure in these countries has a significant impact on OFDI of Chinese firms.

Table 4.2 compares the corporate income tax rates in the top ten countries that attract the most OFDI from China.

Table 4.2 *Corporate Income Tax Comparison in Main Belt and Road Countries*

	Statutory Rate (%)	Special Rates
Cambodia	20	30% for oil and coal development enterprises, 5% for insurance and reinsurance enterprises
Kazakhstan	20	None
Indonesia	25	None
Laos	24	26% for tobacco enterprises
Malaysia	25	None
Pakistan	33	35% for banks, 25% for small enterprises
Singapore	17	None
Thailand	20	None
Turkey	25	None
Vietnam	22	None
average	23.3	None

Data Source: Deloitte tax database.

From Table 4.3, one can *see* that for corporate income tax purposes, the ten countries all apply a proportional tax rate, and specific tax rates are set for certain industries in Cambodia, Laos and Pakistan are different. The average tax rate of the ten countries is 23.3%, which is slightly less than the 25% rate of China's corporate income tax.

Table 4.3 *Personal Income Tax Rates in the Main Belt and Road Countries*

	Statutory Rate (%)
Cambodia	0/5/10/15/20
Kazakhstan	10/(5/15)/(10/20)
Indonesia	5/15/25/30

---

2. Ministry of Commerce, http://fec.mofcom.gov.cn/article/tjsj/tjgb/201512/20151201223579.shtml.

	Statutory Rate (%)
Laos	0/5/10/15/20/24
Malaysia	0-26
Pakistan	(5-20)/ (10-25)
Singapore	(2-20)/15
Thailand	0/10/20/30/37
Turkey	0/10/20
Vietnam	(5-35)/20/ (0.1-25)

Data Source: Deloitte tax database.

The other countries' personal income tax rates are all cumulative and different tax rates are provided for different types of income. For statistical purposes, taking the average tax personal income tax progressive rates for residents as a comparison, Cambodia's tax rate is 10%, Indonesia's is 18.75%, Kazakhstan's is 10%, Malaysia's is 10.8%, Pakistan's is 12.5%, Singapore's is 10.4%, Thailand's is 19.4% and Vietnams' is 20%. The personal income tax rates in Indonesia, Thailand and Vietnam are relatively high. According to the relevant documents of the State Administration of Taxation on China's personal income tax, the average tax rate for personal income tax in China is 24%, which is higher than the average tax rate of the above-mentioned top investment countries.

Table 4.4 Goods and Services Tax Comparison in the Main Belt and Road Countries

Country	Type		Tax Rate
	VAT	Sales Tax	Statutory Tax Rate (%)
Cambodia	√		10
Kazakhstan	√		12
Indonesia	√	√	10
Laos	√		10
Malaysia		√	10
	Service Tax		6
Pakistan		√	16
Singapore,	√		7
Thailand	√		7
Turkey	√		3.6 + 2.4
Vietnam	√		0, 5, 10
		√	10-70

Data Source: Deloitte tax database.

As shown in Table 4.4, VAT is levied in eight countries – all of the ten except Malaysia and Pakistan. Malaysia levied a services tax and sales tax before 1 April 2015, followed by a single consumption tax of 6% at the standard tax rate, while a 16% sales tax is levied in Pakistan. Indonesia and Vietnam collect VAT and sales tax at the same time at different rates, but Indonesia levies sales tax on luxury goods. The remaining countries, namely Cambodia, Kazakhstan, Laos, Singapore and Thailand, are levying only VAT without levying sales tax.

4 CONCLUSION

The area of foreign direct investment in China is mainly concentrated in South Asia and Southeast Asia, which will greatly contribute to China's economic growth and regional development. The corporate income tax rates of the main Belt and Road countries is less than the corporate income tax rate in China. Their personal income tax is levied at progressive tax rates, and the average tax rate is also less than that in China. The turnover tax in the main Belt and Road countries is VAT, and the tax rate is generally less than the standard VAT rate of 17% in China. These attractive tax systems help to explain why Chinese investment mainly goes to these countries, and understanding each country's specific tax policy can help Chinese enterprises that invest aboard.

REFERENCES

R. Morck, B. Yeung & M. Zhao, *Perspectives on China'5 Outward Foreign Direct Investment*, 39 J. Intl. Bus. Studies 3, at 337–350 (2008).

Yang & Zhiyong, *The Fiscal and Tax Policy in One Belt and One Road Initiative*, The Tax Research Journal 6 (2015).

CHAPTER 5

Preferential Treatment under Chinese Tax Treaties with Belt and Road Countries and Disputes Regarding Their Application

Cui Xiaojing[*]

1	Introduction
2	Preferential Treatment under Tax Treaties
	2.1 Interest Article in Tax Treaties
	2.2 Dividends Article in Tax Treaties
	2.3 Royalties Article in Tax Treaties
3	Impact of the OECD/G20 BEPS Project on the Application of Preferential Treatment under Tax Treaties
	3.1 Provisions on Treaty Shopping under BEPS Action 6
	3.2 The Connotation and Application Requirements of the LOB Rules
	3.3 Connotation and Application Requirements of the PPT Rules
	3.4 Suggestions for Balancing Compliance with the BEPS Project and Access to Treaty Benefits
4	Empirical Analysis of the Preferential Tax Treaties Used by Chinese Going-Global Enterprises
	4.1 Case of Chinese Unicom Red Chip Company: Dividend Discount
	4.1.1 Facts of the Case
	4.1.2 Analysis of the Legal Issues
	4.2 Case of Huaxin Cement Limited Company
	4.2.1 Facts of the Case
	4.2.2 Analysis of the Legal Problems Involved
	4.3 Case of Jerry Petroleum Company

---

[*] The Chinese version of this paper has been published in China Legal Science 2017(2).

           4.3.1 Facts of the Case
           4.3.2 Analysis of the Legal Issues Involved
5   Solution to Address Disputes Regarding Tax Treaties Benefits
     5.1 Local Relief in the Host Country as the Main Solution
     5.2 Diplomatic Protection as Auxiliary Solution
     5.3 MAP Between Contracting Countries
6   Conclusion

1   INTRODUCTION

With the advancement of the Chinese Belt and Road Initiative, the stock of Chinese foreign investment is growing. In 2015, Chinese enterprises invested directly in forty-nine countries along the Belt and Road, which amounted to a total investment of USD 14.82 billion, and year-on-year growth of 18.2%. This investment is directed mainly to Indonesia, Kazakhstan, Laos, Russia Singapore and Thailand. Regarding overseas contracted projects, in 2015, Chinese enterprises signed 3,987 contracts in sixty countries along the Belt and Road. The total value of these contracts worth USD 9264 million, accounting for 44.1% of the total newly signed construction contracts abroad, and representing a year-on-year growth of 7.4%; the completed business turnover was USD 69.26 billion, which was over 45% of the total and a year-on-year growth of 7.6%.[1]

Chinese enterprises enjoy opportunities but also face many challenges in the implementation of the Belt and Road Initiative, especially in the field of international taxation. When enterprises go global, on the one hand they may face double taxation, they might not enjoy the preferential tax treatment to which they are entitled; and there are tax risks such as tax discrimination and unfair treatment. On the other hand, they are faced with the problem of how to resolve tax disputes with local tax authorities in the process of investment.

2   PREFERENTIAL TREATMENT UNDER TAX TREATIES

An international tax treaty is a written treaty to coordinate the allocation of taxing rights and interests and to facilitate international tax administrative assistance between jurisdictions.[2] In order to avoid double taxation of income and property and to prevent tax evasion, countries generally enter into bilateral tax treaties. Since China began its first negotiations with Japan for an income tax treaty (tax treaty) in January 1981, China has officially signed 1 multilateral tax treaty and 102 income tax treaties, 98 of which are already in force. China has also signed tax arrangements with two special administrative regions, Hong Kong and Macao, and signed an income tax treaty with

---

1. CN: Min. of Commerce, *2015 Economic and Trade Cooperation with 'The Belt and Road' countries,* http://www.mofcom.gov.cn/article/tongjiziliao/dgzz/201601/20160101239881.shtml (accessed 2 Jul. 2016).
2. *See* the editor in chief of Liao Yixin: 'international tax law', higher education press, 2008, sixtieth pages.

Chapter 5: Tax Treaties Preferential Arrangements: China and BRI Countries

Taiwan.[3] As seen in Figure 5.1, China currently has signed tax treaties with fifty-four of the sixty-four Belt and Road countries,[4] and this tax treaty network covers most Belt and Road countries and regions. As a result, the infrastructure work of the Belt and Road international tax administration has been established.

Figure 5.1 Amount of Tax Treaties Between China and Belt and Road Countries

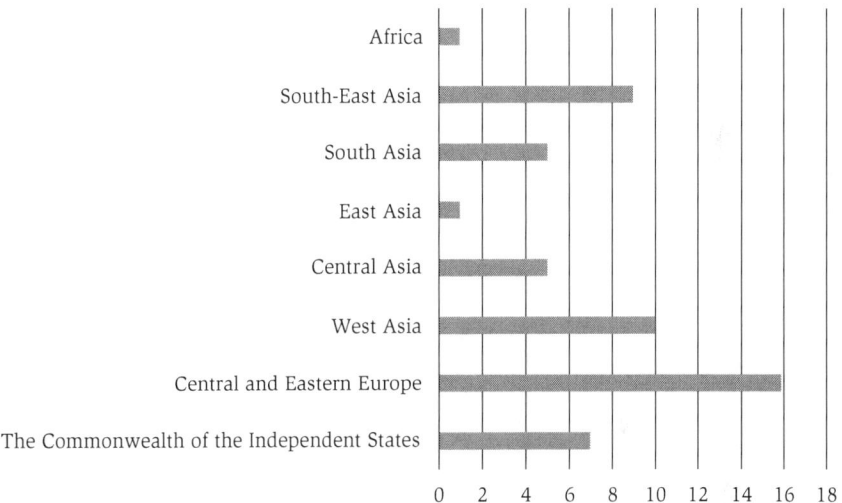

Tax treaties fall under the umbrella of international law. Bilateral tax treaties are negotiated by the governments of the two contracting parties and become effective after being ratified by their respective legislative procedures. Therefore, they are legally binding on the contracting governments. Under the principle of *Pacta Sunt Servanda* and international common practice, when a tax treaty is not consistent with domestic

---

3. *See* CN: State Administration of Taxation, http://www.chinatax.gov.cn/n810341/n810770/index.html (accessed 28 Nov. 2016).
4. Fifty-four countries signed The Belt and Road National Tax Agreement with China:
   - nine countries in Southeast Asia: Indonesia, Malaysia, Philippines, Singapore, Thailand, Brunei, Vietnam, Laos, Kampuchea;
   - five countries in South Asia: Nepal, India, Pakistan, Bangladesh and Sri Lanka;
   - five Central Asian countries: Kazakhstan, Turkmenistan, Kyrgyzstan, Uzbekistan and Tajikistan;
   - ten countries in Western Asia: Iran, Turkey, Syria, Israel, Saudi Arabia, Bahrain, Qatar, Oman, Arabia United Arab Emirates and Kuwait.
   - the sixteen countries of Eastern Europe: Albania, Bosnia and Herzegovina, Bulgaria, Croatia, Czech Republic, Slovakia, Estonia, Lithuania, Hungary, Latvia, Macedonia, Montenegro, Romania, Poland, Serbia, Slovenia;
   - the seven countries of the CIS: Russia, Belarus, Ukraine, Moldova, Georgia, Azerbaijan and Armenia;
   - the one East Asian countries: Mongolia;
   - the one African countries: Egypt;
   - there are ten countries that have not yet signed tax treaties with China, namely Burma, East Timor, Bhutan, Maldives, Afghanistan, Iraq, Jordan, Palestine, Yemen and Lebanon.

tax law, the tax treaty is to prevail over domestic tax law.[5] There are similar provisions under Article 58[6] of the Chinese Corporate Income Tax Law and Article 91[7] of the Tax Administration Law, such that the legal effect of a bilateral tax treaty in China is higher than that of domestic tax law, and the treaty will prevail in application.

Tax treaties are international agreements that deal with cross-border tax issues. They can effectively eliminate double taxation between host countries and China and reduce the overall tax expense of going-global enterprises. Because a tax treaty prevails over domestic law, it is not affected by any changes to domestic tax law; therefore, generally speaking, such a treaty can create a more transparent and more certain tax environment for those enterprises. In addition, tax treaties provide preferential treatment (treaty benefits) for going-global enterprises which help to reduce their tax burden and enhance their competitiveness in the host country. For example, tax treaty provisions on dividends, interest and royalties require the host country to impose a reduced tax rate; the articles on shipping, air and land transportation, property income, government services, and students provide that the host countries must offer tax exemption; the provisions on permanent establishments, operating profit, independent personal services and employment income raise the threshold of the host country, constraining the host country's authority to collect tax under its domestic tax law.

This chapter analyses the preferential treatment for passive investment income, including interest, dividends and royalties, under Chinese tax treaties with Belt and Road countries.

2.1 Interest Article in Tax Treaties

The term 'interest' in a tax treaty usually refers to income from debt claims, whether or not secured by a mortgage or carrying the right to share in the debtor's profits. This includes interest from government bonds, bonds and debentures, including premiums and bonuses. However, penalties for late payment are not included in the concept of interests.

The interest article of a tax treaty usually limits the source state's right of taxation by specifying a reduced tax rate that may be imposed. Under the interest article of Chinese tax treaties with Belt and Road countries, the interest arising in one contracting state and paid to a resident of the other contracting state, may be taxed not only in the other state, but also in the contracting state in which the interest originates under the law of that contracting state. When taxed under the tax law of the state in which the

---

5. 'The tax agreement prevails over the domestic tax law' is not the common view and practice of all countries. In some countries, the law clearly stipulates that the government has the right not to comply with the provisions of the tax agreement, or when the intention is not clear, it will be ruled by the court; in some countries, the provisions of the tax treaties and domestic tax laws are in the same level, if the two appear to be in conflict, then whatever is stipulated more recently shall prevail.
6. Article 58 of Corporate income tax law stipulates that where Chinese tax treaties with foreign countries differ from domestic law, the tax treaties will prevail.
7. Article 91 of the law of tax collection and administration stipulates: 'where the treaties and agreements concluded by People's Republic of China with foreign countries have different provisions, the treaties and agreements shall prevail'.

interest arose (except for the provisions of the tax treaties with the Czech Republic, Israel, Kuwait, Laos, Singapore, Tajikistan and the United Arab Emirates, in which the interest tax rate is lower than 10%), the reduced tax rate is 10% in the tax treaties with the other forty-seven countries.

In addition, under the interest article of tax treaties with most Belt and Road countries, interest arising in one contracting state but obtained by the government of the other contracting state, its administrative agencies or local authorities and its central banks or financial institutions that belong entirely to the government, as well as interest obtained by a resident of the other contracting state, where the claim is indirectly funded by the other contracting state's government, administrative agencies or local authorities and the central bank or financial institutions which belong entirely to the government, the interest will be tax exempt in the contracting state. Some tax treaties also cover interest arising from loans guaranteed or insured by a wholly government-owned financial institution, such as the tax treaties with Czech Republic, Estonia, Latvia, Syria, Tajikistan and Turkmenistan.

In the Chinese tax treaties with Azerbaijan, Brunei, Czech Republic, Indonesia, Laos, Malaysia, Oman, Pakistan, Singapore, Thailand, Turkey, Turkmenistan and Vietnam, the financial institutions that may benefit from tax exemption are listed in detail. In this regard, Chinese financial institutions include: the People's Bank of China, the National Development Bank of China, the Development Bank of China, the Import and Export Bank of China, the Agricultural Development Bank of China, the Chinese National Social Security Fund Council, the Chinese Export and Credit Insurance Corp., the China International Trust Investment Company, the Bank of China (head office), the Construction Bank of China, the Agricultural Bank of China, and the Industrial and Commercial Bank of China.

In practice, most financial institutions transfer the tax burden on interest to the borrower by signing tax-included contracts, but the interest tax exemption can still greatly improve the competitiveness of financial institutions. Moreover, in many cases, because borrowers are often subsidiaries that Chinese enterprises have established in the interest source state, the application of tax exemption on interests to these subsidiaries also helps to reduce their tax burden and reduce the cost of financing. The Chinese tax treaties with Bosnia and Herzegovina, Israel and Slovenia contain no provision for tax exemption of interest on the loans for financial institutions owned by the government or national central bank. Therefore, when Chinese going-global enterprises invest in these countries, they should pay attention not only to the applicable tax treaty, but also their domestic laws, and make full use of the preferential treatment under both the applicable tax treaty and domestic laws. When there is no definite provision in the applicable tax treaty or protocol, the enterprise should consult the tax authorities of the host country.

2.2 Dividends Article in Tax Treaties

The term 'dividends' in a tax treaty usually refers to the gains obtained from shares or the right to share in the profit as the result of a non-creditor relationship, and the gains from other corporate rights that are deemed to be income from shares and is also taxable under the law of the contracting state in which the profit-sharing company is resident. The dividends article of a tax treaty usually limits the taxing rights of the source state by specifying a reduced tax rate. The tax treaties differ from one country to the next as regards the standard of allocating the right of taxation.

Under the Chinese tax treaties with Albania, Azerbaijan, Bahrain, Bangladesh, Belarus, Bosnia and Herzegovina, Hungary, India, Indonesia, Iran, Israel, Kazakhstan, Kyrgyzstan, Malaysia, Nepal, Pakistan, Poland, Qatar, Romania, Russia, Slovakia, Sri Lanka, Turkey, Uzbekistan and Vietnam, when a dividend of the contracting state resident company is paid to a resident of the other contracting state, if the recipient is the beneficial owner of the dividend, the tax may not exceed 10% of the total dividend. In China-Egypt treaty, the applicable tax rate is 8%, while the rate is 7% in the treaty between China and the United Arab Emirates. The tax rate is 5% in the treaties between China and Brunei, Bulgaria, Croatia, Laos, Kuwait, Macedonia, Mongolia, Montenegro, Oman, Saudi Arabia, Serbia and Slovenia.

In addition, under Chinese tax treaties with Belt and Road countries, the source states tax the beneficial owner in different rates according to the different proportion of the shares that the company paying the dividend holds.[8] The higher the proportion of the shares in the dividend paying company, the lower the tax rate applicable in the source state. Chinese tax treaties with some countries have limitations on the nature of the beneficial owners of dividends, such as the tax treaties with Singapore, Tajikistan and Turkmenistan. The beneficial owners of dividends may only be corporations, excluding partnerships.

In the process of going global, if a Chinese enterprise finds that the source state imposes a higher withholding tax rate on dividends than the applicable treaty rate, the dividends paid to domestic shareholders may benefit from a lower rate by applying for preferential tax treatment overseas, and the income tax paid in accordance with the tax treaty rate may be credited in the home country.

---

8. Specifically, it includes:

   (1) 0% (dividends beneficiary owners directly or indirectly own dividend paying companies at least 50% shares and invest EUR 2 million in the company): Georgia;
   (2) 5% (dividends beneficiary owners directly or indirectly own dividend paying companies at least 10% shares and invest EUR 100 thousand in the company): Georgia;
   (3) 5% (the beneficial owner of the dividends is a company, partnership and except direct ownership of the company paying the dividends of shares at least 25% cases): Singapore, Tajikistan, Turkmenistan, Armenia, Syria, Czech Republic, Estonia, Latvia, Lithuania, Ukraine, Moldova, and the national agreement (the beneficial owner of the dividends paid directly with the dividend shares less than 25% cases at a rate of 10%);
   (4) 10% (dividends holders are directly entitled to pay at least 10% shares of the dividend company): Philippines (with the above national agreement, the beneficial owner of dividends has the right to pay dividends directly, the company's share is less than 10%, the tax rate is 15%).
   (5) 15% (the beneficial owner of the dividends is a company, not including a partnership, and has at least 25% shares of the company paying the dividends (case): Thailand and the national agreement stipulates the beneficial owner of the dividends have direct payment of dividends of shares of the company less than 25% cases at a rate of 20%).

2.3 Royalties Article in Tax Treaties

The term 'royalties' usually refers to money paid as remuneration for the use of, or the right to use literary, artistic or scientific works, including film, radio or television broadcasting film, tape copyrights, patents, trademarks, designs or models, drawings, secret formulas or processes, as well as money paid as remuneration for the use of, or the right to use industrial, commercial or scientific equipment, scientific experience and information received as consideration. The Chinese tax treaties with Georgia, Tajikistan and Turkmenistan stipulate that the concept of royalties does not include payments for the use of, or the right to use the other industrial, commercial and scientific equipment. The royalties article usually limits the tax rights of the source state by specifying a reduced tax rate.

Most Chinese tax treaties with Belt and Road countries stipulate that, when royalties arising in a contracting state and paid to a resident of the other contracting state are taxed in the contracting state in which the royalties arose, under the law of that contracting state, if the beneficial owner of the royalties is a resident of the other contracting state, the tax payable may not exceed 10% of the gross amount of the royalties. In the tax treaties with various other Belt and Road countries, the rate is lower or higher than 10%. For example, in the treaty with Georgia, the applicable tax rate is 5%; Latvia and Romania, 7%; Egypt and Tajikistan, 8%; Pakistan, 12.5%; and Nepal and Thailand, 15%.

There are different types of royalties with different tax rates in some Chinese treaties, for example under the tax treaty with Poland, for the use of, or the right to use industrial, commercial or scientific equipment, the applicable tax rate for the remuneration is 7%, but for the use of, or the right to use literary, artistic or scientific work, including film, radio or television broadcasting film, tape copyrights, patents, proprietary technology, trademarks, designs, models, drawings, secret recipes and secret programs, the tax rate is 10%. With the exception of certain countries,[9] the tax rate for royalties under Chinese tax treaties with forty-two Belt and Road countries is 10%. In addition, the Chinese tax treaty with Malaysia contains a special rule under which,

---

9. Specifically, it includes: (1) Georgia: 5%; (2) Laos: 5% (limited to Laos, 10% in China); (3) Romania: 7%; (4) Latvia: 7%; (5) Poland: 7% (limited to the use, the right to use industrial, commercial, scientific equipment to pay a variety of payments. To use or the right to use literary, artistic or scientific works, including film, radio or television broadcasting film, tape copyright, patents, proprietary technology, trademarks, designs, models, drawings, secret recipe, secret program to pay all money as reward for the tax rate of 10%); (6) Egypt: 8%; (7) Tajikistan: 8%; (8) Pakistan: 12.5%; (9) Thailand: 15%; (10) Nepal: 15%; (11) Philippines: 15% (limited to the right to use or have the right to use literary, artistic or scientific works, including films, videos, television or radio the copyright of the tapes paid by various payments. Pay to use or the right to use the patent, trademark, design or model, drawings, secret formula or process as well as the use of, or the right to use, industrial, commercial, industrial, commercial or scientific equipment, scientific experience as all kinds of money reward information applicable tax rate is 10%); (12) Malaysia: 15% (limited to the right or the right to use literary or artistic works, including film, radio or television broadcast, film and tape, the copyright paid by the various payments. To use or the right to use the patent, proprietary technology, trademarks, design or model, drawings, secret formula or scientific program, copyright, or use, the right to use industrial, commercial or scientific equipment or related industrial, commercial or scientific experience and information received as a consideration for the applicable tax rate 10%).

where the royalties obtained by a Chinese resident are subject to movie leasing tax under Malaysia's movie leasing tax law, the fee is exempt from such tax in Malaysia.

Under Chinese bilateral tax treaties with Belt and Road countries, when tax treaty provisions and domestic tax laws are inconsistent, if the treaty rate is less than the tax rate prescribed under domestic tax laws and regulations, the treaty rate will prevail; if otherwise, the domestic laws and regulations will prevail. Therefore, when Chinese enterprises make investments in Belt and Road countries with which China has signed tax treaties, they first should be familiar with the provisions of the applicable tax treaty, especially the preferential treatment of interest, dividends, royalties and other relevant items of income, and obtain a lower tax rate by applying overseas for benefits under the applicable tax treaty.

In order to prevent the abuse of tax treaties, anti-tax avoidance provisions are often included in the interest, dividends and royalties articles, such as beneficial owner provisions, the principal purpose test (PPT) and a limitation on benefits (LOB).[10] Therefore, going-global enterprises should pay special attention to these provisions when designing their overseas investment structures, so as to avoid being identified as abusing tax treaties and therefore not entitled to tax treaty benefits.[11]

At present, ten Belt and Road countries do not have tax treaties with China, namely: Afghanistan, Bhutan, Burma, East Timor, Iraq, Jordan, Lebanon, Maldives, Palestine and Yemen. If a going-global enterprise invests in a country that has not signed a tax treaty with China, tax will be paid solely in accordance with the domestic law of the host country.

3 IMPACT OF THE OECD/G20 BEPS PROJECT ON THE APPLICATION OF PREFERENTIAL TREATMENT UNDER TAX TREATIES

Due to the restriction and influence of various factors, countries lack effective cooperation and coordination in tax collection and the management of transnational economic activities. Taxpayers take advantage of the tax differences among jurisdictions and the mismatch of rules to carry out lawful tax planning, which artificially causes taxable profits to 'disappear' or profits to be transferred to low-tax countries (regions) with little or no substantive business activities, resulting in a serious erosion of the tax base and damage to the interests of tax collection in the relevant countries. This caused not only by the increasingly serious erosion of the tax base and the loss of tax sources but also by the distortion of market resource allocation and damage to the environment of fair competition. Especially in the era of the digital economy, a variety of new tax planning methods adopted by multinationals has made this problem more serious and prominent.

---

10. For example, article 23 of 'double taxation and anti-tax avoidance and evasion treaty between China and Russia' (signed on 13 Oct. 2014, in effect from 9 Apr. 2016).
11. *See* 'Using Tax Treaties to help 'Belt and Road' Enterprise 'Going Global'', PwC China: http://www.pwccn.com/webmedia/doc/635731546577072907_chinatax_news_jul2015_34_chi .pdf (accessed 22 Jun. 2016).

Chapter 5: Tax Treaties Preferential Arrangements: China and BRI Countries

In September 2013, the G20 summit commissioned the OECD to start the implementation of an international tax reform project, namely the OECD/G20 Base Erosion and Profit Shifting (BEPS) project. The purpose of this project is to modify international tax rules; curb multinationals' avoidance of global tax obligations and erosion of national tax bases; and coordinate and equitably balance tax collection and tax allocation among countries in transnational economic activities.

After three years' discussion, in October 2015, the OECD released fifteen final reports under the Action Plan, as well as an explanatory statement. These results were approved in November of the same year by the G20 summit in Antalya, and many countries – including China – are committed to the implementation of the output of the BEPS project. The BEPS Action Plan and the measures in the Final Reports represent the first substantive change in international tax rules by the international community in over almost 100 years. With the official implementation of the output of the BEPS project, at present, the international community and individual countries have gradually entered into a post-BEPS era in which they are now translating BEPS outputs into domestic implementation.

Therefore, against the new background of changing international tax rules and domestic laws, the preferential arrangement in Chinese tax treaties with Belt and Road countries will face new challenges. When a Chinese enterprise makes an investment along the Belt and Road, on the one hand it should make full use of existing preferential treaty provisions to maximize tax benefits; on the other hand, because existing preferential tax treaties will absorb the new constraints and adjustments under the BEPS project, Chinese enterprises will face constraints from these new conditions while seeking to maximize tax benefits and interests. The prominent and immediate issue to be resolved concerns how to seek a balance between ensuring China's compliance with the BEPS project outputs on the one hand, and maintaining the interests of enterprises to continue to enjoy preferential treatment and facilitate their investment in Belt and Road countries on the other hand.

3.1 Provisions on Treaty Shopping under BEPS Action 6

Regarding the preferential provisions of tax treaties and the specific application thereof, the main problems and challenges faced by Chinese enterprises in seeking and realizing the maximization of those treaty benefits lie in the stricter regulatory requirements imposed by BEPS Action 6 in response to the problem of treaty shopping. Under BEPS Action 6, to prevent the abuse of tax treaty benefits, the minimum standard is – at least in bilateral tax treaties – that effective rules should be adopted to deal with treaty shopping. First, the title and preamble of a treaty should clarify that the parties to the treaty intend to prevent the creation of conditions for non-taxation or reduced taxation caused by evasion of taxes, including treaty shopping.

Second, to implement the common will of the contracting states, the treaty will:

- combine the use of the principal purpose test (as a general anti-abuse rule) and a limitation on benefits (as a specific anti-abuse rule);

- incorporate the principal purpose test; or
- incorporate a limitation on benefits, complemented by mechanisms against conduit arrangements, for example by applying the principal purpose test to conduit financing arrangements.

Entities that serve only as conduits and transfer gains to investors in a third country are not allowed to enjoy treaty benefits. These different rules have their own functions and roles: specific anti-abuse rules can provide greater certainty, but can deal only with known tactics of abuse; general anti-abuse rules have less certainty of judicial principles, but are able to deal with unknown or unsolved transactions of abuse. These two methods to resolve treaty abuse are equally effective, but due to the different legal environment and policy orientation, therefore, while the minimum standards can ensure that the abuse of a treaty can be effectively countered, countries have flexibility to determine what rules to use.

3.2 The Connotation and Application Requirements of the LOB Rules

In 2002, OECD issued a report on restricting the entitlement to treaty benefits.[12] This report asserted that the conventional method could only serve as a guiding principle, and that more specific rules should be implemented to deal with treaty shopping As a result of this report, new provisions were added to paragraphs 10, 11 and 12 of the OECD Income and Capital Model Convention and Commentary (OECD Model Commentary) on Article 1 regarding 'improper use' of the Convention. OECD adopted the entire LOB provision based on the 1996 US Model Convention (US Model), and an objective-oriented anti-abuse provision (paragraph 21.4 of the OECD Model Commentary on Article 1) based on the UK practice. A LOB provision was also included in the BEPS Action 6 Discussion Draft published in 2014,[13] which is more detailed than the LOB provision recommended in Article 20(1) of the OECD Model.

The purpose of the LOB provision is to prevent the residents of a third country from obtaining the preferential treatment enjoyed by the residents of a contracting state under the reciprocal treaty. It is mainly based on the objective criteria of a legal nature, ownership and daily activities of the residents of the contracting states to classify the scope of residents that are entitled to enjoy treaty benefits. The basic concept is that tax incentives are applicable only to taxpayers that have real commercial purposes or are fully connected with the residence state. On the surface, each item of the LOB provision is very different, but the essence of them all points to these two important factors. The provision provides for the scope of 'qualified residents' that may enjoy treaty benefits, including 'qualified residents', companies or entities that meet the test on active operating activities, entities that meet the exemption provisions at the discretion of the competent authorities, entities that meet the requirement of a 'derivative benefits'

---

12. OECD, *Restricting the Entitlement to Treaty Benefits* (OECD 7 Nov. 2002).
13. OECD, Discussion Draft, *BEPS Action 6: Preventing the Granting of Treaty Benefits in Inappropriate Circumstances* (OECD Publishing 14 Mar. 2014).

provision (the newly added BEPS Action 6).[14] It can be seen that the application scope of LOB provision under BEPS Action 6 has been expanded, so that some normal transactions or arrangements will not be excluded from tax treaty benefits. On the other hand, the requirements under the provision of limited taxation of interest are more stringent, and the crackdown on treaty shopping is thereby strengthened.

The LOB rules are more detailed, which can provide an objective standard for the competent authorities to make determinations; reduce the difficulty of application; and reduce execution time and expense. However, at the same time, the provision is more complex, and its application needs to consider the interaction between many other treaties. This compounds the complexity of treaties, and increases the possibility of tax arbitrage, so it is suitable to apply the PPT rules in practice to supplement the LOB rules.

3.3 Connotation and Application Requirements of the PPT Rules

Paragraph 9.5 of the OECD Model Commentary on Article 1 sets a guiding principle: if the principal purpose of certain transactions or arrangements is to obtain better tax status, and obtain better treatment, then it is in violation of the objectives and purpose of relevant provisions, and therefore it should not be granted treaty benefits. Article 21.4 of the Commentary on Article 1 provides a sample clause for the PPT rules, 'A guiding principle is that the benefits of a double taxation convention should not be available where a main purpose for entering into certain transactions or arrangements was to secure a more favourable tax position and obtaining that more favourable treatment in these circumstances would be contrary to the object and purpose of the relevant provisions.'

Compared with the PPT rules in the OECD note, BEPS Action 6 clearly suggests that the PPT rules be included in the OECD Model, and explain the key terms in the article in detail, and use the examples to guide the court to explain this subjective principle. The Preventing the Granting of Treaty Benefits in Inappropriate Circumstances, Action 6-2015 Final Report (Final Report of BEPS Action 6) stipulates a proposed Article X (7) of the OECD Model as follows:

> Notwithstanding the other provisions of this Convention, a benefit under this Convention shall not be granted in respect of an item of income or capital if it is reasonable to conclude, having regard to all relevant facts and circumstances, that obtaining that benefit was one of the principal purposes of any arrangement or transaction that resulted directly or indirectly in that benefit, unless it is established that it reflects a genuine economic activity or that granting that benefit in these circumstances would be in accordance with the object and purpose of the relevant provisions of this Convention. [OECD, *Action 6 Final Report*, at 55]

> Notwithstanding the other provisions of this Convention, a benefit under this Convention shall not be granted in respect of an item of income or capital if it is reasonable to conclude, having regard to all relevant facts and circumstances, that

---

14. State Administration of Taxation: 'Preventing Improper Grant of Preferential Tax Treaties (Action Plan No. 6)', China Tax Press, 2015, p. 21.

obtaining that benefit was one of the principal purposes of any arrangement or transaction that resulted directly or indirectly in that benefit, unless it is established that granting that benefit in these circumstances would be in accordance with the object and purpose of the relevant provisions of this Convention.[15]

The provisions on the PPT rules in the Final Report of BEPS Action 6 do not require that obtaining the treaty benefits be the *sole* purpose of a special arrangement; it requires only that it be *one of* the main purposes. The concept of treaty benefits includes all restrictions on the taxation right of the source state (such as tax relief, exemption, deferred tax or refund) under Articles 6 to 22 of the treaty, eliminating double taxation under Article 23 and non-discriminatory protection of national residents and residents of a contracting state in Article 24, and other similar restrictions. However, if it is possible to prove that the preferential treatment accords with the purpose and objective of the relevant provisions of the applicable treaty, the PPT rules are not applicable.

3.4 Suggestions for Balancing Compliance with the BEPS Project and Access to Treaty Benefits

The BEPS project puts forward new frameworks and requirements for shaping and deepening international tax cooperation. China needs to participate in the further adjustment and implementation of the BEPS project at the international level. The Belt and Road Initiative, which the Chinese government has proposed, injects new vigour and vitality into Chinese enterprises, strongly promotes foreign investment by Chinese enterprises and creates conditions and convenience for enterprises to further enhance their competitiveness on the international market. However, while Chinese enterprises make investment in Belt and Road countries, it is the time that the BEPS project should be implemented in various countries. International cooperation on anti-tax avoidance targeted at developed countries will bring about huge challenges and impacts for Chinese businesses attempting to go global. Countries have been revising their domestic tax laws to implement the output of the BEPS project, and the investment structure of Chinese going-global enterprises could be in conflict with laws against cross-border tax avoidance and tax evasion in various countries after their tax laws are revised.

More importantly, with the deepening of Chinese advances in trade and investment in Belt and Road countries, China needs to further improve and strengthen cooperation with countries as regards anti-tax evasion, properly balancing the appeal of their tax benefits, according to the BEPS project's framework and requirements. However, one needs to be aware of the effects of strictly following the BEPS project's framework and requirements regarding Chinese tax benefits, particularly the potentially adverse effects. Therefore, it is necessary to research further and adopt a flexible and creative cooperation and implementation strategy according to the BEPS project, as well as further improve and strengthen cooperation with Belt and Road countries on

---

15. Previously cited 12, State Administration of Taxation book, p. 79.

Chapter 5: Tax Treaties Preferential Arrangements: China and BRI Countries

anti-tax avoidance through the inclusive framework. At the same time, China should better support the development of the Belt and Road Initiative and the growth of Chinese enterprises.

Consider the example of Chinese enterprises investing in Kazakhstan. Chinese enterprises often choose the path of indirect investment by setting up intermediate holding companies, which are often based in Singapore. This is because the China-Kazakhstan tax treaty provides that the dividends Chinese enterprises receive from Kazakhstan are subject to 10% corporate income tax as non-residents, while the Kazakhstan-Singapore tax treaty provides that for dividend and bonuses from Kazakhstan, Singapore businesses need to pay only a 5% withholding tax. Under the China-Singapore tax treaty, the dividends received by Chinese resident enterprises from Singapore are not subject to corporate income tax as non-residents. In this way, a Chinese enterprise that wants to invest in Kazakhstan can first set up an intermediate holding company in Singapore, and then invest into Kazakhstan through the intermediate holding company. This will save the 5% corporate income tax as a non-resident (Figure 5.2).

Figure 5.2 Kazakhstan Investment Framework

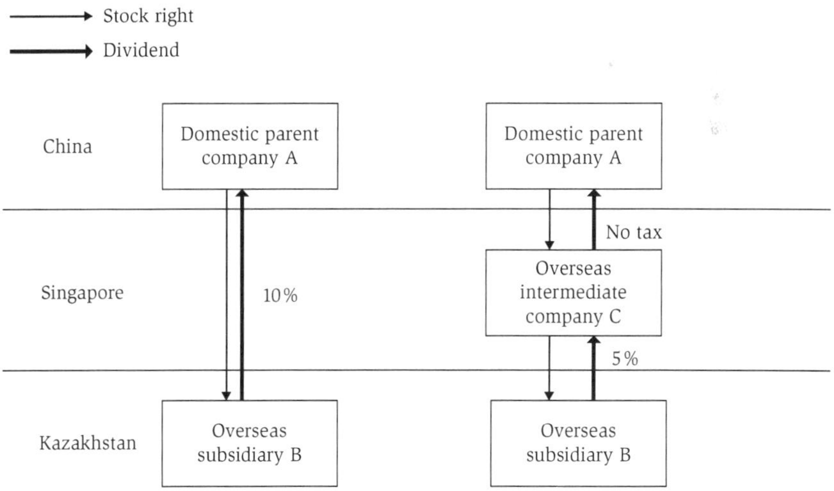

According to the requirements of BEPS Action 6, if Kazakhstan strengthens the regulation of intermediate holding companies, Chinese enterprises will bear 5% of the income tax more than Singapore enterprises do without having to change the China-Kazakhstan tax treaty. This will increase the tax burden of Chinese enterprises and, furthermore, affect their competitiveness on the international market – all while China has not obtained any tax benefits from it. This is not conducive to the development of the Belt and Road Initiative and the growth of enterprises. In fact, there may be various reasons and considerations for a country to provide differential tax treatment to different countries; in fact it does affect and distort the market environment of fair competition. Therefore, to solve the treaty shopping problem, China must put the market environment with fair competition into perspective. In this regard, China should carry out specific cooperation and coordination with Kazakhstan as regards the implementation of BEPS Action 6. The basic strategies and methods include:

(1) adjusting the preferential tax rate for dividends, interest and royalties that resident enterprises are entitled to enjoy in the original tax treaty, to a preferential level compared with other countries in future. Do include a most-favoured-nation treatment provision in future regional tax coordination between China and Kazakhstan, providing that Chinese enterprises automatically obtain preferential tax rates;
(2) without changing the original income tax rate for non-resident enterprises, China should seek an exemption or loosened regulation for Chinese enterprises under BEPS Action 6.

For example, according to the connotation and application requirements of the PPT rules, if one can prove that granting the tax benefit is in line with the purpose of the relevant provisions of the treaty, the PPT rules are not applicable. In the face of the unfair tax environment that Chinese enterprises encounter, China could engage in consultations and negotiations with the host country to ensure that Chinese enterprise investment and specific arrangements are in accordance with the purpose and objective of the tax treaty, so as to avoid being characterized as treaty shopping and subsequently being denied preferential tax treatment.

Therefore, Chinese enterprises must take into account the change in Kazakhstan's domestic tax laws and regulations when making investments, especially the new amendment regarding anti-tax treaty abuse under domestic law, according to the LOB and PPT rules proposed in the BEPS Action 6 Final Report. Chinese enterprises must redesign their own transactions, and never simply set up a number of intermediate holding companies for the sake of tax avoidance. Going-global enterprises should strengthen the whole investment structure and commercial purposes according to anti-treaty abuse rules in the host countries, in order to ensure that the holding company in the intermediary state has a reasonable business purpose, has substantial business activities, independent of its people and property. This will help to avoid tax risk and save tax expense.

On the other hand, countries should make adjustment accordingly in the high-level design of national tax benefit distribution systems, especially to start with negotiations with Belt and Road countries regarding the revision of tax treaties. This should first be based on the principle of mutual benefit and reciprocity. It is necessary to select those countries with a larger number of Chinese foreign direct investments now or in future, and countries that have relatively higher levels of investment directly into China, and lower the tax rate to 5% to 8% (from the existing 10%) on dividends, interest and royalties. More preferential tax treatment, on the one hand, makes Chinese enterprises no longer need to lower their taxes by establishing intermediate holding companies in third countries, thereby avoiding a potential anti-avoidance investigation triggered by tax planning arrangements. Meanwhile, under the precondition of complying with the BEPS project requirements, China can exercise its tax sovereignty rights

Chapter 5: Tax Treaties Preferential Arrangements: China and BRI Countries

to decide the tax rate, tax type and scope of taxation under its domestic laws, save capital structure expense and tax expense for enterprises, further promoting the investment by Chinese enterprises in Belt and Road countries.

4 EMPIRICAL ANALYSIS OF THE PREFERENTIAL TAX TREATIES USED BY CHINESE GOING-GLOBAL ENTERPRISES

Because foreign investment by Chinese enterprises is still in its infancy, some going-global enterprises do not understand tax treaties. Indeed, some are not even aware of their existence, to speak nothing of the ways and tactics to maximize tax treaty benefits. According to a survey conducted by the Beijing municipal office of State Administration of Taxation in 2014 of 281 going-global enterprises, nearly 90% had never received the proper tax treatment abroad under applicable tax treaties. There is little consultation applied by taxpayers with other countries about tax disputes. This chapter takes interest, dividends and royalties as an example, and makes an empirical analysis of relevant cases, with a view to providing guidance for Chinese going-global enterprises to maximize their enjoyment of tax benefits.

4.1 Case of Chinese Unicom Red Chip Company: Dividend Discount

4.1.1 Facts of the Case

The actual name of Chinese Unicom Red Chip Company is Chinese United Network Communications (Hong Kong) Limited Company, and it belongs to Chinese Unicom Group listed in Hong Kong. The Hong Kong Stock Exchange has so-called 'red chip' and 'blue chip' stock. Red-chip companies are those Hong Kong-listed companies the largest holding power of which is directly or indirectly affiliated to institutions or enterprises from Mainland China, i.e., Chinese enterprises listed on the Hong Kong Stock Exchange. The headquarters and actual administration of Chinese Unicom Red Chip Company are located at Financial Street, Xicheng District, Beijing. Wei Yanwei, the chief of Large Enterprises and International Tax Management Department of Xicheng District Tax Bureau in Beijing stated that although Chinese Unicom Red Chip Company is listed in Hong Kong, it is also a Chinese resident enterprise. Under the regulation of National Taxation Administration (2009 No. 82), overseas registered Chinese-invested enterprises are to be characterized as resident enterprises in China. Based on 'actual management standards', Chinese Unicom Red Chip Company was identified as a Chinese resident in November 2010.

In March 2011, based on corporate tax data, the Large Enterprises and International Tax Management Department of Xicheng District Tax Bureau in Beijing learned that, in 2009, China Unicom signed a strategic alliance agreement and mutual investment equity subscription agreement with a Spanish telecommunications company, Telefónica Internacional S.A.U (Telefónica), with the two companies holding each other's shares. In May 2011, Telefónica distributed dividends to Chinese Unicom Red Chip Company four times. Under Spanish tax law, Telefónica withheld and remitted tax on the dividends. The tax rate was 18% before 31 December 2009, and 19% thereafter. Telefónica withheld a total of EUR 22.64 million (approximately CNY 210 million).

It seems reasonable to obtain dividends from foreign shares and pay taxes under local law. However, Chinese Unicom Red Chip Company was identified as a Chinese resident enterprise from 1 January 2008; it should enjoy tax treaty treatment accordingly. China and Spain signed an income tax treaty early in November 1990, Article 10 of which provided that the source state is to cap the tax rate for dividends at 10%. When a Spanish resident pays dividends to a Chinese resident, the tax rate should not exceed 10% of the total dividend. Accordingly, the Xicheng District Tax Bureau stated that China Unicom should enjoy a preferential rate of 10% on income. The company agreed with this, and actively pursued relevant procedures, and jointly asserted its own tax interests and national tax sovereignty with the tax department.

In April 2011, Chinese Unicom Red Chip Company communicated with the Spanish tax authorities on many occasions to apply for treatment under the applicable tax treaty. Chinese Unicom Red Chip Company also requested that the authorities refund the Spanish tax from 2009 to 2011, which was more than the required minimum, totalling EUR 10.62 million.[16]

4.1.2 *Analysis of the Legal Issues*

The focal issue of the Chinese Unicom Red Chip Company case is tax residence status. If any Chinese resident goes abroad to engage in business activities, it may request the related treatment stipulated in the applicable tax treaty. Because the tax treaty is applicable only to 'the residents of contracting states', going-global enterprises must first prove their Chinese tax residence status. Because Chinese Unicom Red Chip Company is listed in Hong Kong, and this place of registration is not in the mainland of China, it could not be seen as resident enterprise of Mainland China without a special procedure to indicate its identification. However, if it were identified as a Mainland China resident enterprise under the mainland corporate income tax rules, the applicable tax treaty benefits would be completely different.

Under regulations of the National Taxation Administration, going-global enterprises should complete the application form for a Chinese tax residence certificate and submit it to the local taxation administration in the foreign jurisdiction. The Chinese tax authorities responsible for such matters under the provisions of the application matters, in accordance with the corporate income tax law, individual income tax law and tax treaties for residents, render an opinion on the applicant's Chinese residence certificate which is issued by the Chinese Director General of Taxation. Residence certificates for Chinese companies are issued by the tax authorities of the place where the taxpayer's headquarters is located.[17]

---

16. Liu Guangming et al., *How nearly 100 Million Yuan of Overpayments Are Returned to China from Spain*, China Revenue News (29 Aug. 2011), 5th edition.
17. According to the Notice of the State Administration of Taxation on Relevant Matters Concerning the Issue of 'the Identity Certification of Chinese Tax Residents' on 28 Jun. 2016 (No. 40 of 2016

Chinese Unicom Red Chip Company's way to safeguard its own rights began with the Chinese tax residence certificate. The Xicheng District tax bureau studied Chinese Unicom Red Chip Company, and immediately issued a notification to the enterprise in order to remind the enterprise to apply for a Chinese tax residence certificate as soon as possible, and timely apply for treaty benefits with the Spanish tax authorities.

4.2 Case of Huaxin Cement Limited Company

4.2.1 *Facts of the Case*

As a key project in the Belt and Road Initiative, Huaxin Cement Limited Company established a subsidiary, Yawan Company, in Tajikistan which was responsible for carrying out the business in Tajikistan. It was reported that in December 2012, the Yawan Company took a USD 78 million loan for a period of seven years from the National Development Bank of China, paid interest of USD 3.94 million in 2013, paid income tax of USD 470,000 at the rate of 12% under Tajikistani domestic law, paid interest of USD 4.45 million in 2014 and did not pay income tax. However, under the China-Tajikistan tax treaty, the interest could be tax exempted. After application of the tax exemption by Yawan Company to the Tajikistan Tax Bureau, the latter replied on 3 November 2014 and agreed that the annual interest would be taxed at the 8% rate stipulated by the tax treaty, but not including taxes payable on interest in 2013 and 2014. To this end, Yawan Company repeatedly communicated with the Tajikistan Tax Bureau, seeking to exempt the 2014 interest from income tax under the tax treaty and obtain a tax refund for 2013.

However, the Tax Bureau did not agree and urged Yawan company to pay USD 530,000 for the withholding tax on interest in 2014; otherwise it would be subject to penalties. Because at that time the Yawan Company had signed a loan agreement for the USD 100 million investment in a second-tier project with the National Development Bank of China, if it could not benefit from tax treaty treatment, the company would have to pay nearly USD 5 million income tax. Therefore, because efforts to cooperate failed, Huaxin Cement Company had to request help from the local tax authorities, namely the Tax Bureau of Huangshi City.

On 2 February 2015, the Tax Bureau of Huangshi called the National Tax Bureau of Hubei Province to report the problem. On 4 February 2015, the National Tax Bureau of Hubei Province fully collected the information and reported the details to the National Taxation Administration. After having been informed, the National Taxation Administration immediately launched a Mutual Agreement Procedure (MAP) under the tax treaty; wrote to the Tajikistan Tax Bureau; and requested a tax exemption on the interest paid by Yawan Company to the National Development Bank of China under the tax treaty. Through efforts to cooperate by the Chinese embassy in Tajikistan, the

---

by the State Administration of Taxation). The domestic and overseas branches of Chinese resident enterprises shall, through their head office, apply for the issuance of 'Certificate of Resident of Tax Resident' in any one calendar year in which they constitute the tax resident in China.

Tax Bureau of Tajikistan confirmed that it received the letter, and finally agreed to grant the tax exemption under the tax treaty.

This has brought approximately USD 5 million in profit for Yawan Company. Thus, through the joint efforts of the Tax Bureau of Hubei Province and the Tax Bureau Huangshi, which lasted thirty-six days, Hubei's first case to safeguard its rights in taxation on the road to investment in a Belt and Road country, was finally settled.[18]

4.2.2 Analysis of the Legal Problems Involved

The first issue in the Huaxin Cement Company case is to determine whether the interest should be paid in Tajikistan. In this case, Yawan Company is a resident enterprise in Tajikistan. It obtained loans from the National Development Bank of China, and paid interest to the National Development Bank of China. Under the China-Tajikistan tax treaty, the interest is deemed to arise in Tajikistan (under Article 11(6)).[19] Article 11(2) of the tax treaty stipulates that the interest that arises in one contracting state and is paid to a resident of the other contracting state, may also be taxed in the state where the interest arises under the laws of the state. However, if the interest beneficiary is a resident of the other contracting state, the tax may not exceed 8% of the total interest. Therefore, under the above provisions, the interest paid by Yawan Company to the National Development Bank of China is taxable under Tajikistani domestic law, and the income tax is to be paid at 8% (the treaty tax rate) instead of 12% (the domestic tax rate).

However, under Article 11 section 3 of the tax treaty, notwithstanding the provisions of Article 11 section 2, interest arising in a contracting state and paid to the government, local authorities, the central bank or any financial institution wholly owned by the government of the other contracting state, or interest arising from one contract state and paid for a loan that is guaranteed and insured by the government, local authorities, central banks of the other contracting state or financial institutions wholly owned by the government, is entitled to tax exemption in the first mentioned contracting state. As the National Development Bank of China is a tax-exempt financial institution under the above provisions, the interest paid by Yawan Company to the National Development Bank of China should enjoy tax exemption in Tajikistan.[20]

At present, among the fifty-four Chinese bilateral tax treaties with Belt and Road countries, forty-nine stipulate that the source state of interest must grant a tax exemption to, or does not enjoy the right to tax interest of the other contracting state, an administrative subdivision or a local authority and the central bank or financial institutions wholly owned or controlled by government. Furthermore, twelve of those tax treaties have specified the scope of 'financial institutions completely owned and controlled by the government', namely the Development Bank of China, the

---

18. Zhu Yan et al., *Cross Border Taxpayers Should Pay Special Attention to the Taxation*, China Tax Newspaper, A01 (23 Mar. 2015).
19. Article 11(6), China-Tajikistan tax treaty ('if the interest payer is the resident of one contracting state, the interest shall be deemed as have occurred in this contracting state'.).
20. Tax treaty between China and Tajikistan.

Agricultural Development Bank of China and the Export Import Bank of China; some of these treaties include the National Social Security Fund Council, the China Investment Corp. and other policy non-bank financial institutions.[21] The remaining thirty-seven tax treaties[22] contain only an exemption principle, without explicitly specifying a list of financial institutions. In addition, five tax treaties, namely those with Bosnia and Herzegovina, Israel, the Philippines, Russia and Slovenia, do not grant a tax exemption for interest paid to financial institutions controlled or owned by the government.

On the other hand, recently, newly signed treaties and revised tax treaties have relaxed the scope of financial institutions owned or controlled by the government, from the original 'full ownership' to 'main ownership', and the scope of financial institutions that are granted tax exemption is gradually expanding. Taking the revised China-Romania tax treaty (signed on 4 July 2016) as an example, paragraph 3 of Article 11 stipulates that notwithstanding the provisions of paragraph 2, interest arising in a Contracting State and beneficially owned by a resident of the other Contracting State shall be taxable only in that other State to the extent that such interest is paid: a) in respect of indebtedness arising as a consequence of the sale on credit of any equipment, merchandise or services; or b) on any loan of whatever kind granted by a financial institution of that other State; or c) to that other State or a political subdivision, local authority or administrative – territorial unit thereof, or any entity wholly or mainly owned by that other State. The term 'mainly owned' refers to ownership of more than 50%.

The tax treaty with Cambodia (signed on 13 October 2016) also stipulates the same. For the purpose of paragraph 3, Article 11, the understanding of 'any financial

---

21. For example, the tax treaty with Pakistan includes only the People's Bank of China and Bank of China; the tax treaty with Turkey includes the People's Bank of China, Bank of China and Industrial Bank of China International Trust and Investment Corporation; the tax treaty with Laos and Oman stipulates that only the People's Bank of China, the State Development Bank of China, the Export-Import Bank of China and the Agricultural Development Bank of China; and Indonesia Agreement on Tax stipulates that "any financial institution" refers to the China Development Bank Corporation, the Agricultural Development Bank of China, the Export-Import Bank of China, the National Council for Social Security Fund and the China Investment Corporation; the tax treaty with Brunei includes the People's Bank of China, the State Development Bank of China, the Export-Import Bank of China, the Agricultural Development Bank of China, the National Council for Social Security Fund; the tax treaty with Singapore, Turkmenistan and Tajikistan includes the People's Bank of China, the China Development Bank, the Agricultural Development Bank of China, the Export-Import Bank of China, the National Council for Social Security Fund and the China Export & Credit Insurance Corporation; the exchange of Notes with Malaysia tax treaty also includes the China Development Bank Corporation, the Agricultural Development Bank of China, the Export-Import Bank of China, the National Council for Social Security Fund, the China Export & Credit Insurance Corporation, the China Investment Corporation and the silk Road Fund Co., Ltd.; Agreement with Azerbaijan tax includes: the State Development Bank of China, the Export-Import Bank of China, the Agricultural Development Bank of China, the National Council for Social Security Fund, the Bank of China, the Construction Bank of China, the Industrial and Commercial Bank of China and the Agricultural Bank of China.
22. Including Thailand, Vietnam, Nepal, India, Bangladesh, Sri Lanka, Kazakhstan, Kyrgyzstan, Uzbekistan, Egypt, Mongolia, Belarus, Ukraine, Moldova, Georgia, Armenia, Albania, Croatia, Czech Republic, Slovakia, plus Leah, Estonia, Lithuania, Hungary, Latvia, Macedonia, Montenegro, Romania, Poland, Serbia, Kuwait, the United Arab Emirates, Bahrain, Qatar, Saudi Arabia, Syria, Iran.

institution or statutory body mainly owned by the Government of the other Contracting State' in China refers to: the National Development Bank of China, the Agricultural Development Bank, the Import and Export Bank of China, the National Social Security Fund Council, the China Export and Credit Insurance Corp., the China Investment Corp., Industrial and Commercial Bank of China, the Bank of China, the Construction Bank of China, the Agricultural Bank of China, and any institutions or legal entities that are mainly owned by the Chinese government, and which the competent authorities of the two contracting states may agree at any time.

4.3 Case of Jerry Petroleum Company

4.3.1 *Facts of the Case*

Yantai Jerry Petroleum Company (referred to here as Jerry Company) is a locally listed company based in Yantai, Shandong Province. In 2010, Jerry Company established a wholly owned subsidiary in Kazakhstan, leasing its own equipment to the subsidiary and charging a leasing fee. The total price of the equipment was approximately CNY 19.56 million, and the leasing income was approximately CNY 53 million over six years. The Kazakhstani tax authorities become aware that the subsidiary paid a huge amount of fees to the parent company, and therefore immediately withheld 15% income tax from the leasing fee paid overseas under its domestic tax law.

In 2011, when Yantai Tax Bureau was making the final settlement for income tax of Jerry Company, it questioned whether Article 12 of the China-Kazakhstan tax treaty stipulated that for the leasing income obtained from the Kazakhstani investment, royalties are to be taxed at 10%. Jerry Company submitted a tax refund application to the competent tax authorities in Kazakhstan, but the Kazakhstani competent tax authorities insisted in applying domestic law and rejected Jerry Company's application. The company's effort to protect its rights was very passive in Kazakhstan. The Tax Bureau of Yantai selected key personnel to intervene decisively, under the article concerning MAP of the China-Kazakhstan tax treaty, and coached the enterprise on how to complete the application for a MAP, submitted the request to the Chinese tax administration via the provincial tax bureau and started negotiation procedures with Kazakhstan.

After rounds of intense bilateral consultations and negotiations, Kazakhstan finally agreed to offer the refund. On 20 February 2012, the State Administration of Taxation issued a notice to Jerry Company, stating that Kazakhstan must tax the leasing income at 10% under the royalties article of the tax treaty. Jerry Company could pay CNY 2.65 million less to Kazakhstan. Kazakhstan also notified Jerry Company that it agreed to impose a 10% leasing tax rate on Jerry's leasing income obtained in Kazakhstan and was prepared to refund the excess tax collected previously. Therefore, the income tax liability was reduced to CNY 5.3 million (from CNY 7.95 million). Kazakhstan also agreed that, in future, the maximum rate under the tax treaty would be applied directly without the taxpayer having to seek a refund. Having received the notice from the Kazakhstani tax authorities, Jerry Group prepared files and submitted its tax refund application.[23]

4.3.2 Analysis of the Legal Issues Involved

This case involves the tax rate applicable to income from related-party equipment leasing and the means of tax collection and payment. Jerry Company and its subsidiaries in Kazakhstan are tax residents of China and Kazakhstan, respectively. They may apply the China-Kazakhstan tax treaty. Under Article 12 of that treaty, equipment leasing fees are royalties.[24] Kazakhstan has the right to levy taxes, and it may impose tax under its national laws, i.e., at the 15% tax rate.[25] However, Jerry Company is the recipient and ultimate beneficiary of the leasing fee from the equipment. Kazakhstan should apply a maximum rate of 10% when it levies taxes under its own law.[26] At the same time, as the tax treaty does not stipulate how to execute these tax rate caps, the host countries apply the rate in accordance with the relevant provisions of domestic law, some countries give refund after collection, and some countries apply the tax cap when the taxpayer makes a declaration. But in recent years in the negotiation of a new tax treaty or amendment of an old tax treaty, China normally seeks to have it stipulated that the tax cap will be applied directly rather than in the form of a refund after collection, so as to reduce the tax expense of going-global enterprises.

This suggests that Chinese enterprises need to actively understand and take advantage of preferential treatment provided by tax treaties, and clarify the relationship between tax treaties and domestic tax laws in the process of going global. When a tax treaty and domestic tax law are not consistent, most countries generally stipulate that the treaty will prevail. If the treaty tax rate is less than the rate under domestic law, the preferential tax rate under the tax treaty is allowed (although there are exceptions, the United States). When a treaty is given the priority, the knowledge and application thereof can bring significant tax benefits for enterprises.

5 SOLUTION TO ADDRESS DISPUTES REGARDING TAX TREATIES BENEFITS

In the case of Huaxin Cement, the relevant interest should enjoy tax exemption in Tajikistan. The Yawan Company consulted with the Tajikistan Tax Bureau many times, but the latter not only refused to grant a tax exemption for 2014 and refund the interest income tax paid in 2013 but even urged Yawan company to pay interest accrued taxes of USD 530,000 in 2014. The enterprises represented by Huaxin Cement

---

23. Zhang Tongpeng, *Five Shandong 'Going Global' Companies Telling How to Crack Three Corporate Tax Revenue Problems*, China Tax News (22 May 2015), B1.
24. Article 12(3).
25. Article 12(1) & (2) China-Kazakhstan tax treaty.
26. Article 12(2) China-Kazakhstan tax treaty ('but if the recipient is the beneficiary of the royalty fee, then the tax payable shall not exceed 10% of the total amount of the royalty fee'.).

Company face the issue of how to safeguard their rights when they have tax disputes with the tax authorities in the host country in the process of going global. In the theory and practice of international tax law, enterprises can generally start with the following ways to safeguard their rights.

5.1 Local Relief in the Host Country as the Main Solution

In the long history of international practice, as for how to resolve disputes between foreign investors and host countries, the territorial supremacy of host countries has been universally respected and recognized by the international community. Among them, for the majority of developing countries that have suffered external interference and coercion over the course of history, they particularly care about the territorial supremacy as hosts when resolving disputes and conflicts of interest with foreign investors. They maintain that disputes need to be resolved by local relief from the host country, as is required by domestic law and foreign policies. Most Belt and Road countries are developing countries, and their territorial superiority as host countries should obviously be highly respected by China, Chinese enterprises and individual investors. In the event of disputes with Belt and Road countries, individual investors and Chinese enterprises should fully respect and make use of Belt and Road countries' local relief to resolve the disputes.

However, there are obvious deficiencies in the awareness and ability of Chinese enterprises and individual investors to apply the legal rules to seek local relief in the host country. To this end, the Chinese government should strengthen and improve the awareness and ability of Chinese enterprises and individual investors to pursue local relief options in the host country from many perspectives. From the perspectives of individual investors and Chinese enterprises, they should further strengthen the awareness and ability to utilize domestic and international tax law experts to timely prevent and control tax disputes; when disputes arise, taxpayers should be able to rely on the support of tax law experts at home and abroad to help resolve tax disputes by pursuing local relief options in the host countries. From the perspective of the Chinese domestic support system, the Chinese government can provide support and assistance for Chinese enterprises and individual investors to use host-country local relief options through establishing and using various consulting and service mechanisms. In this regard, the State Administration of Taxation has established two support institutions for international tax law and policy services, namely, the 12366 Beijing Tax Service Centre and the Shanghai Tax Service Centre.

5.2 Diplomatic Protection as Auxiliary Solution

Diplomatic protection refers to the responsibility of a country to invoke another country's responsibility in the name of the state through diplomatic actions or other peaceful solutions due to the internationally wrongful act of another country that has inflicted harm upon the first country's nationals, so as to enable the country to fulfil its responsibilities. Generally speaking, whether to exercise diplomatic protection is a right of the state decided at its own discretion, not the obligation for its citizens. There are three prerequisites for the exercise of diplomatic protection. *First*, the damage to nationals in a foreign country must be caused by the international wrongful act of the foreign country. *Second*, the requesting state must be able to prove that the victims are its own nationals. *Third*, the local relief options must have been exhausted.

A request for diplomatic protection may be filed without the exhaustion of local relief options if: (i) there is no reasonable and available local relief, or local relief options provide no reasonable possibility of such remedy, (ii) the relief process involves undue delay, and that delay is caused by the country which is alleged to be responsible, (iii) the victim is apparently precluded from pursuing local relief and (iv) the state alleged to be responsible has conceded the exhaustion of local relief. In the judgment in the Diallo case in May 2007 (preliminary objection), the International Court of Justice once again confirmed the two principles of nationality and exhaustion of local relief which are universally recognized conditions for the exercise of diplomatic protection.

As a rule of customary international law, with the development of international practice and the draft articles on diplomatic protection compiled and adopted by the International Law Commission in 2006, there have been some new developments in the diplomatic protection system and its interpretation. Furthermore, the exemption rules have increased such as the standard of nationality; rights and responsibilities; and the demand for local judicial relief. China has actively participated in the whole process of international legislation of Draft Articles on Diplomatic Protection and put forward its own proposal and position for it.

At the same time, facing the huge outbound flow of enterprises and citizens, China is still exploring ways and means to effectively protect overseas interests, and overseas interest protection still has a long way to go. In short, the diplomatic protection system and its interpretation are undergoing new changes, but the exercise requirements and basic framework have not changed fundamentally, especially as regards the exhaustion of local relief requirement. Therefore, addressing disputes over preferential tax treatment via diplomatic protection remains limited to harsh conditions. Moreover, as diplomatic protection covers a wide range of areas, with a high level of political sensitivity, China is unlikely to readily resort to using diplomatic protection to resolve disputes on tax treaty benefits, especially between Belt and Road countries.

5.3 MAP Between Contracting Countries

The MAP under tax treaties opens up an effective international relief channel for going-global enterprises and helps to properly resolve the tax disputes abroad for such enterprises. Chinese tax treaties with Belt and Road countries include a mutual agreement provision, which stipulates that when authorities of the contracting parties cannot reach an agreement regarding the interpretation or application a tax treaty provision, or one country's tax collection practice leads to double taxation, they may consult together to resolve the international tax dispute.

In the case of Huaxin Cement, Huaxin Cement disagreed that its subsidiary company must pay Tajikistani tax on the interest it pays to the China National Development Bank, but that rather it should benefit from tax exemption in that country. This dispute is eligible to request that the Chinese authorities launch a MAP. At the same time, under section 1 and section 2 of Article 26 of the China-Tajikistan tax treaty, Huaxin Cement may also take the case of Tajikistan to the competent authorities of China without considering the relief options under domestic law. If the Chinese competent authorities think the dispute is reasonable and cannot unilaterally resolve it, the Chinese competent authorities should attempt to consult with the competent authorities of Tajikistan, so as to avoid taxes that are not in conformity with the treaty.[27] This is why, when Huaxin Cement experienced ineffective cooperation with the Tajikistan tax authorities, it took the initiative to seek relief from the Chinese tax authorities. Thus, the provincial tax authorities applied to the State Administration of Taxation to launch a MAP under the tax treaty, and eventually the company was able to obtain treaty benefits in the form of tax exemption.

Although Huaxin Cement ultimately achieved a successful outcome in safeguarding its rights, the beginning of the process was not smooth. Huaxin Cement first sought protection from the Chinese embassy, but the tax authorities in Tajikistan ignored diplomacy. Just like Huaxin Cement, when overseas rights are blocked, the first resort of a going-global enterprise is to approach the local consulate for diplomatic protection. However, most developing countries in which Chinese enterprises invest generally require the pursuit of domestic relief first. Although these countries do not recognize diplomatic protection, they are willing to address disputes in accordance with the domestic legal system, including the implementation of MAP under bilateral tax treaties. This means that when an enterprises goes global, if tax disputes with the tax authorities of the invested country occur, such enterprises must apply to the Chinese tax authorities for a mutual agreement; the procedure does not need to be launched under the pre-condition of exhaustion of relief. Rather, the enterprise can appeal directly to the competent authorities of China, and this is more conducive to the protection of the legitimate rights of resident enterprises in China.

In addition, the terms of the MAP article in current Chinese tax treaties do not clearly stipulate, in cases where the Chinese tax authorities initiate a MAP, what is the timeframe within which the other state's competent authorities must reply. Therefore, it is not conducive to resolving disputes in timely manner. This is also the reason why

---

27. Article 26 China-Tajikistan tax treaty ('if a person believes that one or both of the Contracting States to take measures to lead or will lead to the tax does not comply with the provisions of this agreement, cannot consider the state's domestic legal remedies for the parties to present his case the residents of the competent authorities, or if the case belongs to the first paragraph of article twenty-five, can I submit to the competent authorities of the Contracting States of its nationals. The case must be submitted within three years from the date of the first notice of tax measures that are not in conformity with the provisions of this agreement. Two, if the above-mentioned competent authorities consider that the opinions are reasonable and cannot be satisfactorily resolved unilaterally, they should try to resolve each other with the competent authorities of the other Contracting States, so as to avoid taxes that are not in conformity with the agreement. The agreement reached should be enforced and not subject to the time limit of the domestic laws of the States parties'.).

the tax authorities in Tajikistan finally confirmed receipt of the letter after multiple parties had attempted to communicate and cooperate with the tax authorities in China. Therefore, it is suggested that the feedback limits and other procedural obligations shall be stipulated in the MAP rules.

In order to standardize the implementation of tax treaty negotiation procedures, the State Administration of Taxation issued 'Measures for the Implementation of Tax Treaty Negotiation Procedures' (No. 56 Announcement of State Administration of Taxation in 2013, hereinafter referred to as the Measures). The Measures stipulate the applicable object, applicable circumstances, case receiving tax authorities, application procedures and legal force of the consultation outcomes. Under Article 9 of the Measures, Chinese residents in any of the following circumstances may request a MAP:

- disagreement on residence status, especially where a dual-resident status needs to be confirmed through mutual negotiation procedures under the tax treaty;
- disagreement on determining the existence of a permanent establishment, or attribution of profits and deduction thereto;
- disagreement on the exemption or applicable tax rate for income or property;
- violation of a tax treaty's non-discrimination provisions which is likely to have, or has already given rise to tax discrimination;
- disputes on interpreting and applying other provisions of the tax treaty which cannot be settled on their own; and
- other cases where double taxation is likely to occur, or has already occurred. Under Article 4 of the Measures, the Chinese State Administration of Taxation is responsible for MAP; the National Tax Bureau of provinces, autonomous regions, municipalities directly under the central government or local tax bureaus (referred to here as the provincial tax authorities) and the tax authorities at all levels below are responsible for assisting the State Administration of Taxation with mutual agreement related to their jurisdictions.

In summary, when there is a controversy regarding preferential tax treatment between the enterprises and Belt and Road countries, there are a variety of alternative dispute resolution possibilities. Among them, seeking diplomatic protection from a Chinese consulate is subject to strict conditions, and the host country is often not willing to accept this extreme type of solution which is escalated to diplomatic levels between countries. China is unlikely to easily turn an ordinary tax dispute into a highly sensitive dispute between countries, especially with Belt and Road countries. Therefore, when there are disputes in the preferential tax treatment between enterprises and Belt and Road countries, seeking a consulate's diplomatic protection is not the best route.

According to the strategy and reality of the Belt and Road Initiative, the MAP and local relief from the tax authorities in the host country will be the basic approach. At present, the MAP between two tax authorities is a dispute resolution method that Chinese enterprises are familiar with and accustomed to using. Moreover, the Huaxin Cement case also indicates the effectiveness of this approach. In China, more than 190 cases of bilateral consultations at present have been carried out, which have eliminated international double taxation of nearly CNY 30 billion for multinational enterprises. In 2015 alone, the State Administration of Taxation consulted with India, Indonesia, Tajikistan and other Belt and Road countries and reduced the overseas tax burden by approximately CNY 270 million for Chinese enterprises.

However, the MAP between two tax authorities is only a procedure for tax administration cooperation between two sides, and it has inevitable institutional limitations for resolving all kinds of tax disputes effectively. If relying only on MAP, Chinese enterprises are bound to be in a very passive position once the negotiations become ineffective or even have completely failed.

Compared to the MAP between two tax authorities, the host country's administrative or judicial relief options have special advantages both in procedure and in substance, which can provide enterprises with a more stable and predictable tax dispute settlement process and rulings. Moreover, through active and proficient use of local administrative or judicial relief, host countries can improve their administrative and judicial capacity and legal system development, so as to achieve a win-win outcome between the interests of enterprises and the objectives of the Belt and Road Initiative. However, the Huaxin Cement case exposed the lack of awareness and ability of Chinese enterprises to make use of legal provisions to seek local relief. That is not conducive to safeguarding enterprises' own tax benefits in Belt and Road countries fully and effectively, and it is not conducive for China to play a model role in the development of the rule of law in Belt and Road countries. Therefore, in the long run, in the face of potential disputes regarding application of preferential tax treatment in Belt and Road countries, Chinese enterprises must strengthen their awareness and ability to use legal provisions to seek local relief.

6 CONCLUSION

Actively promoting the Belt and Road Initiatives provides a broad platform for going-global enterprises to carry out cooperation in industrial capacity and equipment manufacturing. At the same time, the OECD/G20 BEPS project has put forward a new framework and requirements for shaping and deepening international tax cooperation, and China needs to further its active participation in the adjustment and implementation of the outputs of the BEPS project at the international level, and properly balance the tax interest of various parties.

Against the dual background of such opportunities and challenges, going-global enterprises urgently need to build international tax awareness, understand international tax practice, be familiar with relevant tax treaties, make active use of reciprocal treatment under tax treaties and the negotiation of bilateral tax procedures to reduce their tax expense and address tax disputes. Such enterprises should actively and skilfully use relief offered by host countries, so as to maintain and protect their own interests.

When Chinese companies actively go global, they need to timely understand the progress regarding the BEPS project by local tax authorities in jurisdictions where subsidiaries are located; evaluate the substance of intermediate holding companies using the existing shareholding structure and the certainty of enjoying tax treaty benefits; fully consider whether their contractual arrangement matches the essence of transaction; and strengthen the ability of subsidiaries to bear risk and manage business. When designing top-level tax treaties, China should be mindful of strengthening tax coordination and cooperation with Belt and Road countries, giving greater tax preferences to each other, in order to promote the economic prosperity and development of Belt and Road countries.

CHAPTER 6

Going-Global Enterprises: Tax Planning for Cross-Border Earnings in Belt and Road Countries

Cao Mingxing & Liu Qichao[*]

1 Introduction
2 The New Opportunity for Chinese Going-Global Enterprises to Invest Abroad Against the Background of the Belt and Road Initiative
   2.1 General Performance of Chinese Going-Global Investment
   2.2 Major Investment Destinations and Industrial Models of Going-Global Enterprises along the Belt and Road
3 Comparison of the Tax Rates in Key Destinations for Investment by Going-Global Enterprises along the Belt and Road
   3.1 Comparison of Corporate Income Tax Rates
   3.2 Comparison of Tax Rates in Chinese Tax Treaties with Key Investment Destinations
4 Three Tax Planning Approaches for Going Global Enterprises Regarding Cross-Border Earnings Against the Background of the Belt and Road Initiative
   4.1 The Legal Issues of International Tax Planning for Cross-Border Income
   4.2 Three Tax Planning Approaches for Going Global Enterprises in Terms of Cross-Border Earnings

---

[*] Cao Mingxing, Doctor of Laws, Director of China International Tax Center at Central University of Finance and Economics; Liu Qichao, Shanghai Pudong New Area Division of State Administration of Taxation, part-time as an associate researcher at the International Tax Center in the Central University of Finance and Economics & Research Center of Finance and Taxation Law in the China University of Political Science and Law.

            4.2.1   Active Income from Foreign Operations: General
                    Contracting and Sub-Contracting of Construction Projects
            4.2.2   Passive Income from Foreign Investment in High-, Medium-
                    and Low-Tax Jurisdictions
            4.2.3   Passive Income from Foreign Investment: Intangible Assets
                    4.2.3.1 Software Sales and Licensing
                    4.2.3.2 Setting up Foreign Subsidiaries for Intangible
                             Assets
5   Conclusion

1   INTRODUCTION

As a Chinese poem reads, 'Bells kept ringing in the distant desert, and that must be the camels carrying white silk to the west.' From these words of Zhang Ji, a Tang dynasty poet, one can imagine the bustling scenes along the ancient silk routes. The German geographer Ferdinand von Richthofen might never have imagined that the Silk Route, so named by him in 1877, would be revived in the twenty-first century and reshape world political and economic relationships. One thousand years ago, the Silk Route brought prosperity to the cities of the Han and Tang dynasties; now the Belt and Road Initiative will benefit the world through China's economic contribution and enrich the meaning of going global.

In 2002, China put forward its going-global initiative at the 16th National Congress of the Communist Party. In 2007, it was mentioned to 'adhere to the basic state policy of opening to the outside world and ensure better coordination in pursuing the bring-in and go-global strategies' at the 17th Communist Party National Congress. In 2012, it was mentioned to 'accelerate the pace of going global, and enhance the ability of enterprises to operate internationally, and cultivate a number of world-class multinational corporations' at the 18th Communist Party National Congress. In 2013, the Belt and Road Initiative based on the theme of the going-global initiative to creating a community of shared interests and the so-called Towards a Community of Shared Future for Mankind among different countries.

Against this background, it crucial to encourage and assist going-global enterprises to engage in tax planning with regard to their foreign-source income.

2   THE NEW OPPORTUNITY FOR CHINESE GOING-GLOBAL ENTERPRISES TO INVEST ABROAD AGAINST THE BACKGROUND OF THE BELT AND ROAD INITIATIVE

2.1 General Performance of Chinese Going-Global Investment

Since China implemented the going-global initiative, the amount of the direct investment by Chinese enterprises has maintained a rapid pace of growth. According to statistics, China's outward foreign direct investment reached USD 2.7 billion in 2002, and reached USD 107.84 billion in 2013 – an increase of nearly forty times over twelve years. Chinese outward foreign direct investment ranked third in the world for two years in a row. The stock of foreign direct investment has reached USD 6,604.8 billion, ranking 11th in the world.

In terms of the scale of investment, in 2014, domestic investors in China effected USD 116 billion in investment (including USD 13.110 billion in the financial sector and USD 102.89 billion in non-financial sectors) into 6,128 foreign enterprises in 156 countries and regions around the world, and used USD 119.56 billion of foreign direct investment (FDI). Considering the reinvestment that is financed from third parties other than China and foreign investment, the scale of China's outward foreign direct investment was expected to be approximately USD 140 billion in 2014 – approximately USD 20 billion more than that of the inbound FDI.

In terms of the number of investments, as at the end of 2013, there were 15,300 total investors in China that were directly invested in 25,400 enterprises established abroad. This figure had soared to 32,819 by the end of 2014.

According to the 'Report on Chinese Enterprises Globalization (2014)' by the Center for China and Globalization, the further clarification of the going-global initiative at the Third Plenary Session of the 18th Communist Party National Congress, as well as the launch of the Belt and Road Initiative, has provided Chinese enterprises with significant opportunities to go global. Various indicators reveal that China has become a net exporter of capital, and the Belt and Road Initiative is accelerating the pace of going global by Chinese enterprises.

2.2 Major Investment Destinations and Industrial Models of Going-Global Enterprises along the Belt and Road

Most of the countries along the Belt and Road are developing countries and emerging economies. Among the sixty-four countries, only seven can be categorized as having an advanced economy under the IMF definition, namely the Czech Republic, Estonia, Israel Latvia, Singapore, Slovakia and Slovenia.[1] In addition to China, these sixty-four countries are as follows:[2]

- Russia, Mongolia and five countries in Central Asia: Kazakhstan, Kyrgyzstan, Mongolia, Russia, Tajikistan, Turkmenistan and Uzbekistan;
- eleven countries in Southeast Asia and West Asia: Brunei, Cambodia, East Timor, Indonesia, Malaysia, Philippines, Singapore and Thailand;
- eight countries in South Asia: Afghanistan, Bangladesh, Bhutan, India, Maldives, Nepal, Pakistan and Sri Lanka;

---

1. Ren Li Bo, *New Space for Foreign Investment: Rank of 'Belt and Road' countries Investment Value* (Social Sciences Literature Publishing House March 2015), at 38–39.
2. The Belt and Road is a route for expansion, and is not limited to these stated sixty-four countries. For example Duisburg in Germany and Madrid in Spain are the terminal stations of the Yu Xin-Europe and the Yi-Xin-Europe railway, respectively. They both actively participate in the Belt and Road Initiative. Britain's joining the AIIB also shows that the Belt and Road is a global opportunity provided by China.

- sixteen countries in Central and Eastern Europe: Albania, Bosnia and Herzegovina, Bulgaria, Croatia, Czech Republic, Estonia, Hungary, Latvia, Lithuania, Macedonia, Montenegro, Poland, Romania, Serbia, Slovak Republic and Slovenia;
- sixteen countries in North Africa: Bahrain, Egypt, Iran, Iraq, Israel, Jordan, Kuwait, Lebanon, Oman, Palestine, Qatar, Saudi Arabia, Syria, Turkey, the United Arab Emirates and Yemen; and
- Georgia and five other CIS countries: Armenia, Azerbaijan, Belarus, Georgia, Moldova, and Ukraine.

As the financial crisis in 2008 damaged the economy of developed countries, the amount of foreign investment has been declining. Therefore, Belt and Road countries have not absorbed much FDI. However, since 2008, China's investment in countries along the Belt and Road has been rapidly increasing. In 2013, China's investment into countries along the Belt and Road reached USD 12.634 billion, three times more than the figure for 2008 (Table 6.1). By the end of 2013, the stock of China's investments in the countries along the Belt and Road was USD 57.417 billion, accounting for 1.3% of the total FDI absorbed by Belt and Road countries.[3]

Table 6.1 FDI Absorbed by Belt and Road Countries in 2008–2013[4]

	FDI Absorbed by Belt and Road Countries (USD Billion)	FDI from China (% of Total FDI Absorbed by Belt and Road Countries) (USD Billion)
2008	407.227	4.134 (1%)
2009	273.686	4.528 (1.7%)
2010	310.674	7.743 (2.5%)
2011	348.918	9.929 (2.9)
2012	342.486	13.322 (3.9%)
2013	341.18	12.634 (3.7%)

In 2013, regarding Chinese FDI flows, ten of the top twenty countries and regions are Belt and Road countries. This fully reveals the important position of the countries along the Belt and Road in Chinese foreign direct investment (see Table 6.2).

---

3. Ren Li Bo, *New Space for Foreign Investment: Rank of 'Belt and Road' Countries Investment Value* (Social Sciences Literature Publishing House March 2015), at 53–54.
4. UNCTAD, http://unctad.org/en/Pages/Home.aspx (accessed 20 May 2015); CN: Ministry of Commerce, National Bureau of Statistics, State Administration of Foreign Exchange, *Statistical Communiqué on China's Outward FDI in 2013* (China Statistics Press September 2014).

Table 6.2 Chinese Foreign Direct Investment: Belt and Road Countries among the Top 20[5]

Ranking	Country/Region	FDI Flow (USD billion)	%
6	Singapore	2.03	1.9
7	Indonesia	1.56	1.5
10	Russia	1.02	0.9
13	Kazakhstan	0.81	0.7
14	Laos	0.78	0.7
15	Thailand	0.76	0.7
16	Iran	0.75	0.6
17	Malaysia	0.62	0.4
19	Cambodia	0.50	0.4
20	Vietnam	0.48	8.6
Total		9.31	

According to the 'Guidelines for Foreign Investment and Cooperation Country Areas (Regions)' and 'Country Trade Report' issued by the Ministry of Commerce, the Belt and Road countries that absorb more FDI from China have four main characteristics: (i) abundant natural resources, (ii) poor transportation facilities, (iii) good diplomatic relations with China and (iv) relatively close geographical location. These characteristics coincide with the characteristics of major Chinese investment industries in 2013 along the Belt and Road (Europe and Asia), which include leasing and business services, financing, wholesaling and retailing, mining, transportation, warehousing and postal services.

From a theoretical perspective, preferential tax policies and tax rates will directly affect the investment of going-global enterprises in the countries along the Belt and Road.[6] In practice, tax risks arising from tax administration and the differences between industries is the topic of most concern for current going-global enterprises. Therefore, enterprises should do well in international tax planning based on researches on the key countries and industries along the Belt and Road to enhance their competitiveness and influence.

---

5. CN: Ministry of Commerce, National Bureau of Statistics of China, State Administration of Foreign Exchange, *2013 Statistical Bulletin of China's Outward Foreign Direct Investment* (China Statistics Press September 2014).
6. R. Gropp & K. Kostial, *The Disappearing Tax Base: Is Foreign Direct Investment (FDI) Eroding Corporate Income Taxes?*, IMF Working Paper (2000).

3 COMPARISON OF THE TAX RATES IN KEY DESTINATIONS FOR INVESTMENT BY GOING-GLOBAL ENTERPRISES ALONG THE BELT AND ROAD

3.1 Comparison of Corporate Income Tax Rates

The authors have selected the top sixteen countries/regions along the Belt and Road based on share of FDI from China (Hong Kong, Singapore, Russia, Kazakhstan, Indonesia, Thailand, India, Pakistan, Vietnam, Saudi Arabia, Malaysia, Turkey, Hungary, Egypt, Poland and Uzbekistan)[7] and compare their corporate income tax rates (*see* Table 6.3).

Table 6.3 Corporate Income Tax Rates of Key Investment Destinations (Countries/Regions) Along the Belt and Road[8]

Country/Region	Corporate Income Tax (%) (2015)	Corporate Income Tax for Non-Resident Enterprises (%)	Law
Hong Kong	16.5%	16.5%	Inland Revenue Ordinance (Chapter 112 of the Hong Kong Ordinance), section 14, paragraph 8, section 15, paragraph 8
Singapore	17%	17%	Income Tax Law, Chapter 43 (1)(a) & (8)
Russia	20%	20%	Tax Code, Articles 284, 306 (6)
Kazakhstan	20%	20%	Tax Code 2008, Article 147
Indonesia	25%	25%	Income Tax Act 7 of 1983, Chapter 17 1b (as amended on 2 September 2008)
Thailand	20%	20%	Corporate Income Tax Law, Article 3
India	33.99% (30% plus 10% service fee & 10% education tax)	33.99% (30% plus 10% service fee & 10% education tax)	Chapters 2, 4 & 28 of the Income Tax Act, 1961; Finance Act 2011, Chapter 2, section. 1, Part 1; Finance Act, 2013, Chapter 2, section. 1, Part 1
Pakistan	33%	33%	Income Tax Regulations, 2001, Chapter 1, Part 1, paragraph 2

---

7. Considering the complexity of the access to the information, the authors have made some adjustments to the countries selected (excluding countries such as Iran and the United Arab Emirates). Hong Kong is not a Belt and Road country, but it is included because a large number of going-global enterprises invest there. Due to the length of this chapter, the authors do not specify the quantum of FDI from China.
8. The tax rates for mergers and acquisitions in the key investment destinations (countries/regions) along the Belt and Road are the same as the numbers in Table 6.3.

Country/Region	Corporate Income Tax (%) (2015)	Corporate Income Tax for Non-Resident Enterprises (%)	Law
Vietnam	22%	22%	Corporate Income Tax Law 14 of 2008, Article 10; Enterprise Income Tax Law 9 of 2003; Decree 24 of 2007, Article 9
Saudi Arabia	20%	20%	Income Tax Act 2004, Articles 7a.1 & 7a.3

3.2 Comparison of Tax Rates in Chinese Tax Treaties with Key Investment Destinations

According to statistics, China has signed tax treaties with fifty-three out of sixty-four Belt and Road countries and has completed the revision of its tax treaties with Estonia, Latvia, Russia, Singapore and Uzbekistan. The treaties with Malaysia and Pakistan were negotiated, while negotiations with India and Romania were expected to commence in the second half of 2015, with steady progress.[9] From the perspective of the applying law, making full use of bilateral consultations under bilateral tax treaties can resolve tax disputes such as double taxation. The use of tax treaties can also properly deal with the issue of foreign income tax credits, and such treaties are of great importance to cross-border taxation problem such as the determination of a permanent establishment, as well as dividends, bonuses and royalties (*see* Table 6.4) obtained from abroad.

Consider the example of a Chinese company acquiring a US company. In the process of foreign investment, Chinese companies often choose countries (regions) such as Hong Kong and Singapore as the location for an intermediate holding company to achieve the goal of tax optimization. Hong Kong does not charge income tax on foreign-source dividends and does not charge withholding tax on dividends paid abroad. However, if enterprises blindly invest in Hong Kong, they might overlook the fact that there is no tax treaty between the United States and Hong Kong. So after an acquisition, a US company must withhold and remit 30% withholding income tax to the Hong Kong company (subsidiary) in China under US domestic tax law. If a direct acquisition is done by a company in mainland China, the withholding tax on dividends is only 10% under the China-United States bilateral tax treaty.[10] The full use of tax rates specified in treaties can help going-global enterprises to effectively reduce their tax expense related to international investment and thus enhance their competitiveness.

---

9. CN: State Administration of Taxation, Intranet, *Development of the Belt and Road Initiative by the Inland Revenue Department's Innovation Concept* (accessed 24 May 2015).
10. Ye Hong, You Jiang, Zheng Tiancheng & Zhang Tong, *Typical Tax Risks and Coping Strategies for Chinese M&A by Chinese Enterprises*, International Taxation in China 4 (2015), at 24.

Table 6.4 Tax Rates in Chinese Tax Treaties with Key Investment Destinations along the Belt and Road[11]

Country/Region	Dividends (%)	Interest (%)	Royalties (%)
China Hong Kong	10	7	7
Singapore	10	10	10
Russia	10	10	10
Kazakhstan	10	10	10
Indonesia	10	10	10
Thailand	20	10	15
India	10	10	10
Pakistan	10	10	12.5
Vietnam	10	10	10
Saudi Arabia	5	5	15
Malaysia	10	10	10
Turkey	10	10	10
Hungary	10	10	10
Egypt	8	10	8
Poland	10	10	10
Uzbekistan	10	10	10

4 THREE TAX PLANNING APPROACHES FOR GOING GLOBAL ENTERPRISES REGARDING CROSS-BORDER EARNINGS AGAINST THE BACKGROUND OF THE BELT AND ROAD INITIATIVE

4.1 The Legal Issues of International Tax Planning for Cross-Border Income

An ancient Chinese saying goes,' A long journey can be covered only by taking one step at a time.' Similarly, there is an Arabic proverb which says that the Pyramids were built by piling one stone upon another. In Europe, there is also the saying that' Rome wasn't built in a day.' The Beat and Road Initiative is a great undertaking which requires dedicated efforts. The Belt and Road Initiative involves many aspects of cooperation between China and the sixty-four countries along Belt and Road, such as policy connectivity. The legal systems of some countries are very different from that of China, resulting in the risk of legal information asymmetry. At the same time, in some countries, the law is not complete enough, such that the laws and regulations are often amended, and some countries could discriminate against foreign or foreign-funded

---

11. Institute of Tax Research, International Bureau of Taxation, *Foreign Tax System Summaries*, 4th edition (China Tax Press October 2012); PricewaterhouseCoopers, *Worldwide Tax Summaries* (2014), available at www.pwc.com/gx/en/tax/corporate-tax/worldwide-tax-summaries/taxsummaries.jhtml; CN: International Taxation Bureau, Tax Treaties (in Chinese), available at http://www.chinatax.gov.cn/n810341/n810770/index.html (accessed 5 January 2016).

enterprises when enforcing the law. Some countries might even have some additional control over multinational corporations depending on their own political and economic interests.[12]

On 19 May 2015, the UN released the World Economic Situation and Prospects 2015, which reported that there were still downside risks to the global economy because of the upcoming normalization of US monetary policy; the continued instability of the eurozone; the potential spillover effect of political conflicts; and some problems in emerging economies. It estimated that the global economic growth rate in 2015 was expected to be only 2.8%.[13] The severe economic situation exacerbated tax issues related to investment in Belt and Road countries. If enterprises do not pay enough attention to legal issues, are not familiar with foreign tax laws or lack enough professionals in the field of tax law, they could unintentionally violate local tax laws and rules – which could ultimately affect the profit from the investment.

In general, Belt and Road countries mainly apply a civil law system or common law system; some include a small part of the Islamic law system. According to the Belt and Road coverage, most East Asian countries such as Mongolia; Central Asian countries other than Afghanistan; Southeast Asian countries such as Laos, Myanmar and Thailand and; Russia; Iraq; and most European countries except the United Kingdom and Ireland, all apply a continental legal system. India, Pakistan and other Asian countries, as well as the United Kingdom, Ireland and other European countries apply a common law system. Compared with a continental law system, a common law system is more about following judicial precedent, rather than emphasizing the legal code in the course of a judicial trial. That is to say, under common law, the precedent of a case is legally binding on subsequent cases.

In the case of India Vodafone–Hutchison Telecom brand acquisition, a well-known international accounting firm advised Vodafone Group to adopt a fair tax burden term, so the parties to the transaction each bear the tax burden in mergers and acquisitions, as well as possible responsibility in the event of future tax disputes. However, this requirement was ultimately 'balanced' out. The core of this erroneous decision is that the parties considered India to be a jurisprudential country like the United Kingdom, while in fact the Inland Revenue Department in India had never implemented such law of this kind with regard to wholly offshore equity deals.[14] In addition, Afghanistan and most of the Middle East countries (except Iraq and Saudi Arabia) have implemented Islamic law.[15] The legal system differs from one country to the next, which leads to different ways of handling disputes and creates a number of legal risks.

---

12. Wang Yiwei, 一带一路的机遇与挑战 (*The Opportunities and Challenges of Belt and Road*) (People's Press April 2015), at 135–136.
13. *See* United Nations: the global economy is expected to grow 2.8% in 2015, http://news.xinhuanet.com/fortune/2015-05/21/c_127826633.htm (accessed 21 May 2015).
14. Deng Haoran, *The Tax Risk and Control of the Localization of Overseas FDI) Eroding Corporate Income Taxes?*, International Taxation in China 4 (2015), at 20.
15. Islamic law refers to the basic legal system such as 'legal tradition', 'legal family' or 'legal group' formed by Islamic countries. The main contents include, for example, Muslim obligations, land ownership, debt law, family law, inheritance law and criminal law.

Therefore, through appropriate transnational investment agreements and international tax planning, combined with a skilled application of tax laws and tax treaties in China, going-global enterprises can make their investments in countries along the Belt and Road more internationally competitive.

4.2 Three Tax Planning Approaches for Going Global Enterprises in Terms of Cross-Border Earnings

At present, the basic Chinese laws and rules on the foreign income tax credit mainly consist of the Enterprise Income Tax Law and the Implementation Regulation of the Enterprise Income Tax Law (as formulated by the State Council). However, specific implementation measures are included in The State Administration of Taxation on Offshore Enterprises (Cai Shui [2009] No. 125 Document); the Operation Guide for Overseas Income Tax Credit of Enterprises (State Administration of Taxation No. 1, 2010 Notice); a Circular of the State Administration of Taxation on Improving the Tax Service and Administration for Chinese Enterprises Going Global (Guo Shui Fa [2010] No. 59); a Circular of the State Administration of Taxation on the Development of Tax Service and Management about Implementing the Belt and Road Initiative (China SAT Circular [2015] No. 60). The Chinese foreign income tax credit follows the principle of the supremacy of tax treaties. If there are differences between a signed tax treaty and the above laws and regulations, the jurisdiction to tax should be determined in accordance with the applicable tax treaty.

To carry out international tax planning in the countries along the Belt and Road, it is important that the tax departments of the Going Global Enterprises be closely integrated into the business model rather than being apart from the actual business operations. The first step is to compare and analyse the corporate income tax required of each type of entity and the amount of export tax or dividend withholding income tax that the local enterprises must pay when distributing profits, in order to minimize the local tax burden. Second, regarding the tax credit, Chinese resident enterprises must know whether profits repatriated from abroad are subject to Chinese enterprise income tax and whether the tax paid abroad may be fully credited. Finally, regarding international tax planning, enterprises should seek to reduce the foreign tax burden as much as possible through the arrangement of the organizational structure and business activities; to increase the creditable amount of income tax; and to defer or reduce the Chinese enterprise income tax that must be paid.[16]

---

16. The international tax planning examples of cross-border income for investing countries along the Belt and Road are all derived from or adapted from the cases by Cao Mingxing et al. Cao Mingxing, Yu Hai & Li Na, *International Tax Planning and Management for Cross-Border Income Based on China's Current Tax Law System* (China Tax Press December 2014), at 34–40.

4.2.1 Active Income from Foreign Operations: General Contracting and Sub-Contracting of Construction Projects

Going-global enterprises have carried out a large number of construction projects in the form of general contracting or sub-contracting in countries along the Belt and Road. For example, a Chinese resident enterprise is a general contractor of a construction project in Central Asian Country B, with a total contract value of 80 million and an estimated cost of 60 million. Under relevant rules in Country B, a foreign contractor must set up a project department locally as a permanent establishment, and use the simple collection method to compute corporate income tax, which is levied as 2% of the contract value (requisition and subcontracting fees may not be deducted). Permanent establishments will no longer be subject to profit remittance tax when remitting their after-tax profits out of Country B. The Chinese resident enterprise can build the project entirely on its own, or by using its wholly owned subsidiary in Hong Kong. The profits earned by the Hong Kong subsidiary may be used for other items and not repatriated to China for the time being. The Chinese resident enterprise is only taxed on profits derived from Hong Kong (assuming that the profits from Country B fulfil the requirement for tax exemption).

Query: How do Chinese going-global enterprises structure this project to minimize the total tax burden?

Generally speaking, if the foreign tax burden is relatively low, a proper entity should be considered to undertake all activities or business operations with a mother-son-grandson or so-called sandwich structure, recognizing the profit in the jurisdiction with a lower tax rate and not transferring that profit back to China for the time being, in order to defer Chinese corporate tax on foreign profit. Following the above concepts, the authors compare the pros and cons of the following two Alternatives 6.1A and 6.1B.

First, the Chinese resident enterprises implement all of the contracts as the general contractor as shown below:

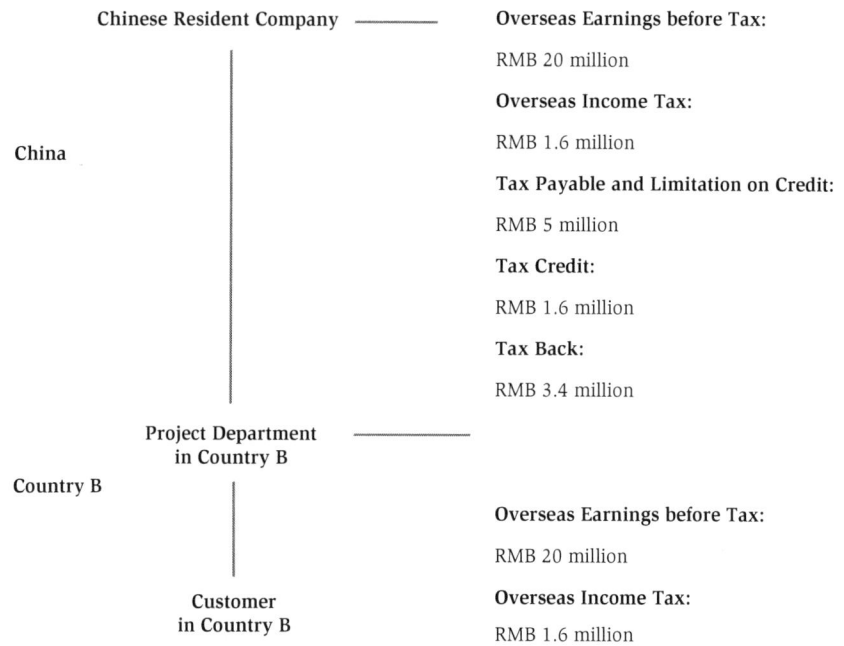

The corporate tax burden under this Alternative 6.1A is 5 million (3.4 + 1.6 = 5).

Chapter 6: Tax Planning Approaches for Cross-Border Earnings: BRI perspective

The Alternative 6.1B, as shown below, is to establish a subsidiary in Hong Kong as the general contractor which implements all the contracts:

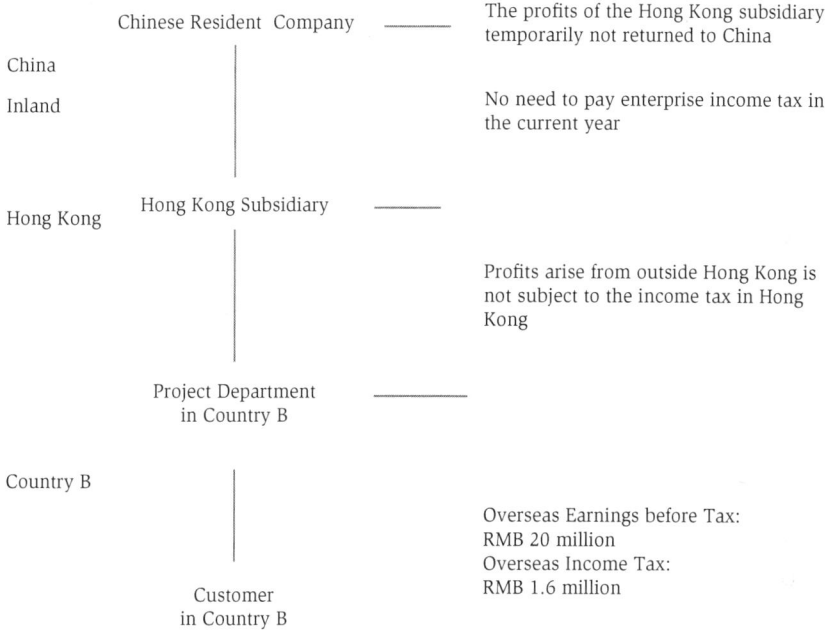

The total corporate tax burden under this Alternative 6.1B is 1.6 million.

Therefore, the key to international tax planning for going-global enterprises that carry out general contracting and subcontracting operations is to obtain foreign-source income from subsidiaries in low-tax jurisdictions, so as to defer Chinese enterprise income tax.

4.2.2 Passive Income from Foreign Investment in High-, Medium- and Low-Tax Jurisdictions

The Belt and Road runs through the continents of Asia and Europe. At one end is the active East Asian economic circle, while at the other end is the developed European economic circle. In between, the vast hinterland has huge potential in economic development. In this vast area, if resident enterprises invest indirectly in more than one country, in some host countries they will inevitably encounter higher or lower tax rates than those in China, thus affecting their normal cross-border tax credits.

For example, a Chinese company planning to set up a subsidiary in Hungary (a Hungarian company) is expected to a earn pre-tax profit of EUR 10 million a year and that profit will be returned to China after paying Hungarian corporate income tax. Assuming a Hungarian corporate income tax rate of 10%, repatriation of dividends to China is exempt from withholding tax. The Chinese resident company previously established a wholly owned subsidiary (a company) in Poland. The Polish company owns a German company with an annual pre-tax profit of EUR 10 million and pays 30% of German corporate income tax. Under Polish tax law, Polish income tax is not imposed on foreign dividends, and Polish companies are not subject to Polish withholding tax on dividends distributed abroad. In addition, following the EU Parent-Subsidiary Directive, when a certain equity ownership level is reached, German and Hungarian companies need not pay withholding tax in Germany or Hungary when they pay a dividend to a Polish company. So what is the difference in taxation when a Chinese resident company or a Polish company establishes a subsidiary in Hungary?

China's foreign income tax credit rules follow the principle of an overall credit on a per-country basis, and its credit principle is applicable only to first-tier foreign enterprises. If second-tier and third-tier foreign enterprises are located in different countries and the tax burdens are different from China (higher or lower than 25%), the investment profit in different foreign tax jurisdictions may be consolidated into one subsidiary via a structural arrangement of the shareholding and remitted back to China so as to reduce Chinese enterprise income tax on profit from the foreign investment. Based on the above ideas, a comparison is presented, below, of the pros and cons of two Alternatives 6.2A and 6.2B.

Chapter 6: Tax Planning Approaches for Cross-Border Earnings: BRI perspective

First, the Chinese resident company could establish a subsidiary in Hungary as shown below:

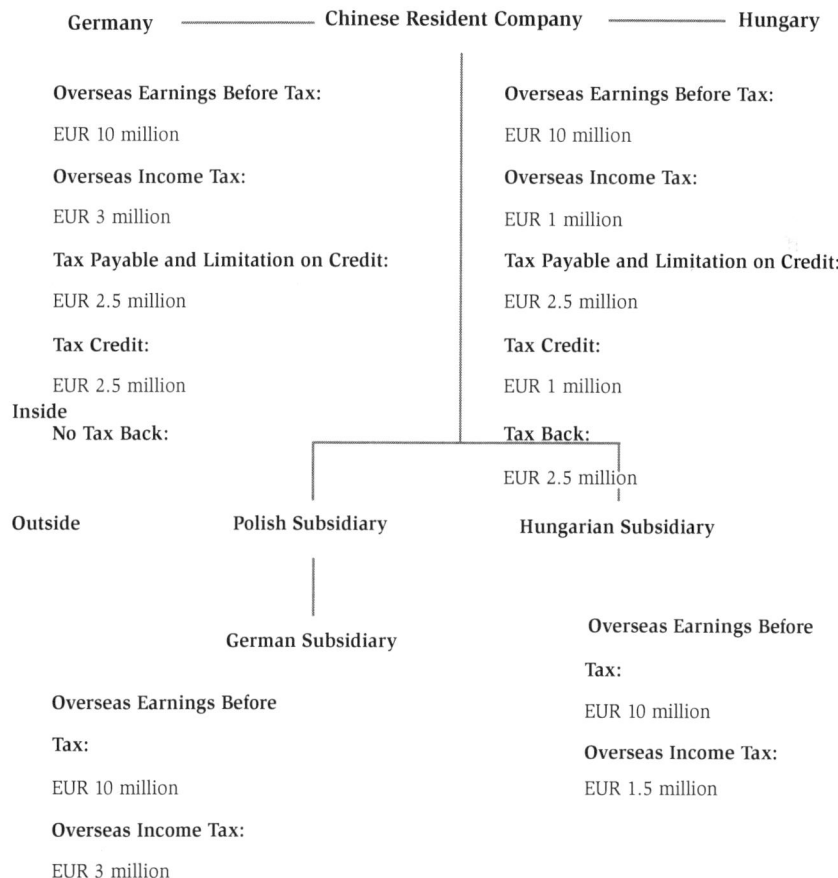

The total corporate tax burden under Alternative 6.2A is 5.5 million (3 + 1 + 1.5 = 5.5).

Second, the Polish subsidiary could establish a subsidiary in Hungary as in Alternative 6.2B below:

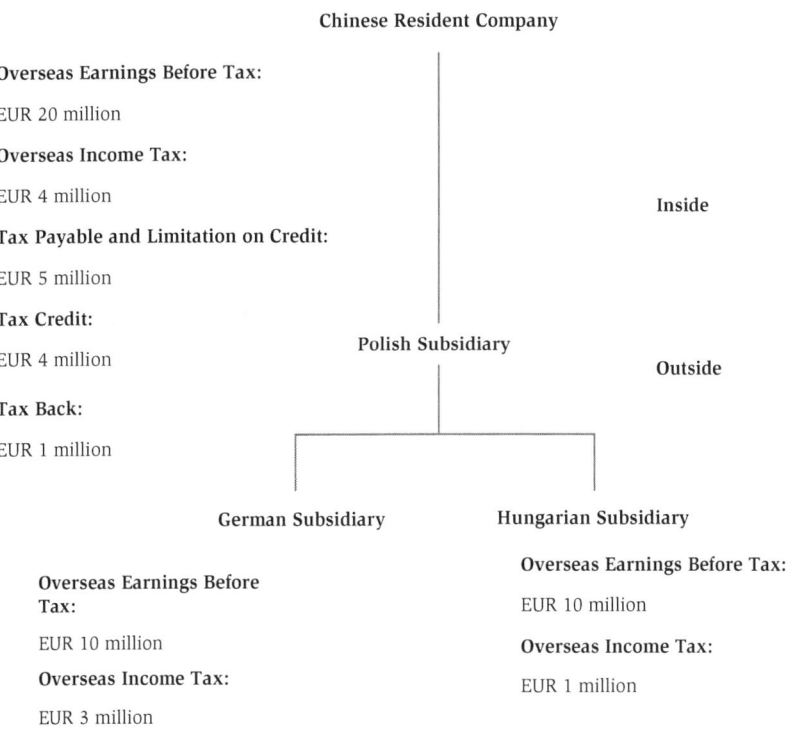

The total corporate tax burden under Alternative 6.2B is USD 5 million (3 + 1 + 1 = 5).

Therefore, the key point for international tax planning by going-global enterprises as regards their indirect investment into the countries along the Belt and Road is to neutralize the profits from high-tax and low-tax jurisdictions through first-tier foreign subsidiaries in order to increase the foreign tax credit limitation and the tax credit with regard to foreign-source income, and to reduce Chinese corporate income tax.

4.2.3 *Passive Income from Foreign Investment: Intangible Assets*

At present, the high-tech sector has become a key sector for going-global enterprises. The passive foreign-source income related to intangible assets consists mainly of royalties, but in certain special circumstances, it can also be in the form of, for example, sales revenue from goods, rental of equipment or technical service fees. Under Chinese tax treaties and agreements, the term 'royalties' is generally defined as income from 'the use of, or the right to use, any copyright of literary, artistic or scientific work including cinematograph films, or films or tapes for radio or television broadcasting, any computer software, patent, trade mark, design or model, plan, secret formula or process, or for the use of, or the right to use, industrial, commercial or scientific equipment or for information concerning industrial, commercial or scientific experience'.[17] Typically, Chinese resident enterprises realize foreign income from intangible assets through software sales and software licensing, or by setting up foreign companies to hold intangible assets.

4.2.3.1 Software Sales and Licensing

For software sales and licensing, Chinese resident enterprises usually export their software to foreign companies in two types of transactions: one is to provide software separately to a foreign company in the form of a CD-ROM or Internet transmission, while the other is to embed the software in machinery and equipment and export it to foreign companies. Enterprises can obtain software sales revenue once at the time of exporting or obtain an entry fee and installation fee when exporting, and then charge an annual software license fee again in the software use period.

Regarding international taxation, when a Chinese resident enterprise exports its software to a foreign company and obtains the above income, it is essential to determine whether such income is subject to host country withholding tax or customs duties.

Generally speaking, software embedded in imported equipment or imported in the form of CD-ROMs falls within the scope of customs duties, while 'software licensing fees' paid by a local company are just subject to withholding taxes other than customs duties. In the case of a gap between the customs duty rate and the withholding tax rate, for software exports the tax planning issue arises as to how to choose the transaction arrangement with the lowest tax burden. In addition, when a Chinese resident enterprise obtains revenue from software exports, it must pay Chinese enterprise income tax, and – depending on the specific circumstances of the transactions – may obtain a foreign tax credit. As the scope of the foreign income tax credit is limited to the foreign-source income derived by the Chinese resident enterprise, if the Chinese resident enterprise licenses the software to a foreign company, the software license fees obtained are to be categorized as foreign-source income (i.e., from outside China) and thus the foreign withholding tax should be deductible.

For example, a Chinese resident company exports a production line to a wholly owned Indian holding subsidiary and provides the system software needed to operate the equipment. The software is valued at USD 10 million and no cost may be deducted for purposes of Chinese enterprise income tax. The tax rate applicable to Chinese resident enterprises is 25%, and exporting software (including licensing) is exempt from VAT and sales tax. The Indian subsidiary is subject to 30% corporate income tax, the withholding tax for dividends is 0% and the tariff rate is 10%. The subsidiary's pre-tax profit for the year before deducting the cost of the software and import duties

---

17. Agreement between the Government of the Republic of Singapore and the Government of the People's Republic of China for the Avoidance of Double Taxation and the Prevention of Fiscal Evasion with Respect to Taxes on Income. 1 Jan. 2008.

(if any) is USD 20 million. Assuming that the Indian customs and tax authorities stipulate that if the imported equipment contains software, the price of the software will be included in the customs import declaration price of the equipment and will be subject to customs duties. If the software is not included in the equipment but is permitted to be used by a foreign company, the software license fees should constitute royalties and a payment of 10% withholding income tax. An Indian company may deduct the software license fees and import duties (if any) once in the same year. Consider the following comparison of two Alternatives 6.3A and 6.3B for taxation.

Under Alternative 6.3A below, the Chinese resident company embeds the software in the equipment and exports it to an Indian subsidiary:

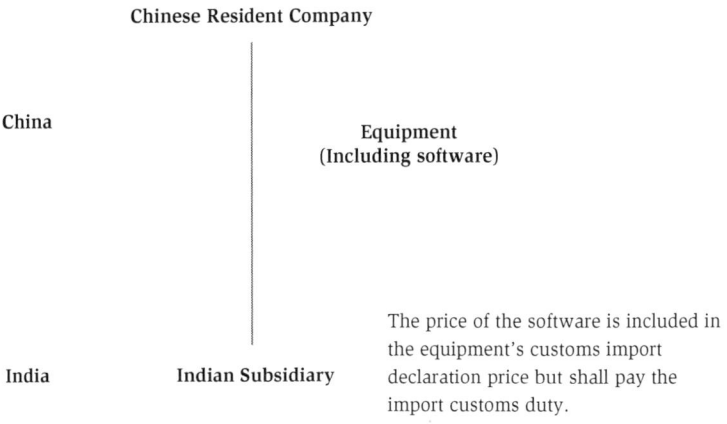

The tax burden under Alternative 6.3A is USD 6.2 million (2.5 + 1 + 2.7 = 6.2).

Under Alternative 6.3B below, the Chinese resident company separately licenses the software to the Indian subsidiary:

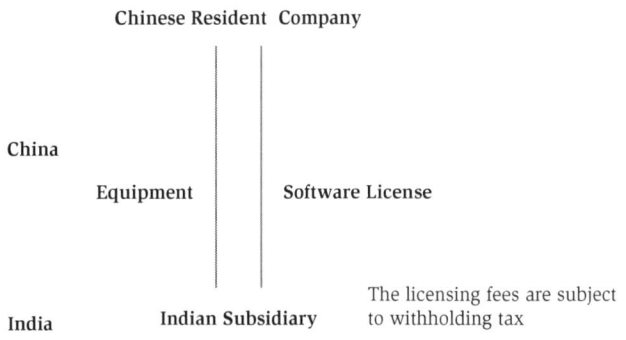

The tax burden under Alternative 6.3B is USD 5.5 million (1 + 1.5 + 3 = 5.5).

The key difference in the taxation of the above two Alternatives 6.3A and 6.3B is that the enterprises are to pay customs duty (Alternative 6.3A) or withholding tax

Chapter 6: Tax Planning Approaches for Cross-Border Earnings: BRI perspective

(Alternative 6.3B) for the income from the software export. If it pays customs duty, the tax is borne by the Indian subsidiary, but may offset the local corporate income tax; if it pays withholding tax, the tax burden is on itself, but it may deduct the Chinese corporate income tax. In this case, due to the relatively low deductible cost for resident Chinese enterprises and the fact that the income tax rate in India is higher, the overall tax burden can be reduced by adopting Alternative 6.3B (paying withholding tax).

4.2.3.2 Setting up Foreign Subsidiaries for Intangible Assets

In order to protect their intellectual property, multinational corporations typically set up subsidiaries in Hong Kong, the Netherlands or Switzerland, for example; inject intangible assets such as trademarks, software or technology; and then license them to foreign companies. With regard to international tax planning, if a Chinese resident company sets up an intangible asset company in a low-tax jurisdiction, it can defer Chinese enterprise income tax to a certain extent while avoiding the burden of the Chinese business tax on licensing income from trademarks, technology and other intangible assets. At the same time, withholding taxes on royalties can also be reduced if there is a favourable tax treaty between the country of the intangible asset company and the licensee's country.

For example, a Chinese resident company directly holds 100% of an Indian company and a Hong Kong company. At present, the Chinese resident company plans to develop a technology (cost CNY 1 million) that will be licensed to the Indian company. The Chinese resident company is subject to 25% corporate income tax, and technology licensing income requires the payment of a 5% business tax; however the income derived from entrusted technology development can be free of tax, and technology development income up to CNY 5 million is exempt from corporate income tax. Assume that a Hong Kong company obtains the license fee for technology paid by the Indian company, and this income is free of Hong Kong income tax. The pre-tax profit of the Indian company in the next five years is CNY 10 million, with 30% corporate income tax and 10% withholding tax for dividends and royalties. The profits of the subsidiaries in Hong Kong and India are used in other foreign investment projects and will temporarily not be repatriated to China. The currency mentioned above is CNY, and the time value of the currency is not considered. Consider the following comparison, as well as the similarities and differences between the tax implications of the following two Alternatives 6.4A and 6.4B.

Alternative 6.4A: The Chinese resident company directly licenses the technology to the Indian company and charges a fee of CNY 5 million for five years in total as shown below:

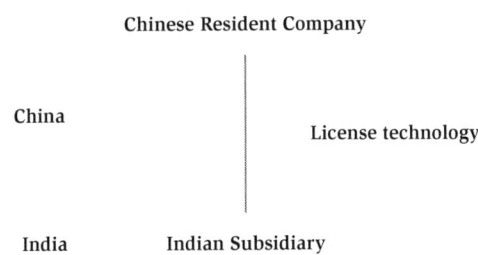

The tax burden under Alternative 6.4A is USD 2.69 million (0.5 + 0.25 + 0.44 + 1.5 = 2.69).

Alternative 6.4B: The Hong Kong subsidiary entrusts the Chinese resident company to develop a technology, which costs USD 2 million. Then the Hong Kong subsidiary licenses the technology to the Indian subsidiary, and charges a fee of CNY 5 million for five years in total as below:

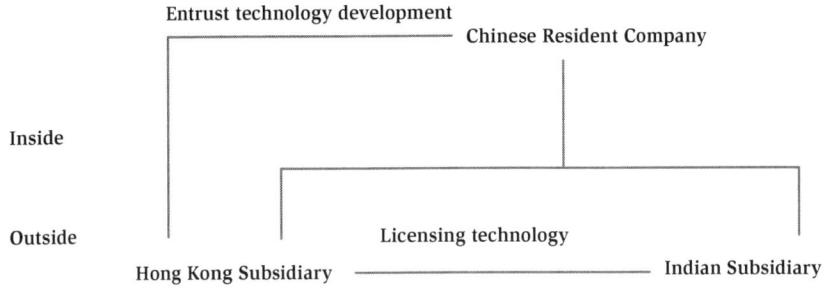

The tax burden under Alternative 6.4B is USD 2 million (0.5 + 1.5 = 2).

Here, Alternative 6.4B can lower the Chinese corporate income tax by entrusting the Chinese resident company to develop technology through the Hong Kong subsidiary and then license it to the Indian subsidiary.

5 CONCLUSION

Although the Belt and Road initiative provides great opportunities for going-global enterprises, it also poses a serious challenge in the international tax planning for cross-border income. In accelerating the pace of going global, one should clearly understand that the key destination and means of investment by going-global enterprises will change with the orientation of national policies and the establishment of bilateral and multilateral cooperation mechanisms; the design of international tax planning and business investment structure will be changing following the change of

Chapter 6: Tax Planning Approaches for Cross-Border Earnings: BRI perspective

the tax treaties signed by China and Belt and Road countries in the aspects of countries, number, contents or other elements. However, the only unchanged thing should be the firm determination to continuously serve going-global enterprises and deeply research on the approaches of international tax planning and management.[18]

---

18. In this chapter, the international tax planning methods for various items of cross-border income of going-global enterprises are not mentioned in order to advocate that going-global enterprises evade taxation in China. Instead, the authors seek to help Chinese enterprises implement appropriate investment structures and international tax planning in Belt and Road countries, so as to reduce their overall tax burden, thereby enhancing international competitiveness and influencing China's going-global enterprises.

CHAPTER 7
International Tax Coordination under the Belt and Road Initiative

Wenjing Wang* & Hongyu Lai**

1 Introduction
2 Basic Economic Circumstances of Countries along the Belt and Road
    2.1 Population Density
    2.2 Economy Level
    2.3 International Trade and Investment
    2.4 Comparison of Economic Factors along the Belt and the Road
3 Chinese Bilateral Tax Treaties with Countries along the Belt and Road
4 International Tax Proposals to Boost Implementation of the Belt and Road Initiative
    4.1 International Tax Rules Should Be Top-Level Designed under the Belt and Road Initiative
    4.2 The Tax Treaty Network Should Be Improved on a Timely Basis
    4.3 Tax Policies for Outward-Oriented Economic Development Should Be Implemented in China
    4.4 A Tax Coordination Mechanism for the Cross-Border Economic Cooperation Zone Should Be Explored

---

* The author can be reached at wwj@cufe.edu.cn. This chapter is translated and modified based on the authors' article published in the *Journal of International Taxation in China* (in Chinese), with some amendments and deletions.
** The author can be reached at daisy_lai.cufe@foxmail.com.

1 INTRODUCTION

In 2013, the 'Decision of the Central Committee of the Communist Party of China on Some Major Issues Concerning Comprehensively Deepening the Reform' put forward the proposal of 'promoting the construction of the Silk Road Economic Belt and the Maritime Silk Road, and forming a new pattern of opening up in all directions' in China. In 2015, the Chinese government promulgated the 'Vision and Actions on Jointly Building the Silk Road Economic Belt and twenty-first Century Maritime Silk Road' and clearly outlined the regional development outlook and feasible path under the Belt and Road Initiative. And the First Belt and Road Forum for International Cooperation was held in 2017 – a sign of existing achievements. The economic and tax circumstances in countries along the Belt and Road vary significantly. Therefore, this chapter mainly focuses on those differences, especially the ones among countries along the Belt and along the Road.

2 BASIC ECONOMIC CIRCUMSTANCES OF COUNTRIES ALONG THE BELT AND ROAD

The Belt and Road Initiative can be characterized as having a wide range of geographic scope; diversification of economy and society; and pan-regional win-win cooperation. In order to make a comparative analysis, the authors choose sixty-four countries along the Belt and Road as the research sample and further classified these countries into six categories:

- eleven countries of Southeast Asia (Brunei, Cambodia, East Timor, Indonesia, Laos, Malaysia, Myanmar, the Philippines, Singapore, Thailand and Vietnam);
- eight countries of South Asia (Afghanistan, Bangladesh, Bhutan, India, Maldives, Nepal, Pakistan and Sri Lanka);
- sixteen countries of West Asia and North Africa (Bahrain, Egypt, Iran, Iraq, Israel, Jordan, Kuwait, Lebanon, Oman, Palestine, Qatar, Saudi Arabia, Syria, Turkey, the United Arab Emirates and Yemen);
- five countries of Middle Asia (Kazakhstan, Kyrgyzstan, Tajikistan, Turkmenistan and Uzbekistan);
- eight countries of the Commonwealth of Independent States (CIS) and related countries (Armenia, Azerbaijan, Belarus, Georgia, Moldova, Mongolia, Russia and Ukraine); and
- sixteen countries of Central and Eastern Europe (Albania, Bosnia and Herzegovina, Bulgaria, Croatia, Czech Republic, Estonia, Hungary, Latvia, Lithuania, Macedonia, Montenegro, Poland, Romania, Serbia, Slovakia and Slovenia).

Furthermore, the authors make two further categorizations. First, countries along the Silk Road Economic Belt include the five countries in Middle Asia, the Commonwealth of Independent States and Georgia, Mongolia, the sixteen countries in Central and Eastern Europe, as well as some Western Asian countries (such as Iran and Turkey). In this chapter, these countries are referred to as countries along *the Belt*. Second, the countries along the twenty-first Century Silk Road mainly include eleven countries in Southeast Asia, eight countries in South Asia, most of West Asia and Egypt. Similarly, they are referred to as countries along *the Road*.

2.1 Population Density

The land area of the sixty-four countries along the Belt and Road is nearly one-third of the total area of all countries of the world, while the total population along the Belt and Road is approximately 3.151 billion, accounting for approximately 43.4% of the total global population in 2014.[1]

The land area covered by the Silk Road Economic Belt is even broader and runs through the vast hinterland of the Eurasian continent. The land area covered by the twenty-first Century Maritime Silk Road is relatively small but radiates extensively over the waters of the South Pacific and Indian Oceans. From the perspective of the land area proportion, Mongolia and Russia account for 40% of the total area of the sixty-four countries along the Belt and Road. Therefore, eight countries of CIS, Georgia and Mongolia occupy almost half of the land area along the Belt and Road. The group with the lowest land share is the sixteen countries of Central and Eastern Europe, which has only 3%.[2]

According to 2014 data from the World Bank, the population of countries along the Road is relatively larger, while the population along the Belt is relatively small. In terms of population composition, the eight countries in South Asia account for the largest share, totalling over one-half of the population among all countries along the Belt and Road. The population in the five Central Asian countries is the lowest, at only 2%. Both the sixteen countries of Central and Eastern Europe and the eight countries of the Commonwealth of Independent States and related countries have a share of the population, at less than 10%.[3]

In contrast, the population densities in the countries along the Belt and Road are quite different, with the population densities of Asian countries being significantly higher. The population density along the Road is generally higher than that along the Belt. The Belt covers almost two-thirds of the land area along the Belt and Road, but the population share is less than one-third.

---

1. The values are calculated based on data from the World Bank WDI database. In order to ensure the unity of statistical standards, this chapter adds up all accessible country data as total population and total area. See http://databank.worldbank.org/data/reports.aspx?source=world-development-indicators.
2. The values are calculated based on data from the World Bank WDI database. *See* http://databank.worldbank.org/data/reports.aspx?source=world-development-indicators.
3. *Ibid.*

2.2 Economy Level

In terms of total economic output, there are large gaps among countries along the Belt and Road. According to the World Bank (the WDI database), the total GDP of the 64 countries along the Belt and Road in 2013 was approximately USD 13.2202 trillion, accounting for approximately 1.37 times China's GDP in 2013. The total GDP of 62 countries along the Belt and Road (due to a lack of GDP data for Syria and Palestine) in 2014 was approximately USD 12.9883 trillion, accounting for approximately 1.25 times China's GDP in 2014. From the GDP percentages of different groups in 2014, the fourteen countries in West Asia and North Africa (excluding Syria and Palestine) is approximately 29.2% of the total GDP of sixty-two countries along the Belt and Road, accounting for the highest share. However, the share of five Asian countries is the lowest, at 2.66%. In addition, if the CIS country group were not to include Russia, the GDP of the remaining seven countries would account for only 2.55%, and the share of GDP for the sixteen countries in Central and Eastern Europe also has a relatively low value.[4]

GDP values vary greatly among countries along the Belt and Road. The top three countries in terms of GDP rank in 2014 are, in order, India, Russia and Indonesia. The last three countries in terms of GDP rank are, in order, East Timor, Bhutan and Maldives. Among them, India's GDP is approximately 1,446 times that of East Timor. The GDP of Russia and India are both higher than the total GDP values of 16 Central and Eastern European countries. The average GDP value of 62 countries along the Belt and Road is approximately 3.3 times the median value, indicating that there are significant gaps in economic level among countries along the Belt and Road, and the number of countries with a lower GDP value is relatively large.[5]

Regarding per capita income level, there are also obvious gaps among countries along the Belt and Road. Based on the indicator of gross national income per capita (GNI per capita) for 2014 as calculated by the World Bank and its national income level classification,[6] and bearing in mind the absence of data on East Timor and Palestine, eighteen of the sixty-two countries are characterized as being at the high-income level, twenty-one countries are at the upper-middle-income level, twenty countries are at the lower middle-income level and three countries are at the low-income level. The GNI per capita values vary widely among countries along the Belt and Road. The arithmetic mean in different income groups is higher than its median, meaning that there are relatively more countries at a lower income level within each group. China's GNI per capita in 2014 is USD 7,380, slightly higher than the median of the upper-middle-income group and below the arithmetic mean and population weighted average value of the group.

---

4. *Ibid.*
5. *Ibid.*
6. *See* https://data.worldbank.org/.

2.3 International Trade and Investment

From the perspective of import and export trade, according to the WDI database,[7] the average value of trade and service imports for sixty-one countries along the Belt and Road (due to a lack of data on East Timor, Palestine and Myanmar) was approximately USD 84.73 billion in 2014; and the average value of trade and service exports was approximately USD 93.524 billion.[8] The average value of imports on GDP is approximately 52.58%, while that of exports on GDP is approximately 50.11% according to 2014 data. According to 2014 data from the WDI database, China's import value was approximately USD 1.96 trillion, while its export value was approximately USD 2.34 trillion[9] – much higher than the average and median values above. On the whole, many countries along the Belt and Road rely on international trade and services for economic development.

Regarding capital flow, according to the WDI database, the net inflow value of foreign direct investment in the sixty-two remaining countries in 2014, accounted for approximately 3.54% of GDP on average, (bearing in mind the absence of data on Syria and Palestine). According to the WDI database, China's net foreign direct investment inflows in 2014 accounted for approximately 2.8% of GDP, less than the average share noted above (3.54%). With regard to the net direct investment outflow, the average value of its percentage of GDP in 2014 for the forty-nine remaining countries (excluding missing country data) was approximately 1.44%.[10] The top three countries ranked by net outflow of direct investment are Singapore, Kuwait and Hungary. According to the WDI database, China's net direct investment outflows as a share of GDP was approximately 1.72% for 2013.[11]

2.4 Comparison of Economic Factors along the Belt and the Road

Countries along the Belt and the Road obviously differ as regards land area, population, level of economic development, and scale of international trade and investment. There are tremendous spaces for win-win cooperation between China and countries along the Belt and Road.

First, the economic aggregates along the Belt and the Road are generally in balance. However, the total economic output of countries along the Road is slightly higher than that of the other countries along the Belt. China has a much higher economic output level and trade scale than many countries along the Belt and Road. As most countries along the Belt and Road have a high degree of dependence on the

---

7. http://databank.worldbank.org/data/reports.aspx?source=world-development-indicators.
8. Some of the sixty-one remaining countries still do not have data for 2014, so the authors chose the retrievable data for the most recent year as a substitute. *See* http://databank.worldbank.org/data/reports.aspx?source=world-development-indicators.
9. *See* http://databank.worldbank.org/data/reports.aspx?source=world-development-indicators.
10. Some of the forty-nine remaining countries still do not have data for 2014, so the authors chose the retrievable data for the latest year as a substitute. *See* http://databank.worldbank.org/data/reports.aspx?source=world-development-indicators.
11. *See* http://databank.worldbank.org/data/reports.aspx?source=world-development-indicators.

international economy, one can expect that China has had sufficient opportunities to induce economic radiation effects for countries along the Belt and Road which could enhance economic cooperation under the Initiative. The economic gaps among the countries also create space for cooperation.

Second, as a whole, GNI per capita in countries along the Belt is relatively higher than that of countries along the Road. From the perspective of per capita income level, China is basically at a medium level among countries along the Belt and Road, and therefore it has relevant cooperation space with other countries in medium-income, higher-income and lower-income levels.

Third, the average values of net foreign direct investment inflow on GDP and net direct investment outflow on GDP in countries along the Road are slightly higher than those in the countries along the Belt as a whole. The proportion of China's cross-border capital flow on its GDP is relatively close to the average level of the countries along the Belt and Road. Therefore, it is feasible to promote the cooperation between China and countries along the Belt and Road.

3 CHINESE BILATERAL TAX TREATIES WITH COUNTRIES ALONG THE BELT AND ROAD

Among countries along the Belt and Road analysed in this chapter, ten have not signed bilateral tax treaties with China as at November 2017, namely Afghanistan, Bhutan, East Timor, Iraq, Jordan, Lebanon, Maldives, Myanmar, Palestine and Yemen. Most of these countries are located along the Road. Among them, Jordan has signed more than 100 bilateral tax treaties, mostly with EU and developed countries. There are very few bilateral tax treaties signed by the nine remaining countries. Afghanistan and Maldives have signed no tax treaties with any other country. Bhutan has signed only one tax treaty, with India. Cambodia has signed tax treaties with three countries. East Timor has signed only one tax treaty, with Portugal. Lebanon has signed tax treaties with four countries, while Yemen has signed tax treaties with five countries. Myanmar has signed tax treaties with nine countries. Although no bilateral tax treaty has been signed with Maldives or Lebanon, China has signed an aviation agreement with Maldives and an aviation and sea transport agreement with Lebanon, which contain tax-exempt provisions on corporate income tax, personal income tax and indirect tax.

Looking at the signing date of current bilateral tax treaties, most of the Chinese agreements with countries along the Belt and Road to avoid double taxation were signed during the period from the 1980s to the beginning of the twenty-first century. Since 2005, China has separately signed tax treaties with Azerbaijan, Czech Republic, Georgia, Saudi Arabia, Syria, Tajikistan and Turkmenistan. China has renegotiated its tax treaties with Russia and Singapore. However, among the tax treaties that are currently in force, there are still some that were signed in the 1980s to which no amendments have been made since 2000. In the meantime, the international tax situation has changed significantly. The forms of international tax evasion are more complex and variable. International tax coordination efforts not only remain

Chapter 7: BRI Corporate Income Tax Laws and Tax Treaties - Comparison

concerning as regards the issue of avoiding double taxation but also pay more attention to preventing base erosion and profit shifting.

4 INTERNATIONAL TAX PROPOSALS TO BOOST IMPLEMENTATION OF THE BELT AND ROAD INITIATIVE

4.1 International Tax Rules Should Be Top-Level Designed under the Belt and Road Initiative

Designing international tax coordination and cooperation rules at the highest level helps to achieve a continuous and stable coordination effect under the Initiative. Although there are difficulties in reaching consensus on international tax coordination and cooperation among countries along the Belt and Road, as the initiator and core participant of the Belt and Road initiative, it is necessary for China to combine the goals of the Initiative with the OECD/G20 BEPS initiative, in order to design international tax coordination and cooperation rules under the Belt and Road Initiative. The rules under the Initiative should pay more attention to bilateral and multilateral tax coordination and cooperation, considering the economic and tax characteristics of countries along the Belt and Road and that the essential aim is to achieve a win-win situation. The rules should include at least the following elements: (i) principles of coordination and allocation of tax benefits (including income tax and value added tax) realized in future under the Initiative, (ii) principles of cooperation in international tax collection and administration under the Initiative, (iii) tax dispute negotiation principles and (iv) principles of tax coordination as regards the special cooperation issues under the Initiative.

At an operational level, this chapter suggests the design of corresponding coordination rules according to the economic and tax characteristics of the countries along the Belt and Road. In particular, in view of the significant differences in tax collection levels between countries along the Belt and the Road, when China discusses tax rules with most countries along the Belt, it should focus on strengthening tax collection and administration, and tax dispute negotiation.

4.2 The Tax Treaty Network Should Be Improved on a Timely Basis

Overall, a Chinese international tax treaty network with countries along the Belt and Road has basically taken shape. With the promotion of the Belt and Road Initiative, China still needs to improve its current tax treaty network in four regards. First, China should renegotiate some of its bilateral tax treaties with countries along the Belt and Road, in order to take into account the current new international economic and tax situation and the cooperation prospects under the Belt and Road Initiative. By renegotiating the tax treaties, China and countries along the Belt and Road could be encouraged to reach a new consensus on international tax coordination so as to achieve deep economic and tax cooperation.

Second, considering the implementation of the Belt and Road Initiative, China should actively improve the contents of bilateral tax treaties by signing protocols, in order to better coordinate bilateral tax benefits.

Third, China should push forward negotiations on bilateral tax treaties with countries along the Belt and Road that have not yet signed a tax treaty with China.

Fourth, China could attempt to promote the tax information exchange network with countries along the Belt and Road and step up deep cooperation in the field of international tax collection and administration.

4.3 Tax Policies for Outward-Oriented Economic Development Should Be Implemented in China

The economic and tax differences among countries along the Belt and Road have created win-win cooperation opportunities. Building a diversified outward-oriented economy in China and encouraging Chinese enterprises to go global into areas along the Belt and Road are feasible developments under the Initiative. The authors suggest that tax collection and services should be strengthened, and special tax incentive policies should be implemented in China. First, for example, permanent establishment provisions; limited interest rates for dividends, interest and royalties; and tax sparing provisions in bilateral tax treaties, have provided effective guarantees for enterprises to avoid double taxation.

However, there are still many Chinese going-global enterprises that fail to take full advantage of tax treaties. The authors suggested that the Chinese tax authorities should step up publicity regarding tax treaties to going-global enterprises in order to help them make effective use of these beneficial tax treaties.

Second, the Chinese tax authorities should also step up tax collection and service work for going-global enterprises, including both the management of tax-related information and the coordination of enterprises' overseas tax disputes.

Third, in the case of Chinese enterprises investing and operating in countries with less tax transparency (i.e., a lower nominal rate but higher non-tax burden), when the Chinese tax authorities calculate the overseas tax credits for enterprises, the authors suggest the non-tax burden should be taken into account in order to reduce the total burden.

Fourth, considering that the nominal corporate income tax rate in China is higher than that in most countries along the Belt and Road (especially in the countries along the Belt), there may be some difficulties in attracting low-tax countries to invest in certain industries in China. Tax incentives to attract foreign investment should be piloted in specific industries in China. In the short term, direct tax incentives such as direct tax cuts or exemption could be adopted. In the medium to long term, indirect tax incentives could be emphasized, and the dependence on preferential tax policies should be gradually reduced. Especially for those countries that have tax sparing provision in their tax treaties, the above-mentioned preferential tax policies will effectively attract enterprises from these countries to invest in China.

4.4 A Tax Coordination Mechanism for the Cross-Border Economic Cooperation Zone Should Be Explored

In order to take advantage of cross-border economic cooperation zones under the Belt and Road Initiative, China needs to clarify the principle of cross-border coordination of tax revenues and explore a special cross-border tax coordination mechanism to implement more convenient and preferential tax policies. In view of the differences in tax systems among the countries analysed here, the authors suggest that a simple tax system could be introduced in the cross-border economic cooperation zone. Tax administration in the zones should also be simplified. At present, the problem that still cannot be solved concerns whether the operating modes of cross-border economic cooperation zones across China should be unified and whether the applicable tax policies in different zones should be the same in future. Taking into account the reality of the differences among the border areas, the authors suggest granting local governments a certain degree of discretion in order to make tax coordination more effective under the Initiative.

CHAPTER 8
Analysis of Financial and Tax Operations in Five Central Asian Countries

Wei Tong, Jie Lei & Yaqiong Tian[*]

1	The Reform of Public Finance Systems and Policy Changes of the Five Central Asian Countries
	1.1 Kazakhstan
	1.2 Uzbekistan
	1.3 Kyrgyzstan
	1.4 Tajikistan
	1.5 Turkmenistan
2	Financial State of the Five Central Asian Countries
	2.1 Kazakhstan
	2.2 Uzbekistan
	2.3 Kyrgyzstan
	2.4 Tajikistan
	2.5 Turkmenistan
3	Fiscal Comparison Between the Five Central Asian Countries and Major Economies of the World
	3.1 The Size of Fiscal Revenue and Expenditure
	3.2 The Proportion of Fiscal Revenue and Expenditure in GDP
	3.3 Comparison of Per Capita Fiscal Revenue and Expenditure
References	

---

[*] Wei Tong, Doctor of Economics, Doctoral tutor, Institute of Finance and Economics Research, Central University of Finance and Economics; Jie Lei and Yaqiong Tian, PhD students of world economics, Institute of Finance and Economics Research, Central University of Finance and Economics.

1 THE REFORM OF PUBLIC FINANCE SYSTEMS AND POLICY CHANGES OF THE FIVE CENTRAL ASIAN COUNTRIES

In recent years, in order to promote their own economic development and broaden their sources of revenue, as well as maintain balanced fiscal revenue, the five Central Asian countries have on the one hand increased their financial input, accelerated infrastructure construction, reduced the tax burden, and created a favourable environment for the development of enterprises, and on the other hand, their governments are committed to strengthening the linkages between the states' medium-term strategic plans and budget decisions, and improving the performance of fiscal expenditure so that the state's financial and economic conditions will be improved.

1.1 Kazakhstan

In 2012, Kazakhstan formulated the 'Kazakhstan-2050 Strategy'. According to this strategy, Kazakhstan introduced a more open tax policy, which simplifies tax declaration procedures by improving customs management and organization, providing more preferential treatment to taxpayers and enterprises in the fields of production and new technologies, encouraging and attracting domestic and foreign investment.

As an important source of fiscal revenue, asset legalization policies have been implemented more extensively in Kazakhstan in recent years.[1] By 1 January 2017, citizens can voluntarily disclose their private funds, real estate and other property, so as to obtain the amnesty and immunity to the declared property. However, after 1 January 2017, the property of all citizens in Kazakhstan needs to be fully publicized. Government can take necessary measures to find out the sources of income and tax payment and determine the assets and accounts of the citizens wherever they are based. The implementation of this policy is of great significance to promoting the re-entry of property and capital into the market and further cracking down on the shadow economy.

With regards to fiscal expenditure, Kazakhstan has always been implementing the fiscal policy of 'acting according to one's own measures and seeking truth from facts.' That is, with limited increases in fiscal revenue, all the fiscal expenditures will be fully liquidated, including inefficient or ineffective fiscal expenditure items, and projects that can be solved by the market. Meanwhile, in order to ease the pressure on fiscal spending, Kazakhstan also vigorously promotes the PPP model of development and introduces private investment into the investment and construction of livelihood projects.

---

1. In Kazakhstan, the legalization of assets began in 2001 and contributed USD 480 million to the government revenue. The second phase was in 2006–2007 and contributed USD 7 billion revenue. The third phase was in 2014–2016 and currently receives 662 billion KZT of revenue (about USD 2 billion).

1.2 Uzbekistan

In order to ensure the rapid and steady growth of economy, Uzbekistan has been continuously pushing forward the tax reform to reduce the tax burden on enterprises and citizens. According to data from the Economy Ministry in Uzbekistan, the tax revenue has decreased by about half in total GDP from 41% in 1996 to 20.5% in 2013, by simplifying and improving the tax system.

To reduce the tax burden, Uzbekistan's government has reduced the tax rates in various degrees for small and medium-sized enterprises, including tax rates in industrial field, unified social rates, corporate income rate and personal income tax rate. In 2012, the tax rate for small and medium-sized industrial businesses was reduced to 5%, 6% lower compared with the tax rate of 13% in 2005; the personal income tax rate was reduced from 10% to 7.5% in 2015, while small and micro enterprises and farmers witness a drop in unified social fee rate from 25% to 15%, and this rate in the construction field was also reduced from 6% to 5%.

In addition, since 2009, Uzbekistan has also begun to charge differentiated profit taxes for different business activities of commercial banks. At present, the validity of this policy is extended to 2020. According to the regulation, in the fiduciary investment projects of three years and above, the profit tax rate is 80% for commercial banks with a share of 30–40%, 75% for those with a share of 40%–50%, and 70% for those with a share of more than 50%.[2] Besides, Uzbekistan will take further steps to develop the indices of land tax, consumption tax, tobacco tax and alcohol tax.

1.3 Kyrgyzstan

According to 'Kyrgyzstan's Stable Development Strategy for 2013–2017', released in 2012, Kyrgyzstan will promote macroeconomic development, achieve a balanced budget, and ensure the sustainability of debt scale and promote the structural economic reform. These are the three overarching strategic objectives for the country's financial and economic development. To reach these goals, Kyrgyzstan sets the task for reforming the medium-term fiscal system as follows:

(a) Increase investment in infrastructure and energy

The fiscal deficit is a persistent problem for Kyrgyzstan and is also a major impediment to the growth of Kyrgyzstan government investment. With slow economic growth and declining Somme exchange rate, the government had to increase its investment in infrastructure construction through international loans. According to statistics, in 2015–2017, under the impetus of large-scale government investment, the country's GDP will increase 7.4% annually.

Most of the international loans that Kyrgyz government receives are from the Export-Import Bank of China, the Asian Infrastructure Investment Bank, the World

---

2. Дифференцированные ставки налога в Узбекистане продлены до 2020 года. 2015-5-11. http://ria.ru/economy/20150511/1063848513.html

Bank, the Islamic Development Bank and the Swiss government. 35% of the loans borrowed from China are in the form of grant, and the rest are preferential facilities.

(b) Implement rigorous tax policy

In response, the measures taken by Kyrgyzstan government include: reducing tax breaks and raising the rate of value-added tax collection, phasing out business taxes, narrowing the scope of application for the simplified tax regimes, and simplifying the system of accounting statements. In addition, Kyrgyzstan government also plans to rebuild the national tax service management system and strengthen tax supervision.

(c) Optimize the expenditure structure

In order to maximize financial savings, Kyrgyzstan government proposes to reduce recurrent expenditures and raises capital expenditures. Except for the social subsidy for low-income groups, the other expenditures, such as the expenditures on goods and services, and the salaries of civil servants will be gradually reduced. In the meantime, Kyrgyzstan will also improve the government procurement mechanism and increase the efficiency of budget subsidies in all economic sectors, which are the priorities for its fiscal reform.

1.4 Tajikistan

In September 2012, Tajikistan reviewed and passed the new basic tax law. This law reduces the current tax categories from twenty-one items to ten items, of which the national tax is reduced from seventeen items to eight items, the local tax from four items to two items, and some tax types of similar nature are consolidated. A number of tax categories, such as retail sales taxes, have been cancelled.

In February 2016, Tajikistan government proposed to amend the 2012 Edition of the Tax Code and it is primarily oriented towards simplifying the tax system and reducing the tax burden. The specific directions are as follows: (a) Implement the regressed social fee system. That is, when the salary reaches a certain level, the social fee rate drops and the tax burden on employers does not increase, so as to increase the willingness and possibility of raising the salary of employees. (b) Reduce the tax burden on SMEs in order to expand production, as well as increase job opportunities and investment attractiveness.[3]

The starting point for launching this tax reform lies in the fact that numerous fiscal and tax experts and government officials in Tajikistan regard it as both unrealistic

---

3. Правительственная комиссия рассматривает поправки в Налоговый кодекс Таджикистана. 2016-2-3. http://www.avesta.tj/sociaty/38180-pravitelstvennaya-komisiya-rassmatrivaet-popravki-v-nalogovyy-kodeks-tadzhikistana.htm.

and undesirable to rely solely on increasing tax revenue to supplement fiscal funds. The increase in fiscal revenue depends on a number of factors,[4] such as increasing industrial capacity, the viability and creativity of enterprises, the ability to attract foreign capital, and improving the efficiency and transparency of fiscal spending.

1.5 Turkmenistan

In November 2015, Turkmenistan passed the 'Turkmenistan's National Budget in 2016', a bill which sets the main tasks of the state budget as continuing to promote economic diversification, reforming the fiscal and taxation system and ensuring that the budgetary policy is consistent with the macroeconomic policies identified in 'Outline of Economic Development in Turkmenistan's National Societies (2011-2030)' and 'Outline of Socio-Economic Development in Turkmenistan (2012-2016)'. In order to promote economic development and social stability, Turkmenistan also proposed to further improve production efficiency, enhance the competitiveness of enterprises in light of the changes in the domestic and international climate, make effective use of investments, foster the country's technological innovation, and create more jobs.

According to the budget law, Turkmenistan's budget will set the main goal of expenditures as increasing the standard of living for the citizens, improving citizens' welfare, expanding spending on social services such as education and healthcare.[5] Timely and targeted budget expenditure is the important principle for budget policy in Turkmenistan.

Generally speaking, all five Central Asian countries have carried out various fiscal and taxation reforms. However, judging from the paces of fiscal reforms in those countries, result-oriented budget reform is proceeding more slowly failing to build a good connection between budget reform and national strategy, and the establishment of the modern financial system is not progressing fast enough. From the perspective of the reform stages, the five Central Asian countries are also mainly concentrated in the tax system reform. Because the fiscal revenue is not high, there are only limited means of using fiscal and tax policies to promote social and economic development.

2 FINANCIAL STATE OF THE FIVE CENTRAL ASIAN COUNTRIES

The five Central Asian countries have set up market economy one after another and given a facelift to the financial system. However, due to the differences in natural endowment and economic development level, there are always differences in the fiscal profiles among the five Central Asian countries since the independence among them.

---

4. Эксперт: Увеличение объема госбюджета только за счет налогов - дорога в никуда. 2015-11-2.
   http://nm.tj/economy/35168-ekspert-uvelichenie-obema-gosbyudzheta-tolko-za-schet-na logov-doroga-v-nikuda.html.
5. Принят Государственный бюджет Туркменистана на 2016 год. 2015-11-23.
   http://www.minfin.gov.tm/addhtml/news.html.

2.1 Kazakhstan

Kazakhstan enjoys sound fiscal performance after a series of reforms. As shown in Figure 8.1, it had maintained steady growth in fiscal revenue and expenditure during 2008–2015, except the year of 2009, which witnessed a decrease due to the financial crisis. The fiscal revenue was KZT 7,711.2 billion in 2015, an increase of 90.85% comparing to that in 2008. And the fiscal expenditure was KZT 8,626.9 billion, an increase of 97.24%, which is slightly higher than the growth of fiscal revenue.

From 2008 to 2011, the growth of fiscal deficit was slow in Kazakhstan, while there was a dramatic and consistent expanding state from 2011 to 2015. In 2015, the fiscal deficit was increasing 61.05% comparing to 2011. The number was only KZT 568.6 billion in 2011, and reached the highest point in 2014, which was KZT 1,086.7 billion. Then there is a slightly slowdown in 2015, down to KZT 915.7 billion.

Figure 8.1 Fiscal Revenue and Expenditure of Kazakhstan During 2011–2015 (Unit: KZT 100 million)

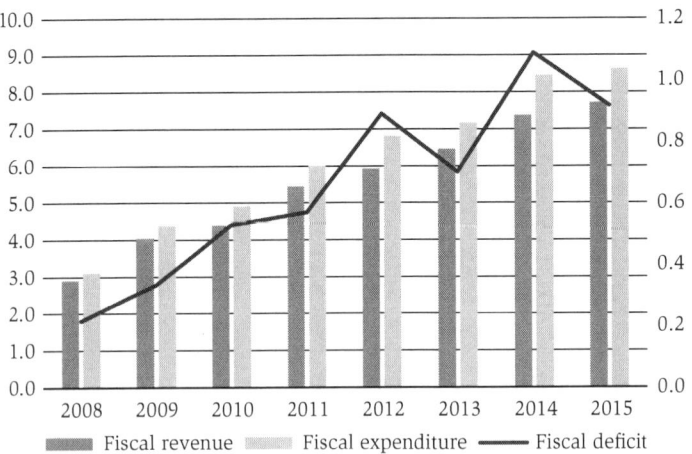

Data source: Ministry of Finance of Kazakhstan.

Kazakhstan's fiscal revenue mainly consists of tax, non-tax, sales of fixed assets, transfer payments and budget loan. The various revenue sources have gained increases to varied degrees in 2015, compared with 2014. The tax revenue reached KZT 4,883.9 billion in 2015, accounting for 63.34% of total fiscal revenue and representing an increase of 8.1% year on year; non-tax revenue was KZT 224.8 billion, accounting for 2.92% and representing an increase of 10.6% year on year; transfer payment accounts for a large portion in Kazakhstan's fiscal revenue, which was KZT 2,456.4 billion, or 31.86% of the total revenue. Besides, sales of fixed assets have generated KZT 69.7 billion of revenue while budget loan generated KZT 68.2 billion.

In 2015, the total fiscal expenditure was KZT 8,626.9 billion in Kazakhstan, which still mainly focuses on three livelihood fields, namely social relief, social security and medical care. The expenditures were KZT 1,713.5 billion, KZT 1,364.7 billion and KZT 863.9 billion, respectively, covering about half of the total fiscal expenditure. Other expenditure items were: culture, sports and tourism with payment of KZT 293.8 billion, housing and utilities with payment of KZT 443.3 billion, agricultural forestry and fisheries with payment of KZT 376 billion, transport and communication with payment of KZT 681.7 billion.

Kazakhstan's national debts consist of government debt (internal and foreign debt), central bank debt and local government debt. According to the released data of Kazakhstan's Ministry of Finance, by 1 January 2016, the total fiscal debt was KZT 8,240.8 billion, in which government debt was KZT 7,947.2 billion, accounting for 96.44%; and central bank debt was KZT 291.1 billion, accounting for 3.53%. We can see from Figure 8.2 that the government debt remains dominant in the national debt, and its proportion even reached 99.57% in 2014.

The growth rate of Kazakhstan's national debt was slower from 2012 to 2014, but government debt had ballooned from 2014 to 2016(including foreign debt), which led to a drastic increase of national debt. By 1 January 2016, Kazakhstan's national debt increased by 46.9% year on year. According to the data of International Monetary Fund (IMF), from 2012 to 2015, Kazakhstan's national debt accounts for 12.4%, 12.9% and 14.5% of GDP respectively. The proportion of foreign debt is high, respectively, accounting for 67.3%, 64.7 and 71.2% of the total debt.

Figure 8.2   Kazakhstan's National Debt Structure During 2012–2016
(Unit: KZT 100 million)

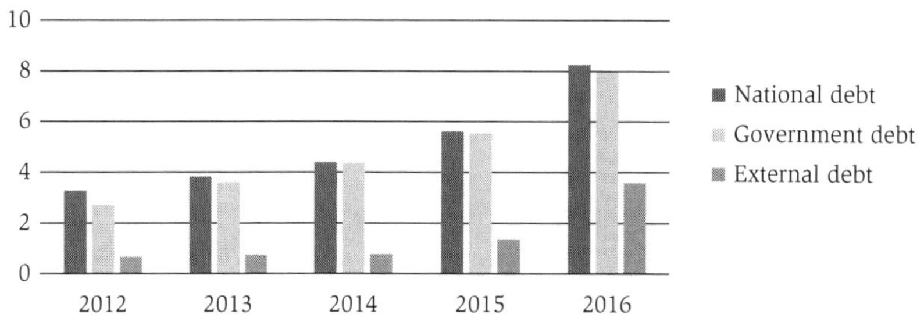

Data source: Ministry of Finance of Kazakhstan.

2.2 Uzbekistan

In recent years, the fiscal performance in Uzbekistan has been sound. The fiscal revenue and expenditure have gone up steadily each year, and the revenue was always high than expenditure, producing fiscal surplus. According to Figure 8.3, the fiscal revenue was UZS 36,492.7 billion, which was 4.16 times higher than that in 2008, and fiscal expenditure was UZS 36,289.8 billion, which was 4.43 times higher than that in 2008, and was slightly higher than the growth of fiscal revenue.

Figure 8.3 Budgetary Revenue and Expenditure of Uzbekistan in 2008–2015 (Unit: UZS 100 million)

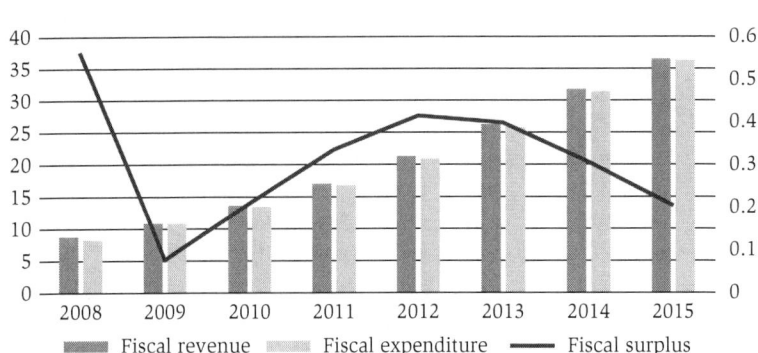

Data source: Ministry of Finance of Uzbekistan.

At the same time, from 2008 to 2015, the fiscal surplus in Uzbekistan showed significant fluctuations. In the wake of the financial crisis, the fiscal surplus fell sharply from UZS 563.7 billion in 2008 to UZS 76.3 billion in 2009, down by 86.46%. From 2009 to 2012, Uzbekistan fiscal surplus had gradually climbed up to a record high in eight years – UZS 413.7 billion. But from 2013, the surplus began to decline, 203.9 billion in 2015, falling by 48.9% comparing with 2013 (UZS 397.1 billion). Comparing with 2009, the fiscal revenue in 2015 increased 2.4 times, the expenditure increased 2.4 times and the fiscal surplus increased 1.7 times.

The Uzbekistan's fiscal revenue consists of direct tax, indirect tax, resource and property tax etc. In 2015, direct tax was UZS 8,798.5 billion, accounting for 24.1% of total revenue; and indirect tax was about UZS 19,193.8 billion, accounting for 52.6%. The indirect tax includes value added tax, consumption tax, customs tax and transport tax etc., in which value added tax made up more than half of the total. Resource and property tax was about UZS 4,816.1 billion, 13.2% of total revenue, while other revenue was UZS 3,684.4 billion, accounting for 10.1% of total revenue.

Uzbekistan's fiscal expenditure largely goes to social investment, aiming at rationalizing primary distribution and developing education and medical care. As Figure 8.4 shows, in 2014–2015, the structure of Uzbekistan's fiscal expenditure was stable: welfare and social security account for 58.8% and 58.7% respectively, economic development account for 10.7% and 10.6%, central investment expenditure account for 5.1%, and maintaining the operation of government, executive bodies, and judicial arms account for 4.5% and 4.4% respectively.

Figure 8.4 Fiscal Expenditure Structure of Uzbekistan (Unit: UZS 100 million)

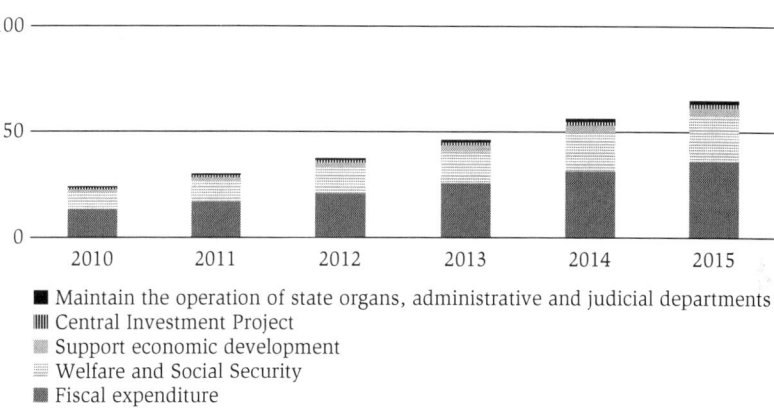

- Maintain the operation of state organs, administrative and judicial departments
- Central Investment Project
- Support economic development
- Welfare and Social Security
- Fiscal expenditure

Data source: Ministry of Finance of Uzbekistan.

In recent years, Uzbekistan's national debt has been spiralling up rapidly. The national debt was USD 5.45 billion in 2014, up by 11.9% compared with USD 4.87 billion in 2013. Though the national debt kept increasing, according to Figure 8.5, the national debt to GDP kept decreasing constantly, from 21% in 2006 to 9% in 2014, and the ratio was kept between 8.5 and 9% from 2011 to 2014.

Figure 8.5 Uzbekistan's National Debt and Its Proportion in GDP (Unit: UZS 100 million)

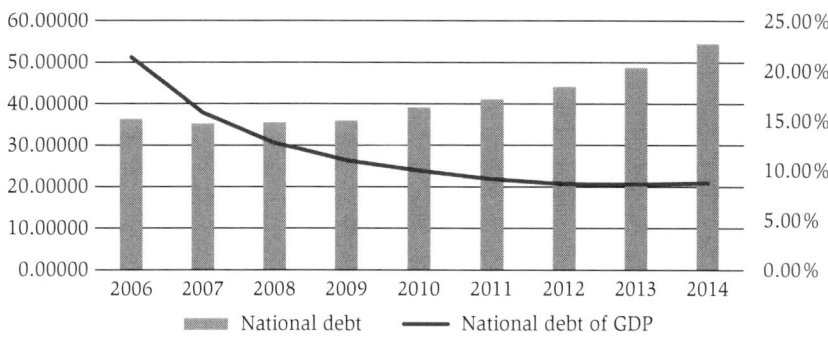

Data source: http://ru.tradingeconomics.com/uzbekistan/indicators.

2.3 Kyrgyzstan

In order to solve the long-time fiscal deficit, in recent years Kyrgyzstan has implemented tight fiscal policies and strictly controlled fiscal expenditure, which transformed the country's fiscal profile.

Figure 8.6 Fiscal Revenue and Expenditure of Kyrgyzstan During 2008–2015
(Unit: KGS 100 million)

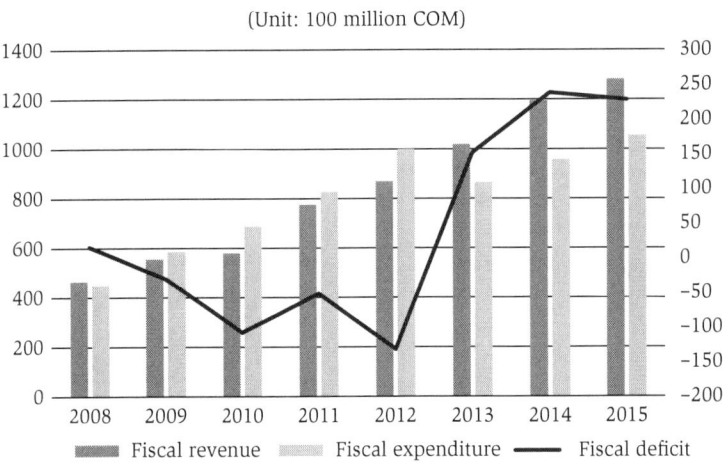

Data source: Ministry of Finance of Uzbekistan and National Bureau of Statistics.

As shown in Figure 8.6, Kyrgyzstan fiscal revenue had maintained its growth momentum from 2008 to 2015. It had increased by 175%, from KGS 46.6 billion in 2008 to KGS 128.1 billion in 2015. In a span of five years from 2008 to 2012, the fiscal expenditure growth had doubled. In 2013, the size of expenditure had shrunk to 87% of the previous year, yet it bounced back to the growth trajectory afterwards.

In 2015, fiscal expenditure was KGS 105.3 billion, up by 134% compared with 2008, yet it was way behind the growth rate of the fiscal revenue. What worth to be noted in 2013 is that the fiscal revenue exceeded fiscal expenditure for the first time, which generated a fiscal surplus (KGS 15.2 billion), and reached KGS 23.8 billion and KGS 22.8 billion in the recent two years.

In 2015, total fiscal expenditure was KGS 105.3 billion. As shown in Figure 8.7, it mainly focused on education, social relief, national defence, public security and medical care, and the input in each of area was KGS 25.4 billion, KGS 24.8 billion, KGS 14.9 billion and KGS 12.7 billion respectively.

Chapter 8: Financial and Tax Operations in the Five Central Asian Countries

Figure 8.7   Fiscal Expenditure Breakdown of Kyrgyzstan in 2015
(Unit: KGS 100 million)

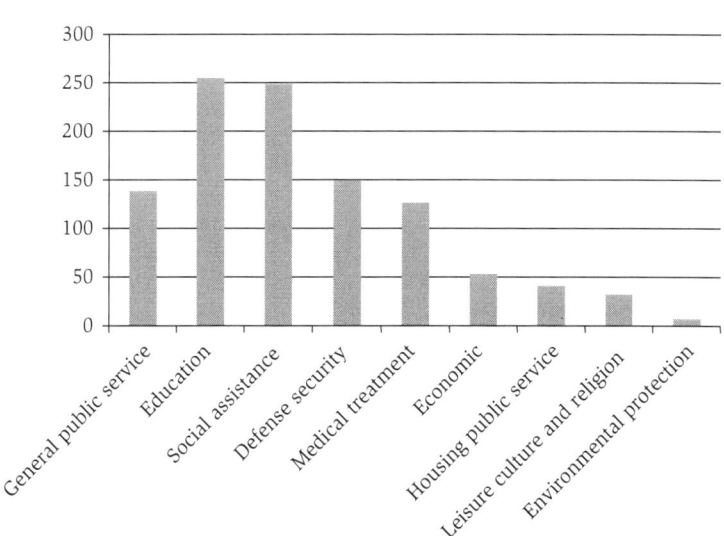

Data source: Ministry of Finance of Kyrgyzstan

However, in spite of the fiscal balance, the government debt was actually enormous, which was a major impediment to the economic development in Kyrgyzstan.

Figure 8.8 The National Debt of Kyrgyzstan during 2006–2014
(Unit: KGS 100 million)

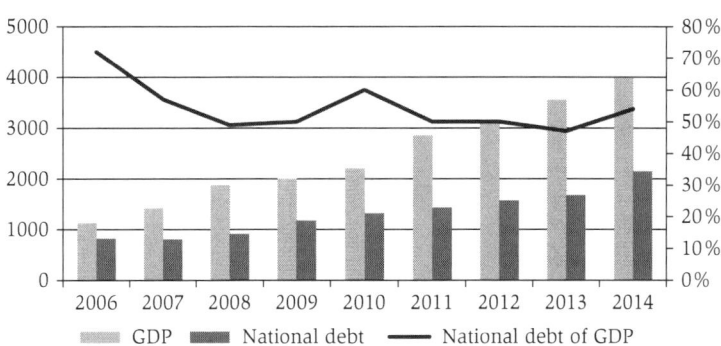

Data source: Bureau of statistics of Kyrgyzstan.

As shown in Figure 8.8, from 2006 to 2014, the GDP was constantly increasing, but the national debt was also increasing year by year. In 2006, the country's debt was

KGS 82.3 billion, while it went up to KGS 214.8 billion in 2014, up by 161%. The ratio of national debt (containing secured debt) of Kyrgyzstan in GDP decreased from 100% in 2003 to 49% in 2008. Then inflicted by the financial crisis, the ratio bounced back to 60% in 2010. Thanks to the government's countermeasures against the crisis, the debt level came back to the level in 2008(47%). However, it climbed back to 54% in 2014.

In fact, since large-scale conflict erupted in Kyrgyzstan in 2010, its economic situation became worse. As the size of foreign debt kept expanding, the country was no longer capable of paying back the debt independently. Thus, in 2012, the Kyrgyzstan parliament adopted the amendment to the National Debt Act to cap the size of foreign debt. According to the amendment, the foreign debt shall not exceed 50% of GDP. However, according to the data published by Kyrgyzstan's Ministry of Finance, by the end of 2015, the foreign debt reached 64.5% of GDP, exceeding the provisions of the National Debt Act in reality.

2.4 Tajikistan

Since the economic crisis in 2008, the fiscal revenue and expenditure of Tajikistan have maintained a stable rise. It has achieved the surplus; moreover, the growth rate of surplus in the last two years has exceeded the growth rate of the fiscal revenue and expenditure. As shown in Figure 8.9, in 2014 Tajikistan's fiscal revenue was TJS 14.4 billion with a year-on-year growth of 17.5%, of which tax revenue was 8.4 billion and non-tax revenue was TJS 1.1 billion; the fiscal expenditure was TJS 13.2 billion with a year-on-year growth of 13.8%. Compared with 2009, Tajikistan's fiscal revenue and expenditure increased by 140% and 132% respectively in 2014. In 2009–2014, Tajikistan's fiscal surplus has been increasing from TJS 264 billion in 2009 to TJS 123.3 billion in 2014, representing an increase of 3.7 times.

Figure 8.9 Fiscal Revenue and Expenditure of Tajikistan During 2009–2014 (Unit: TJS 100 million)

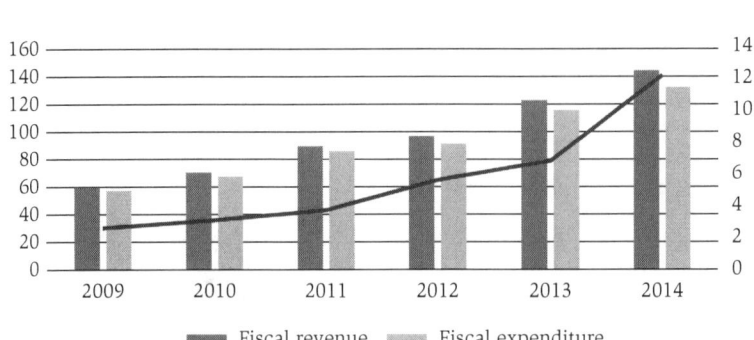

Data source: Bureau of Statistics of Tajikistan.

Chapter 8: Financial and Tax Operations in the Five Central Asian Countries

Tajikistan's fiscal revenue includes national revenue and local revenue which are both composed of tax revenue and non-tax revenue. Among them, the tax revenue mainly includes income tax, social tax, property tax (including land), sales tax, value added tax, consumption tax, goods, services tax, and so on. The national revenue is mainly based on value-added tax which accounts for about half of the national revenue, while the local revenue is mainly based on income tax which accounts for about 45% of the local revenue.[6]

The government of Tajikistan consistently adheres to the principle of low deficit. In 2009–2014, Tajikistan's fiscal expenditure accounts for about 30% of GDP and the annual average variation is about 2%. The fiscal expenditure of Tajikistan mainly goes to salaries, social security and subsidies, interest payment, and so on. In recent years, the change in its expenditure structure is primarily caused by the continuous growth in social security expenditure.

Tajikistan's foreign debt comes mainly from the World Bank, the Asian Development Bank and the Export-Import Bank of China. In recent years, Tajikistan's foreign debt has been slowly rising. In 2013, the foreign debt reached a record high of USD 2.19 billion, which increased by nearly 30% compared with 2009. In 2014, the foreign debt declined to around USD 2.1 billion. As shown in Figure 8.10, thanks to better economic development, as well as the external investment in agriculture, energy, transport, healthcare and education, Tajikistan's foreign debt as a share of GDP was spiralling down from 36% in 2009 to 23% in 2014.

Figure 8.10 Tajikistan's Foreign Debt and Its Share in GDP During 2009–2014 (Unit: USD 100 million)

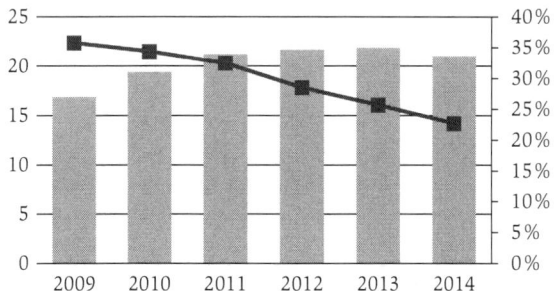

Data source: Ministry of Finance of Tajikistan.

At the same time, the debt servicing ratio of Tajikistan has been rising since 2010 (Figure 8.11). The growth of precious metals, transport facilities and natural gas exports, as well as the consequent increase in the fiscal revenue, are the main factors contributing to the improvement of the national solvency.

---

6. The data comes from the Ministry of Finance of Tajikistan from January to September 2014.

Figure 8.11 Debt Servicing Ratio of Tajikistan During 2008–2014 (Unit: %)

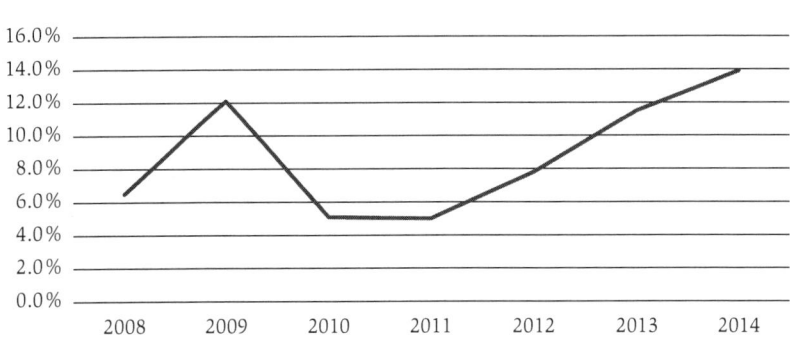

Data source: Ministry of Finance of Tajikistan.

Tajikistan obtains international loans from both multilateral lenders and bilateral lenders. As Figure 8.12 shows, in 2014, Tajikistan's multilateral loans included: USD 327 million from the World Bank, USD 1.47 billion from the IMF, USD 277 million from the Asian Development Bank, USD 3 million from the European Bank for Reconstruction and Development, USD 119 million from the Islamic Development Bank, USD 0.38 billion from the OPEC Fund, USD 70 million from the Eurasian Stability and Development Fund (formerly Eurasian Economic Community Anti-Crisis Fund).

Figure 8.12 Multilateral Lenders of Tajikistan in 2014 (Unit: %)

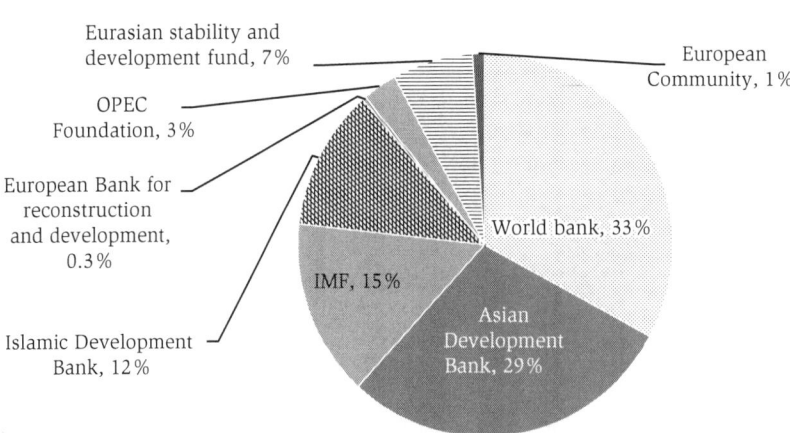

Data source: Отчет о состояниигосударственногодолгана 2014 год.

As Figure 8.13 shows, the bilateral lenders of Tajikistan have changed considerably from 2006 to 2014. In 2006, Uzbekistan and Russia were the largest lenders of Tajikistan, of which the former accounted for 40% and the latter accounted for 16%. In 2014, China became the largest lender of Tajikistan, accounting for 84% of the total,

Chapter 8: Financial and Tax Operations in the Five Central Asian Countries

while Uzbekistan dropped to 1%. The United States dropped from 9% in 2006 to 1% in 2014 and Kazakhstan dropped from 6% in 2006 to 0.2% in 2014.

Figure 8.13 Bilateral Lenders of Tajikistan in 2006 and 2014 (Unit: %)

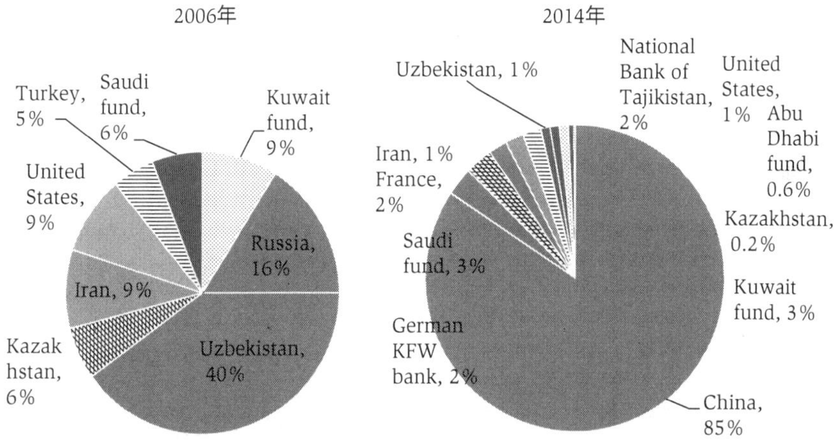

Data source: Отчет о состояниигосударственногодолгана 2014 год.

As of March 2015, Tajikistan's un-liquidated obligations had mounted to USD 2.096 billion. Among them, the bilateral debts were USD 1.045 billion and accounted for 49.86% of the total; the multilateral debts were USD 833 million and accounted for 39.74%; other obligations, including the guaranteed debt, were USD 218 million and accounted for 10.4%.

2.5 Turkmenistan

Turkmenistan's fiscal revenue and expenditure have long been volatile. The fiscal revenue fiercely fluctuates, while the fiscal expenditure has been rising. As a result, the deficit problem is serious.

As Figure 8.14 shows, Turkmenistan had the highest fiscal revenue of USD 2.39 billion in 2012 and the lowest revenue of USD 380 million in 2014. The difference was a jaw-dropping USD 2.01 billion. The fiscal expenditure hiked from USD 2.07 billion in

2009 to USD 3.25 billion in 2014 with an increase of 57%. Due to the excessively low fiscal revenue and ever-increasing fiscal expenditure, the fiscal deficit skyrocketed to USD 2.87 billion with a year-on-year increase of 22.1%.

Since 2011, Turkmenistan's national debt has soared. As Figure 8.14 shows, Turkmenistan's national debt soared from USD 2.9 billion in 2011 to USD 8.7 billion in 2013. There was a slight decrease in 2014 but still as high as USD 8.1 billion. Turkmenistan's national debt as a share of GDP is consistent with the growth trajectory of the size of the national debt. The share was 2.81% in 2008, 21.1% in 2013, and it dropped slightly to 16.8% in 2014.

Figure 8.14 *Turkmenistan's National Debt and Its Share in GDP During 2008–2014 (Unit: %)*

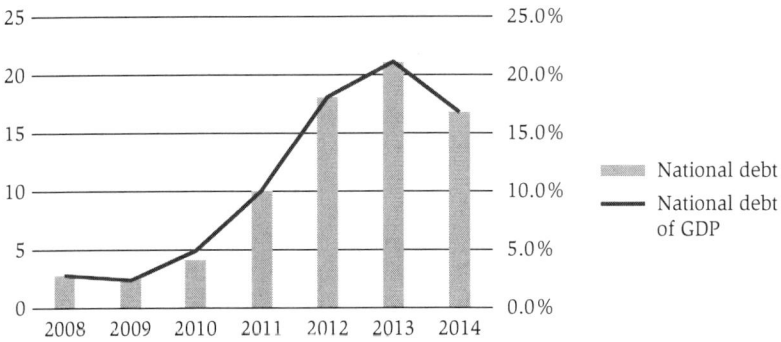

Data source: https://ru.tradingeconomics.com/.

From the above analysis, the fiscal and economic developments of the five Central Asian countries have the following characteristics:

(a) Except for Turkmenistan, the public finance of the other four countries run smoothly and the fiscal revenues and expenditures have been steadily increasing year by year. In Uzbekistan, Tajikistan and Kyrgyzstan, the revenues exceed the expenditures, which result in the fiscal surplus. Among them, the growth of Tajikistan's fiscal surplus is rising continuously, while that of Uzbekistan's surplus is slowing down. In Kazakhstan and Turkmenistan, the fiscal expenditures exceed the revenues, which result in the fiscal deficit. The fiscal deficit of Turkmenistan is more serious and has the risk of further expansion.

(b) The expenditure primarily goes to people's livelihood. The Central Asian countries all focus their fiscal expenditure on the social fields closely related to the life of the citizens during their economic transitioning, such as education and medical treatment. Even Kyrgyzstan, which adopts a tightened fiscal policy, does not reduce government subsidies for low-income groups.

(c) Debt scale is expanding. The debts of the Central Asia countries are expanding constantly. Among them, in Kyrgyzstan and Turkmenistan, the debt problem is more serious and the national debt as a share of GDP is relatively higher. Uzbekistan and Tajikistan are also pressed by national debt, but the shares of national debts in GDP are declining constantly. Kazakhstan's national debt was stable before 2014, but its debt has soared in the past two years with a further upward trend. At the same time, it is noteworthy that in 2014 China became the largest lender of Tajikistan. We must pay close attention to the economic development, the fiscal revenue and expenditure and the fiscal deficit of Tajikistan to protect China's creditor's right from being harmed.

3 FISCAL COMPARISON BETWEEN THE FIVE CENTRAL ASIAN COUNTRIES AND MAJOR ECONOMIES OF THE WORLD

In 2008–2014, the size of fiscal revenue and expenditure of the Central Asian countries was on the rise, but still at a low level compared with the major economies of the world.

3.1 The Size of Fiscal Revenue and Expenditure

From 2008 to 2014, Kazakhstan's fiscal revenue was between USD 2 billion and USD 45 billion, and Uzbekistan's fiscal revenue was between USD 6 billion and USD 14 billion. Kyrgyzstan, Tajikistan and Turkmenistan had smaller fiscal revenues. Among them, the fiscal revenue of Kyrgyzstan and Tajikistan was between USD 1 billion and USD 3 billion, while Turkmenistan's fiscal revenue in 2010 was only USD 390 million (shown in Table 8.1).

Table 8.1 The Fiscal Revenue of the Central Asian Countries and Sino-Russia (Unit: USD 100 million)

	Kazakhstan	Uzbekistan	Kyrgyzstan	Tajikistan	Turkmenistan	Russia	China
2008	239.9	62.8	11.8	–	21.8	5447.0	8969.0
2009	272.3	70.8	12.4	13.4	15.8	4496.6	10035.9
2010	297.8	82.9	12.3	16.0	3.9	5260.3	12589.0
2011	366.7	95.0	16.7	18.8	10.6	6477.1	16489.0
2012	394.0	107.3	18.3	20.3	23.9	7601.8	18815.7
2013	420.5	117.2	20.6	25.9	6.2	7468.1	21315.7
2014	403.9	131.0	20.3	27.6	3.8	4757.7	22631.9

Data source: Ministry of Finance and Bureau of Statistics of each country.

On the size of fiscal expenditure, the size of fiscal expenditure of the Central Asian countries is basically in line with the size of their income. From 2008 to 2014, Kazakhstan's fiscal expenditure was between USD 25 billion and USD 50 billion, meanwhile Uzbekistan's fiscal revenue was between USD 5 billion and USD 13 billion. However, Kyrgyzstan, Tajikistan, Turkmenistan, had a rather smaller size, between USD 1 billion and USD 3.5 billion (shown in Table 8.2).

Table 8.2 The Fiscal Revenue of the Central Asian Countries and Sino-Russia (Unit: USD 100 million)

	Kazakhstan	Uzbekistan	Kyrgyzstan	Tajikistan	Turkmenistan	Russia	China
2008	257.7	58.7	11.4	–	14.6	4761.4	9153.6
2009	294.8	70.3	13.1	12.8	20.7	5306.2	11175.7
2010	333.6	81.6	14.6	15.3	21.9	5780.3	13615.0
2011	405.0	93.2	17.8	18.0	25.0	6213.4	17342.0
2012	453.2	105.2	21.1	19.1	26.1	7515.2	20211.7
2013	466.1	115.4	17.6	24.5	29.7	7727.3	23130.8
2014	463.5	129.7	16.2	25.2	32.5	4908.0	24472.4

Data source: Ministry of Finance and Bureau of Statistics of each country.

Compared with Russia and China's fiscal revenue and expenditure, the Central Asian countries have a relatively low budget. Take 2014 as an example, the share of the fiscal revenue and expenditure in the GDP of Tajikistan, Kyrgyzstan and Turkmenistan was less than 1% compared with that in China and Russia. The proportion of Kazakhstan and Uzbekistan was relatively large. The former was about 10% of Russia and 2% of China, and the latter was about 3% of Russia and 1% of China.

3.2 The Proportion of Fiscal Revenue and Expenditure in GDP

Apart from Turkmenistan, the Central Asian countries' fiscal revenue and expenditure account for between 20% and 45% of GDP. Tajikistan and Kyrgyzstan's fiscal revenue and expenditure account for a larger share of GDP than Kazakhstan and Uzbekistan. In 2014, the share in Tajikistan and Kyrgyzstan was 36.16% and 30.67% respectively, higher than 19.85% in Kazakhstan and 25.59% in Uzbekistan. Turkmenistan's fiscal revenue and expenditure as a share of GDP was lower than that of other Central Asian countries and fluctuated between 1% and 22%. In 2014, it was only 1.09%.

Compared with Russia, the fiscal revenue of the Central Asian countries as a share of GDP during 2008–2013 was lower than that of Russia's. In 2014, the shares in the Central Asian countries and Russia changed. The share in Russia has declined significantly to 23.60% in 2014. Therefore, in 2014, Kyrgyzstan and Tajikistan's fiscal revenue as a share of GDP was higher than Russia. Uzbekistan was close to Russia, but Kazakhstan and Turkmenistan were below it.

At the same time, except for Turkmenistan, the fiscal revenue of the Central Asian countries as a share of GDP was similar to that of China. In 2014, China's fiscal

Chapter 8: Financial and Tax Operations in the Five Central Asian Countries

revenue accounted for 26.75% of GDP. Uzbekistan's share was basically the same as that of China. Kyrgyzstan and Tajikistan were higher than that of China and Kazakhstan was lower.

With regards to the fiscal expenditure as a share of GDP, except for Turkmenistan, other Central Asian countries' fiscal expenditure as a share of GDP is between 20% and 45%. Tajikistan's fiscal expenditure as a share of GDP is higher than that of Kazakhstan and Uzbekistan. In 2014, Tajikistan's fiscal expenditure accounted for 33.07% of GDP, higher than 22.77% in Kazakhstan and 25.35% in Uzbekistan and 24.55% for Kyrgyzstan, which was between Kazakhstan and Uzbekistan. Turkmenistan's fiscal expenditure as a share of GDP, which was 9.24% in 2014, was lower than that of other countries in Central Asia, fluctuating between 9% and 15%.

The fiscal expenditure of the Central Asian countries in 2008–2013 was lower than that of Russia's fiscal expenditure as a share of GDP. In 2014, those proportions changed remarkably. The share in Russia plunged to 24.34%. Such ratio in Tajikistan was higher than that of Russia. Uzbekistan, Kyrgyzstan and Kazakhstan shared a similar proportion with Russia, yet Kazakhstan's share was slightly lower than Russia's.

The share of fiscal expenditure in GDP in those Central Asian countries was comparable to that in China. In 2014, the share in Tajikistan was higher than that in China, and the numbers in the other four countries were lower than that in China (shown in Figure 8.15).

Figure 8.15 Central Asian Countries, Sino-Russia's Fiscal Expenditure as a Share in GDP During 2008–2014

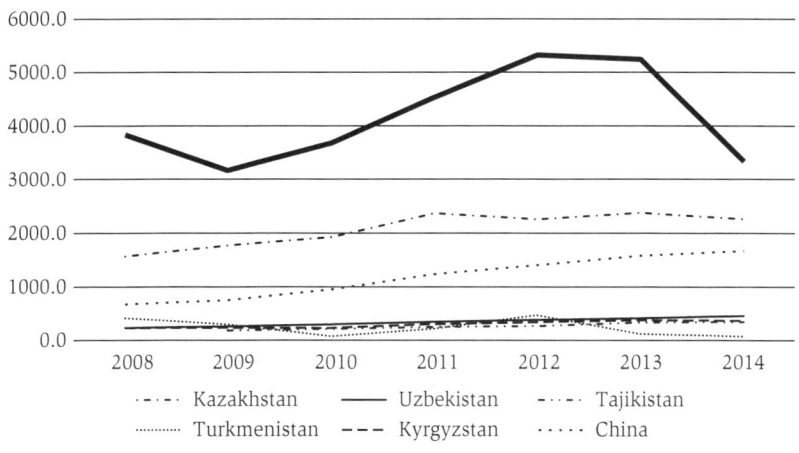

Data source: Ministry of Finance and Bureau of Statistics of each country.

3.3 Comparison of Per Capita Fiscal Revenue and Expenditure

In terms of per capita fiscal revenue, Kazakhstan stands out and its per capita fiscal revenue is between USD 1,500 and USD 2,500, much higher than that of the other four Central Asian countries. The per capita fiscal revenue of Uzbekistan, Turkmenistan, Kyrgyzstan and Tajikistan is under USD 500. Among them, Turkmenistan's figure fluctuates severely, hitting bottom at USD 72.6.

Taking 2014 as an example, Kazakhstan's per capita fiscal revenue was USD 2,256.6 in that year, but per capita fiscal revenue of Uzbekistan, Kyrgyzstan, Tajikistan was equivalent to 20%, 16%, 15% of Kazakhstan's number. Turkmenistan's per capita fiscal revenue was low, equivalent to only 3% of Kazakhstan's revenue (shown in Table 8.3).

Table 8.3   The Central Asian Countries Per Capita Fiscal Revenue (Unit: USD)

	Kazakhstan	Uzbekistan	Tajikistan	Turkmenistan	Kyrgyzstan	China	Russia
2008	1567.7	227.4	–	410.9	222.1	674.4	3835.9
2009	1768.4	253.8	179.1	291.9	230.2	749.7	3168.9
2010	1921.2	294.0	207.5	72.6	224.3	946.5	3678.6
2011	2366.1	338.3	247.3	212.2	298.6	1233.6	4532.6
2012	2251.3	377.7	260.3	468.8	332.9	1400.8	5315.9
2013	2375.7	408.3	328.0	120.6	375.2	1579.4	5240.8
2014	2256.6	453.2	340.7	73.7	362.0	1669.4	3338.7

Data source: Ministry of Finance and Bureau of Statistics of each country.

Compared with Russia, Central Asian countries' per capita fiscal revenue is far lower than Russia's. For example, in 2014 per capita fiscal revenue of Russia was 1.5, 7.4, 9.4, 9.8 and 45.3 times that of Kazakhstan, Uzbekistan, Tajikistan, Kyrgyzstan and Turkmenistan respectively.

Although the per capita fiscal revenue of Uzbekistan, Kyrgyzstan and Tajikistan is low, the operation is relatively stable. By contrast, Turkmenistan's figure fluctuates a lot.

It is worth noting that per capita fiscal revenue of Kazakhstan is higher than that of China, and the number in 2014 was 1.35 times that of China. The rest four's are lower than that of China. In 2014, per capita fiscal revenue of China was 3.7, 4.7, 4.9, 22.6 times that of Uzbekistan, Kyrgyzstan, Tajikistan and Turkmenistan respectively.

Overall, the five Central Asian countries' fiscal revenues and expenditures are on an upward trend. Kazakhstan and Uzbekistan have larger scale of fiscal revenues and expenditures than the other three countries in Central Asia. But compared with the world's major economies, Central Asian countries have a smaller scale. Due to the low level of economic development in Central Asia, the proportion of fiscal revenue and expenditure in GDP fluctuate downward. At the same time, the fiscal system of the Central Asian countries is still in the making, the institutions are still not sound enough, the duties of the government and enterprises are not clearly defined, and the concentration of government is high. Therefore, the proportion of fiscal revenue in GDP of each country is basically in line with the fiscal strength of developing countries.

Due to the differences in economic development levels, population, and tax systems in the Central Asian countries, per capita fiscal revenue between countries is varied. Kazakhstan is the most prominent performer, with its per capita fiscal revenue more than three times that of other Central Asian countries in 2014. Uzbekistan, Kyrgyzstan and Tajikistan have low per capita fiscal revenue, but run relatively smoothly. The per capita fiscal revenue of Uzbekistan is slightly higher than that of Kyrgyzstan and Tajikistan, while Turkmenistan's figure is low.

Despite the differences in the level of economic development of the Central Asian countries, their fiscal profile represents the characteristics in developing countries. Governments are also committed to enhancing the ability of finance over the regulation and control of the macro-economy, creating a stable and favourable tax and fiscal environment for the economic development of the country.

REFERENCES

Дифференцированные ставки налога в Узбекистане продлены до 2020 года. 2015-5-11. http://ria.ru/economy/20150511/1063848513.html

Правительственная комиссия рассматривает поправки в Налоговый кодекс Таджикистана 2016-2-3. http://www.avesta.tj/sociaty/38180-pravitelstvennaya-komissiya-rassmatrivaet-popravki-v-nalogovyy-kodeks-tadzhikistana.html

Эксперт: Увеличение объема госбюджета только за счет налогов – дорога в никуда 2015-11-2. http://nm.tj/economy/35168-ekspert-uvelichenie-obema-gosbyudzheta-tolko-za-schet-nalogov-doroga-v-nikuda.html

Принят Государственный бюджет Туркменистана на 2016 год. 2015-11-23. http://etoday.kz/finances/11822-prinyat-gosudarstvennyy-byudzhet-turkmenistana-na-2016-god.html

'Отчёт по исполнению Государственного бюджета 2009-2014 года республики Таджикистан' http://minfin.tj/

'Исполнение государственного бюджета республики узбекистан за 2007-2014 год' https://www.mf.uz/

'Отчет о состояниигосударственногодолгана 2014 год'. http://minfin.tj/

CHAPTER 9

The Role of Border Crossing Procedures in the Transportation of Goods along the New Silk Road: The Impact of Technical and Administrative Requirements

Jasmin Kollmann

1 Introduction
2 One Belt One Road Initiative: Transport Aspects
    2.1 The Silk Road Economic Belt: The Initiative
    2.2 Transport by Road
3 International Organizations Promoting Road Transport along the Silk Road
    3.1 International Road Transport Union
    3.2 The UN Economic and Social Commission for Asia and the Pacific
    3.3 The UN Economic Commission for Europe
    3.4 Central Asia Regional Economic Cooperation Programme
4 Cross-Border Trade and Customs Issues along the Silk Road
    4.1 Trade Facilitation Agreements
        4.1.1 Shanghai Cooperation Organization Agreement on Facilitation of International Road Transport
        4.1.2 Basic Multilateral Agreement on International Transport for the Development of the Transport Corridor Europe-Caucasus-Asia
    4.2 Customs Agreements
        4.2.1 TIR Convention
        4.2.2 Economic Cooperation Organization Transit Transport Framework Agreement
        4.2.3 Eurasian Economic Union

4.3 Convention on the Contract for the International Carriage of Goods by Road
4.4 Bilateral Agreements Facilitating International Trade and Customs along the Silk Road
5 Tackling Bottlenecks along the Silk Road
5.1 Current Status of Border Crossings Efficiency
5.2 Recommendations for Trade Facilitation
6 Conclusion

1 INTRODUCTION

This chapter deals with China's newly launched One Belt One Road Initiative. Also known as the New Silk Road project, One Belt One Road focuses on establishing a trade channel between China and the European Union.[1] In principle, there are two possibilities for shipping goods from China to Europe: the maritime route, known as the Maritime Silk Road, and the land route, known as the Silk Road Economic Belt. As for the Maritime Silk Road, the focus of the Chinese government lies in expanding the already existing waterways between China and Europe.[2] For the sake of this research project, the Maritime Silk Road will not be analysed.

The land route does not consist of only one possible way for transport, but again more alternatives. On the one hand, transport can take place by road; on the other hand, goods can be shipped by rail. Finally yet significantly, transport by pipeline is also possible, as it is being used to import gas from Kazakhstan and Turkmenistan to China.[3] These gas sales and purchases are governed by specific agreements.[4] An analysis of the implications of such agreements is beyond scope of this chapter.

This chapter will show that, in spite of various trade and transit agreements, a variety of issues are still hindering cross-border trade. Now that the Chinese government and also private companies invest in infrastructure projects in Central Asia, legal aspects of cross-border trade must be harmonized, with customs procedures being one critical factor among them. Thus, considerable work remains to be done in order to enable timely and efficient transport of goods.

Shipment by road will be the main point of analysis. First, the Silk Road Economic Belt Initiative will be described, with a special focus on showing how transport by road

---

1. K. Bradsher, *Hauling New Treasure along the Silk Road*, The New York Times (21 Jul. 2013). For more information on the maritime Silk Road, *see* R. Wang & C. Zhu, *Annual Report on the Development of the Indian Ocean Region (2015): 21st Century Maritime Silk Road* (Springer 2016).
2. For more information on the maritime Silk Road see the book of Wang / Zhu "Annual Report on the Development of the Indian Ocean Region (2015): 21st Century Maritime Silk Road", Springer, (2016).
3. J. Fishelson, *From the Silk Road to Chevron: The Geopolitics of Oil Pipelines in Central Asia*, J. Rus. & Asian Studies (2007), available at http://geohistory.today/geopolitics-pipelines-central-asia/ (accessed 30 Jan. 2016).
4. N. Yodogawa & A. Peterson, *An Opportunity for Progress: China, Central Asia, and the Energy Charter Treaty*, Texas J. Oil, Gas, & Energy Law, at 113, 120 (2013). For more information, *see* http://www.cnpc.com.cn/en/FlowofnaturalgasfromCentralAsia/FlowofnaturalgasfromCentral Asia2.shtml (accessed 14 Sep. 2018).

can be undertaken between China, Iran, Kazakhstan, Kyrgyzstan, Russia, Tajikistan, Turkmenistan, and Uzbekistan. In particular, potential obstacles hindering multilateral trade, such as restrictive transport regulations, will be presented. The following section will cover different international organizations that have launched projects in order to promote trade and transport between various countries along the Silk Road. Next, the analysis will focus on trade and customs issues along the Silk Road, assessing trade and transit agreements in the Central Asia region. As it is unlikely that one single carrier will undertake a journey all the way from China to Europe, imposing a focus will be necessary. The main emphasis will be on selected bilateral agreements between the above-mentioned countries, as road transport is usually focused on regional transport. Finally, the current status of border performance is the subject of a closer analysis, and recommendations are offered on how to improve this current status.

2 ONE BELT ONE ROAD INITIATIVE: TRANSPORT ASPECTS

2.1 The Silk Road Economic Belt: The Initiative

Over the last few decades, Central Asian countries lagged behind in terms of economic development. Currently, Kazakhstan, Kyrgyzstan, Tajikistan, Turkmenistan and Uzbekistan are moving at different speeds towards a market economy and privatization of state-owned enterprises. Gradually, the region as a whole is progressing towards integration and market liberalization, with the motor of development being the oil, gas and mining sector.[5]

Despite this recent economic upswing, the geographic remoteness of the Central Asia region has been seen as an obstacle to the development of infrastructure and trade. The fact that most of the countries are landlocked and that the closest seaport is at considerable distance leads to high transport costs. Nevertheless, transport is one of the most significant factors for economic development in a region. Therefore, investment in infrastructure, such as rail, roads and pipelines, is necessary to exploit trade and investment opportunities. Most Central Asian countries are stepping aboard this train, but the openness of individual economies remains varied.[6]

In order to take advantage of the centrality of Kazakhstan, Kyrgyzstan, Tajikistan, Turkmenistan and Uzbekistan, China's leader Xi Jinping presented the newly launched Silk Road project in autumn 2013. It is a collection of land and maritime routes, forming a transport corridor between China and Europe. Nevertheless, besides being a functional channel from Asia to the European Union, the Silk Road project also focuses on boosting economic development in the countries concerned. It covers many different investment projects, mainly focusing on infrastructure.[7]

---

5. United Nations Conference on Trade and Development, *Investment Guide to the Silk Road*, at 3 (2014).
6. *Ibid.*, at 4 (2014).
7. M. Schüller & T. Nguyen, *Vision einer maritimen Seidenstraße: China und Südostasien*, GIGA Focus Global 7, at 1, 2 (2015); M. Kaczmarski, *The New Silk Road: A Versatile Instrument in China's Policy*, OSW Commentary 161, at 1 (2015).

China's Silk Road project also aims to foster maritime possibilities of transport. Currently, it is still true that shipping goods via maritime transport causes few problems regarding border crossing. However, because only thirty ports carry out 80% of world trade, making use of these means of transport causes bottlenecks and delays, in cases when goods are shipped to remote harbours.[8] Therefore, the following sections are focused on transport by rail and by road.

2.2 Transport by Road

Transport by road is the most basic form of transport in every country. Therefore, because geographically China has a land connection with Europe, it used to rely on road transport. Especially countries in the Central Asia region heavily rely on transport by road, as it is at everyone's disposal and even remote regions can be reached. Modernization and expansion of road networks has already been commenced, yet considerable effort is needed in order to achieve a modern and efficient land transport route between China and Europe.[9]

Even though some of the infrastructure still needs to be build or modernized, cross-border transport by road can already be undertaken in the Central Asia region. Already more than 143,000 km of highways interconnect East and Central Asian countries with linkages to Europe.[10] The Asian Highway project, established by countries in Asia and Europe, as well as the United Nations Economic and Social Commission for Asia and the Pacific (ESCAP), aims to improve the current network of highways. It focuses on making use of already existing connections and adding missing legs only when necessary. The map below provides an overview over the most significant highway connections between China and Europe:[11]

---

8. IRU, *Euro-Asian Road Transport Links – Reopening the Silk Road*, available at https://www.iru.org/sites/default/files/2016-01/en-ar-2011.pdf (accessed 14 Sep. 2018).
9. R. Khan, *Transport Network in the Middle East Region: A Spatial Analysis*, 1 Intl. J. Sci. Engg. & Research 3, at 93–97 (2013).
10. United Nations Economics and Social Commission for Asian and the Pacific (ESCAP), *Review of Developments in Transport in Asia and the Pacific 2013*, at 9 (2013).
11. ESCAP, *Asian Highway Route Map* (6 Nov. 2014), available at http://www.unescap.org/resources/asian-highway-routemaphttp://www.unescap.org/sites/default/files/AH-map_GIS.pdf (accessed 3 Feb. 2016).

Chapter 9: Role of Cross-Border Procedures in Goods Transportation

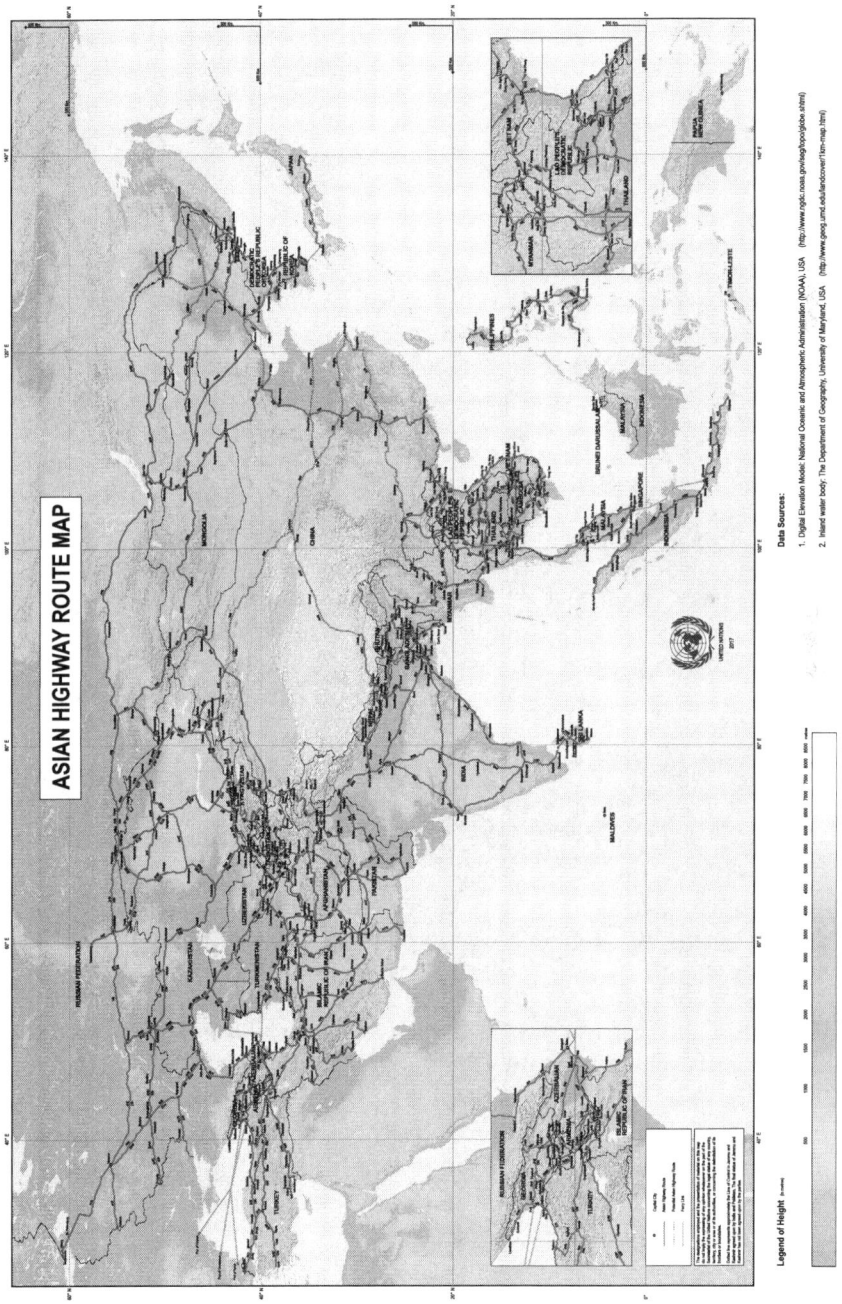

The map shows that, starting from the Chinese city of Urumqi, China has road connections to Kazakhstan, Kyrgyzstan and Pakistan,[12] and is then further linked to Iran, Tajikistan, Turkmenistan and Uzbekistan.[13] One of the most critical routes is the AH5, running 10,380 km (16,705 miles) from Shanghai via Kazakhstan, Kyrgyzstan, Uzbekistan, Turkmenistan, Azerbaijan and Georgia to the border between Turkey and Bulgaria. Even though these highways represent only a relatively small portion of the total length of all roads in that region, these highways connect the most important cities.[14]

The quality of highways within the Asian Highway Network varies, so the highways were classified into four groups. *Primary* highways are access-controlled highways and consist of asphalt or cement concrete pathways; *Class I* highways have four or more lanes and *Class II* highways only have two lanes. Both have pathways consisting of asphalt or cement concrete. *Class III* highways have two lanes and the pathways consists of double bituminous treatment.[15] Member countries of the Asian Highway Network invest in upgrading their roads, and it can be assumed that the Chinese government will also continue to do so in the course of the Silk Road project.[16]

In the case of cross-border transport of goods, mainly transport by sea is used, due to the cost advantages and reduced administrative burden. Nevertheless, land transport remains critical for landlocked countries and regional transport. With land transport, the issue arises that different countries have different rules on, for example, road-transport-related law, admission to the occupation, market access for transport of goods, transit systems, border control and customs, and road safety. These differing rules cause restrictions and can serve to hinder cross-border transport. Therefore, international organizations are concerned with facilitating the legal framework in order to enable smooth and efficient ways of transporting goods.

3 INTERNATIONAL ORGANIZATIONS PROMOTING ROAD TRANSPORT ALONG THE SILK ROAD

Transport is among the most critical factors for the development of a country or a region. Transport by road has the advantages that even remote areas can be reached and small loads can be transported relatively inexpensively. A variety of international organizations thus engage in establishing projects and initiatives to promote road transport along the New Silk Road. An overview if provided here of the most significant

---

12. For a more detailed map of China's highways, *see* http://www.unescap.org/sites/default/files/China%20AH%20map.pdf (accessed 3 Feb. 2016).
13. *See* http://www.unescap.org/sites/default/files/Kazakhstan%20AH%20map.pdf; http://www.unescap.org/sites/default/files/Kyrgyzstan%20AH%20map.pdf; http://www.unescap.org/sites/default/files/Turkmenistan%20AH%20map.pdf; http://www.unescap.org/sites/default/files/Uzbekistan%20AH%20map.pdf (accessed 3 Feb. 2016).
14. ESCAP, *Review of Developments in Transport in Asia and the Pacific 2013*, at 10 (2013).
15. ESCAP, *Review of Developments in Transport in Asia and the Pacific 2005*, at 64–67 (2005).
16. ESCAP, *Review of Developments in Transport in Asia and the Pacific 2013*, *supra* n. 13, at 10–13. For more information, *see* the website of the IRU: https://www.iru.org/en_history_and_mission (accessed 2 Feb. 2016).

Chapter 9: Role of Cross-Border Procedures in Goods Transportation

international organizations facilitating cross-border road transport along the Silk Road. Although each organization is described briefly, the main focus is on their specific Silk Road-related initiatives.

3.1 International Road Transport Union

The International Road Transport Union (IRU) focuses on upholding the interests of road transport operators to ensure economic growth and prosperity, and aims to facilitate road transport worldwide.[17] Even though road freight transport is generally not used for long distance transport of goods, it can be used for the shipment of goods to the nearest port or freight rail station and for shorter distance transport. For road freight transport, the IRU offers a range of services, such as providing information on road transport regulations, transport security and legal services.[18] As of February 2016, all countries along the Silk Road have at least one organization that is a member of the IRU.[19]

Regarding the Silk Road, the IRU also made efforts to remove obstacles to traffic across the Eurasian continent. In fact, the role of the IRU is not to enable one single truck to take a 10,000 km journey from China to Europe by road. Rather, the short and middle-distance interconnection of different businesses in one supply chain in different Central Asian countries should be enabled. Nevertheless, the integration of various economies along the Silk Road leads to a reduction in obstacles. More specifically, with the New Eurasian Land Transport Initiative (NELTI), the IRU focuses on promoting commercial deliveries of industrial and consumer goods across the Eurasian landmass.[20] Within the framework of the NELTI project, three main routes of transport were established and possible problems were monitored. Goods were shipped along these three roads using Transports Internationaux Routiers (TIR) procedures.[21] The three main routes are shown in the map below.[22]

---

17. For more information please visit the homepage of IRU: https://www.iru.org/en_history_and_mission (last viewed on 2 Feb. 2016)
18. *See also* https://www.iru.org/what-we-do (accessed 14 Sep. 2018).
19. For more information on members of IRU, *see* https://www.iru.org/en_iru_members (accessed 2 Feb. 2016).
20. *See also* http://www.iru-nelti.org/ (accessed 3 Feb. 2016).
21. NELTI, *Final Report: Analysis of Monitoring Data Collected on NELTI Project Routes in 2008-2009*, at 8 (2009).
22. *Ibid.*, at 11.

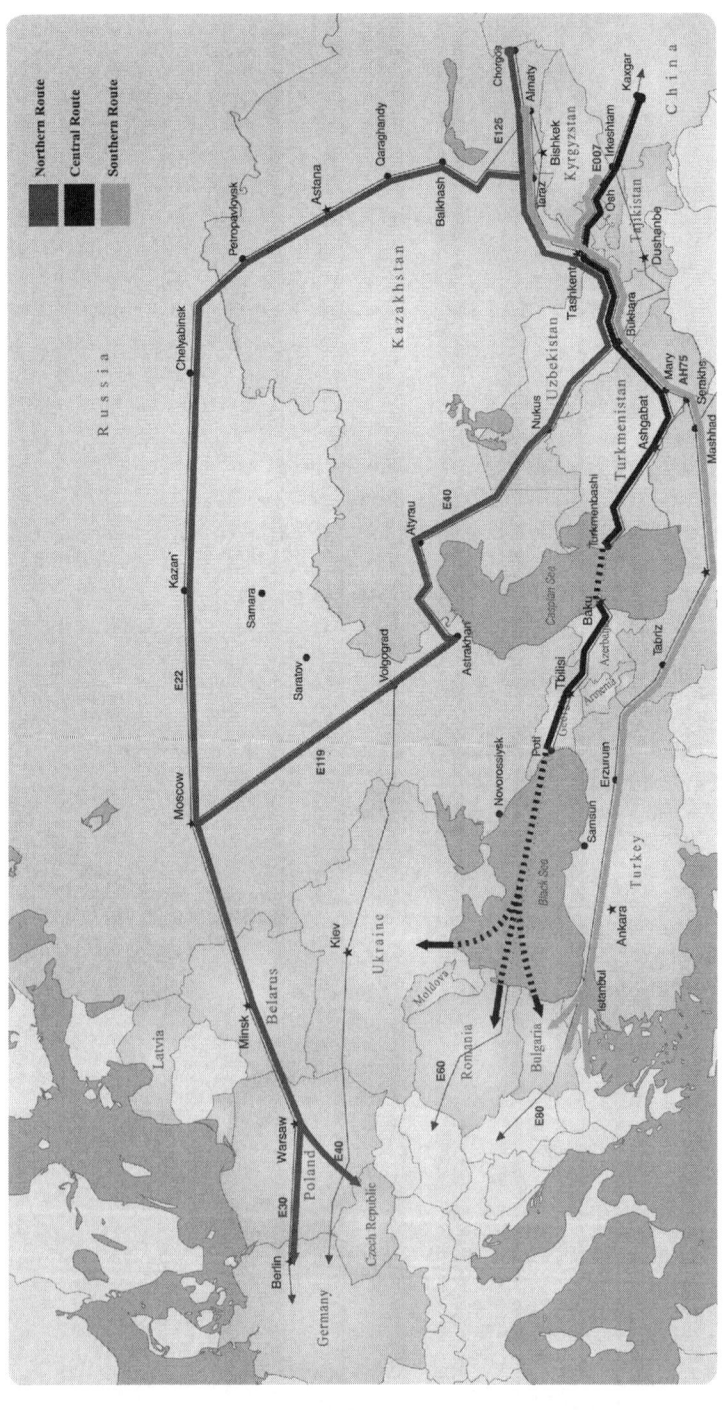

The *Northern route* stretches from the Chinese borders via Uzbekistan, Kazakhstan, Russia and Belarus to the European Union.[23] It is reported that on the northern route the average truck speed was 489 km/day, which is significantly less than the average intra-European speed of approximately 750 km/day.[24] The major problems were poor road conditions, unofficial payments at border crossing and long waiting times at boarders, reaching up to 96 hours at the border between Kyrgyzstan and Uzbekistan.[25]

The *Central route* starts in China, at the border with Kyrgyzstan and leads to Europe via Turkmenistan, Azerbaijan and Georgia.[26] Thus, some parts of this route need to be undertaken by ship via the Caspian Sea and Black Sea. Even though the distance of the Central route is only approximately 5,100 km, compared to 6,300 km for the northern route, an equal or even greater number of days of travel time were reported.[27] This is due to the fact that the average speed is 366 km/day. Waiting times at borders, peaking at 144 hours at the border crossing between Turkmenistan and Azerbaijan at the Turkmenbashi port, and at the Caspian Sea and Black Sea were reported.[28]

The *Southern route* is the shortest with only approximately 4,000 km, because its starting point is in Kyrgyzstan.[29] Nevertheless, also a connection to China is possible, as it would be the same track as the central route. It leads through Uzbekistan, Turkmenistan, Iran and Turkey all the way to the European Union.[30] The average operating speed was 255 km/day. This number is so low because the southern route has high waiting times and high border crossing payments at most of the borders, with the longest waiting time being 122 hours at the border of Iran and Turkmenistan.

Furthermore, driving restrictions may delay operations within one country. For example, drivers may operate only between 6 a.m. and 9 p.m. in Iran.[31]

The common underlying issue for all three routes is that there are significant obstacles to the development of road transit through Central Asia. On the one hand, poor conditions of roads, as well as poorly equipped carriers, prevent efficient and profitable operations.[32] On the other hand, local carriers are making use of outdated logistics operations systems, which hinder timely cargo handling.[33]

Nevertheless, for western provinces of China, making use of land route transportation can still be a better option than transporting goods to China's harbours located on the Eastern coast of China. Even though there might not be waiting times at borders, domestic road tolls are the main fee in transportation cost, comprising 30–50% of

---

23. *Ibid.*
24. *Ibid.*, at 12.
25. *Ibid.*, at 12–13.
26. *Ibid.*, at 13.
27. *Ibid.*, at 13.
28. *Ibid.*, at 14.
29. *Ibid.*, at 15.
30. *Ibid.*
31. *Ibid.*, at 15.
32. M. Emerson & E. Vinokurov, *Optimisation of Central Asian and Eurasian Trans-Continental Land Transport Corridors*, 7 EU Central Asia Monitoring Working Paper, at 10 (2009).
33. *Ibid.*

transport cost.[34] More precisely, charges are due mainly on Chinese highways, so drivers prefer to use overland roads where no tolls are due but travel times are longer.[35]

Overall, the NELTI project leads to several conclusions. Depending on which destination in Europe needs to be reached, one of the three routes can be chosen accordingly. Compared to European standards, the travel time is significantly higher along each of the routes. This can be explained by differing conditions of roads,[36] as well as differing waiting times and unofficial payments at border crossings. Furthermore, also specific transport permissions are required in order to be allowed to undertake transportation of goods in a foreign country. Thus, the NELTI project shows that even though there are already existing roads connecting China to Europe, they need to be modernized. Additionally and more critically, border crossing and customs procedures seem to be an even bigger obstacle. These issues will be analysed below.[37]

From a policy perspective, it is not yet clear as to which of the routes will be the preferable option for China. The answer to this question depends mainly on China's political relations in the Asian region. In recent years, China changed its position regarding the inclusion of India in its Silk Road project.[38] Also, over the last few years, Sino-Russian competition has been growing, with the aim of limiting the other party's influence in Central Asia.[39] On the other hand, with the Arab Spring movement it is not certain whether a more southern route would feature fewer impediments to international transport. Thus, politically, the central route seems to be the safest and most stable possibility.

3.2 The UN Economic and Social Commission for Asia and the Pacific

The ESCAP works, among other things, in the area of transport, as well as trade and investment, and provides technical assistance and capacity building to Member States.[40] Also, statistics and reports can be found on the organization's website. The ESCAP has fifty-three Member States, including Azerbaijan, China, Georgia, Iran, Kazakhstan, Kyrgyzstan, Pakistan, Russia, Tajikistan, Turkey, Turkmenistan and Uzbekistan, as well as nine associate members.[41] Its main work in the area of transport

---

34. F. Chen & C.-Y. Lee, *Logistics in China*, in *Handbook of Global Logistics*, at 3, 10 (J. Bookbinder ed., Springer 2013).
35. *Ibid.*, at 11.
36. *See* the previous section on the classification of Asian Highways.
37. *See* section 4 (Cross-Border Trade and Customs Issues along the Silk Road).
38. S. Blank, *Russia, China, India and Central Asia*, 2 Comillas J. Intl. Relations 3, at 13, 17–20 (2015).
39. *Ibid.*, at 17–20.
40. For more information, *see* website of ESCAP: http://www.unescap.org/about (accessed 6 Mar. 2016).
41. *See* website of UNESCAP http://www.unescap.org/about/member-states (accessed 6 Mar. 2016).

is to strengthen national capacities to develop physical access to movement of goods and people and to facilitate cooperation between different regions, with a special focus on road transport.[42]

The ESCAP is responsible for implementing the Asian Highway project, which includes thirty-two participating countries. Its aim is to enhance development of road transport infrastructure in order to promote international and bilateral trade.[43] One of the achievements has been the implementation of commonly used names, as well as classifications and designs of the highways.[44] The ESCAP not only assists in construction of infrastructure, but also facilitates the effective use thereof by transport operators. The methods that were undertaken in order to tackle non-physical barriers to cross-border transportation and to improve efficiency at border crossings, will be described below.[45]

The Regional Strategic Framework[46] is an initiative by ESCAP Member States to facilitate international road transport. It aims at establishing a legal regime and technical capacity for countries in the Central Asia region.[47] It provides legal assistance for establishing and entering into international conventions on transport facilitation, as well as harmonization and coordination of legislation and agreements on transport facilitation.[48]

The Regional Strategic Framework identified a variety of issues and provides recommendations on how to commonly approach facilitation. First, the issue was described that transport permits are often issued for one single trip undertaken by one single vehicle on a predetermined route only.[49] Similarly, visa issuance for road vehicle drivers is subject to national legislation and bilateral agreements on visas. Procedures are complicated and difficult, and sometimes even require the application for visas in person at embassies. Frequently, only single-entry visas are issued.[50] Furthermore, vehicles can be permitted to cross borders without the use of a financial guarantee of some kind. Additionally, major charges can be due for the use of the documents and guarantees issued under this system. This goes together with the necessity to purchase vehicle insurance at each border.[51] Lastly, yet significantly, technical standards on vehicle weight and dimensions differ between Asian countries. At border crossings, weighing and inspections are often conducted.[52]

---

42. IRU, *TRANSLex: Handbook on Road Transport Facilitation, Legislation and Practices*, at 40 (2004).
43. IRU; 'TRANSLex: Handbook on Road Transport Facilitation, Legislation and Practices', (2004), p.41.
44. *Ibid.*
45. *See* section 4. (Cross-Border Trade and Customs Issues along the Silk Road).
46. Regional Strategic Framework for the Facilitation of International Road Transport of 14 Jun. 2013.
47. ESCAP, *Review of Developments in Transport in Asia and the Pacific 2013*, supra n. 13, at 42.
48. *Ibid.*
49. ESCAP, *Ministerial Declaration on Transport Development in Asia and the Pacific on the Regional Strategic Framework for the Facilitation of International Road Transport*, at 8 (2012).
50. ESCAP, *Ministerial Declaration on Transport Development*, supra n. 45, at 8–10.
51. *Ibid.*, at 10–12.
52. *Ibid.*, at 11–12.

The result of the above-mentioned issues is delays in the delivery of goods and sometimes the mandated changing of vehicles or drivers at border crossings. The ESCAP recommends that its Member States access already existing international conventions relating to transport facilitation, or conclude bilateral or multilateral agreements.[53]

3.3 The UN Economic Commission for Europe

The UN Economic Commission for Europe (the UN Commission), similar to the ESCAP, is one of five regional commissions of the United Nations.[54] It aims at promoting economic integration in the pan-European region, among other things, also in the area of transport. In cooperation with the ESCAP, it launched the Euro-Asian Transport Links project, which identified Euro-Asian road and rail routes for priority development and cooperation, and aims at making these overland connections operational.[55]

In its expert group report on Euro-Asian Transport Linkages, the UN Commission evaluated Euro-Asian transport flows and identified non-physical obstacles to trade and transport.[56] Similar to other projects, the conclusion was drawn that it is not only geographic limitations and poor infrastructure that hinder trade in Central Asia. Non-physical obstacles such as non-harmonized regulations, policies and procedures can also cause major impediments, with the main bottlenecks for transportation and trade being border crossing points.[57]

Apart from this major focus on transport in Central Asia, the UN Commission is responsible for major agreements regarding road transport, such as the Convention on the Contract for the International Carriage of Goods by Road (CMR Convention),[58] dealing with legal issues regarding transport and freight. Other agreements with contracting parties from Central Asia include conventions and agreements on the road traffic,[59] establishing standard traffic rules, on road signs and signals,[60] on the work of crews of vehicles in international transport,[61] as well as agreements on border crossing

---

53. ESCAP, *Review of Developments in Transport in Asia and the Pacific*, at 43 (2013). For details on the agreements, see section 4, below.
54. For more information, see the website of the UN Economic Commission for Europe (UNECE) at http://www.unece.org/mission.html (accessed 4 Feb. 2016).
55. See the website of UNECE http://www.unece.org/trans/main/eatl.html (accessed 4 Feb. 2016).
56. UNECE, *Euro-Asian Transport Linkages, Phase II: Expert Group Report* (2012).
57. *Ibid.*, at 151.
58. Convention on the Contract for the International Carriage of Goods by Road (CMR Convention) of 19 May 1956. CMR is an abbreviation of the French title of the convention, *Convention relative au contrat de transport international de marchandises par route*.
59. Convention on Road Traffic of 8 Nov. 1968.
60. Convention on Road Signs and Signals of 8 Nov. 1968.
61. European Agreement concerning the Work of Crews of Vehicles Engaged in International Road Transport (AETR) of 1 Jul. 1970.

Chapter 9: Role of Cross-Border Procedures in Goods Transportation

facilitation.[62] The agreements regarding the transport of dangerous goods by road[63] and of perishable foodstuffs[64] set minimum requirements for their international carriage. The impact of selected agreements will be described below.[65]

Table below shows the status of accession of states along the Silk Road to the above-mentioned international conventions:

---

62. *Convention on the International Transport of Goods under Cover of TIR Carnets* (TIR Convention) (14 Nov. 1975); *Customs Convention on the Temporary Importation of Commercial Road Vehicles* (18 May 1956); *Customs Convention on Containers* (2 Dec. 1972); *International Convention on the Harmonization of Frontier Controls of Goods* (21 Oct. 1982). TIR stands for *Transports Internationaux Routiers* (International Road Transports).
63. European Agreement concerning the International Carriage of Dangerous Goods by Road (ADR) (30 Sep. 1957).
64. Agreement on the International Carriage of Perishable Foodstuffs and on the Special Equipment to be Used for such Carriage (ATP) (1 Sep. 1970).
65. *See* Chapter 4. (Cross-Border Trade and Customs Issues along the Silk Road).

	Road Traffic (1968)	Road Signs and Signals (1968)	TIR (1975)	Temporary Importation of Vehicles (1956)	Containers (1972)	Harmonization of Frontier Controls of Goods (1982)	CMR (1956)	AETR (1970)	ADR (1957)	ATP (1970)
Afghanistan			X							
Azerbaijan	X	X	X	X	X	X	X	X	X	X
China					X					
Georgia	X	X	X		X	X	X	X		X
Iran	X	X	X			X	X			
Kazakhstan	X	X	X		X	X	X		X	X
Kyrgyzstan	X	X	X	X	X	X	X	X		X
Pakistan	X	X	X							
Russia	X	X	X		X	X	X	X	X	X
Tajikistan	X	X	X			X	X	X	X	X
Turkey	X		X	X	X	X	X	X	X	X
Turkmenistan	X	X	X				X	X		
Uzbekistan	X	X	X	X	X	X	X	X		X

3.4 Central Asia Regional Economic Cooperation Programme

The Central Asia Regional Economic Cooperation (CAREC) programme brings together Afghanistan, Azerbaijan, China, Kazakhstan, Kyrgyzstan, Mongolia, Pakistan, Tajikistan, Turkmenistan and Uzbekistan. It aims at reintegrating the economies of the Central Asian continent by means of facilitating regional cooperation in the areas of transport, trade facilitation, trade policy and energy.[66] Ultimately, economic corridors between China and the Central Asia countries should be established.[67]

A variety of different projects were implemented in the area of transport and trade facilitation, such as improving physical connectivity by investing in road networks and border-crossing points, as well as measures for customs modernization.[68] Similar to other initiatives in the Central Asia region, the CAREC programme focuses on improving road transport infrastructure, as well as enhancing transport connectivity.[69] It makes use of the same roads as the Asian Highway project.[70] Regarding road transport, by 2014, 1,450 km of highways were constructed or improved.[71] Additionally, the simplification of border crossing procedures and documentation, as well as visa requirements are being facilitated.[72] As of 2014, the average time taken to clear a border-crossing point was 14.1 hours and the average cost of border-crossing clearance amounted to USD 172.[73] However, the use of TIR carnets[74] has led to significantly lower costs and shorter amounts of time needed to undergo customs procedures.[75] Similarly, the economic union between Armenia, Belarus, Kazakhstan, Kyrgyzstan and Russia[76]

---

66. *See* the website of CAREC programme, http://www.carecprogram.org/index.php?page=carec-program (accessed 16 Mar. 2016).
67. Asian Development Bank, *CAREC 2020: A Strategic Framework for the Central Asia Regional Economic Cooperation Program 2011–2020*, at 13 (2012). For the distinction between transport, logistics and economic corridors, *see* P. De, *Economic Corridors and Regional Economic Integration*, in *Developing Economic Corridors in South Asia*, at 15, 16–19 (P. De & K. Iyengar eds., Asian Development Bank 2014).
68. Asian Development Bank, *CAREC 2020*, supra n. 63, at 3.
69. *Ibid.*, at 12.
70. For a detailed map and a description of the corridors developed under CAREC, *see* Asian Development Bank, *Central Asia Regional Economic Cooperation Corridor Performance Measurement and Monitoring: A Forward-Looking Retrospective*, at 9–12 (2014).
71. CAREC Secretariat, *Development Effectiveness Review 2014*, at 7 (2015).
72. Asian Development Bank, *CAREC 2020*, supra n. 63, at 12. Investments in infrastructure include technical equipment, such as x-ray scanners at the international border crossing. CAREC Secretariat, *Development Effectiveness Review 2014*, supra n. 67, at 8.
73. CAREC Secretariat, *Development Effectiveness Review 2014*, at 9–12 (2015). For a list of the examined border posts, *see* Asian Development Bank, *Central Asia Regional Economic Cooperation Corridor Performance Measurement and Monitoring: A Forward-Looking Retrospective*, at 31 (2014). However, when comparing the current data to baseline data in 2010, no real progress can be seen. Compare Asian Development Bank, *Central Asia Regional Economic Cooperation Corridor Performance Measurement and Monitoring: A Forward-Looking Retrospective*, at 48 (2014).
74. For details, *see* section 4.2.1.
75. *Compare* Asian Development Bank, *Central Asia Regional Economic Cooperation Corridor Performance Measurement and Monitoring: A Forward-Looking Retrospective*, at 35 (2014).
76. For details, *see* section 4.2.3.

led to a decrease in time and costs for border crossings within the economic union, but increased the same figures for shipments entering into the economic union.[77]

Regarding trade, the CAREC programme encourages CAREC countries to reduce tariff and non-tariff barriers, as well as institutional impediments, by accessing WTO agreements and accepting the standards laid out by the WTO.[78] Results are ambivalent due to the newly established economic union between Armenia, Belarus, Kazakhstan, Kyrgyzstan and Russia. On the one hand, it is reported that half of the CAREC countries reduced their average tariffs and eliminated discrepancies between taxes applied to domestic products and to imports.[79] On the other hand, when crossing the external border of the Eurasian economic union, higher duties and taxes than before the establishment of the economic union are due.[80]

To summarize, there is a variety of international organizations, all aimed at promoting and facilitating road (and rail) transport in Central Asia. The initiatives of these organizations are similar and often overlapping. This means that there is an evident case for coordination between all those programmes and initiatives. Bundling resources and providing mutual assistance with a best practice analysis would be beneficial for all parties involved. Even though political interests might differ, it is common ground that infrastructure and trade liberalization play a key role in facilitating trade.[81] Nevertheless, the programmes are far from being fully coordinated. Currently, all the initiatives undertake different new investments in Central Asia, which leads to a change in the environment. Thus, all these multiple programmes necessarily need to be aligned in order to ensure coherence of actions.[82]

4 CROSS-BORDER TRADE AND CUSTOMS ISSUES ALONG THE SILK ROAD

This section will now deal with different legal agreements. The first part focuses on agreements that generally enable cross-border transport of goods and set requirements for doing so. The second part focuses on customs agreements regulating issues for the cross-border shipment of goods and vehicles engaged in cross-border transport. Next, the third part deals with the CMR Convention, which – in contrast to the previously mentioned agreements – does not ask countries to bring their national rules in line with the agreements, but specifically offers guidance for parties engaging in road transport. Lastly, a summary follows that focuses on China's situation regarding the agreements

---

77. *Compare* Asian Development Bank, *Central Asia Regional Economic Cooperation Corridor Performance Measurement and Monitoring: A Forward-Looking Retrospective*, at 36 (2014).
78. *Ibid.*, at 12.
79. CAREC Secretariat, *Development Effectiveness Review 2014*, at 13 (2015).
80. Asian Development Bank, *Operationalizing Economic Corridors in Central Asia: A Case Study of the Almaty-Bishkek Corridor*, at 14–18 (2014).
81. *See also* N. Wana Ismail & J. Mohd Mahyideen, *The Impact of Infrastructure on Trade and Economic Growth in Selected Economies in Asia*, 553 ADBI Working Paper, at 3 (2015).
82. C. Rastogi & J.-F. Arvis, *The Eurasian Connection: Supply-Chain Efficiency along the Modern Silk Route through Central Asia*, at 18 (World Bank Publications 2014).

Chapter 9: Role of Cross-Border Procedures in Goods Transportation

described. It analyses gaps in their coverage and takes into account whether such gaps are taken into account in bilateral agreements.

4.1 Trade Facilitation Agreements

4.1.1 Shanghai Cooperation Organization Agreement on Facilitation of International Road Transport

Countries of the Central Asia region have also developed regional agreements to facilitate the movement of goods, people and vehicles across borders. One of these is the Agreement on Facilitation of International Road Transport of the Shanghai Cooperation Organization (SCO).[83] SCO Member States are China, Kazakhstan, Kyrgyzstan, Russia, Uzbekistan and Tajikistan, while its observer states are Afghanistan, India, Iran, Mongolia and Pakistan.[84] The Agreement on Facilitation of International Road Transport has not yet entered into force, because not all parties have ratified the agreement.[85]

The main purpose of this Agreement is the simplification and harmonization of documentation, procedures and requirements concerning international road transportation. It permits carriers to engage in international road deliveries in the SCO Member States by using a vehicle registered in one Member State.[86] For the performance of such road transport, only one single standard permit is necessary, which can be issued by the competent authorities of any of the Member States.[87] This permit exempts the carriers from payments related to the possession or use of vehicles and related to the

---

83. This agreement was signed at the annual summit of the Member States of the Shanghai Cooperation Organization held in Dushanbe, Tajikistan on 11–12 Sep. 2014. It is available in Russian and Chinese.
84. See website of the SCO http://eng.sectsco.org/about_sco/ (accessed 14 Sep. 2018).
85. Tajikistan ratified the Agreement on 21 Jan. 2015. A. Yuldoshev, *Tajikistan ratifies SCO agreement on international road transport facilitation*, Internetnews Tajikistan (21 Jan. 2015), available at http://news.tj/en/news/tajikistan-ratifies-sco-agreement-international-road-transport-facilitation (accessed 28 Mar. 2016). Kazakhstan ratified the Agreement on 10 November 2015. *Kazakhstan ratifies SCO Agreement on Facilitation of International Road Transport*, AKIpress (10 Nov. 2015), available at http://pclo.akipress.com/news:568192/ (accessed 28 Mar. 2016). However, other member state's ratification was not reported yet. See A. Lu, *China Welcomes SCO Expansion, Calls for Upholding 'Shanghai Spirit'*, Xinhua (7 Nov. 2015) (Xi Jinping called on Member States to quicken the implementation), available at http://news.xinhuanet.com/english/201507/11/c_134402081.htm (accessed 28 Mar. 2016).
86. Secretariat of Shanghai Cooperation Organization, *The Agreement among the Governments of the SCO Member States on International Road Transportation Facilitation*, at 5 (Beijing 2015), available at http://www.unescap.org/sites/default/files/6b)%20-%20The%20Agreement%20between%20the%20Governments%20of%20SCO%20member%20states%20on%20facilitation%20of%20international%20road%20trans port%20by%20SCO.pdf (accessed 13 Jun. 2016).
87. *Agreement among the Governments of the SCO Member States on International Road Transportation Facilitation*, supra n. 82, at 5.

maintenance and use of roads in other Member States.[88] However, in order to obtain these benefits, specific roads, as stipulated in the Annex of the Agreement, must be used.[89]

4.1.2 Basic Multilateral Agreement on International Transport for the Development of the Transport Corridor Europe-Caucasus-Asia

The Basic Multilateral Agreement on International Transport for Development of the Europe-Caucasus-Asia Corridor was signed 1998 in Baku and entered into force in March 2000. It was initiated by and receives funding from the European Union. It is the key document establishing the legal basis for the development of economic relations, trade and transport between the parties to the agreement, namely Armenia, Azerbaijan, Bulgaria, Georgia, Iran, Kazakhstan, Kyrgyzstan, Moldova, Romania, Tajikistan, Turkey, Ukraine and Uzbekistan.[90] China, Russia and Pakistan are not parties to this agreement.

The Multilateral Agreement aims at facilitating access to the international market of road hauling; facilitating international transport of goods; ensuring traffic safety and security of goods; and harmonizing transport policy and the legal framework in the field of transport.[91] It forbids levying taxes and duties except from: (i) customs obligations and payments for transport, (ii) use of transport infrastructure and (iii) services related to transport.[92] More significant, however, is its most favoured nation clause,[93] under which preferential terms and tariffs between two Member States must also be applicable between these states and all other states that are parties to the agreement.

Without using technical specifications, the Technical Annex of the Basic Multilateral Agreement on International Transport stipulates that technical details of road vehicles are to be in accordance with national laws of the Member States. Thus, to harmonize technical aspects, this agreement is of little help for international carriers, as it merely refers them to national rules. Nevertheless, regarding customs duties, charges and taxes, motor fuel and lubricants in standard tanks of a vehicle, as well as spare parts and tools designated for repair of the damaged motor-vehicle are mutually

---

88. Ibid., at 6.
89. ESCAP, *SCO Member States Agreement on Facilitation of International Road Transport* (11 Sep. 2014), available at http://www.unescap.org/announcement/sco-member-states-agreement-facilitationinternational-road-transport (accessed 13 Jun. 2016).
90. *See* website of the TRACECA corridor, http://www.traceca-org.org/en/traceca/basic-documents/ (accessed 14 Mar. 2016). TRACECA is an abbreviation for Transport Corridor Europe-Caucasus-Asia.
91. Article 3 Basic Multilateral Agreement on International Transport for Development of the Europe-Caucasus-Asia Corridor.
92. Article 5 Basic Multilateral Agreement on International Transport for Development of the Europe-Caucasus-Asia Corridor. This means that goods in transit shall not be subject to value added tax.
93. Article 6 Basic Multilateral Agreement on International Transport for Development of the Europe-Caucasus-Asia Corridor.

exempt.[94] Customs procedures and documentation are to be harmonized and be brought in line with the TIR Convention, the International Convention on the Harmonisation of Frontier Controls on Goods and the Customs Convention on Containers.[95] To date, these goals of the Basic Multilateral Agreement on International Transport have not been reached, so harmonization has still not been achieved.[96] In brief, the Transport Corridor Europe-Caucasus-Asia (TRACECA) remains to be strengthened and modernized, as regards both corridor development and overall policy discussion.[97]

4.2 Customs Agreements[98]

4.2.1 TIR Convention

The Convention on International Transport of Goods under Cover of TIR Carnets (the TIR Convention) is a multilateral treaty simplifying and harmonizing administrative formalities of international road transport. It establishes an international customs transit system in order to move goods in sealed containers from a customs office of departure in one country through intermediate countries to a customs office of destination in another country without checks at intermediate borders.[99] In order for this system to function efficiently, precautionary measures, such as customs control, are undertaken at the office of departure.[100] The Convention applies to all modes of transport, provided that some portion of the journey is made by road.[101] If a transport carrier wishes to make use of the TIR procedure, it is necessary to obtain a TIR carnet. This customs document is valid internationally and, among other things, represents a financial guarantee for the payment of the suspended duties and taxes.[102] The TIR Convention currently has sixty-nine parties, including Azerbaijan, Georgia, Iran,

---

94. Article 8 Technical Annex on International Road Transport.
95. *See* Technical Annex on Customs and Documentation Procedures.
96. *See*, e.g., a later document of the TRACECA Intergovernmental Commission. *Action Plan for 2013–2015*, Appendix 10 to 10th Anniversary IGC Conference, available at http://www.tracecaorg.org/fileadmin/fm-dam/pdfs/til_igcmeets/10th/en/Appendix_10_Action_Plan_2013-2015_eng.pdf (accessed 14 Sep. 2018). *See also* TRACECA, *Regional Road Safety Action Plan*, at 5–8; 20–22 (with a detailed overview), available at http://www.traceca-org.org/fileadmin/fmdam/pdfs/til_igcmeets/9th/en/Regional_Road_Safety_Action_Plan_Eng.pdf (accessed 14 Mar. 2016).
97. European Commission, *Extension of the Major transEuropean Transport Axes to the Neighbouring Countries – Guidelines for transport in Europe and Neighbouring Regions*, COM (2007) 32 final; European Commission, *The EU and Its Neighbouring Regions: A Renewed Approach to Transport Cooperation*, COM (2011) 415 final.
98. It is acknowledged that also the Greater Mekong Subregion Cross-Border Transport Agreement (GMS CBTA) includes issues regarding the non-physical measures for cross-border land transport. The agreement promotes the reduction in the amount of time spent in crossing borders. However, apart from China, all other ratifying countries are located in South East Asia. Therefore, this agreement will not be analysed in depth.For further information, *see* Asian Development Bank, *Greater Mekong Subregion Cross-Border Transport Facilitation Agreement: Instruments and drafting history* (2011).
99. UNECE, *Euro-Asian Transport Linkages, Phase II: Expert Group Report*, supra n. 52, at 151.
100. *Ibid.*
101. *See* e.g., http://www.unece.org/trans/tir/about.html (accessed 22 Mar. 2018).
102. *Ibid.*

Kazakhstan, Kyrgyzstan, Russia, Turkey, Turkmenistan and Uzbekistan, as well as almost all countries on the European subcontinent.[103] China is currently not yet a party to the TIR Convention.

The TIR system is based on six essential principles. First, using *secure vehicles and containers* implies that the commodities are to be carried by vehicles or containers that can be sealed and are approved by customs authorities. Second, an *international chain of guarantee* secures duties and taxes in case of irregularities. Third, all parties to the TIR Convention *mutually recognize customs controls*. Furthermore, the *TIR carnet* – a harmonized document accepted by all customs authorities of the members of the TIR Convention – accompanies the goods on their journey. What is more, both transport operators and national issuing and guaranteeing associations may *access the TIR system*. Finally, SafeTIR provides for an electronic control and tracking system for TIR carnets.[104]

Thus, in theory, when using a TIR carnet, one might think that interventions and delays at border crossing should no longer be an issue in international transport. Moreover, as it is not necessary to pay customs duties or taxes at an international border, in principle no payments would need to be made.[105] Thus, times for transit procedures of goods should be minimized, allowing exporters to choose the most appropriate form of transport.[106] However, various studies have revealed a different picture.[107] Apart from poor infrastructure, the most commonly reported obstacle in Central Asian cross-border transport was waiting times and unofficial payments at borders.[108]

Even though customs procedures are an expression of the sovereignty of countries, transit countries that are signatories of the TIR Convention are, in principle, intended to undertake customs control only in case of abuse.[109] However, as the NELTI project of the IRU has shown, many obstacles remain. Despite conventions on the harmonization of customs control,[110] in practice, customs regulations in Central Asian countries differ in terms of both requirements and procedures.[111] A further complexity along the Silk Road is caused by the fact that most of the customs authorities use

---

103. *See* treaty collection of the United Nations, available at https://treaties.un.org/Pages/ViewDetails.aspx?src=TREATY&mtdsg_no=XI-A-16&chapter=11&lang=en (accessed 4 Feb. 2016).
104. IRU, *Key Principles of TIR*, available at https://www.iru.org/en_iru_tir_key-principles (accessed 4 Feb. 2016).
105. H.R.A. Shirsavar et al., *The Role and Impact of the TIR's Convention on the Facilitation of Legitimate Trade*, 14 Middle-East J. Sci. Research 11, at 1414, 1417 (2013).
106. *Ibid*.
107. *See especially* NELTI, *Final Report*, *supra* n. 19, at 8 (stating that all shipments were governed by TIR procedures). *See also* A. Diener, *Parsing Mobilities in Central Eurasia: Border Management and New Silk Roads*, 56 Eurasian Geography & Econ., at 376–380 (2015).
108. *See* section 2.3. (Transport by Road).
109. H.R.A. Shirsavar et al., *The Role and Impact of the TIR's Convention on the Facilitation of Legitimate Trade*, 14:11 Middle-East J. Scientific Research, 1414, 1416 (2013).
110. *International Convention on the Simplification and Harmonization of Customs Procedures* (Revised Kyoto Customs Convention) (3 Feb. 2006); *International Convention on the Harmonization of Frontier Controls of Goods* (21 Oct. 1982).
111. NELTI, *Final Report*, *supra* n. 19, at 25.

different computer systems, some of which are not kept up to date.[112] This leads to a lacking flow of information and to uncoordinated approaches by customs authorities.[113] Finally yet significantly, changes in customs regulations are not always communicated to all parties concerned.[114]

4.2.2 Economic Cooperation Organization Transit Transport Framework Agreement

The Economic Cooperation Organization (ECO) has initiated several projects on energy, trade, transportation, agriculture and drug control. Its Member States are Afghanistan, Azerbaijan Iran, Kazakhstan, Kyrgyzstan, Pakistan, Tajikistan, Turkey, Turkmenistan and Uzbekistan. China is not a member of the ECO.[115]

The ECO Transit Transport Framework Agreement was signed in Almaty on 9 May 1998 between nine ECO Member States (all but Uzbekistan; to date, Turkmenistan has failed to ratify). It first came into force on 19 May 2006.[116] Its aim is to facilitate movement of goods and passengers, and it provides for cooperation in the area of customs fraud and tax evasion.[117]

The ECO Transit Transport Framework Agreement grants transit through the territories of the Member States on prescribed routes and exempts transit by motor vehicles from customs duties, taxes and other charges.[118] Moreover, it provides drivers of vehicles engaged in international transport operations with multiple entry and transit visas valid for one year 'with a right of staying on the territory of each Contracting Party for 15 days in transit for each trip'.[119] Additionally, the Agreement provides for a mutual recognition of driving licenses.[120] However, regulation of transportation permits and temporary admission of means of transport are still subject to the domestic law of each Member State.[121] Annex 4 of the Transit Transport Framework Agreement specifies technical requirements for road vehicles.[122] It shows

---

112. *Ibid.*, at 25–26.
113. M. Polner, *Coordinated Border Management: From Theory to Practice*, 5 World Customs J. 2, at 49, 52–55 (2011).
114. NELTI, *Final Report*, *supra* n. 19, at 26.
115. *See* website of ECO at http://www.eco.int/general_content/85059-Member-States.html?t = General-content (accessed 14 Sep. 2018).
116. USAID Trade Project, *Legal & Policy Gap Analysis for Economic Cooperation Organization Transit Transport Framework Agreement*, at 3 (2014).
117. Article 2 ECO Transit Transport Framework Agreement.
118. Articles 4 & 5 ECO Transit Transport Framework Agreement.
119. Article 12 ECO Transit Transport Framework Agreement.
120. Article 20 ECO Transit Transport Framework Agreement (but correspondence with the Convention on Road Traffic of 1968 is required).
121. *See* Articles 15–17 ECO Transit Transport Framework Agreement.
122. Turkmenistan and Uzbekistan are not members of the ECO Transit Transport Framework Agreement. For China (2014), Georgia (2015) and Russia (2015) the information was taken from IRU, *IRU Maximum weights and dimensions*, available at https://www.iru.org/apps/infocentre-itemaction?id = 2255&lang = en, https://www.iru.org/apps/infocentre-item-action?id = 292&lang = en, https://www.iru.org/apps/infocentre-item-action?id = 325&lang = en (accessed 13 Jun. 2016).

the maximum permissible axle loads per vehicle category in the different Member States as shown in the table below.

	Single Axle	Tandem Axle	Triple Axle	Maximum Permissible Laden Weight (tonnes)
Afghanistan	10	16	22	36
China*	11.5	–	–	49
Azerbaijan	10	16	22	36
Georgia*	10			44
Iran	13	20	26	40
Kazakhstan	8	13.2	18.8	36
Kyrgyzstan	10	16	22	36
Pakistan	12	22.5	33	40
Russia*	11.5	20	26	44
Tajikistan	8	14	22	36
Turkey	10	16	22	40
Turkmenistan*	6	10	13	36
Uzbekistan*	8	16	24	40

All parties to the ECO Transit Trade Framework Agreement signed and ratified the TIR Convention. Regarding customs procedures, the Agreement also stipulates an attempt to harmonize customs procedures and customs documents, like goods declarations for customs transit as well as customs seals and fastenings.[123] For efficient clearance at land border stations, the establishment of adequate facilities at borders, as well as the provision of mutual administrative assistance during business working hours is encouraged.[124]

Even though the ECO Transit Trade Framework Agreement entered into force approximately ten years ago, most of its member countries still fail to properly implement its provisions. The biggest problems are that border stations designated for traffic in transit are not provided with sufficient resources to manage the increasing volume of trade and transit. Moreover, there is no transparent mechanism for the provision of visas and transport permits for foreign truck drivers and service providers.[125] In brief, one can conclude that the agreement contains rules and procedures aimed at promoting transit facilitation, and lays down minimum technical requirements for the construction and maintenance of infrastructure. Nevertheless, a timely and efficient implementation of all the proposed measures will be of key importance for flows of goods and services in the Central Asia region in future.

---

123. Articles 29-30 ECO Transit Transport Framework Agreement.
124. Articles 9 and 10 ECO Transit Transport Framework Agreement.
125. USAID Trade Project, *Legal & Policy Gap Analysis for Economic Cooperation Organization Transit Transport Framework Agreement*, at 14-17 (2014).

4.2.3 Eurasian Economic Union

The Eurasian Economic Union originated out of the Eurasian Economic Community and the Eurasian Customs Union, and is established between Armenia, Belarus, Kazakhstan, Kyrgyzstan and Russia.[126] Further potential participants could be Tajikistan and Uzbekistan.[127] Customs unions are characterized by removing all trade barriers within the union and harmonizing members' external trade policies.[128] An economic union is characterized by a higher degree of integration, comprising the free movement of labour and capital between, and the unification of the monetary and fiscal policies of the Member States.[129]

Originally, when the customs union was established, its priorities were the elimination tariffs and duties among the participating states and the establishment of a common external tariff policy, as well as the elimination of non-tariff trade barriers.[130] As a result, border controls were lifted between the Member States in 2011, and other restrictions to trade are gradually being abolished.[131] Even before this step, free trade agreements between the Member States led to a duty-free trade in goods. Nevertheless, with the Eurasian Economic Union, more efficient border crossing, simplified payments and reduced corruption have led to a significant increase in trade among the Member States.[132]

The Member States adopted a common external customs tariff, which in fact was a replication of Russian external tariffs.[133] For Armenia, Kazakhstan and Kyrgyzstan this was a substantive increase in tariffs, as those countries originally had a much lower tariff structure.[134] This harmonized customs tariff led to a decrease in time and costs needed for border crossings within the economic union, while at the same time it led

---

126. *See* the website of the Eurasian Economic Union.
127. I. Krotov, *Customs Union between the Republic of Belarus, the Republic of Kazakhstan and the Russian Federation within the Framework of the Eurasian Economic Community*, 5 World Customs J., at 129 (2011). Tajikistan's main obstacle to Eurasian Economic Union integration is the lack of necessary infrastructure, especially roads. Moreover all major trade routes pass through Uzbekistan. In case only Tajikistan aims at entering the Eurasian Economic Union, modernizing its roads and establishing new direct connections to Kyrgyzstan would be necessary. *See also* S. Olimova, *Tajikistan's Prospects of Joining the Eurasian Economic Union*, 165 Rus. Analytical Digest, at 15 (2015). Nevertheless, in an opinion poll the majority of participants from Uzbekistan and Kyrgyzstan and also from Turkmenistan thought that it was advisable to join the Eurasian Economic Union. *See* Opinion Poll; Appendix to 165 Rus. Analytical Digest, at 21–25 (2015).
128. F. Wang, *The Role of Customs in the Economic Integration of East Asia: Problems and Proposals*, 8 World Customs J., at 35, 37 (2014).
129. *Ibid.*
130. Igor Krotov, *Customs Union between the Republic of Belarus, the Republic of Kazakhstan and the Russian Federation within the framework of the Eurasian Economic Community*, 5 World Customs J., at 129, 130–133 (2011).
131. H.-M. Wolffgang, G. Brovka & I. Belozerov, *The Eurasian Customs Union in transition*, 7 World Customs J., at 93, 94 (2013).
132. *Ibid.*, at 95.
133. *Ibid.*
134. D. Tarr, *The Eurasian Economic Union of Russia, Belarus, Kazakhstan, Armenia, and the Kyrgyz Republic: Can It Succeed Where Its Predecessor Failed?*, 54 Eastern European Economics, 1, 4 (2016).

to an increase in the same figures from external shipments entering into the union.[135] Among the states of the Eurasian Economic Union, trade was promoted, but simultaneously this led to a decrease in imports from the rest of the world.[136] Thus, Russia can be seen as profiting the most from the common customs policy of the Eurasian Economic Union. On the other hand, Russia acceded the WTO in 2012 and, as a result, had to lower the common external tariff of the Eurasian Economic Union.[137]

With the creation of the Economic Union, the free movement of goods, capital, services and people, together with common economic, transport and fiscal policies, is aimed at in the future.[138] In fact, not only common external tariffs, but also administrative integration promote trade facilitation. Nevertheless, functionality of the Eurasian Economic Union is highly volatile.[139] Due to the late accession of Armenia and Kyrgyzstan, coordination problems among Member States have been arising.[140] Furthermore, regarding the progress in reducing non-tariff barriers has been rather slow to date. A system of common standards regarding documents and mutual-recognition agreements still needs to be established.[141] The Eurasian Economic Union has already taken some steps forward with regard to integration, but it is too early to expect a functioning single market after only one year.[142] Additional reforms are necessary, but they will take time.

4.3 Convention on the Contract for the International Carriage of Goods by Road

The Convention on the Contract for the International Carriage of Goods by Road (CMR Convention) represents an effective, complex and far-reaching regulation of transportation of cargo in the contracting states and beyond. Currently, it has fifty-five contracting parties, but China and Pakistan are not members of the CMR.[143] The CMR Convention applies to international carriages of goods by road when the place of taking over of the goods and the place designated for delivery are situated in two different countries, one which is a contracting country.[144]

---

135. *Compare* Asian Development Bank, *Central Asia Regional Economic Cooperation Corridor Performance Measurement and Monitoring: A Forward-Looking Retrospective*, at 36 (2014); Tarr, *supra* n. 130, at 13.
136. Tarr, *supra* n. 130, at 4.
137. *Ibid.*, at 6.
138. This level of integration has not been reached yet. *See* statement of the Eurasian Economic Commission, *Domestic Markets Operation Department Has Been Formed in the EEC* (1 Mar. 2016), available at http://eec.eaeunion.org/en/nae/news/Pages/01-03-2016-3.aspx (accessed 18 Mar. 2016).
139. S. Roberts & A. Moshes, *The Eurasian Economic Union: A Case of Reproductive Integration?*, 32 Post-Soviet Affairs, at 1, 4–5 (2015).
140. *Ibid.*, at 16.
141. Tarr, *supra* n. 130, at 18–20. E.g., driving licenses should be recognized automatically.
142. *Compare* e.g., the slow process of economic integration in the European Union.
143. *See* website of the UNECE, http://www.unece.org/trans/maps/un-transport-agreements-andconventions-26.html (accessed 10 Mar. 2016).
144. Article 1 *Convention on the Contract for the International Carriage of Goods by Road* (CMR Convention).

In principle, this Convention regulates the content of an international contract of carriage and outlines the main obligations of the carrier of the goods in international transport. It provides for a common standard regarding international transport in goods.[145] When making use of the CMR Convention, charges relating to the carriage, including customs duties, must be included in the consignment contract.[146] On the other hand, local cross-border movements in Central Asia are less structured and less formal, and thus, they are not subject to the same international standard.[147] More specifically, for local movements, (i) whether the carrier can be held liable for delays at border crossings and (ii) whether customs duties and other charges are included in the contract of carriage, are subject to negotiation between the parties to the contract of carriage.[148] Thus, not only factual waiting times and significant charges at border crossings, but also legal implications can impede efficient cross-border trade. As such, contracts of carriage concluded under the CMR Convention are important for ensuring liability and service quality of carriers operating along the Silk Road.[149] In essence, by adhering to the principles of the CMR Convention, transit through the Central Asia region meets a minimal set of standards, which in turn leads to increased legal certainty and trustworthiness between the contracting parties.

4.4 Bilateral Agreements Facilitating International Trade and Customs along the Silk Road

More than 100 bilateral and regional agreements related to international road transport have been signed in the Central Asia region.[150] As most of the agreements and initiatives described in the previous section involve only the Central Asian states, China is excluded from the benefits of those agreements. Furthermore, China has, to date, accessed neither the TIR Convention nor the CMR Convention. Therefore, China has signed bilateral or multilateral agreements on trade and cross-border transport with neighbouring countries.[151] Furthermore, China has established specific offices responsible for border crossing administration.[152]

China's bilateral transport agreements are similar to a great extent and cover the transport of both passengers and goods by road. They contain the commitment to facilitation and national approval for vehicles engaged in bilateral traffic, as well as

---

145. Rastogi & Arvis, *supra* n. 78, at 52.
146. Article 6(1)(i) *CMR Convention*.
147. Rastogi & Arvis, *supra* n. 78, at 52.
148. *Ibid.*
149. *Ibid.*, at 55–57 (2014).
150. ESCAP, *Review of Developments in Transport in Asia and the Pacific*, 45 (2013).
151. Bilateral agreements on road transport exist with Kazakhstan (1992), Uzbekistan (1993), Kyrgyzstan (1994), Tajikistan (2008), Pakistan (1993) and Russia (1992). The two multilateral agreements in the region were concluded between China, Pakistan, Kazakhstan, Kyrgyzstan (1995) and China, Kyrgyzstan, Uzbekistan (1998). *See* IRU, *Road Transport in the People's Republic of China*, at 48 (IRU 2009).
152. IRU, *TRANSLex*, *supra* n. 39, at 466.

rules on border posts, routes and procedures that were mutually agreed. Furthermore, a reciprocal exemption from duties and taxes is granted, specifically including fuel, lubricants and spare parts, but user charges and tolls may be imposed on the basis of national rules. The contracting parties usually agree to improve infrastructure at border crossings and to unify customs procedures. Additionally, there is an aim to establish a uniform set of freight documents. However, many of these provisions are merely frameworks for more precise actions to be undertaken by the competent authorities of the countries.[153] Thus, the existence of a bilateral transport agreement represents a first step towards facilitating transport, but follow-up actions and implementation of the agreement in good faith are even more critical.

At the 17th EU-China Summit, the European Union and China agreed in a memorandum of understanding on further investments in the Silk Road project.[154] A special focus was placed on improving infrastructure links between Europe and China. This will be achieved by developing synergies between relevant initiatives and projects, and bundling sources of funding for investment in transport in Central Asia.[155] Once again, a proper implementation of this memorandum is necessary in order to ensure competitive transport infrastructure in Central Asia.

5 TACKLING BOTTLENECKS ALONG THE SILK ROAD

5.1 Current Status of Border Crossings Efficiency

So far, this chapter has shown that there are a variety of bilateral and multilateral agreements governing trade and transport along the Silk Road. Each of the projects aims at removing obstacles to free trade along the Silk Road. Some initiatives focus on factually improving infrastructure, such as modernizing and expanding the current system of highways. Other agreements rather focus on removing administrative barriers, such as visa requirements and mutual recognition of documents, and the introduction of common standards for customs requirements.

Improving the efficiency of border crossings is a critical step towards easing economic and social barriers to trade and transport between countries. Table below shows the efficiency of border crossings operations. The columns *burden of non-tariff barriers* and *burden of customs procedures* rate the countries on a scale from 1 (= extremely high burden) to 7 (= extremely low burden). Non-tariff barriers include health and product standards, as well as technical and labelling requirements. The burden of customs procedures measures the efficiency of customs procedures related

---

153. Ibid., at 469.
154. European Commission, *EU-China Summit Joint Statement: The Way Forward after Forty Years of EU-China Cooperation*, at 1 (29 Jun. 2015).
155. European Commission, *EU-China Summit Joint Statement*, supra n. 150.

Chapter 9: Role of Cross-Border Procedures in Goods Transportation

to the entry and exit of goods. The column *trade tariffs* indicates the weighted average tariff rate levied on imports of goods, including preferential rates applied to any other country.[156] Data are taken from the Global Competitiveness Report 2015–2016 issued by the World Economic Forum.[157] The columns *export* and *import time* and *cost* in the below table contain relevant numbers for the land supply chain from the point of origin to the buyer's warehouse:[158]

---

156. World Economic Forum, *The Global Competitiveness Report 2015–2016*, at 68 (2015). There is no distinction between the mode of transport.
157. The report did not contain any data for Afghanistan.
158. For this section, data are taken from World Bank, *Connecting to Compete 2014, Trade Logistics in the Global Economy: The Logistics Performance Index and Its Indicators* (2014). Again, no distinction is made between rail and road exports and imports.

	Burden of Non-Tariff Barriers (Rank on Scale of 1 to 7)	Burden of Customs Procedures (Rank on Scale of 1 to 7)	Trade Tariffs (Rank)	Export Time / Distance	Export Cost (USD)	Import Time / Distance	Import Cost (USD)
Afghanistan	–	–	–	–	–	–	–
Azerbaijan	4.4 (60)	3.2 (122)	7.4 (88)	–	–	–	–
China	4.2 (78)	4.2 (56)	11.0 (117)	2 days 24 8 km	683	2 days 137 km	514
Georgia	5.2 (6)	5.5 (9)	0.8 (4)	1 day 75 km	1,000	1 day 75 km	1,000
Iran	4.1 (99)	3.3 (117)	27.3 (140)	6 days 612 km	1225	5 days 553 km	1,500
Kazakhstan	4.5 (45)	4.2 (55)	5.5 (73)	–	–	–	–
Kyrgyzstan	4.3 (77)	3.5 (97)	10.9 (116)	14 days 3500 km	5,000	5 days 3,500 km	5,000
Pakistan	4.0 (106)	3.4 (111)	17.5 (137)	4 days 417 km	970	4 days 515 km	1,307
Russia	4.0 (108)	3.6 (88)	5.7 (76)	11 days 3,500 km	3,162	15 days 3,500 km	4,472
Tajikistan	4.0 (112)	3.9 (73)	5.7 (75)	–	–	–	–
Turkmenistan	–	–	–	–	–	–	–
Uzbekistan	–	–	–	18 days 3,500 km	5,000	18 days 3,500 km	5,000

This table indicates that despite recent efforts to facilitate trade, a considerable amount of time and money is still needed for border crossings. For all Central Asia countries, the burden of customs procedures and the burden of non-tariff trade barriers were rated in the mid-field. In the three categories for burden of non-tariff barriers, burden of customs procedures and trade tariffs, all countries but Kazakhstan rank in the bottom half of all examined countries (140 in total).

5.2 Recommendations for Trade Facilitation

Even though regional agreements aim at granting preferential trade conditions (although this might not be reflected in the table above, as the column 'trade tariffs' indicates the weighted average of all imports), non-tariff obstacles to trade continue to hinder efficient border crossings between countries situated along the Silk Road. Consistently, this table reveals that for all countries, the burden of non-tariff barriers is higher than the burden of customs procedures.

The high cost and time of cross-border transport of goods is caused by several factors. The necessity to have transport documents, vehicle documents and a driving license that are accepted in each of the Central Asia countries, as well as a visa for each country, leads to a high level of complexity. It is often not clear which regulations can be applied and how different border authorities administer the respective customs procedures. There is a possibility that the border crossing process could be disturbed by collusive customs administration. Delays and long waiting times can lead to a lack of mutual trust from shippers and customers. These issues have already been identified by international organizations.[159]

Although many agreements[160] aim at a simplification and harmonization of rules and standards applicable in cross-border transport, these common standards often take a long time to be implemented. Thus, the volume and impact of bureaucratic procedures and corruption still needs to be decreased.[161] A change is necessary, so that border authorities do not rely only on their own controls and certificates. As a first step, customs documents must be shared among authorities.[162] A further way could be to establish joint border controls and coordinate the work of national government agencies among themselves as well as customs authorities of different countries.[163]

In a long run, even higher levels of integration can be reached by sharing responsibilities for different tasks of the border control process.[164] One form of such a shared responsibility could be joint border controls at a joint border post.[165] On a more technical level, customs authorities should make use of the same software, which

---

159. *See* section 3.
160. *See* section 4.
161. *See also* Andrew Grainger, *Trade Facilitation: A Conceptual Review*, 45 J. World Trade, at 39, 42 (2011).
162. Polner, *supra* n. 109, at 53.
163. Grainger, *supra* n. 157, at 46.
164. Polner, *supra* n. 109, at 53.
165. *Ibid.*, at 57–58.

should generate a standardized format of documentation.¹⁶⁶ Such a standardized software could simplify the mutual recognition of border recognition documentation.¹⁶⁷

Furthermore, cross-border trade benefits from easily accessible and also understandable laws. This means that the customs tariffs should be publicly available and easy to understand.¹⁶⁸ Additionally, carriers should be informed about which documents are necessary for conducting cross-border operations Central Asia countries and how such documents can be obtained. In order to deal with language differences, documents should be standardized and simplified so that government authorities are able to process documents in other languages.¹⁶⁹

Another measure to decrease waiting times at border crossings would be to coordinate working hours and to provide customs authorities with sufficient staff and financial resources in order to handle long queues efficiently. A further aspect of managing such a high workload is to focus customs controls on suspicious movements rather than enforcing blanket controls on a specific percentage of all traffic.¹⁷⁰

Needless to say, working procedures need to be aligned and best practices should be shared and adapted by other countries. However, in order to effectively implement all of the above-mentioned recommendations, political goodwill is necessary. Simply entering into bilateral or multilateral agreements without undertaking follow up work to improve the current situation, no progress can be made. In order to be able to ship goods more effectively over the land route from China to Central Asia and further onward, a higher level of political commitment is necessary.

6 CONCLUSION

The last few decades have witnessed an exponential growth in trade all around the globe. Central Asia has largely been an outsider to this development. Now, with the One Belt One Road Initiative of the Chinese government, this circumstance has changed. Central Asia has not remained untouched by global trade and transport initiatives. This chapter shows that there is already a wide-ranging variety of projects that focus on facilitating trade and transport in Central Asia.

---

166. Grainger, *supra* n. 157, at 42; E. Gwardzińska, *The Standardisation of Customs Services in the European Union*, 6 World Customs J., at 93–94 (2012).
167. Gwardzińska, *supra* n. 162, at 96–97.
168. Grainger, *supra* n. 157, at 49. For companies exporting from the EU, it is possible to access all relevant information at http://madb.europa.eu/madb/indexPubli.htm. This database gives a detailed overview of the customs tariffs for each country and product. Additionally, other barriers, such as declaration requirements and financial restrictions, can be found. The author is not familiar with whether such databases also exist for other countries that wish to export along the Silk Road.
169. *Compare*, for example, the practice of European Union. For cooperation among national authorities common forms are used in different language version. These forms are all structured in the same way. By means of ticking boxes the competent authorities of one country can process a request from a different country even though not making use of a common language.
170. Grainger, *supra* n. 157, at 49.

Facilitating trade requires not only tangible infrastructure, but also other elements such as a good business and regulatory environment, transparency and customs management. Even though many projects focus on the same areas of problems along the Silk Road, the initiatives are mostly conducted in an uncoordinated way and therefore, many agreements propose solutions for the same problems. These suggestions are, however, in many cases non-binding recommendations. This leads to a situation where countries are faced with many different sets of non-binding rules, where making domestic law compliant with one agreement could lead to a violation of the remaining agreements. This means that not the quantity of rules, but the quality and the degree of harmonization is critical. Instead of facilitating trade, a so-called 'spaghetti bowl' of trade agreements would merely create obstacles to economies' meeting their full growth potential.

But not only countries face compliance problems. More significantly, logistics providers operating along the Silk Road are forced to comply with differing national sets of rules in order to be allowed to cross borders and to use highways in the different countries. While being compliant with the differing maximum weight and height specifications is relatively easy (it is necessary to comply with the strictest requirement), visas, customs clearance certificates and transportation documents might differ from country to country, including as regards the language in which they are issued. Because of this administrative burden, costs associated with the cross-border transport of goods increase. The reduction of documents for international transport would thus lead to a reduction in cost and time for exports via the Silk Road.

In order to overcome these issues, it is suggested that further research focus on improvements in operational efficiency. Moreover, research could aim at providing support to develop effective multinational infrastructure policies. Therefore, it is necessary to conduct further research about the detailed situation regarding how the above-mentioned agreements could be simplified and harmonized. It is suggested to focus on an analysis of the feasibility as to whether one single a multinational instrument could serve as an 'umbrella agreement' in order to bring order to the chaos of the currently existing variety of agreements.

A comparison with the experience of the European Union reveals that regional integration evolves over time, and that current arrangements are subject to revision and ultimately may lead to the regional organizational change. China's reform and opening period have shown that prosperity and wealth can be achieved only by international cooperation. Similarly, Central Asia countries also need to open up their infrastructure and start aligning their border crossing requirements with international standards. To realize aims of the Belt and Road Initiative, internationally recognized rules that are accepted by all countries, must be followed. Thus, only stronger cooperation will lead to mutual benefits across the region.

CHAPTER 10
Transfer Pricing Issues Related to the One-Belt-One-Road Project

Raffaele Petruzzi, Mirna Solange Screpante, Claire (Xue) Peng, Norbert Roller & Vladimir Tyutyuryukov[*]

1 Introduction
2 Relevant Areas of Study
   2.1 Manufacturing Activities
   2.2 Services and Financial Transactions
   2.3 Intangible Property
   2.4 Cost Contribution Arrangements
   2.5 Documentation
   2.6 Advance Pricing Arrangements
3 Conclusion and Proposals

1 INTRODUCTION

One of the most challenging topics that One-Belt-One-Road (OBOR) countries will face is related to transfer pricing laws and their interpretation. From a general perspective, the history of OBOR countries has been linked with trading activities originated back in the first century BC; however a comparison of the commercial activities back then with

---

[*] The authors are very grateful to all participants of the Conference 'The One Belt One Road Initiative: The Tax Aspects', held on 9–11 May 2017 at WU (Vienna University of Economics and Business) and to all the participants of the International Tax Forum on 'The One Belt one Road Initiative' held on 17 Apr. 2018 at WU (Vienna University of Economics and Business), for their insightful comments and suggestions. Moreover, the authors would like to thank Prof. Dr Jeffrey Owens, Head of the WU Global Tax Policy Center at the Institute for Austrian and International Tax Law at WU for his precious support and feedback in drafting this article. The views expressed here are those of the authors and do not necessarily represent or reflect the views of their organizations.

those of today unsurprisingly shows a dramatically different scenario. The geographical fragmentation of the activities of multinational enterprises (MNEs) and, thus, of their global value chains, has created a new trade reality which was unknown before. This fragmentation has deepened the interdependency of trade relations and, thereby, generated many implications for transfer pricing.

The transfer pricing environment in OBOR countries is extremely diversified. Most countries are in an early stage as regards the implementation of transfer pricing rules, while some others are much more advanced.[1] This fact, despite constituting a disadvantage, might constitute also a great advantage, since reaching a common understanding on these topics would be easier. For example, countries such as Armenia, Azerbaijan, Bahrain, Brunei, Kuwait, Moldova, Syria, the United Arab Emirates and Uzbekistan do not have transfer pricing rules in their tax systems. For these countries transfer pricing rules might be seen as something complicated and costly to implement, but it should be born in mind that definitely the benefits are higher than the costs for two main reasons. First, protecting the tax base by domestic measures such as general or specific anti-avoidance rules might not be sufficient to the same extent than transfer pricing rules. Second, tax administrations might take different views on how to allocate profit among associated entities that could lead to double taxation (and, hence, a worst investment climate in the country). These rules, nevertheless, should balance, on the one hand, simplicity (where possible), certainty and clarity and, on the other, a fair and balanced taxation.

In this regard, there is also a reality to take into account and it is that most OBOR countries are non-OECD countries and, in many cases, they could be considered as developing countries, which make necessary to take a different viewpoint on what matters since developing countries are primarily concerned with the erosion of the tax base rather with the shifting of profits mainly due to its character as capital importing countries. This could lead to an exacerbated protection of the tax base which, on the one hand, makes transfer pricing issues quite unique, and on the other hand, the corresponding solutions and guidance as regards for those issues might derive from a review of not only the OECD Transfer Pricing Guidelines for Multinational Enterprises and Tax Administrations (OECD Guidelines),[2] but also the United Nations Practical Manual on Transfer Pricing for Developing Countries (UN Manual)[3] and the Transfer Pricing Handbook recently released by the World Bank Group (World Bank Handbook).[4]

When analysing specific transfer pricing topics, some common issues can be identified. First and foremost, among the most common transfer pricing issues that will impact the OBOR countries are those related to manufacturing activities. In their pursuit of profit maximization, MNEs are always seeking locations that could minimize

---

1. S.T.Y. Sim, *A Different Take on Transfer Pricing in Asia*, 22 Asia-Pac. Tax Bull. 4, (2016).
2. OECD, *Transfer Pricing Guidelines for Multinational Enterprises and Tax Administrations* (OECD Publishing 10 Jul. 2017).
3. UN, Dept. of Econ. & Soc. Affairs, *United Nations Practical Manual on Transfer Pricing for Developing Countries* (2017).
4. J. Cooper, R. Fox, J. Loeprick & K. Mohindra, *Transfer Pricing and Developing Economies: A Handbook for Policy Makers and Practitioners* (World Bank Group 2016).

their costs of production. Typically, western countries have, in the past, relocated their manufacturing activities to Asian countries, especially China. However, given the recent trend generating an increase in manufacturing expenses in China, many MNEs are moving manufacturing factories out of that country. Therefore, it is reasonable to anticipate that they will find landing places in the OBOR neighbouring countries. Equally foreseeable, MNEs will implement business restructurings in order to optimize their supply chain structures. All these changes will imply relevant transfer pricing considerations. These issues will be analysed in section 2.1.

Another relevant transfer pricing issue concerns transactions involving intra-group services (including financial transactions). Indeed, these transactions will also play a relevant role within the OBOR countries, considering that, seen globally, they are of crucial significance for the sustainable and efficient operation of MNEs' businesses and, certainly, they are expected to be a critical topic for the businesses operating therein. For example, according to the Asian Development Bank, Asia's infrastructure construction will see a financing gap of USD 8.3 trillion in 2010–20.[5] In order to compensate this gap, an enormous amount of internal financing in the form of, for example, intra-group loans, credit guarantees and cash pooling, will be provided within the OBOR countries. These topics will be analysed in section 2.2.

Moreover, transfer pricing issues related to intangible property (IP) are well known as a difficult area considering their relevant contribution to value creation of an MNE and the high complexity of their practical implementation, which has opened new challenges in the implementation of the arm's length principle. Many MNEs have indeed decreased their investments in physical or working capital assets and now focus their resources more on developing IP. Addressing transfer pricing issues involving intangibles could have a major impact in the OBOR region if value creation and economic activities are taken into account in determining the transfer pricing outcomes. These topics will be analysed in section 2.3.

In the context of the development of goods, services and IP, transfer pricing issues related to CCAs will also need to be carefully considered. This will be analysed in section 2.4.

A crucial role will be also played by the laws and regulations that will define the relevant transfer pricing documentation. Such laws and regulations, indeed, will need to strike the right balance between, on the one hand, the aim of having a tool that provides a complete illustration of MNEs' transfer pricing policies and their implementation and, on the other, the necessity of generating an outcome that will be useful for the recipients of the documentation (i.e., tax administrations). These topics will be analysed in section 2.5.

Finally, the changes and challenges mentioned above, as well as the more transparent environment enhanced by transfer pricing documentation, will fundamentally need to be supported by relevant tools aimed at avoiding or minimizing disputes between the relevant players (i.e., MNEs and tax administrations of the countries in

---

5. EY, *Finance & Infrastructure Lead New Wave of the Belt and Road Investment* (15 Sep. 2015), http://www.ey.com/cn/en/newsroom/news-releases/news-ey-2015-finance-and-infrastructure-lead-new-wave-of-the-belt-and-road-investment (accessed 25 Apr. 2017).

which they operate). To this end, the development of efficient and effective advanced pricing agreement (APA) programmes will be fundamental. This will be analysed in section 2.6.

This chapter will address the above-mentioned topics by providing, first, a background on each one, taking into account the main features from a general international perspective as well as those specifically related to OBOR countries, and, then, some conclusions and proposal for future developments.

2 RELEVANT AREAS OF STUDY

2.1 Manufacturing Activities

Manufacturing activities give rise to some of the most common kind of transactions around the world. In general, businesses can operate with three types of models, namely toll manufacturers, contract manufacturers and full-fledged manufacturers. Toll and contract manufacturers operate in a quite similar way. They are limited-risk service providers, producing goods strictly under specifications and selling everything back to the principal. Other than plant, machinery and routine manufacturing skills, they do not own valuable IP, such as patents and secret formulas. The main difference between the two business models is seen in the fact that the toll manufacturer does not bear any inventory risk, while the contract manufacturer procures and owns raw materials and takes title to the finished products, thereby bearing the related inventory risks. In contrast, the functions of a full-fledged manufacturer cover, for example, manufacturing, procurement, inventory management and customer negotiations, as well as sometimes research and development (R&D) and marketing activities. Furthermore, a full-fledged manufacturer generally possesses various inventory and valuable IP,[6] such as industrial/technical know-how and secret formulas. As a result, the risks undertaken by a full-fledged manufacturer are substantial and material.

For transfer pricing purposes, the nature of transactions between related parties arising from the manufacturing activities should comply with the arm's length principle. This often requires the performance of an accurate comparability analysis, by means of a comparison between terms and conditions agreed between related parties and those agreed between unrelated parties. Due to the differences in risk profiles, it is the general understanding that toll and contract manufacturers are, in principle, remunerated with relatively low but stable returns, while full-fledged manufacturers can claim the residual profits (or suffer considerable losses). In this context, the comparable uncontrolled price (CUP) method, the cost-plus method and the transactional net margin method (TNMM), typically applied in practice, rely heavily on

---

6. Another type of manufacturer that literature often mentions is the licensed manufacturer. The functional profile of a licensed manufacturer is generally the same as that of a full-fledged manufacturer. However, a licensed manufacturer does not perform R&D activities, and does not have product- or manufacturing-related intangibles. For production purpose, the licensed manufacturer uses intangibles via license agreements with an associated entity or third party.

comparables data. As a result, two main issues are often identified, especially within developing countries, namely the lack of comparables data[7] and the allocation of location savings.[8]

Regarding the lack of comparables data, developing counties are faced with a shortage of commercial databases, publicly available, for the purpose of finding comparables data. It is undisputed that the likelihood of non-OECD countries not having access to a commercial database with company financial or pricing of transactions is much higher than that of OECD countries. The main reasons are that those countries do not have resources available to purchase databases and/or lack skilled personnel to manage and operate these databases. Furthermore, for some countries that have access to these databases, the data that are relevant to their audit may not be sufficient. In 2015, 106 countries had no more than ten independent records with revenue and net margin information, and thirty countries had approximately 10-100 such records. Many OBOR strategic countries, including Albania, Armenia, Azerbaijan, Bahrain, Belarus, Brunei, Croatia, Georgia, Iran, Kyrgyzstan, Laos, Moldova, Mongolia, Nepal, Qatar, Syria, Tajikistan, Turkmenistan, Uzbekistan, and the United Arab Emirates were on that list. The issues are caused by the fact that these countries do not have proper financial registries where local companies can record their corporate financial information that could be also used for transfer pricing analyses. This issue, to some extent, often ends up with tax administrations using 'secret comparables' in tax audits. However, such use of secret comparables may infringe the tax secrecy of taxpayers the tax data of which are taken for assessment use, and, in addition, the assessed taxpayers would not be able to properly defend their results because they lack access to the secret data.[9] As a result of the conflicting interests against taxpayers' rights, the use of secret data could discourage MNEs from establishing business operations in the concerned jurisdictions, potentially harming the success of the OBOR project.

In China, tax administrations may use public information (e.g., the databases of the National Bureau of Statistics and the Bureau van Dijk), as well as non-public

---

7. For guidance on these topics, *see* The Platform for Collaboration on Tax, *Discussion Draft: A Toolkit for Addressing Difficulties in Accessing Comparables Data for Transfer Pricing Analyses* (January 2017); European Commission, Dir.-Gen. Taxation & Customs, EU JTPF, *Report on the Use of Comparables in the EU* (Oct. 2016), JTPF/007/2016/FINAL/EN.
8. For guidance of these topics, *see* OECD, *Transfer Pricing Guidelines for Multinational Enterprises and Tax Administrations* (OECD Publishing 2010), D.6.1. Location savings, amended by OECD, *Aligning Transfer Pricing Outcomes with Value Creation – Actions 8–10 Final Reports*, OECD/G20 Base Erosion and Profit Shifting Project (OECD Publishing 5 Oct. 2015); UN, *Practical Manual on Transfer Pricing for Developing Countries*, supra n. 3, paras. B.2.3.47.-B.2.3.2.61.; Cooper et al., *World Bank Transfer Pricing Handbook*, supra n. 4, p. 218-219.
9. The OECD is generally opposed to the use of secret comparables. OECD Guidelines (2016), para. 3.36. The view of the UN is rather flexible (UN, *Practical Manual on Transfer Pricing for Developing Countries*, supra n. 3, paras. B.1.6.30.-B.1.6.32) that the tax authorities may use secret comparables in a transfer pricing audit; however, the tax authorities should (within limits of confidentiality) disclose the data to the taxpayer so as to assist the taxpayer in defending itself against an adjustment. The World Bank Transfer Pricing Handbook contends that, in practice, non-pubic information is often used by tax administrations for risk-assessment purposes, rather than for transfer pricing adjustments, and such information is practically useful to establish a safe harbour margin. Cooper et al., *World Bank Transfer Pricing Handbook*, supra n. 4, at 1501-51.

information, to prove compliance with the arm's length principle during transfer pricing audits.[10] To do so, they may collect secret comparables during transfer pricing audits to use them as comparables in other audits in the same industry.

Likewise, the law of Kazakhstan envisages the use of the following sources of information on market prices (in the order of priority): (i) officially recognized sources of information, (ii) stock exchange quotations, (iii) price information maintained by Kazakh state authorities and (iv) software issued by the authorities, information provided by taxpayers and other sources of information.[11] However, a major challenge for taxpayers in Kazakhstan is that the process leading to transfer pricing assessments undertaken by tax authorities is often non-transparent, and the tax authorities typically do not disclose either the source of data used or the methodology they have applied.[12] In Russia, the databases used are RUSLANA and SPARK. Taxpayers may use foreign comparables, although local data are preferred. In addition, the use of a 'secret source of information' or information that is inaccessible under Russian law is explicitly prohibited, unless the information is derived from tax audits.[13] Therefore, both tax administrations and taxpayers may rely only on publicly available sources of information. In contrast, sources on comparables data are not yet available for Georgia or Belarus.

Regarding the allocation of location savings, tax administrations in OBOR countries may tend to use foreign comparables that are often more available, however adjusted in order to consider the specific geographical conditions by virtue of 'location savings'. The views on this topic from the OECD and the UN have been more aligned by the OECD/G20 BEPS project. As a general rule, local comparables, if available, should override foreign comparables, and the arm's length nature of a transaction should be determined by reference to the former kind of comparables.[14] In this context, there will be no need to perform a separate adjustment to account for location savings. However, foreign comparables, adjusted to take into account location savings, could be used to derive the arm's length nature of a transaction when local comparables are absent.[15] Finally, if there are no comparables at all, the proposed solution would lead to splitting the benefits derived from location savings between the involved enterprises based on the bargaining power of each.[16]

---

10. 第三十七条，《国家税务总局关于发布〈特别纳税调整及相互协商程序管理办法〉的公告》（国家税务总局公告2017第6号），2017年3月17日。
11. **KZ**: Law 67-IV, Article 18.
12. A. Zhabbarov & A. Kulisheva, *New Transfer Pricing Law in Force*, **17** Intl. Transfer Pricing J. 4, at 304 (2010).
13. E. Veter, H. Hansen & R. Radzhabov, *New Transfer Pricing Rules*, **18** Intl. Transfer Pricing J. 5, at 340 (2011).
14. OECD, *Actions 8-10 Final Reports*, supra n. 8, para. 1.142; UN, *Practical Manual on Transfer Pricing for Developing Countries*, supra n. 3, para. B.2.3.2.50.
15. OECD, *Actions 8-10 Final Reports*, supra n. 8, para. 1.143; UN, *Practical Manual on Transfer Pricing for Developing Countries*, supra n. 3, para. B.2.3.2.50.
16. OECD, *Actions 8-10 Final Reports*, supra n. 8, para. 1.143; UN, *Practical Manual on Transfer Pricing for Developing Countries*, supra n. 3, para. B.2.3.2.56. More often than not, this solution is applied in cases of full-fledged manufacturers, where comparables might often not be available. As a result, the compensation usually requires a more detailed study of its contribution to the value chain, behind which are functions, risks and assets.

On the other hand, some countries (especially developing countries, which certainly include quite a number of OBOR countries) assert that the economic benefits arising from location savings should accrue to the country where the operations actually take place. The Chinese tax authorities, for example, are a leading proponent of such view. Particularly, the Chinese tax authorities provide a six-step approach to determine the transfer price for a Chinese enterprise to allow for the location-savings benefits.[17] The application of this six-step approach will align the profitability, which is equal to full cost mark-up multiplied by the margin, of the Chinese enterprise with that of the foreign enterprise, which is mostly selected from developed countries.[18] Ultimately, all the benefits derived from location savings are officially allocated to the Chinese enterprise. The approach taken by the Chinese tax authorities may generate concerns for MNEs that have manufacturing activities out in China, due to the deviations of this approach from the international standards set out by the OECD and the UN. On the other hand, Chinese MNEs investing abroad could face similar challenges from local jurisdictions declaring location savings.

India is also known to apply the concept of location savings quite often in practice. The Indian tax authorities hold that transfer prices determined by virtue of good local comparables, if available, are at arm's length and capture the effects of location savings.[19] Both China and India leave the option open of applying the profit split method in this context.[20]

In addition, an increasing number of countries are exploring the application of location savings in their domestic transfer pricing laws. The tax administrations in South Africa and Vietnam, for example, following the practice of China and India, are currently considering the use of the concept of location savings in their tax audits.[21,22] In effect, issues surrounding location savings again highlight the problem of the insufficient availability of local comparables data, which to some extent results in an overuse and potential misuse of foreign comparables in practice.

2.2 Services and Financial Transactions

Intra-group services include a vast variety of transactions, ranging from management and administrative services to marketing services, technical services, as well as intra-group financial transactions. A review of the arm's length nature of intra-group services normally requires a two-steps analysis.[23] The first step is to determine the

---

17. UN, *Practical Manual on Transfer Pricing for Developing Countries*, supra n. 3, para. B.2.4.4.9.
18. Ibid.
19. UN, *Practical Manual on Transfer Pricing for Developing Countries*, supra n. 3, para. D.3.7.4.
20. *Ibid.*, paras. B.2.4.6.13. and B.3.7.3.
21. *Ibid.*, para. D.5.8.4.
22. VN: Quy định về quản lý thuế đối với các doanh nghiệp có giao dịch liên kết (Regulations on the Tax Administration of Enterprises with Related-Party Transactions) (21 Nov. 2016), Article 6(3)(d).
23. For guidance of these topics, *see* OECD, *Transfer Pricing Guidelines* (2010), Chapter VII, 'Special Considerations for Intra-Group Services', amended by *Action 8–10 Final Reports*; UN, *Practical Manual on Transfer Pricing for Developing Countries*, supra n. 3, Chapter B.4., 'Intra-Group Services'; Cooper et al., *World Bank Transfer Pricing Handbook*, supra n. 4, at 205–209; EU

chargeability of the concerned intra-group activities via the so-called 'benefit test'. Pursuant to this test, two conditions are to be satisfied, namely: (i) the activity at stake has provided or is expected to provide economic value to the concerned parties and (ii) a third party in comparable circumstances would have been willing to pay for the provision of the activity or would have performed the activity in-house.[24] In particular, shareholder activities,[25] mere duplications of services[26] and the provision of incidental benefits[27] are not classified as chargeable intra-group services under this test.

The second step, then, is the determination of the arm's length compensation for the chargeable services in three further steps, namely assessing costs of the concerned service; choosing the proper charging method (direct or indirect) to allocate the costs; and applying the most appropriate transfer pricing method to calculate the proper amount of remuneration. In this regard, the CUP method, the cost-plus method and the TNMM are used most frequently in practice. Within this framework, safe harbour rules, in the specific context of low value-adding services[28] and minor expenses,[29] could be applied in certain cases.

Regarding the specific category of financial services, the above-mentioned general principles apply equally in order to obtain their arm's length nature. Nevertheless, special considerations should be paid as regards the category of arrangement. In this context, the CUP method is often applied to locate the arm's length rate of interest or credit rating, although the cost-plus method and profit split method could also prove useful. For example, for intra-group interest rates, the information derived from third-party syndicated loans, price quotes[30] and other information contained in publicly available databases[31] can be beneficial;[32] for intra-group financial guarantee fees, instead, the information derived from third-party financial guarantees, price quotes,[33]

JTPF. *See* European Commission, Dir.-Gen. Taxation & Customs, EU JTPF, *Report on Cost Contribution Arrangements on Services not Creating Intangible Property* (2012), JTPF/008/FINAL/2012/EN.
24. OECD, *Transfer Pricing Guidelines* (2010), para. 7.6; OECD, *Actions 8–10 Final Reports, supra* n. 8, para. 7.6; UN, *Practical Manual on Transfer Pricing for Developing Countries, supra* n. 3, para. B.4.10.
25. OECD, *Actions 8–10 Final Reports, supra* n. 8, para. 7.9; UN, *Practical Manual on Transfer Pricing for Developing Countries, supra* n. 3, paras. B.4.2.13.–B.4.2.17.
26. OECD, *Actions 8–10 Final Reports, supra* n. 8, para. 7.11; UN, *Practical Manual on Transfer Pricing for Developing Countries, supra* n. 3, paras. B.4.2.18.–B.4.2.20.
27. OECD, *Actions 8–10 Final Reports, supra* n. 8, para. 7.12; UN, *Practical Manual on Transfer Pricing for Developing Countries, supra* n. 3, paras. B.4.2.21.–B.4.2.24.
28. OECD, *Actions 8–10 Final Reports, supra* n. 8, paras. 7.43–7.65; UN, *Practical Manual on Transfer Pricing for Developing Countries, supra* n. 3, paras. B.4.5.3.– B.4.5.10.
29. UN, *Practical Manual on Transfer Pricing for Developing Countries, supra* n. 3, paras. B.4.72-B.4.13.5.
30. These quotes, however, may not be accepted as the primary method in certain jurisdictions. Nevertheless, they could still be used as a corroborative method.
31. For example., Thomson Reuters Loan Connector™, Bloomberg Professional® and information found on the websites of stock market exchanges.
32. For more detailed guidance on this topic, *see* R. Petruzzi, *Transfer Pricing Aspects of Intra-Group Financing* (Wolters Kluwer 2016).
33. These quotes, however, may not be accepted as the primary method in certain jurisdictions. Nevertheless, they could still be used as a corroborative method.

bankers' acceptances, credit default swap fees, letter of credit fees, commitment fees, various types of insurance, as well as put options can be beneficial.[34]

In the context of the OBOR countries,[35] the topic of intra-group services (including financial transactions) plays a relevant role. The Chinese tax authorities, as an echo to the BEPS project, have amended the domestic transfer pricing guidelines to ensure alignment with international standards, following the release of Bulletin 42,[36] Bulletin 64[37] and Bulletin 6.[38] Concerning intra-group services, the benefit test will be taken into account to assess the deductibility of service payments, and in particular shareholder activity, duplicated activities and incidental benefits are non-chargeable.[39] In particular, the enhancement of the credit rating which is solely attributable to being part of an MNE group, will not be characterized as an intra-group service.[40]

Singapore suggests a 5% mark-up on 'routine services' provided by the parent or a group service company for 'business convenience and efficiency reasons',[41] and a 0% margin on cost pooling arrangements.[42] As regards the related cross-border loans, an internal comparable between the Singaporean associated entity and the third-party entity is strictly preferred in comparison to an internal comparable with a third-party bank.[43] It is also prescribed that the arm's length interest rate usually consist of a base reference rate[44] and a credit spread or margin.[45,46] Instead of conducting a detailed transfer pricing analysis, taxpayers may choose to apply the indicative margin to each related-party loan that does not exceed SGD 15 million at the time the loan is obtained or provided.[47]

Russian transfer pricing rules do not include a safe harbour rule on low value-adding services. However, regarding intercompany loans, the interest for tax purposes is defined by law and, therefore, interest rates that are not within the defined

---

34. For more detailed guidance on this topic, see Petruzzi, supra n. 32.
35. A study by the Chinese Ministry of Commerce shows that, in the first half of 2015, Chinese enterprises invested in 48 countries along the OBOR zone, totaling USD 7.05 billion, mainly in the ASEAN region, Russia and Kazakhstan. For reason of materiality, the analysis of this section is deliberately focused on the ASEAN region, Russia and Kazakhstan.
36. CN:《国家税务总局关于完善关联申报和同期资料管理有关事项的公告》（国家税务总局公告2016第42号），2016年6月29日。
37. CN:《国家税务总局关于完善预约定价安排管理有关事项的公告》（国家税务总局公告2016第64号），2016年10月11号。
38. CN:《国家税务总局关于发布〈特别纳税调整及相互协商程序管理办法〉的公告》（国家税务总局公告2017第6号），2017年3月17号。
39. CN: 第三十五条，《国家税务总局关于发布〈特别纳税调整及相互协商程序管理办法〉的公告》（国家税务总局公告2017第6号），2017年3月17号。
40. CN: 第三十五条，《国家税务总局关于发布〈特别纳税调整及相互协商程序管理办法〉的公告》（国家税务总局公告2017第6号），2017年3月17号。
41. SG: IRAS, *IRAS e-Tax Guide: Transfer Pricing Guidelines* (2017), paras. 12.26–12.27.
42. *Ibid.*, paras. 12.31–12.32.
43. *Ibid.* 13.16.
44. The base reference rate is usually a publicly available rate such as the Singapore Inter-Bank Offered Rate, the London Inter-Bank Offered Rate or prime rates offered by banks.
45. The margin is mainly to compensate the lender for bearing the credit risk of the borrower defaulting on the loan.
46. IRAS, *supra* n. 41, paras. 13.17–13.19.
47. *Ibid.* 13.27–13.34.

range will be subject to standard transfer pricing rules.[48] Specifically, the Russian tax authorities do not assess for transfer pricing purpose: (i) transactions involving the provision of guarantees where all the parties to the transaction are non-bank Russian companies or (ii) transactions involving the provision of interest-free loans between Russian related persons.[49]

In Indonesia, under domestic transfer pricing rules, taxpayers are obligated to charge a market interest rate on loans granted.[50] During a tax audit, the Indonesian tax authorities will assess four aspects of intra-group loans to ensure fairness, namely: (i) analysing whether the debt is needed, (ii) verifying that loans from affiliated parties actually occur, (iii) testing the reasonableness of the debt-to-equity ratio and (iv) testing the reasonableness of the interest rate or other expenses related to intra-group loans.[51] Furthermore, the CUP method can be used to test an interest payment transaction. It is also provided that an intra-group guarantee should also be priced at the market rate. Nevertheless, the Indonesian transfer pricing rules do not distinguish between implicit and explicit guarantees. In that case, taxpayers may use the CUP method to support the arm's length nature of the guarantee.

Vietnamese transfer pricing rules currently do not contain specific provisions on inter-group loans. However, it is suggested that the CUP method is appropriate in establishing the arm's length result under a loan contract.[52] Particularly, where loans are provided by an overseas entity, a Vietnamese company will need to register its medium- and long-term foreign loans (for a term of one year or more) with the State Bank of Vietnam. If local companies fail to do so, the interest expense generated as such is not deductible.

Neither the Indonesian tax authorities nor the Vietnamese tax authorities provide any safe harbour provisions under domestic transfer pricing law. On the other hand, Hungary includes special treatment for low value-adding intra-group services in a non-exhaustive list, taking into account the work of EU JTPF[53] on this matter.

2.3 Intangible Property

IP is defined in the Actions 8–10 Final Reports[54] as 'something which is not a physical asset or a financial asset, which is capable of being owned or controlled for use in commercial activities, and whose use or transfer would be compensated had it occurred in a transaction between independent parties in comparable circumstances'.[55] The transfer pricing issues connected to intra-group transactions involving IP are numerous and of high relevance, considering the increasing importance of their

---

48. RU: Tax Code Articles 43(3) & 269(1).
49. RU: Tax Code, section V.1.
50. ID: Income Tax Law, Article 18.
51. ID: PER-22 of the Directorate General of Taxes Regulation.
52. VN: Transfer Pricing Circular 6.
53. EU JTPF, *Report on Cost Contribution Arrangements on Services not Creating Intangible Property*, *supra* n. 23.
54. OECD, *Actions 8–10 Final Reports*, *supra* n. 8.
55. *Ibid.*, para. 6.6.

value within MNEs.⁵⁶ One of the most relevant of these issues concerns how to attribute the value generated by IP amongst the various members of an MNE, i.e., how to allocate IP-related returns between related parties. Indeed, although the legal ownership of IP might be easily identifiable, the arm's length nature of the allocation of the IP-related returns should rather focus on the specific contribution to the important functions and risks related to the development, enhancement, maintenance, protection and exploitation (DEMPE) of the IP, as the OECD stated in the Actions 8-10 Final Reports.⁵⁷

In this regard, the UN Manual also identifies the importance of the special contributions made with respect to DAEMPE (development or acquisition, enhancement, maintenance, protection and exploitation) of the intangibles involved.⁵⁸ Additionally, the World Bank Handbook supports the DEMPE concept in general, although it underscores the uncertainty and lack of resources for tax administrations to apply the DEMPE concept in practice.

In the context of the OBOR countries, China has come a long way from having a dearth of transfer pricing rules to now being one of the earliest adopters of the outcomes of the OECD/G20 BEPS project despite some divergences. For example, for purposes of Chinese transfer pricing law, 'ownership' is not limited to a strict legal sense. Rather, the Chinese tax authorities typically apply the concept of 'economic ownership', especially in the case of marketing intangibles and IP resulting from R&D activities, in order to preserve China's taxing rights over value created within its boundaries. Furthermore, in the case of marketing intangibles, to the extent that the Chinese enterprise would bear a substantial amount of marketing expenses, the Chinese position is that the Chinese enterprise should be entitled to at least a portion of any excess economic profit associated with the marketing intangibles resulting from the marketing activities within the jurisdiction.⁵⁹ Moreover, although China follows the OECD approach as regards ownership and the DEMPE functions, its view on the functional analysis is broader in the sense that it sets out a 'DEMPEP' approach. This means that it goes one step further by adding 'promotion' to the definition of activities that entitle returns on IP. By adding 'promotion' to the DEMPE standard, China reinforces its view that market premium could rise to the level of a unique and valuable intangible. It emphasizes the contribution of manufacturers and marketers to the enhancement of IP asset value, and downplays the significance of high-level strategic planning and control of IP asset development. In other words, the Chinese approach

---

56. For guidance of these topics, see OECD, *Transfer Pricing Guidelines* (2017), *supra* n. 2, Chapter VI, 'Intangible Property', amended by OECD, *Actions 8-10 Final Reports*, *supra* n. 8); UN, *Practical Manual on Transfer Pricing for Developing Countries*, *supra* n. 3, Part B.5, 'Transfer Pricing considerations for Intangible Property'); Cooper et al., *World Bank Transfer Pricing Handbook*, *supra* n. 4, at 212, Chapter 5, 'Selected Issues in Transfer Pricing' – 'Intangibles').
57. OECD, *Actions 8-10 Final Reports*, *supra* n. 8, para. 6.32.
58. UN, *Practical Manual on Transfer Pricing for Developing Countries*, *supra* n. 3, paras. B.5.3.13.–B.5.3.14.
59. China (People's Rep.), *Transfer Pricing*, Topical Analyses IBFD (accessed 28 Aug. 2016).

deviates from the OECD approach, which pursues to allocate value creation based on decision-making as a control factor, which clearly is more beneficial to developed countries.[60]

The majority of OBOR countries (Albania, Bangladesh, Belarus, Bosnia and Herzegovina, Bulgaria, China, Croatia, Czech Republic, Estonia, Georgia, Hungary, India, Indonesia, Israel, Kazakhstan, Kuwait, Kyrgyzstan, Latvia, Lithuania, Malaysia, Mongolia, Oman, Philippines, Qatar, Romania, Russia, Saudi Arabia, Serbia and Montenegro, Singapore, Slovakia, Slovenia, Sri Lanka, Tajikistan, Turkey, Ukraine and Vietnam) to a greater or a lesser extent, follow the OECD Guidelines. This means that the legal owner of intangibles will be entitled to retain all ex-ante returns derived from the exploitation of such intangibles only if it performs and controls all of the DEMPE functions; provides all assets, including funding, necessary for the DEMPE functions; and assumes all risks related to the DEMPE functions.

Despite the widespread adoption of the OECD Guidelines among OBOR countries, there are some jurisdictions that do not follow the OECD and apply only the transfer pricing rules envisaged under their domestic tax system, such as Egypt, Iran, Macedonia, Nepal, Pakistan, and Turkmenistan. Nevertheless, as regards the allocation of returns on intangibles, they do not have specific rules, which inevitably might trigger disparities among the region when determining the proper transfer price in connection with intangibles, if they do not pursue a move to the OECD/UN (post-BEPS) approach. As mentioned before, countries such as Armenia, Azerbaijan, Bahrain, Brunei, Kuwait, Moldova, Syria, the United Arab Emirates and Uzbekistan do not have transfer pricing rules in their tax systems – which might also be detrimental to OBOR development.

Moreover, as regards the definition of IP, difficulties can arise during a transfer pricing analysis as a result of definitions of the term 'intangibles' that are either too narrow or too broad under domestic laws. On the one hand, if an overly narrow definition is applied, certain IP could fall outside the definition and therefore be able to be transferred or used without separate compensation. On the other hand, if an overly broad a definition is applied, the use or transfer of IP in transactions between associated enterprises could require compensation in circumstances where no such compensation would be provided in transactions between independent enterprises.[61]

2.4 Cost Contribution Arrangements

The OECD defines CCAs as 'special contractual arrangements among business enterprises to share the contributions and risks involved in the joint development, production or the obtaining of IP, tangible assets or services with the understanding that such IP, tangible assets or services are expected to create benefits for the individual

---

60. C. Chi, J. Kondos, S. Liu & K. Liao, *China's New Transfer Pricing Guidelines and BEPS*, in *China – Looking Ahead, Intl. Tax Rev.*, at 19 (2015), http://www.internationaltaxreview.com/IssueArticle/3511707/Archive/Chinas-new-transfer pricing-guidelines-and-BEPS.html (accessed 12 Dec. 2017).
61. UN, *Practical Manual on Transfer Pricing for Developing Countries*, supra n. 3, Part B.2.2.

Chapter 10: TP Issues Related to the Belt and Road Initiative

businesses of each of the participants'.[62] CCAs often pursue two distinctive purposes, namely: (i) the joint development, production or obtaining of assets[63] and (ii) the sharing of costs for obtaining intra-group services.[64] MNEs have used CCAs since 1950s as a cost-effective means of carrying out their activities based on economies of scale and sharing of risks and resources. Their distinct benefit vis-à-vis traditional multilateral agreements or a web of bilateral ones is a more streamlined system of sharing contributions, remuneration and risks.

CCAs can involve numerous transfer pricing issues that must be carefully considered. These include the determination of the participants; their contribution to the CCAs as well as their expected benefits form the CCAs; and the quantification (and classification) of balancing payments and of any payment for entry, withdrawal or termination of the CCA.[65]

As far as the OBOR countries are concerned, there are some recent developments to be considered. China first adopted CCA rules in January 2009 (effective from 1 January 2008)[66] and amended the reporting and administration process in June 2015.[67]

---

62. *See* OECD Guidelines, Chapter VIII ('Cost Contributions Agreements'), amended by the Actions 8–10 Final Reports. OECD, *Actions 8–10 Final Reports*, supra n. 8, at 161.
63. CCAs of the first type resemble joint ventures (or consortia), where the parties partially unite forces, assets and activities to implement a certain project. The practical difference between CCAs and joint ventures (or consortia) is that the former are commonly agreed among related parties, while the latter are agreed among unrelated parties. In OBOR countries, consortia are popular in industries such as mineral extraction and construction, and the respective agreements may be concluded on intergovernmental level or closely observed by the governmental agencies.
64. CCAs of the second type are arrangements where several members of an MNE contribute to the group's internal activities (becoming, in a way, 'cost centres'), while other group members cover their respective costs based on certain allocation keys. These arrangements can cover the use of intangibles owned, IT, logistics, accounting and other management services performed by designated companies of the group. The difference from common arrangements for intra-group services is the more complex nature of relations, whereby the same companies are both providers of some services and recipients of others. The costs are split among members of the group (potentially) benefiting from such intangibles or services in proportion to their sales revenue, profit, number of staff, number of software licenses or other relevant indicator or set thereof. While the 'beneficiaries' regularly pay for such services and use of intangibles, the volume of benefits obtained in a given period does not necessarily correlate with the amounts paid in the same period; however this may happen among independent companies in the case of subscription-type arrangements.
65. For guidance of these topics, *see* OECD, *Transfer Pricing Guidelines*, Chapter VIII, 'Cost Contribution Arrangements', amended by OECD, *Actions 8–10 Final Reports*, supra n. 8); UN, *Practical Manual on Transfer Pricing for Developing Countries*, supra n. 3, paras. 1.6.11–1.6.12 and 7.4.6.13–7.4.6.14; Cooper et al., *World Bank Transfer Pricing Handbook*, supra n. 4, Chapter 5, 'Cost Contribution Arrangements'; EU JTPF, *Report on Cost Contribution Arrangements on Services not Creating Intangible Property*, supra n. 23. Communication from the Commission to the European Parliament, the Council and the European economic and social committee COM (2012) 516 final dated 19 Sep. 2012, http://ec.europa.eu/taxation_customs/sites/taxation/files /resources/documents/taxation/company_tax/transfer_pricing/forum/jtpf/2012/2012-09_co m516_en.pdf). The EU JTPF found that by 1 Jul. 2011, only a few EU Member States had law or guidance on CCAs, namely Denmark, Estonia, Italy, Lithuania, the Netherlands, Spain, Portugal, Slovenia and the United Kingdom. Earlier, it also acknowledged that 'tax auditors ... may not be familiar with such arrangements'.
66. CN: Implementation Measures of Special Tax Adjustments (Guoshuifa [2009] 2).
67. CN: Announcement on Standardizing the Administration of Cost Sharing Agreement (Announcement 45).

These rules allow both of the above-mentioned types of CCAs, and prohibit accrual and payment of any additional royalties for the IP developed or transferred under a CCA. They also include limitation on benefits clauses; establishing five conditions when the respective costs cannot be deducted; namely a lack of economic substance; deviation from the arm's length principle; costs not matching revenues; non-compliance with documentation requirements and reporting requirements; and a timeframe of less than twenty years. The documentation and reporting requirements include a list of minimum contents for a CCA, a list of supporting information and rights of the tax authorities to review the arrangement and amend the price. The emphasis of CCA rules in China is on the deductibility of the incurred expenses.

Among former USSR countries, there are only three that have detailed transfer pricing rules, namely Kazakhstan, Russia and Ukraine, although they do not provide for acceptance of CCAs. Practitioners confirm that in Russia, CCAs are not legally possible due to contract requirements and difficulties with cost justification. As a result, a business is forced to use 'cover' transactions (i.e., bilateral service contracts with management companies or license payments).[68] However, there remains a risk of exposure during tax audits, and in 2013 there were numerous Russian court cases involving this issue. The corporate and tax rules in other former USSR countries (such as Azerbaijan, Belarus, Georgia, Kyrgyzstan, Tajikistan, Turkmenistan and Uzbekistan) contain limited transfer pricing provisions, which are similar in respect of non-acceptance of CCAs, and no publications considered this issue. Armenia and Moldova have no transfer pricing rules and therefore CCAs are not accepted.

Among EU OBOR countries, some have designated CCA rules, such as Estonia, Poland, and Romania, which include detailed provisions on the content of respective documentation (including proof of benefits of domestic company, allocation keys and consistency use thereof, breakdown of costs). Croatia, Czech Republic, Hungary, Latvia, Lithuania, Slovakia and Slovenia normally accept CCAs, but the deductibility of respective costs is determined on a case-by-case basis.

In the maritime OBOR countries, Indonesia briefly touches upon the issue of CCAs in its tax rules, and practitioners believe that the OECD approach is acceptable. Malaysia applies dedicated guidance based on the OECD Guidelines. That guidance contains a chapter on CCAs which sets forth only basic rules (definition, arm's length rule, suggested allocation keys and economic substance); in practice, the tax authorities tend to apply rules on intra-group services instead (if there is no development of IP). Singapore does not have specific rules on CCAs and tends to treat 'service' CCAs as intra-group services (with respective requirements) and 'IP' CCAs as either the acquisition of IP or license fees, depending on the facts of the case.

---

68. R. Avalyan,Антиофшорный Закон вернул лишь шестую часть бизнеса в Россию (Интервью с А.В. Гуськовым) [Anti-Offshore Law Returned Only One Sixth Of Business to Russia (Interview with A.V. Guskov)], in Налоговый учет для бухгалтера [Tax Accounting for Accountants], issue 6, at 11–17 (2016); A. Smekhova,Налоговики стараются не выносить заведомо проигрышные решения (Интервью с М. Орловым) [Tax Officers Tend to Avoid Issuing Definitely Losing Decisions (Interview with M. Orlov)], Российский налоговый курьер (Russian Tax Courier), issue 11, at 86–90 (2014).

Bangladesh, India, Israel, Philippines and Sri Lanka generally accept CCAs and allow the deduction of respective payments; no formal guidance is available. Turkey also generally accepts CCAs, and in 2016 it published Draft Guidance on the subject which is generally a translation of the OECD Guidance. In particular, it requires proof that the services in question were actually necessary for recipient and duly rendered (in addition to the arm's length nature of price and proper documentation).

Albania, Bulgaria, Egypt, Iran, Kuwait, Macedonia, Mongolia, Pakistan, Qatar, Saudi Arabia, Serbia and Montenegro and Vietnam do not have any rules on CCAs, and the local tax authorities may have issues with recognizing such arrangements. A few additional countries, such as Bahrain, Brunei, Oman and the United Arab Emirates, do not have any transfer pricing rules, and provisions on CCAs are thus also absent.

The above review of CCA practice in OBOR countries suggests that the main issues are the limited spread of CCAs and the consequent lack of related experience within the tax authorities. Moreover, in some countries, inexperienced tax officers are suspicious of the nature of CCAs, as there may be no explicit economic benefits for a particular company against incurred costs, especially when there is no direct supplier-customer relationship and no fixed price. This is mitigated in part by rules requiring proof of necessity and actual delivery of the service (as in Turkey). The World Bank Handbook cites the following CCA-specific issues:[69] (i) valuation of buy-in and buy-out payments, (ii) valuation of participants' contributions, for both IP and services, (iii) determination of participants' expected benefits, (iv) determination of the cost base (e.g., inclusion of the costs of employee share options), (v) treatment of tax incentives and government subsidies, (vi) acceptance of different types of ownership of intangibles (i.e., legal, beneficial and economic) and (vii) tax treatment (e.g., withholding obligations) of contributions and balancing payments.

Some comments on the revisions to Chapter VIII of the OECD Guidelines,[70] however, included criticism of the approach based on valuation of participants' contributions as less objective than an approach assessed on participants' costs (which are readily identifiable in accounting records). They additionally pointed out that estimation of (expected) benefits and respective allocation of costs (which may seem more fair) makes the system more complicated for the tax authorities than cost-based allocation (which seems more practical). Another comment emphasized the lack of clarity in the requirements for CCA documentation.

The introduction of CCAs can also require a set of changes to domestic rules on contracts and accounting. Such changes include acceptance of cost recognized by a particular company based on cost sharing agreement (as opposed to traditional price setting) and adjustment of rules on documentary evidence of costs in (tax) accounting. Furthermore, as OBOR countries normally use their official languages for accounting

---

69. Cooper et al., *World Bank Transfer Pricing Handbook*, supra n. 4, at 214–215.
70. OECD, *Comments Received on Public Discussion Draft BEPS Action 8: Revisions to Chapter VIII of the Transfer Pricing Guidelines on Cost Contribution Arrangements (CCAS)* (OECD Publishing 2010), pp.19–20 by Federation of German Industries, p.52 by BUSINESSEUROPE, pp.60–61 by CBI etc.

and reporting purposes, companies interested in using CCAs will have to bear the expense of translating documentation supporting the arrangements.

2.5 Documentation

Every transfer pricing analysis necessitates comprehensive knowledge of the facts and circumstances of the specific case. If facts and circumstances are not known, a reliable assessment cannot be made. The extraordinary volumes of relevant data that must be looked at usually distinguishes transfer pricing cases from other tax cases, and even minor changes in the fact pattern can have a significant influence on the results of such analysis. Thus, a common understanding of the facts and circumstances of a case is essential. Establishing such knowledge is based on the data collected by the taxpayer to substantiate its tax position – in this context, transfer pricing documentation.

Under the BEPS project, Action 13[71] has aimed to re-examine transfer pricing documentation and has developed rules regarding transfer pricing documentation to enhance transparency for tax administrations, taking into consideration the compliance costs for business. This has resulted in a new three-tier approach consisting of: (i) a master file containing standardized information relevant for all group members, (ii) a local file referring specifically to material transactions of the local taxpayer and (iii) a country-by-country report containing information on income, taxes paid and economic activities of the group.[72] Structurally, this builds on Chapter V of the OECD Guidelines, as well as the EU Code of Conduct on Transfer Pricing Documentation[73] in which the concepts of master file and local file were first introduced. The country-by-country report is, instead, something genuinely new in the transfer pricing field; however, it was used before – in slightly different form – for accounting and reporting purposes for groups in specific sectors (e.g., banking and extractives).[74]

This new BEPS standard, as introduced in the paragraph above, involving a three-tier approach to transfer pricing documentation, is not fully endorsed by the UN Manual as revised in 2017. The UN Manual emphasizes that for developing countries, it must be decided – depending on the specific country situation – whether the implementation is useful and doable,[75] while the Manual still acknowledges that related to the UN standards on transfer pricing, documentation should – to the extent

---

71. OECD, *Transfer Pricing Documentation and Country-by-Country Reporting – Action 13: 2015 Final Report*, OECD/G20 Base Erosion and Profit Shifting Project (OECD Publishing 5 Oct. 2015).
72. OECD, Action 13 Final Report, *supra* n. 71, Chapter C.
73. EU Code of Conduct: Resolution of the Council and of the representatives of the governments of the Member States, meeting within the Council, of 27 June 2006 on a code of conduct on transfer pricing documentation for associated enterprises in the European Union (EU TPD), OJ C176 (28 Jul. 2006).
74. European Commission, Country-by-country reporting for specific sectors (banking and extractives) in the EU, available at https://ec.europa.eu/info/business-economy-euro/company-reporting-and-auditing/company-reporting/public-country-country-reporting and https://ec.europa.eu/info/business-economy-euro/company-reporting-and-auditing/company-reporting/transparency-requirements-listed-companies_en.
75. UN, *Practical Manual on Transfer Pricing for Developing Countries*, *supra* n. 3, Chapter B.1.6.6 and C.2.2.3.1.

possible – be in line with OECD standards.[76] Also, the World Bank Handbook does not make any recommendations to implement specific standards (whether it is the new BEPS standard or that of other institutions), but merely describes various approaches.[77] Nevertheless, as the BEPS project created a minimum standard on transfer pricing documentation, and countries in the Inclusive Framework[78] are committed to implement all minimum standards, it will certainly unleash global effects in the coming years.

The master and local files, according to the BEPS standard, are to provide comprehensive data to a tax administration to conduct a transfer pricing examination, while the country-by-country report is conceived as a risk assessment tool. This is stated not only in the respective BEPS final report,[79] but also in section 5 of the Multilateral Competent Authority Agreement on the Exchange of Country-by-Country Reports (Multilateral CAA),[80] as well as in model Competent Authority Agreements to income tax treaties (tax treaties) and tax information exchange agreements as attached to the BEPS Action 13 Final Report. Nevertheless, this clarification should not be misunderstood. While the template is conceived for use in high-level risk assessment regarding transfer pricing and other BEPS-related risks, and tax administrations are not allowed to base adjustments merely on the information received in this specific form, the country-by-country report will certainly have to be available to auditors during a later transfer pricing audit. In addition to these objectives, transfer pricing documentation additionally serves to increase taxpayer awareness and attention to compliance with the arm's length principle.[81]

According to the Action 13 Final Report, the procedure for transmitting the documentation to the tax authorities deviates significantly between the country-by-country report and the master and local files. While the master and local file are directly sent by a local subsidiary of a group to the respective tax authorities, the country-by-country report is sent only by the ultimate parent company of a group to the tax administration of its residence country and is subsequently disseminated to other affected tax administrations via exchange of information mechanisms. Thus, such differences lead to deviations in the date on which documentation is available to tax administrations, as well. While it is up to every single tax administration to define timelines for transmission of the master and local files, the country-by-country report must be submitted within twelve months[82] after the fiscal year of the report, and shared with other authorities within fifteen (eighteen) months.[83]

---

76. *Ibid.*, Chapter B.1.8.12.
77. Cooper et al., *World Bank Transfer Pricing Handbook*, supra n. 4, at 241–268.
78. As at December 2017, there are 110 countries participating in the inclusive framework on BEPS. *See* http://www.oecd.org/tax/beps/inclusive-framework-on-beps-composition.pdf. Many of them participating in the OBOR initiative.
79. OECD, *Action 13 Final Report*, supra n. 71, para. 25.
80. OECD, *Multilateral Competent Authority Agreement on the Exchange of Country-by-Country Reports*, available at http://www.oecd.org/tax/automatic-exchange/about-automatic-exchange/cbc-mcaa.pdf.
81. OECD, *Action 13 Final Report*, supra n. 71, Chapter B.
82. *Ibid.*, Article 5, Annex IV (Model legislation related to Country by Country Reporting).
83. OECD, *MCAA on the Exchange of Country-by-Country Reports*, supra n. 80, section 3.

Transfer pricing documentation regimes are often reinforced with significant penalties. Nevertheless, the new OECD standard does not necessarily foresee penalties and leaves it to the domestic legislature as to whether to implement them or not.[84] In contrast, the EU, which issued a binding directive on country-by-country reporting in 2016,[85] includes the obligation for Member States to foresee penalties, but leaves it open to the Member States to design such rules individually.[86] In any case, when it comes to penalizing groups that are obliged to submit a country-by-country report, it will be difficult to determine penalties that are severe enough to be effective while also not being draconian. At the same time, it is widely acknowledged that – regarding country-by-country reporting – the risk of being negatively rated during a tax administrations risk assessment process and later thoroughly audited will incentivize groups at least as much as penalties to submit accurate data.

Transfer pricing documentation and the country-by-country report as part of it are protected by tax secrecy. The BEPS Action 13 Final Report emphasizes this fact by reiterating confidentiality requirements in Chapter V of the OECD Guidelines, in the model legislation on domestic implementation of country-by-country reporting and in the multilateral competent authority agreement, as well as in the competent authority agreements based on the model tax conventions and model tax information exchange agreements. Nevertheless, certain stakeholders – in particular from civil society[87] and academia – call for publication of country-by-country reports, arguing that only public knowledge of these facts will lead to a push back against overly aggressive taxpayer behaviour. While within the OECD there seem to be no signs to reconsider the confidentiality approach, publication of these reports is more intensely discussed at the level of the EU. In 2016, the Commission proposed to amend the Accounting Directive[88] to oblige groups to publish parts of their country-by-country reports.[89]

OBOR countries have widely deviating transfer pricing frameworks on these topics. Some of them look back on many years of experience in applying transfer

---

84. OECD, *Action 13 Final Report*, *supra* n. 71, Article 7, Annex IV (Model legislation related to Country by Country Reporting).
85. EU Exchange of Information Directive 3: EU Council Directive 2015/2376/EU of 8 Dec. 2015 amending Directive 2011/16/EU as regards mandatory automatic exchange of information in the field of taxation, OJ L 332 (2015).
86. EU Exchange of Information Directive 4: Council Directive (EU) 2016/881 of 25 May 2016 amending Directive 2011/16/EU as regards mandatory automatic exchange of information in the field of taxation, OJ L 146 (2016), Article 25a.
87. *See* e.g., A. Knobel & A. Cobham, *Country-by-Country Reporting: How Restricted Access Exacerbates Global Inequalities in Taxing Rights*, Tax Justice Network (December 2016).
88. EU Accounting Directive: Directive 2013/34/EU of the European Parliament and of the Council of 26 Jun. 2013 on the annual financial statements, consolidated financial statements and related reports of certain types of undertakings, amending Directive 2006/43/EC of the European Parliament and of the Council and repealing Council Directives 78/660/EEC and 83/349/EEC Text with EEA relevance, OJ L182 (29 Jun 2013).
89. According to this approach, information on the following topics should be published: (i) the nature of the activities, (ii) the number of employees, (iii) total net turnover made, which includes turnover made with third parties, as well as between companies within a group, (iv) the profit made before tax, (v) the amount of income tax due in the country as a reason of the profits made in the current year in that country, (vi) the amount of tax actually paid during that year and (vii) accumulated earnings.

pricing rules, while others introduced respective law only quite recently.[90] Accordingly, the capacities of tax administrations vary broadly, as well. Rules on transfer pricing documentation will have to consider such variations and tailor-made approaches will be necessary. Nevertheless, a clear trend towards the implementation of transfer pricing documentation regimes could be observed over the last decade which further accelerated after the release of the BEPS Action 13 Final Report.[91] In addition, it must be recognized that international commitments to different standards deviate between countries (some being OECD, some G20, some Inclusive Framework members), and policies will have to take this into account.

Implementation of country-by-country reporting requires a network of exchange of information rules. Typically, such provisions are implemented through a country's tax treaty network or accession to the Multilateral Convention on Mutual Assistance in Tax Matters. Where such network does not exist (which is still the case for some of the countries participating in OBOR), implementation will have only limited effects, as country-by-country reports of foreign groups will not be transmitted to those countries.

Furthermore, not all OBOR countries' tax administrations are capable of processing transfer pricing documentation provided in English, even though this will be the language of most of the data obtained. Thus, this will lead in the short term to the necessity for taxpayers to provide (costly) translations.

2.6 Advance Pricing Arrangements

An APA is defined as:

> an arrangement that determines, in advance of controlled transactions, an appropriate set of criteria (e.g. method, comparables, an appropriate adjustment thereto, critical assumptions as to future events) for the determination of the transfer pricing for those transactions over a fixed period of time. An APA is formally initiated by a taxpayer and requires negotiations between the taxpayer, one or more associated enterprises, and one or more tax administrations.[92]

An APA can be concluded unilaterally, bilaterally or multilaterally, as questions on transfer pricing issues can occur between a taxpayer and the tax administration of its residence country, as well as between tax administrations of different

---

90. Cooper et al., *World Bank Transfer Pricing Handbook*, supra n. 4, Chapter 6. *See also* e.g., EY Transfer Pricing Surveys (latest publication -http://www.ey.com/gl/en/services/tax/ey-2016-transfer pricing-survey-series), Deloitte Global Transfer Pricing Country Guides (latest publication – https://www2.deloitte.com/us/en/pages/tax/articles/global-transfer pricing-country-guide.html).
91. *See* e.g., KPMG, *BEPS Action 13 Country Implementation Summary*, https://home.kpmg.com/content/dam/kpmg/xx/pdf/2017/04/tnf-beps-action-13-april24-2017.pdf. On implementation of country-by-country reporting, *see* OECD, *Country-Specific Information on Country-by-Country Reporting Implementation*, http://www.oecd.org/tax/automatic-exchange/country-specific-information-on-country-by-country-reporting-implementation.htm.
92. OECD, *Transfer Pricing Guidelines* (2017), supra n. 2, para. 4.123.

jurisdictions.[93] The legal basis for unilateral APAs can be found in the respective domestic tax law, either in transfer pricing law, in specific law on APAs or in general procedural rules. The legal basis for bilateral or multilateral APAs can be found in international treaties such as tax treaties, where provisions implementing Article 25 of OECD or UN Models on the mutual agreement procedure (MAP) usually serve as the basis for such agreements. While some countries consider international treaty provisions on MAPs alone as a sufficient basis for a bilateral or multilateral APA, others require specific domestic implementations.

An APA must be based on the arm's length principle. Regardless of whether an APA is concluded unilaterally, bilaterally or multilaterally, its purpose should be to find a common interpretation of the arm's length principle in a specific situation, rather than to arbitrarily define tax burdens for involved taxpayers. An APA is not a civil law contract, but an instrument of public law. Tax administrations will lack the authority to autonomously reduce or increase a taxpayer's tax burden, and they will certainly be bound by the rule of law to apply their country's transfer pricing law, including the arm's length principle. Nevertheless, it is only rarely the case that a jurisdiction will use favourable and unilateral APAs that go beyond the arm's length principle as an incentive to attract businesses.

Not all OBOR countries provide for the possibility of an APA.[94] The main reasons for being reluctant to introduce APAs can be grouped into three categories, namely: (i) a lack of transfer pricing experience and knowledge, (ii) a lack of capacity and (iii) a lack of trust in such cooperative procedure. Where countries have only recently introduced transfer pricing law or have just started to enforce such rules, they usually need to gain experience before starting an APA programme in order to minimize the risk of locking in transfer pricing positions that are either not in line with international standards and/or are harmful for their country. Some countries that have already gained know-how and experience in the field of transfer pricing still have not implemented APA programmes because of their limited personal capacity in this area and their will to use such limited capacity primarily for tax audits, as only this function promises revenue generating effects. Finally, countries might be reluctant to introduce APA programmes because they do not trust in the specific APA procedure, where taxpayers are typically intensively involved in establishing the assessment of a case and results might depend on the agreement of a taxpayer.

Unfortunately, there are currently not many publicly available data on existing programmes, many countries do not even publish their administrative guidance and there is scarcely any case law available. Such lack of transparency increases the risk

---

93. For guidance of these topics, *see* OECD, *Transfer Pricing Guidelines* (2017), *supra* n. 2, paras. 4.129 & 4.130; UN, *Practical Manual on Transfer Pricing for Developing Countries*, *supra* n. 3, Chapter 3.10; Cooper et al., *World Bank Transfer Pricing Handbook*, *supra* n. 4, Chapter 7.
94. The APA policy of specific countries can be found in the Transfer Pricing Surveys published annually by major firms such as EY, https://www.ey.com/gl/en/services/tax/ey-2016-transfer-pricing-survey-series; KPMG, https://home.kpmg.com/xx/en/home/insights/2013/04/kpmg-global-transfer-pricing-review.html; PwC, https://www.pwc.com/gx/en/services/tax/publications/international-transfer-pricing.html; Deloitte, https://www2.deloitte.com/us/en/pages/tax/articles/global-transfer-pricing-country-guide.html.

that APAs will not be in line with international standards, will be inconsistent with the treatment of other cases or will even be considered as providing preferential taxation in specific cases.

Regarding issues related to APAs, generally, every transfer pricing case should be resolved based on the same set of rules. As such, there should be no distinction between an APA case and any other case, although an APA case is resolved in advance of the concerned transactions while other cases are often handled years later during a tax audit. This earlier resolution can be financially favourable for a tax administration; if during APA negotiations the tax liability of a taxpayer turns out to be higher than according to the taxpayer's initial approach, this will – looking at the time value of money – increase tax revenue for the tax administration. Additionally, the quality of data to which a tax administration has access in an APA procedure is often better than during an audit, and thus allows for a more accurate assessment. For businesses, an APA increases certainty, allowing for more accurate planning. Businesses must plan their undertakings as accurately as possible for internal and external reasons. Internally, a company must know how much resources are available in order to be able to make sound management decisions. Externally, a company must provide a clear picture of its financial situation in order to attract new investors[95] or to satisfy demands of its creditors. Uncertainty counteracts these demands, and thus companies are likely to be interested in the certainty regarding their tax liabilities as provided by APAs.

During negotiations for an APA, the tax administration can obtain in-depth insights into the taxpayer's organization and strategies, allowing the administration to learn and increase its knowledge. APA negotiations are typically held in an open and cooperative atmosphere where the tax administration is working closely with the taxpayer. As the taxpayer initiates an APA procedure, its willingness to share information on the concerned transactions will typically be higher than during an audit procedure. The fact that on the side of the taxpayer the same persons who designed the transfer pricing system of the respective transactions will negotiate the APA, will further improve the quality of information at hand vis-à-vis audits of past transactions. These insights will allow tax administrations personnel to learn more about the thinking of taxpayers, a knowledge that can be used later in different areas of work (e.g., risk analysis, auditing).

Nevertheless, asymmetries in the skill and training level between a tax administration and taxpayers or between different tax administrations can influence outcomes negatively. An APA is the result of a process of negotiations. If the APA is unilateral, these are conducted between a tax administration and a taxpayer; or if the APA is bilateral or multilateral, they are conducted between more than one tax administrations with the involvement of a taxpayer. If there are significant discrepancies between the resources of stakeholders, this will likely influence the outcomes favouring the

---

95. In particular regarding projects with an extraordinary investment volume, such certainty is essential for investor relations. In the past, agreements similar to APAs were even lifted to the level of states treaties in order to comfort investors (e.g., Intergovernmental Agreement on the Nabucco Pipeline Project where agreement was found that profits should be shared according to the length of the pipeline in a specific country).

resource-rich parties. If, for example, one party can rely on the expertise of an economist who is specialized specifically in transfer pricing, while the other party cannot rely on such a person, there is a risk that facts in favour of the latter party's position will be overlooked. Asymmetries (as described above) will also occur in other situations, such as audits and MAPs, and are therefore not an exclusive problem of APA negotiations. However, the cooperative character of an APA procedure could certainly give rise to potentially negative effects.

Offering the opportunity to conclude an APA may increase the attractiveness of a certain jurisdiction for businesses. Business decisions regarding where to locate activities are complex and take into account various aspects. Tax is one of these aspects and in this realm, it is not only the statutory tax rate that companies are considering. In any case, tax certainty and – in particular – a reliable and well-functioning tax administration can positively influence a company's decision to invest in a country, and the availability of an APA can signal this reliability. Accordingly, the BEPS Action 14 Final Report recommends the introduction of (bilateral) APA programmes[96] in its best practices, and a recent joint report from the OECD and IMF on tax certainty refers to APAs as a practical tool for enhancing tax certainty.[97]

Nevertheless, APAs can lead tax administrations to focus scarce resources on compliant rather than non-compliant taxpayers, thus 'squeezing the wrong end'. Tax administrations with very narrow personnel resources may have to wind down their audit attempts in order to be able to run an APA programme, resulting in an overall decrease in collected taxes. At the beginning of a tax administration's work in the field of transfer pricing, personal resources are typically very scarce. If only a very small group of skilled employees is available, the proper allocation of such capacity is extremely critical. Often this group will work in an audit programme first, as this promises countable monetary results while at the same time is a strong signal to the business community. Moreover, audits that are based on prudent risk assessment allow for a focus on taxpayers that are unlikely to be compliant, while taxpayers that reveal their transfer pricing system voluntarily are more likely to be compliant anyway. Thus, introducing an APA programme at an early stage could effort with drawing skilled auditors and result in an unreasonable allocation of scarce resources.

Unilateral APAs are particularly vulnerable to being used in unintended ways. First, the close cooperation between tax administration and taxpayers could lay the groundwork for corruption. The facts that only a small number of tax administration employees will have the skills to verify the integrity of an APA and a domestic appeal procedure is usually ruled out in an APA can further leverage this risk. Second, the broad range of possible interpretations of the arm's length principle could tempt tax administrations to use APAs as a tool for (harmful) tax competition. Especially in European and OECD countries, this opportunity was seen as problematic and countermeasures have been considered already. In the EU, relevant cross-border APAs had to

---

96. OECD, *Making Dispute Resolution Mechanisms More Effective – Action 14: 2015 Final Report*, OECD/G20 Base Erosion and Profit Shifting Project (OECD Publishing 5 Oct. 2015), at 28.
97. IMF/OECD, *Tax Certainty: IMF/OECD Report for the G20 Finance Ministers* (Mar. 2017), available at http://www.oecd.org/tax/g20-report-on-tax-certainty.htm.

be exchanged spontaneously[98] and from 2017, must be exchanged automatically,[99] at the level of the OECD, the BEPS Action 5 Final Report[100] established a new minimum standard on the mandatory exchange of APAs.

Many of the risks mentioned in above can be mitigated through increased transparency. Risks that are rooted in the one-sidedness of unilateral APAs are minimized if all interested jurisdictions are informed at an early stage, and if later APAs are exchanged[101] between the jurisdictions involved in the transactions. Taxpayers are then not able to take different approaches,[102] and thus the risks of unwanted double non-taxation and other forms of misuse are reduced. At the same time, the risk of double taxation is reduced as well, if jurisdictions openly share their opinions. Further transparency will facilitate the closing of the gap in asymmetric situations, this is particularly true when APAs are published and can therefore be studied by anyone who is interested.

3 CONCLUSION AND PROPOSALS

This chapter has analysed various transfer pricing topics that can generate relevant issues in OBOR countries. In general, one of the very first aims is to put on equal footing the understanding of transfer pricing rules among OBOR countries in order to build a bridge between jurisdictions with transfer pricing rules and those without.

Moreover, it would be reasonable to focus further actions on the development and promotion in OBOR countries of two key aspects, namely the improvement of guidance and the dissemination of experience among the various stakeholders. The first part could potentially take place through the implementation of a commonly agreed set of guidelines among OBOR countries. The second part, instead, could take the form of tailoring existing training programmes to the local environments of the target countries. In this context, both international organizations and academic institutions should consider both offering consultations on the development of specific guidelines and training of local tax officers. Additionally, OBOR countries might also consider the establishment of an international forum (e.g., in a similar setting as the EU JTPF) of experts from both governmental institutions and private practice that regularly meets and analyses various pre-defined transfer pricing topics, in order to produce guidance that, although not legally binding, could constitute a useful practical tool to solve specific issues.

---

98. EU Savings Directive: Council Directive 2011/16/EU of 15 Feb. 2011 on administrative cooperation in the field of taxation and repealing Directive 77/799/EEC, OJ L64/1, Article 9.
99. EU Exchange of Information Directive 3, *supra* n. 85.
100. OECD, *Countering Harmful Tax Practices More Effectively, Taking into Account Transparency and Substance – Action 5: 2015 Final Report*, OECD/G20 Base Erosion and Profit Shifting Project (OECD Publishing 5 Oct. 2015).
101. Automatic exchange of APAs is obligatory from 2017 onwards according to the Directive on Administrative Assistance (*supra* n. 98) and is part of the new BEPS minimum standard (*supra* n. **72**).
102. OECD, *Transfer Pricing Guidelines* (2010), para. 4.129 favours information of the other jurisdiction in cases of unilateral APAs; the Action 5 Final Report foresees a sophisticated system of exchange of rulings.

As far as issues related to manufacturing activities are concerned, specifically related to the lack of comparables data and to the allocation of location savings, some of the proposals developed by the Platform for Collaboration on Tax as well as by the EU JTPF could be considered to be implemented also in OBOR countries. To this end, the development of a network of multilateral safe harbours among the various countries could enhance the resolution of numerous issues related to the lack of comparable data and allocation of location savings. In this regard, the benefits of safe harbours are commonly known as being: compliance relief for taxpayers; certainty for taxpayers; and administrative simplicity for the tax administration.[103] However, all the numerous areas of concern should be properly addressed: the potential non-compliance with the arm's length principle; the risk of double taxation by the single tax administration of a specific country; the potential for tax planning opportunities for taxpayers; and potential equity and uniformity issues. Moreover, the development of a database including financial data of MNEs operating in OBOR countries could also be considered as a valid option.

Regarding services and financial transactions, the guidelines provided by international organizations might constitute a good source of reference for tax administrations and taxpayers, as well as practical tools for capacity building in transfer pricing matters. Moreover, also in this case, the development of a network of multilateral safe harbours among the OBOR countries for low value adding services (as well as for some types of financial transactions) and the development of a database including data on services and financial transactions in the OBOR countries could be beneficial solutions.

Regarding IP, the attribution of IP-related returns should be based on a thoughtful analysis of relevant functions, assets and risks related to the D(A)EMPE of such IP. Indeed, if OBOR countries consider legal ownership and contractual agreements as the sole factor in determining the allocation of profits, profits could be shifted improperly to other jurisdictions. Thus, implementing the OECD/UN approach to this matter would have a major effect on the entitlement to retain profits from intangibles. For example, if an entity located in a given OBOR country performs and controls the important value-creating DEMPE functions, it could retain profits independently if the entity that performs the DEMPE functions is the legal owner. Indeed, the mere legal ownership of an intangible will not by itself confer any right to retain all or a portion of ex ante returns derived from the exploitation of such intangibles.[104] On the other hand, if MNEs outside the OBOR provide intangibles to their affiliates in OBOR countries in return for royalties and other payments, those OBOR affiliates, if they contribute to the improvement of the original intangibles or create additional value, might retain some related profits (e.g., by means of a reduction of the royalty payments). In other words, in future, following the OECD/UN approach, the location of DEMPE functions should be considered as a key factor in OBOR countries when undertaking transfer pricing law modifications regarding IP.

---

103. UN, *Practical Manual on Transfer Pricing for Developing Countries*, supra n. 3, D.3.15.; Cooper et al., *World Bank Transfer Pricing Handbook*, supra n. 4, at 136, 318, 319; OECD, *Transfer Pricing Guidelines* (2017), supra n. 2, Chapter IV, section E.
104. OECD, *Actions 8-10 Final Reports*, supra n. 8, at 74, 84.

Moreover, it would be ideal for all countries to follow similar rules in an effort to reach common ground. In this context, the legal framework for IP protection, which is very well developed in the region (including copyright law, patent law, trademark law and laws against unfair competition), should also be carefully considered, as legal ownership is the starting point of the analysis to allocate income on the basis of the arm's length principle.[105] Moreover, regarding the definition of IP, the first action that OBOR countries could take would be to align the definition of intangibles with that suggested by the OECD/UN approach.

Regarding issues related to CCAs, the efforts of the OECD and UN to promote uniform rules on CCAs are commendable, especially considering the fact that the concept is new for many OBOR countries and they will probably 'borrow' rules from international bodies. In practice, when a country adopts rules on CCAs, the use of the OECD approach seems to be common. However, a further enhancement could derive from the promotion of the understanding of both types of CCA (i.e., 'service' and 'development') among the tax authorities in OBOR countries, so that MNEs could expect similar treatment of their subsidiaries and avoid suffering from excessive differences in documentation requirements. A bigger problem in this regard might be that the CCA mechanism might not comply with the local tax or corporate law. Therefore, it is recommended that an update of local laws to allow CCAs, be encouraged.

Regarding transfer pricing documentation, policy makers will have to balance the need of tax administrations for data against the administrative burden and costs for taxpayers. While tax administrations will seek to obtain as much information as possible, it must be borne in mind that every piece of transfer pricing documentation carries additional costs for a taxpayer without creating additional value, and thus has a negative effect on businesses. Therefore, following internationally agreed standards would help to take into account such diverging interests of tax administrations and taxpayers. First, it will allow tax administration to obtain information that was considered sufficient to evaluate transfer pricing by experienced stakeholders that participated in the design of such international standard and, second, preparing transfer pricing documentation according to the same rules and formats from one jurisdiction to the next will allow taxpayers to apply standardized processes and accordingly limit administrative costs. Finally, following international standards regarding transfer pricing documentation usually does not restrict tax administrations from further inquiries during a later tax audit, thus reducing the risk of the tax administrations obtaining incomplete information.

Moreover, it will be useful to require taxpayers to submit their transfer pricing documentation automatically in a timely manner. This will allow tax administrations to use such data not only during tax audits, but also for risk assessment,[106] thus helping

---

105. *See* UN Conference on Trade & Development (UNCTAD), *Investment Guide to the Silk Road 2014*, at 45–58 (2014), available at http://cf.cdn.unwto.org/sites/all/files/pdf/sr_investment _guide_2014.pdf.
106. Under the three-tier OECD approach, the country-by-country report, which is explicitly created as a risk assessment tool, and the master file will be useful sources of information for early risk assessment.

tax administrations to allocate resources most efficiently. Additionally, it will oblige taxpayers to prepare documentation contemporaneously to the actual transactions, thereby increasing the quality of the data and also increasing transfer pricing awareness among taxpayers.[107] However, in some countries, the submission of complete documentation will trigger time limits on future adjustments, and such countries might only oblige taxpayers to prepare documentation contemporaneously, but submit it only upon request.

Penalties for safeguarding transfer pricing regimes will not be needed in every jurisdiction, but will certainly be useful in most. This will depend on he observed level of compliance by taxpayers in a specific jurisdiction. However, the submission of proper transfer pricing documentation can be incentivized in other ways, as well. First, the fact that a failed submission will have effects on the risk assessment of such taxpayers will certainly positively affect submissions and, second, additional incentives, such as a shift in the burden of proof or a broader penalty protection for transfer pricing adjustments, could be built into a documentation regime, as well.

Regarding APAs, introducing a multilateral APA programme in the OBOR region could give businesses an opportunity to reach an agreement with the tax authorities in combination with other tax authorities on the future application of transfer pricing rules to their related-party transactions. Moreover, it provides taxpayers with certainty as regards an appropriate transfer pricing methodology and outcome, enhancing the predictability of the tax treatment of related-party transactions and limiting the prospect of a costly and time-consuming transfer pricing audit. For the tax authorities, an APA provides certainty as regards tax collections and is an effective cooperative compliance mechanism. But for this purpose, a multilateral APA framework compromises four substantive aspects. First, as mentioned, in the context of implementing a multilateral APA, it is highly relevant that transfer pricing rules among OBOR countries be on an equal footing; otherwise a multilateral understanding among tax authorities would be difficult – if not impossible – to achieve.

Second, before and after the submission of a multilateral APA, maintaining robust contemporaneous transfer pricing documentation must be considered by taxpayers, especially in the initial phase, as substantive information requests are to be expected by tax authorities, and the process requires the commitment of substantial resources by the taxpayer.

Third, for the discussion and negotiation phase, it would be advisable to establish specialized transfer pricing units that are separated into functional units within the same tax authority. Each of those special units could work alongside the same special units of the other tax authorities in the other jurisdictions. It could be the case that they overlap in the use of expertise and resources, but to a large degree each functional unit will be individually established. In turn, this would make the multilateral negotiation process much easier and faster, which is not a minor issue when it comes to financial resources. At this stage, it is also relevant to determine the 'critical assumptions' on which the multilateral APAs is based, so that if there is a change in the circumstances

---

107. For the first time explicitly mentioned in Chapter B.I of the Action 13 Final Report. OECD, *Action 13 Final Report, supra* n. 71.

on which a multilateral APA was agreed, the parties will no longer be bound by the multilateral APA. It is critical to distinguish in this phase those critical assumptions which might affect the multilateral APA as a whole, and those that might affect, for example, two or three jurisdictions, depending on the transaction under analysis. Finally, over the term of a multilateral APA, taxpayers should be required to lodge a brief annual report that proves their compliance with the agreed terms and conditions of the multilateral APA.

Finally, OBOR countries should adopt an active stance towards the BEPS initiative, as it already has – and will continue to have – worldwide tax implications. Special consideration should be taken to the digitalization of the economy which technically speaking face many challenges indeed, as the current international tax framework does not fit well. This may result in arbitrary taxation, inequities, double taxation, et cetera. It is also a fact that it seems very difficult, if not impossible, to ring-fence the digitalization of the economy in a meaningful way what could affect equally digitalized and non-digitalized businesses. Within this context, this is a solid opportunity for the region to take domestic tax reforms forward and to establish a more prominent role in the international community in terms of making international tax rules. Moreover, the new standards proposed by the UN and the OECD will bring more enforcement of existing anti-tax avoidance measures and will improve tax transparency. It is clear that the BEPS initiative will undoubtedly influence forthcoming actions over the next few years in the OBOR region.

CHAPTER 11

Tax Treaties Between Belt and Road Countries

Sathi Meyer-Nandi, David Orzechowski & Vladimir Tyutyuryukov

1 Introduction
2 Residency: Article 4 of the OECD and UN Models
    2.1 General Residency Criteria
    2.2 Tiebreaker: Individuals
    2.3 Tiebreaker: Persons Other than Individuals
3 Permanent Establishment: Article 5 of the OECD and UN Models
    3.1 Fixed Place of Business Permanent Establishment
    3.2 Specific Activity Exemptions
    3.3 Agency PE
    3.4 Insurance Undertakings
    3.5 Independent Agent
    3.6 Separate Entity
4 Transportation: Article 8 of the OECD and UN Models
    4.1 General Approach
    4.2 Taxation of the Leasing of Vessels, Vehicles and Containers
    4.3 Land Traffic
    4.4 Further Modifications Found in Article 8 of Chinese Treaties with Belt and Road Countries
5 Dividends: Article 10 of the OECD and UN Models
    5.1 General Taxing Rights
    5.2 Definition of Dividends
    5.3 PE Provision
    5.4 Further Modifications Found in Article 10 of Chinese Treaties with Belt and Road Countries
    5.5 Non-Tax BRI Treaties

6 Interest: Article 11 of the OECD and UN Models
   6.1 General Taxing Rights
   6.2 Definition of Interest
   6.3 PE Provision
   6.4 Determining the Source
   6.5 Arm's Length Interest Rate
   6.6 Further Modifications Found in Article 11 of Chinese Treaties with Belt and Road Countries
7 Royalties: Article 12 of the OECD and UN Models
   7.1 General Taxing Rights
   7.2 Mutual Agreement on Application
   7.3 Definition of Royalties
   7.4 PE Provision
   7.5 Determining the Source
   7.6 Arm's Length Royalties Rate
   7.7 Further Modifications Found in Article 12 of Chinese Treaties with Belt and Road Countries
8 Capital Gains: Article 13 of the OECD and UN Models
   8.1 General Taxing Rights
   8.2 Taxing the Alienation of PE Property
   8.3 Taxing the Alienation of Vessels and Vehicles
   8.4 Taxing the Alienation of Shares
   8.5 Taxing Rights in Other Cases
9 Income from Employment: Article 15 of the OECD and UN Models
   9.1 Article 15 of the OECD and UN Models
   9.2 Article 15(1) and (2) of Chinese Tax Treaties
   9.3 Article 15(3) of Chinese Tax Treaties with Belt and Road Countries
10 Directors' Fees: Article 16 of the OECD and UN Models
11 Method Articles: Article 23 of the OECD and UN Models
   11.1 Article 23A and 23B of the OECD and UN Models
   11.2 Application of the Method Articles in China
   11.3 Taxes Payable under Chinese Tax Treaties
   11.4 Indirect Tax Credit
12 Conclusion
   12.1 Tax Treaty Design Questions
   12.2 Suggestions
   12.3 Harmonization of Construction PE Timeframe
   12.4 Inclusion of Deemed PE for Insurance Undertakings
   12.5 Treatment of Oil and Gas Transportation by Pipeline
   12.6 Special Provision on Interest Income
   12.7 A Common Approach to Anti-Treaty Shopping

Chapter 11: Tax Treaties Between the Belt and Road Countries

1 INTRODUCTION

On 29 December 2014, China created the Silk Road Fund – an investment company controlled by the State Administration of Foreign Exchange, the China Investment Corporation, the Export-Import Bank of China and the China Development Bank. The total capital of this Fund will be USD 40 billion, contributed in instalments. The Silk Road Fund invests in projects in infrastructure, energy and resources, industrial capacity and financial sectors.[1] Total Chinese investment in the Belt and Road Initiative (BRI) is estimated at USD 890 billion, mostly financed through Chinese policy banks, and the payback period will be rather long.[2]

Chinese business has already invested in several project in Belt and Road countries, such as the Kazakhstan-China oil pipeline (from 1997); the Beineu-Bozoi-Shymkent gas pipeline (from 2010); the Kashagan oil field in the Caspian Sea (2013); two refineries and some roads in Kyrgyzstan; roads and a textile park in Tajikistan; a chemical processing plant and a 19.2-km tunnel in Uzbekistan. (Figure 11.1 shows further existing and planned gas pipelines between China, Central Asia and the Middle East, reported as constituting portions of BRI infrastructure.) Specifically, the Silk Road Fund invested in the Karot Hydropower Project in Pakistan; acquired 10% in SIBUR, a Russian gas processing and petrochemicals group; and signed a memorandum of understanding with Russian gas producer Novatek for the purchase of a 9.9% stake in one of its liquefied natural gas projects.[3] The China-Belarus Great Stone industrial park, located next to Minsk National Airport approximately 25 km east of Minsk, is under development.

According to a World Investment Report, by 2016 there were twenty-four Chinese companies on the list of the top 100 non-financial multinational enterprises (MNEs) from developing and transitional economies by foreign assets (along with thirteen Hong Kong companies). For comparison, other Belt and Road countries featured: Singapore, nine MNEs; India, six; Malaysia, five; and Russia, two. Chinese outward foreign direct investment in stock, in absolute terms, grew over thirty times from 2004 to 2016, increasing from USD 44.78 billion to USD 1.36 trillion (growing on average by 33.4% every year).[4] Chinese outward foreign direct investment in stock as a percentage of GDP over the same period increased fourfold, from 2.3% to 12.1%.[5] Mass media reports on China pursuing its business interests in the particular countries included financing and building roads to destinations deemed important for Chinese business; staffing building projects with Chinese employees; and acquiring resources and transporting them into China.

---

1. Silk Road Fund, *Overview*, http://www.silkroadfund.com.cn/enweb/23775/23767/index.html (accessed 12 Feb. 2018).
2. J. Kynge, *How the Silk Road Plans Will Be Financed*, Financial Times (9 May 2016), https://www.ft.com/content/e83ced94-0bd8-11e6-9456-444ab5211a2f (accessed 12 Feb. 2018).
3. J. Chen, *China's $40b Silk Road Fund Signs MoU with Russian Firms*, China Daily (3 Sep. 2015), http://www.chinadaily.com.cn/china/2015-09/03/content_21785297.htm (accessed 12 Feb. 2018); SIBUR, *10% Stake in SIBUR to Be Sold to China's Silk Road Fund* (14 Dec. 2016), http://investors.sibur.com/investor-news/2016/dec/14-12-2016-srf.aspx?sc_lang=en (accessed 12 Feb. 2018).
4. UNCTAD. *FDI outward stock, by region and economy*, 1990–2017, http://unctad.org/en/Pages/DIAE/World%20Investment%20Report/Annex-Tables.aspx (accessed 27 Jun. 2018).
5. *Ibid.*

Figure 11.1   Existing and Planned Gas Pipelines Between China, Central Asia and the Middle East

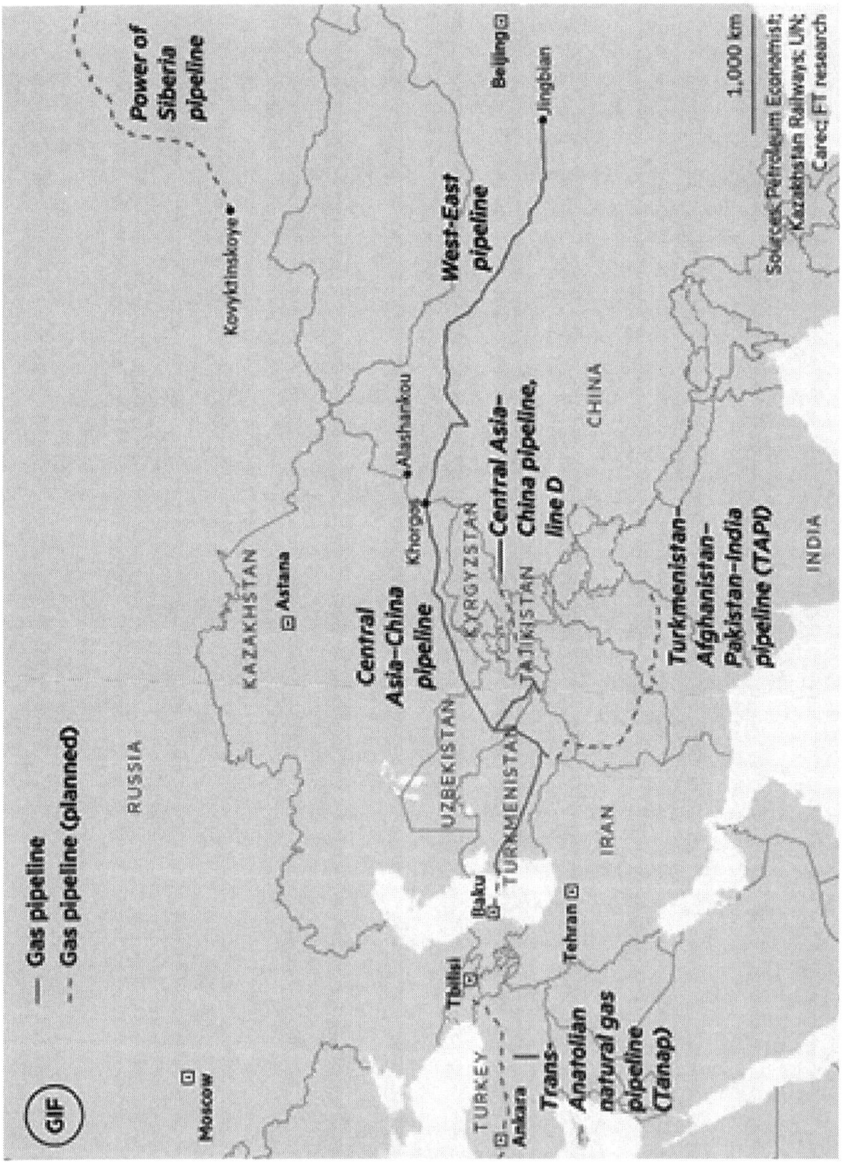

Source: Financial Times.[6]

---

6. Kynge, *supra* n. 2.

China is actively expanding its railroad connections. By January 2017, there were thirty-nine railroad lines connecting fifteen European and sixteen Chinese cities.[7] From 2013 through the beginning of 2017, first freight trains of China Railway Express Co. ran from Yiwu (China) to Zhengzhou (China) to Hamburg (Germany), Madrid (Spain), Riga (Latvia), Warsaw (Poland), London (United Kingdom), as well as to Kaluga region (Russia) and Tehran (Iran). Some of these lines already have weekly connections. Container traffic from China to Europe via Kazakhstan doubled by 2015, with Kazakhstan and Pakistan offering two critical land transport corridors between China and Europe and the Middle East.

The above facts suggest that the main direction of investment and transportation flows is from China into other Belt and Road countries. This chapter presents a comparative analysis of Chinese double taxation avoidance treaties (tax treaties) with fifty Belt and Road countries, namely: Albania, Armenia, Azerbaijan, Bahrain, Bangladesh, Belarus, Bosnia and Herzegovina, Brunei, Bulgaria, Croatia, Czech Republic, Egypt, Estonia, Georgia, Hungary, India, Indonesia, Iran, Israel, Kazakhstan, Kuwait, Kyrgyzstan, Laos, Latvia, Lithuania, Macedonia, Malaysia, Mauritius, Moldova, Mongolia, Oman, Pakistan, Poland, Philippines, Qatar, Romania, Russia, Saudi Arabia, Serbia and Montenegro, Singapore, Slovenia, Sri Lanka, Syria, Tajikistan, Turkey, Turkmenistan, Ukraine, the United Arab Emirates, Uzbekistan and Vietnam. Selected additional tax treaties are considered where appropriate.

This chapter follows the structure of the OECD (2014) and UN Model Tax Conventions (2011) (OECD and UN Models) and compares the respective provision of these Models and the above-mentioned tax treaties. Although covering the vast majority of Belt and Road countries, the authors recognize that there are differences in the scope of Belt and Road countries and, accordingly, some countries might be missing. Thus, the authors' selection constitutes a representative portion. At a future stage, the authors will perform a similar analysis of the remaining treaties between key Belt and Road countries.

2 RESIDENCY: ARTICLE 4 OF THE OECD AND UN MODELS

2.1 General Residency Criteria

Article 1 of the OECD Model (which corresponds with the UN Model) provides for the application of the tax treaty to 'residents' of one or both of the contracting states. As the domestic law of the contracting states is decisive in respect of determining the

---

7. J. Webb, *The New Silk Road: China Launches Beijing-London Freight Train Route*, Forbes (3 Jan. 2017), http://www.forbes.com/sites/jwebb/2017/01/03/the-new-silk-road-china-launches-beijing-london-freight-train-route/2/#56d8a26a7f9d (accessed 12 Feb. 2018); BBC, 'China Freight Train' in First Trip to Barking (3 Jan. 2017), http://www.bbc.com/news/business-38497997; *Silk Road Route Back in Business as China Train Rolls into London*, The Guardian (14 Jan. 2017), https://www.theguardian.com/world/2017/jan/14/china-silk-road-trade-train-rolls-london (accessed 12 Feb. 2018); GAU ARRKO, *Kaluga Region Is Part of New Silk Road. Europe and Asia Becomes Closer* (5 Feb. 2016), http://investkaluga.com/en/media/news/kaluzhskaya-oblast-chast-novogo-shelkovogo-puti--aziya-i-evropa-stali-blizhe/ (accessed 12 Feb. 2018).

residency of an individual or enterprise, there could be a scenario where the taxpayer may qualify as a tax resident in both states. This outcome could give rise to double taxation, leading to suboptimal levels of taxation. In these cases, the tax treaty provides a list of criteria under which the residence state will be determined for tax treaty purposes. The determination of exclusive residency is necessary, as the functioning of the allocation rules and the method article requires that there be only one residence state.[8]

Generally, Article 4 of the OECD Model (which is reproduced by the UN Model with one adjustment, namely the additional criterion of 'place of incorporation') stipulates a list of criteria in its paragraph 1 for determining residency. These include domicile, residence, place of management (to which the UN Model adds 'place of incorporation') or any other criterion of a similar nature. Under the Commentary on the OECD Model, the wording is aimed at covering the various forms of personal attachment to a state, which in the domestic tax laws form the basis of full liability to tax.[9] However, under Article 4(1) of the OECD and UN Models, the treaty residence of a person is still dependent on the domestic tax laws of each contracting state, which may result in a person's being resident in both states. In such cases, Article 4(2) determines a single treaty residence in the case of individuals. Article 4(3) does the same for persons other than individuals.

Chinese tax treaties with Belt and Road countries[10] all include a variant of Article 4 on residency. With regard to the criteria set out in paragraph 1 of the OECD and UN Models, under which a person is resident in a contracting state, the wording of the UN Model (with the additional criterion of place of incorporation) was adopted in the tax treaties with four countries.[11] Additionally, in four other tax treaties,[12] distinct criteria have been added, namely the place of head office and the place of registration. In the remaining tax treaties with Belt and Road countries, the criteria of place of head office and place of registration replace the place of incorporation or the place of management. Conspicuously, the rules on determining residency in the tax treaty with Kuwait have a parallel application. Accordingly, for the purposes of this treaty, the term 'resident of a Contracting State' in the case of Kuwait includes an individual who has his or her domicile in Kuwait and is a Kuwaiti national and a company which is incorporated in Kuwait; in the case of China, on the other hand, a resident is defined as any person

---

8. M. Lang, *Introduction to the Law of Double Taxation Conventions*, 2nd edition, at 77 (Linde 2013).
9. *OECD Model Tax Convention on Income and on Capital: Commentary on Article 4*, para. 8.
10. Albania, Armenia, Azerbaijan, Bahrain, Bangladesh, Bosnia and Herzegovina, Belarus, Brunei, Bulgaria, Croatia, Czech Republic, Egypt, Estonia, Georgia, Hungary, India, Indonesia, Iran, Israel, Kazakhstan, Kuwait, Kyrgyzstan, Laos, Latvia, Lithuania, Malaysia, Macedonia, Moldova, Mongolia, Nepal, Oman, Pakistan, Philippines, Poland, Qatar, Romania, Russia, Saudi Arabia, Serbia and Montenegro, Singapore, Slovakia, Slovenia, Sri Lanka, Syria, Tajikistan, Turkey, Turkmenistan, Ukraine, the United Arab Emirates, Uzbekistan and Vietnam.
11. China-Czech Republic tax treaty (2009); China-Estonia tax treaty (1998); China-Russia tax treaty (2014); China-Syria tax treaty (2010).
12. China-Israel tax treaty (1995); China-Kazakhstan tax treaty (2001); China-Romania tax treaty (2016); China-Singapore tax treaty (2007).

who, under Chinese law, is liable to taxation therein by reason of his or her domicile, residence, place of head office or any other criterion of a similar nature.[13]

2.2 Tiebreaker: Individuals

Insofar as individuals are concerned, the criteria under which the residence state is determined are found in Article 4(2) of the OECD Model (which is also reproduced by the UN Model). This paragraph lists in decreasing order of relevance a number of subsidiary criteria which should be applied if an individual is a resident of both contracting states and the preceding paragraph did not result in a conclusive outcome as regards the ultimate state of residency for treaty purposes. The criteria of permanent home, centre of vital interests, habitual abode and nationality are enumerated in sequence.

With regard to individuals, most Chinese tax treaties[14] with Belt and Road countries are generally identical to the wording of Article 4(2) of the OECD and UN Models. However, the treaty with Singapore stands out, as it is the only one in which Article 4(2)(d) provides that if a person has a habitual abode in both states or in neither of them, and has dual nationality of both states, the question on residency must be settled by mutual agreement.[15]

2.3 Tiebreaker: Persons Other than Individuals

As far as persons other than individuals are concerned, the criterion to determine the residence state is found in Article 4(3) of the OECD Model (which is reproduced by the UN Model). It deals with companies and other bodies of persons, irrespective of whether they are legal persons. It provides that the dual-resident person 'shall be deemed to be a resident only of the State in which its place of effective management is

---

13. *See* Article 4 China-Kuwait tax treaty (1989).
14. Albania-China tax treaty (2004); Armenia-China tax treaty (1996); Azerbaijan-China tax treaty (2005); Bahrain-China tax treaty (2002); Bangladesh-China tax treaty (1996); China-Belarus tax treaty (1995); Brunei-China tax treaty (2004); Bulgaria-China tax treaty (1989); China-Croatia tax treaty (1995); China-Czechoslovakia (Slovakia) tax treaty (1987); China-Egypt tax treaty (1997); China-Estonia tax treaty (1998); China-Georgia tax treaty (2005); China-Hungary tax treaty (1992); China-India tax treaty (1994); China-Indonesia tax treaty (2001); China-Iran tax treaty (2002); China-Israel tax treaty (1995); China-Kazakhstan tax treaty (2001); China-Kyrgyzstan tax treaty (2002); China-Laos tax treaty (1999); China-Latvia tax treaty (1996); China-Lithuania tax treaty (1996); China-Malaysia tax treaty (1985); China-Macedonia tax treaty (1997); China-Moldova tax treaty (2000); China-Mongolia tax treaty (1991); China-Nepal tax treaty (2001); China-Oman tax treaty (2002); China-Pakistan tax treaty (2000); China-Philippines tax treaty (1999); China-Poland tax treaty (1988); China-Qatar tax treaty (2001); China-Romania tax treaty (2016); China-Russia tax treaty (2014); China-Saudi Arabia tax treaty (2006); China-Serbia tax treaty (1997); China-Singapore tax treaty (2007); China-Slovenia tax treaty (1995); China-Sri Lanka tax treaty (2003); China-Syria tax treaty (2010); China-Tajikistan tax treaty (2008); China-Turkey tax treaty (1995); China-Turkmenistan tax treaty (2009); China-Ukraine tax treaty (1995); China-Uzbekistan tax treaty (1996); China-United Arab Emirates tax treaty (1993); China-Vietnam tax treaty (1995); China-Yugoslavia (Bosnia and Herzegovina) tax treaty (1988).
15. Article 4(2)(d) China-Singapore tax treaty (2007).

situated'. However, due to the modifications of the OECD Model in 2017 resulting from the BEPS Project, Article 4(3) of the OECD Model was replaced by the following:

> Where by reason of the provisions of paragraph 1 a person other than an individual is a resident of both contracting states, the competent authorities of the Contracting States shall endeavour to determine by mutual agreement the Contracting State of which such person shall be deemed to be a resident for the purposes of the Convention, having regard to its place of effective management, the place where it is incorporated or otherwise constituted and any other relevant factors.[16]

However, even before the BEPS Project commenced, the 2008 Update to the OECD Model had already introduced an alternative version of Article 4(3), under which the competent authorities of the contracting states could settle the question of residence.

As far as companies are concerned, the exact wording of Article 4(3) of the OECD and UN Models was incorporated into six Chinese treaties.[17] The treaty with Singapore includes a specification, stipulating as an additional rule, that if the place of effective management cannot be determined, the competent authorities of the contracting states must resolve the question by mutual agreement. Furthermore, twenty-one Chinese treaties[18] with Belt and Road countries do not ultimately refer to the place of effective management as the tiebreaker rule, but rather state that the competent authorities of the contracting states are to resolve the issue of residency by means of a mutual agreement procedure. This approach already reflects the changes to the tiebreaker rule envisaged through the BEPS Project and incorporated in the 2017 OECD Model. A modified version of this tiebreaker rule can be found in eight other treaties;[19] referring to the mutual agreement procedure only in the case where a person has the place of effective management of its business in one of the contracting states and the place of the head office of its business in the other contracting state. Additionally, in Chinese treaties with fourteen[20] other Belt and Road countries, the tiebreaker rule refers to the place of the head office rather than the place of effective management.

---

16. OECD, *Preventing the Granting of Treaty Benefits in Inappropriate Circumstances – Action 6: 2015 Final Report*, OECD/G20 Base Erosion and Profit Shifting Project, at 72 (OECD 5 Oct. 2015).
17. Azerbaijan-China tax treaty (2005); China-Czech Republic tax treaty (2009); China-Kuwait tax treaty (1989); China-Romania tax treaty (2016); China-Russia tax treaty (2014); China-Saudi Arabia tax treaty (2006).
18. Albania-China tax treaty (2004); Armenia-China tax treaty (1996); Bahrain-China tax treaty (2002); Belarus-China tax treaty (1995); Brunei-China tax treaty (2004); China-Estonia tax treaty (1998); China-Indonesia tax treaty (2001); China-Kazakhstan tax treaty (2001); China-Kyrgyzstan tax treaty (2002); China-Latvia tax treaty (1996); China-Lithuania tax treaty (1996); China-Moldova tax treaty (2000); China-Nepal tax treaty (2001); China-Oman tax treaty (2002); China-Philippines tax treaty (1999); China-Sri Lanka tax treaty (2003); China-Syria tax treaty (2010); China-Turkmenistan tax treaty (2009); China-Ukraine tax treaty (1995); China-Uzbekistan tax treaty (1996); China-Vietnam tax treaty (1995).
19. China-Egypt tax treaty (1997); Bangladesh-China tax treaty (1996); China-Hungary tax treaty (1992); China-Malaysia tax treaty (1985); China-Pakistan tax treaty (2000); China-Poland tax treaty (1988); China-Serbia tax treaty (1997); China-Yugoslavia (Bosnia and Herzegovina) tax treaty (1988).
20. Bulgaria-China tax treaty (1989); China-Croatia tax treaty (1995); China-Czechoslovakia (Slovakia) tax treaty (1987); China-Georgia tax treaty (2005); China-India tax treaty (1994); China-Iran tax treaty (2002); China-Israel tax treaty (1995); China-Laos tax treaty (1999);

3 PERMANENT ESTABLISHMENT: ARTICLE 5 OF THE OECD AND UN MODELS

3.1 Fixed Place of Business Permanent Establishment

The concept of a permanent establishment (PE) enshrined in Article 5 of the OECD and UN Models is critical to the determination as to whether an enterprise conducting business abroad will be subject to tax on its business activities. Only if a PE is established in a source state, will the profits of an enterprise of one state be taxable in the other state (the source state), and only to the extent that the profits are attributable to the permanent establishment. Article 5(1) of the OECD Model (which is reproduced by the UN Model) generally defines a PE as a fixed place of business through which the business of an enterprise is wholly or partially carried out.

This general definition can be found throughout Chinese tax treaties with Belt and Road countries, with two exceptions,[21] which have a slight twist in the wording, potentially resulting in a higher PE threshold in their definition of fixed place of business. Both treaties explicitly require that the enterprise of the other contracting state carry on the business in the other contracting state at a fixed place of business – rather than referring to business being carried out in the other contracting state through a fixed place of business. The subsequent Article 5(2) through (4) of the OECD Model (which is reproduced by the UN Model) enumerates (not exhaustively) common types of fixed place of business PEs and place of business that do not trigger the existence of a PE. Places of business that specifically can constitute a PE include a place of management; a branch; an office; a factory; a workshop; and a mine, an oil or gas well, a quarry or any other place of extraction of natural resources.

Approximately three-quarters of Chinese tax treaties[22] with Belt and Road countries include the OECD/UN wording of Article 5(2). The remaining treaties have

---

China-Macedonia tax treaty (1997); China-Mongolia tax treaty (1991); China-Qatar tax treaty (2001); China-Slovenia tax treaty (1995); China-Turkey tax treaty (1995); China-United Arab Emirates tax treaty (1993).
21. Albania-China tax treaty (2004); China-Iran tax treaty (2002).
22. Albania-China tax treaty (2004); Armenia-China tax treaty (1996); Azerbaijan-China tax treaty (2005); China-Belarus tax treaty (1995); Bulgaria-China tax treaty (1989); China-Croatia tax treaty (1995); China-Czech Republic tax treaty (2009); China-Czechoslovakia (Slovakia) tax treaty (1987); China-Estonia tax treaty (1998); China-Georgia tax treaty (2005); China-Hungary tax treaty (1992); China-Iran tax treaty (2002); China-Israel tax treaty (1995); China-Kazakhstan tax treaty (2001); China-Kyrgyzstan tax treaty (2002); China-Kuwait tax treaty (1989); China-Latvia tax treaty (1996); China-Lithuania tax treaty (1996); China-Macedonia tax treaty (1997); China-Mongolia tax treaty (1991); China-Oman tax treaty (2002); China-Philippines tax treaty (1999); China-Poland tax treaty (1988); China-Romania tax treaty (2016); China-Russia tax treaty (2014); China-Saudi Arabia tax treaty (2006); China-Serbia tax treaty (1997); China-Singapore tax treaty (2007); China-Slovenia tax treaty (1995); China-Sri Lanka tax treaty (2003); China-Syria tax treaty (2010); China-Tajikistan tax treaty (2008); China-Turkey tax treaty (1995); China-Turkmenistan tax treaty (2009); China-Uzbekistan tax treaty (1996); China-United Arab Emirates tax treaty (1993); China-Vietnam tax treaty (1995); China-Yugoslavia (Bosnia and Herzegovina) tax treaty (1988).

some additional business premises included, such as farms and plantations[23] and vineyards,[24] or other place where agriculture, forestry and plantation activities are carried out;[25] a refinery;[26] a warehouse (in relation to a person providing storage facilities for others);[27] and a sales outlet.[28] The Chinese treaty with India includes a noteworthy feature, stipulating that an installation or structure used for the exploration or exploitation of natural resources constitutes a PE, but only if so used for a period of more than 183 days.[29]

Furthermore, under Article 5(3) of the OECD Model, the PE definition also includes a building site, a construction or an installation project only if it lasts more than 12 months. The UN Model in Article 5(3) is broader, as it is divided into two further sections. Article 5(3)(a) includes in addition to the above, namely assembly projects as well as supervisory activities in connection with a building site, a construction, and an assembly or installation project. Another difference is that the UN Model reduces the minimum duration to six months. The UN Model further includes Article 5(3)(b) (absent in Article 5(3) of the OECD Model). It states that the PE definition further includes the provision of services, including consultancy services, by a company through its staff or other staff employed for this purpose if the activities last for more than 183 days in a 12-month period.

The precise wording of Article 5(3)(a) of the UN Model can be found in Chinese treaties with fourteen countries.[30] The remaining treaties differ as regards their time threshold. Some require 183 days,[31] others 9 months.[32] Then there are some stipulating

---

23. Brunei-China tax treaty (2004); China-Egypt tax treaty (1997); China-India tax treaty (1994); China-Indonesia tax treaty (2001); China-Laos tax treaty (1999); China-Malaysia tax treaty (1985); China-Moldova tax treaty (2000); China-Nepal tax treaty (2001); China-Qatar tax treaty (2001).
24. China-Moldova tax treaty (2000).
25. China-India tax treaty (1994).
26. Bahrain-China tax treaty (2002).
27. Bahrain-China tax treaty (2002); Bangladesh-China tax treaty (1996); China-India tax treaty (1994); China-Indonesia tax treaty (2001); China-Nepal tax treaty (2001); China-Ukraine tax treaty (1995).
28. China-Moldova tax treaty (2000).
29. Article 5(2)(i) China-India tax treaty (1994).
30. Bangladesh-China tax treaty (1996); Brunei-China tax treaty (2004); Bulgaria-China tax treaty (1989); China-Czechoslovakia (Slovakia) tax treaty (1987), China-Indonesia tax treaty (2001); China-Kuwait tax treaty (1989); China-Malaysia tax treaty (1985); China-Pakistan tax treaty (2000); China-Philippines tax treaty (1999); China-Poland tax treaty (1988); China-Saudi Arabia tax treaty (2006); China-Singapore tax treaty (2007); China-Vietnam tax treaty (1995); China-Yugoslavia (Bosnia and Herzegovina) tax treaty (1988).
31. China-India tax treaty (1994); China-Nepal tax treaty (2001); China-Sri Lanka tax treaty (2003).
32. Albania-China tax treaty (2004); China-Oman tax treaty (2002); China-Qatar tax treaty (2001); China-Syria tax treaty (2010).

12 months[33] or 18 months,[34] and others up to 24 months.[35] Further modifications can be found in Chinese treaties with Azerbaijan, Egypt, Georgia, Romania and Sri Lanka. For example, in the case of Egypt, activities falling under Article 5(3)(a) constitute a PE only if the duration is more than 12 months within a 24-month period.[36] The mentioning of assembly projects is absent in the tax treaties with Azerbaijan[37] and Georgia, and supervisory activities are not included in the treaties with Georgia[38] and Romania.[39] Additionally, the treaty with Sri Lanka includes in Article 5(3)(a) a drilling rig or ship used for the exploration or development of natural resources, as long as they last longer than 183 days in a 12-month period.[40] A similar provision can be found in five other Chinese tax treaties, however with different time thresholds (3 months,[41] 6 months[42] and 12 months[43]).

The wording of Article 5(3)(b) of the UN Model can be found in only three treaties.[44] In fourteen treaties,[45] the contracting parties omitted the inclusion of the provision in its entirety. In the remaining treaties, there were some modifications. The most common distinction (found in fourteen treaties)[46] in relation to Article 5(3)(b) is that the time threshold was lowered to a period of six months. In other treaties, these periods range from nine months,[47] to twelve months,[48] eighteen months[49] and even

---

33. Armenia-China tax treaty (1996); Azerbaijan-China tax treaty (2005); Bahrain-China tax treaty (2002); China-Croatia tax treaty (1995); China-Czech Republic tax treaty (2009); China-Estonia tax treaty (1998); China-Hungary tax treaty (1992); China-Iran tax treaty (2002); China-Israel tax treaty (1995); China-Kazakhstan tax treaty (2001); China-Kyrgyzstan tax treaty (2002); China-Laos tax treaty (1999); China-Latvia tax treaty (1996); China-Lithuania tax treaty (1996); China-Macedonia tax treaty (1997); China-Moldova tax treaty (2000); China-Romania tax treaty (2016); China-Serbia tax treaty (1997); China-Slovenia tax treaty (1995); China-Tajikistan tax treaty (2008); China-Turkey tax treaty (1995); China-Turkmenistan tax treaty (2009); China-Uzbekistan tax treaty (1996).
34. Belarus-China tax treaty (1995); China-Mongolia tax treaty (1991); China-Russia tax treaty (2014); China-Ukraine tax treaty (1995).
35. China-United Arab Emirates tax treaty (1993).
36. Article 5(3)(a) China-Egypt tax treaty (1997).
37. Azerbaijan-China tax treaty (2005).
38. China-Georgia tax treaty (2005).
39. China-Romania tax treaty (2016).
40. China-Sri Lanka tax treaty (2003).
41. Azerbaijan-China tax treaty (2005); China-Philippines tax treaty (1999).
42. China-Indonesia tax treaty (2001).
43. China-Croatia tax treaty (1995); China-Kazakhstan tax treaty (2001).
44. China-Nepal tax treaty (2001); China-Romania tax treaty (2016); China-Russia tax treaty (2014).
45. Bahrain-China tax treaty (2002); China-Estonia tax treaty (1998); China-Georgia tax treaty (2005); China-Iran tax treaty (2002); China-Laos tax treaty (1999); China-Latvia tax treaty (1996); China-Lithuania tax treaty (1996); China-Macedonia tax treaty (1997); China-Moldova tax treaty (2000); China-Pakistan tax treaty (2000); China-Qatar tax treaty (2001); China-Serbia tax treaty (1997); China-Syria tax treaty (2011); China-Uzbekistan tax treaty (1996).
46. *Ibid.*
47. Albania-China tax treaty (2004); China-Czech Republic tax treaty (2009); China-Oman tax treaty (2002).
48. Armenia-China tax treaty (1996); China-Hungary tax treaty (1992); China-Kazakhstan tax treaty (2001); China-Kyrgyzstan tax treaty (2002); China-Slovenia tax treaty (1995); China-Turkey tax treaty (1995).
49. Belarus-China tax treaty (1995); China-Mongolia tax treaty (1991); China-Ukraine tax treaty (1995).

twelve months in the tax treaty with the United Arab Emirates.[50] The treaty with India explicitly excludes technical services as defined in its Article 12 from its services PE definition.[51]

3.2 Specific Activity Exemptions

The specific activity exemption included in Article 5(4) of the OECD and UN Model excludes certain activities from constituting a PE. The UN Model has a more limited number of exclusions available from its PE definition, as it does not explicitly exclude facilities solely used for the purpose of delivery and stock maintained only for the purpose of delivery. Otherwise, both the OECD and UN Models correspond in their exempted activities, covering the use of facilities solely for the purpose of storage or display of goods or merchandise belonging to the enterprise;[52] the maintenance of a stock of goods or merchandise belonging to the enterprise solely for the purpose of storage or display;[53] the maintenance of a stock of goods or merchandise belonging to the enterprise solely for the purpose of processing by another enterprise;[54] the maintenance of a fixed place of business solely for the purpose of purchasing goods or merchandise or of collecting information, for the enterprise;[55] the maintenance of a fixed place of business solely for the purpose of carrying on, for the enterprise, any other activity of a preparatory or auxiliary character;[56] and the maintenance of a fixed place of business solely for any combination of above stated activities, provided that the overall activity of the fixed place of business resulting from this combination is of a preparatory or auxiliary character.[57]

However, the provision on specific activity exemption was subject to change in the 2017 OECD Model due to the recommendations resulting from the BEPS Project. According to the BEPS Project recommendations, countries have different options, including making all specific activities subject to an overall 'preparatory or auxiliary' requirement.[58] The future will reveal what China's decision with its Belt and Road country treaty partners will look like.

The list of exempted specific activities was incorporated into one Chinese treaty with a Belt and Road country, reproducing the wording of the UN Model.[59] In contrast, approximately 90%[60] of the treaties reproduce the wording of the OECD Model –

---

50. China-United Arab Emirates tax treaty (1993).
51. Article 5(2)(k) China-India tax treaty (1994).
52. Article 5(4)(a) *United Nations Model Double Taxation Convention between Developed and Developing Countries* (2011).
53. Article 5(4)(b) *UN Model* (2011).
54. Article 5(4)(c) *UN Model* (2011).
55. Article 5(4)(d) *UN Model* (2011).
56. Article 5(4)(e) *UN Model* (2011).
57. Article 5(4)(f) *UN Model* (2011).
58. OECD, *Preventing the Artificial Avoidance of Permanent Establishment Status – Action 7: 2015 Final Report*, OECD/G20 Base Erosion and Profit Shifting Project, at 28–29 (OECD 5 Oct. 2015).
59. China-Iran tax treaty (2002).
60. Albania-China tax treaty (2004); Armenia-China tax treaty (1996); Azerbaijan-China tax treaty (2005); Bahrain-China tax treaty (2002); Bangladesh-China tax treaty (1996); Belarus-China tax

meaning that Article 5(4)(a) and (b) include facilities for the purpose of deliveries, and the maintenance of a stock of goods for the purpose of delivery to fall within the PE exceptions. Other modifications are the inclusion of an additional paragraph including the maintenance of a fixed place of business for the purpose of advertising, or for the supply of information.[61] Additionally, the treaties with India, Pakistan and Vietnam do not include Article 5(4)(f), which excludes a combination of all activities if they can be considered as being of a preparatory or auxiliary nature.

3.3 Agency PE

Article 5(5) specifies the requirements for the establishment of an agency PE. Under the OECD Model, an agent must have, and habitually exercise, in a contracting state an authority to conclude contracts in the name of the enterprise. However, this is the case only if the activities conducted by the agent do not fall within the scope of the specific activities exempted under Article 5(4) of the OECD Model.

The UN Model contains a broader agency PE definition, as it includes an additional subparagraph, stipulating that a person without authority to conclude contracts in the name of the enterprise is nonetheless considered a dependent agent if the person habitually maintains a stock of goods or merchandise from which the person regularly delivers goods or merchandise on behalf of the enterprise.[62] This additional section is aligned witho the previous Article 5(4) of the UN Model, which does not – unlike the OECD Model – include the delivery of stock as an exempted activity.

However, the dependent agent PE definition was subject to change as a result of the BEPS Project. A dependent agent PE will arise not only where a dependent agent concludes contracts in the name of the enterprise, but also contracts for the transfer of, or for the granting of the right to use, property owned by that enterprise, or for the provision of services by that enterprise, where the agent habitually concludes

---

treaty (1995); Brunei-China tax treaty (2004); Bulgaria-China tax treaty (1989); China-Croatia tax treaty (1995); China-Czech Republic tax treaty (2009); China-Czechoslovakia (Slovakia) tax treaty (1987), China-Egypt tax treaty (1997); China-Estonia tax treaty (1998); China-Georgia tax treaty (2005); China-Hungary tax treaty (1992); China-Israel tax treaty (1995); China-Kazakhstan tax treaty (2001); China-Kyrgyzstan tax treaty (2002); China-Kuwait tax treaty (1989); China-Laos tax treaty (1999); China-Latvia tax treaty (1996); China-Lithuania tax treaty (1996); China-Malaysia tax treaty (1985); China-Macedonia tax treaty (1997); China-Moldova tax treaty (2000); China-Mongolia tax treaty (1991); China-Nepal tax treaty (2001); China-Oman tax treaty (2002); China-Philippines tax treaty (1999); China-Poland tax treaty (1988); China-Qatar tax treaty (2001); China-Romania tax treaty (2016); China-Russia tax treaty (2014); China-Saudi Arabia tax treaty (2006); China-Serbia tax treaty (1997); China-Singapore tax treaty (2007); China-Slovenia tax treaty (1995); China-Sri Lanka tax treaty (2003); China-Syria tax treaty (2010); China-Tajikistan tax treaty (2008); China-Turkey tax treaty (1995); China-Turkmenistan tax treaty (2009); China-Ukraine tax treaty (1995); China-Uzbekistan tax treaty (1996); China-United Arab Emirates tax treaty (1993); China-Yugoslavia (Bosnia and Herzegovina) tax treaty (1988).
61. Article 5(4)(e) China-Indonesia tax treaty (2001).
62. Article 5(5)(b) *UN Model* (2011).

contracts, or habitually plays the principal role leading to the conclusion of contracts that are routinely concluded without material modification by the enterprise.[63]

Most Chinese treaties with Belt and Road countries incorporate Article 5(5) of the OECD Model.[64] Only two treaties followed the UN Model with the additional subparagraph (b).[65] There are also treaty-specific modifications. For instance in the Chinese tax treaty with the Philippines, the contracting states do not exclude all activities stipulated in the specific activities exemption in Article 5(4). Rather, only activities limited to the purchase of goods or merchandise for the enterprise are excluded from the agency PE threshold.[66] The treaty with Kuwait contains distinct wording in its Article 5(5), as it also includes persons who regularly secure orders in the other contracting state wholly or almost wholly for the enterprise itself or for the enterprise and other enterprises which control or are controlled by that enterprise.[67]

3.4 Insurance Undertakings

The UN Model has a specific rule on PEs of insurance undertakings in its Article 5(6), stipulating that an insurance company – other than a reinsurer – is deemed to have a PE in the other contracting state if it collects premiums in this other contracting state or insures risks located therein. However, this does not apply to agents of an independent status, who fall within the scope of the subsequent paragraph.

This specific provision on insurance enterprises can be found in only seven Chinese treaties with Belt and Road countries.[68]

---

63. OECD, *Action 7 Final Report, supra* n. 58, at 16.
64. Albania-China tax treaty (2004); Armenia-China tax treaty (1996); Azerbaijan-China tax treaty (2005); Bahrain-China tax treaty (2002); Bangladesh-China tax treaty (1996); Belarus-China tax treaty (1995); Brunei-China tax treaty (2004); Bulgaria-China tax treaty (1989); China-Croatia tax treaty (1995); China-Czechoslovakia (Slovakia) tax treaty (1987); China-Estonia tax treaty (1998); China-Georgia tax treaty (2005); China-Hungary tax treaty (1992); China-India tax treaty (1994); China-Iran tax treaty (2002); China-Israel tax treaty (1995); China-Kazakhstan tax treaty (2001); China-Kyrgyzstan tax treaty (2002); China-Laos tax treaty (1999); China-Latvia tax treaty (1996); China-Lithuania tax treaty (1996); China-Malaysia tax treaty (1985); China-Macedonia tax treaty (1997); China-Moldova tax treaty (2000); China-Mongolia tax treaty (1991); China-Nepal tax treaty (2001); China-Oman tax treaty (2002); China-Poland tax treaty (1988); China-Qatar tax treaty (2001); China-Romania tax treaty (2016); China-Russia tax treaty (2014); China-Saudi Arabia tax treaty (2006); China-Serbia tax treaty (1997); China-Singapore tax treaty (2007); China-Slovenia tax treaty (1995); China-Sri Lanka tax treaty (2003); China-Syria tax treaty (2010); China-Tajikistan tax treaty (2008); China-Turkey tax treaty (1995); China-Turkmenistan tax treaty (2009); China-Ukraine tax treaty (1995); China-Uzbekistan tax treaty (1996); China-United Arab Emirates tax treaty (1993); China-Vietnam tax treaty (1995); China-Yugoslavia (Bosnia and Herzegovina) tax treaty (1988).
65. China-Indonesia tax treaty (2001); China-Pakistan tax treaty (2000).
66. Article 5(5) China-Philippines tax treaty (1999).
67. Article 5(5)(b) China-Kuwait tax treaty (1989).
68. Brunei-China tax treaty (2004); China-Egypt tax treaty (1997); China-Indonesia tax treaty (2001); China-Nepal tax treaty (2001); China-Pakistan tax treaty (2000); China-Sri Lanka tax treaty (2003), China-Vietnam tax treaty (1995).

3.5 Independent Agent

Article 5(6) of the OECD Model and Article 5(7) of the UN Model specify the definition of an independent agent, not triggering an agency PE. Accordingly, no PE is triggered if an enterprise carries on business through a broker, general commission agent or any other agent of an independent status, provided that the person acts in the ordinary course of his/her business. The UN Model, in addition to this wording, specifies that an agent is not regarded as independent if the agent's activities are devoted wholly or almost wholly to one enterprise and the conditions made or imposed between the agent and the enterprise differ from the conditions between independent parties.[69]

However, the independent agent definition in the 2017 OECD Model was subject to modification based on the BEPS Action 7 recommendations – bringing it closer to the UN Model. Accordingly, an agent would not be regarded as 'independent' if such person acts exclusively or almost exclusively for one or more enterprises to which it is closely related.[70]

Twelve Chinese treaties with Belt and Road countries have adopted the OECD Model provision before the 2017 modification.[71] As few as two treaties followed the UN Model.[72] However, the overwhelming majority have implemented a modified version, which includes a shortened version of the UN Model provision, solely stipulating that an agent cannot attain independent status when the activities of such agent are devoted wholly or almost wholly on behalf of that enterprise.[73]

3.6 Separate Entity

The last paragraph of Article 5 (Article 5(7) of the OECD Model and Article 5(8) of the UN Model) states that a subsidiary company in the other contracting state does not, of

---

69. Article 5(7) *UN Model* (2011).
70. OECD, *Action 7 Final Report, supra* n. 58, at 16.
71. Belarus-China tax treaty (1995); Bulgaria-China tax treaty (1989); China-Czech Republic tax treaty (2009); China-Georgia tax treaty (2005); China-Philippines tax treaty (1999); China-Qatar tax treaty (2001); China-Russia tax treaty (2014); China-Serbia tax treaty (1997); China-Slovenia tax treaty (1995); China-Tajikistan tax treaty (2008); China-Turkey tax treaty (1995); China-Ukraine tax treaty (1995).
72. Azerbaijan-China tax treaty (2005); China-Singapore tax treaty (2007).
73. Albania-China tax treaty (2004); Armenia-China tax treaty (1996); Bahrain-China tax treaty (2002); Bangladesh-China tax treaty (1996); Brunei-China tax treaty (2004); China-Croatia tax treaty (1995); China-Czechoslovakia (Slovakia) tax treaty (1987); China-Egypt tax treaty (1997); China-Estonia tax treaty (1998); China-Hungary tax treaty (1992); China-India tax treaty (1994); China-Indonesia tax treaty (2001); China-Iran tax treaty (2002); China-Israel tax treaty (1995); China-Kazakhstan tax treaty (2001); China-Kyrgyzstan tax treaty (2002); China-Kuwait tax treaty (1989); China-Laos tax treaty (1999); China-Latvia tax treaty (1996); China-Lithuania tax treaty (1996); China-Macedonia tax treaty (1997); China-Malaysia tax treaty (1985); China-Moldova tax treaty (2000); China-Mongolia tax treaty (1991); China-Nepal tax treaty (2001); China-Oman tax treaty (2002); China-Pakistan tax treaty (2000); China-Poland tax treaty (1988); China-Saudi Arabia tax treaty (2006); China-Sri Lanka tax treaty (2003); China-Syria tax treaty (2010); China-Turkmenistan tax treaty (2009); China-Uzbekistan tax treaty (1996); China-United Arab Emirates tax treaty (1993); China-Vietnam tax treaty (1995); China-Yugoslavia (Bosnia and Herzegovina) tax treaty (1988).

itself, constitute a PE of its parent company, as a subsidiary is a separate legal entity. However, if the requirements of Article 5(1) are met, i.e., a parent company has space at its disposal in the subsidiary's place of business, or if the requirements of Article 5(5) are met, a subsidiary may nevertheless constitute a PE of the parent company.

Without exception, all Chinese treaties with Belt and Road countries have implemented this provision.

4 TRANSPORTATION: ARTICLE 8 OF THE OECD AND UN MODELS

4.1 General Approach

Article 8 (Alternative A) of the UN Model reproduces Article 8 of the OECD Model, and both consider only the 'operation of ships or aircraft in international traffic' and the 'operation of boats engaged in inland waterways transport'. The exclusive taxing rights are attributed to the state in which the place of effective management of the transport operator is located (and if the place of effective management is aboard a ship or boat, to the state where the home harbour of such ship or boat is located, or where its operator is a resident).

The UN Model also provides an Alternative B, containing a separate paragraph on taxation of the operation of ships in international traffic. This paragraph shifts taxing right to the source state if the shipping activity there is 'more than casual'. Paragraph 13 of the Commentary on this article explains that 'more than casual' means scheduled or planned visits (both regular and irregular, but not fortuitous) of a ship to the source state to pick up freight or passengers. In this case, the source state has the right to tax the respective share of the operator's net profit. None of the analysed tax treaties includes this alternative.

The majority of the reviewed tax treaties refer to the residency of the operating company instead of the 'place of effective management' as foreseen by paragraph 5 of the Commentary on Article 8 of the UN Model.[74] Fifteen tax treaties, however, are based on the place of effective management.[75]

---

74. Albania-China tax treaty (2004); Armenia-China tax treaty (1996); Azerbaijan-China tax treaty (2005); Bahrain-China tax treaty (2002); Bangladesh-China tax treaty (1996); Belarus-China tax treaty (1995); Brunei-China tax treaty (2004); China-Croatia tax treaty (1995); China-Egypt tax treaty (1997); China-Estonia tax treaty (1998); China-Georgia tax treaty (2005); China-India tax treaty (1994); China-Indonesia tax treaty (2001); China-Iran tax treaty (2002); China-Israel tax treaty (1995); China-Kazakhstan tax treaty (2001); China-Kyrgyzstan tax treaty (2002); China-Latvia tax treaty (1996); China-Lithuania tax treaty (1996); China-Malaysia tax treaty (1985); China-Mauritius tax treaty (1994); China-Moldova tax treaty (2000); China-Oman tax treaty (2002); China-Philippines tax treaty (1999); China-Romania tax treaty (2016); China-Russia tax treaty (2014); China-Singapore tax treaty (2007); China-Sri Lanka tax treaty (2003); China-Syria tax treaty (2010); China-Tajikistan tax treaty (2008); China-Turkey tax treaty (1995); China-Turkmenistan tax treaty (2009); China-Ukraine tax treaty (1995); China-Uzbekistan tax treaty (1996); China-Vietnam tax treaty (1995).
75. Bulgaria-China tax treaty (1989); China-Czech Republic tax treaty (2009); China-Hungary tax treaty (1992); China-Kuwait tax treaty (1989); China-Laos tax treaty (1999); China-Macedonia tax treaty (1997); China-Mongolia tax treaty (1991); China-Pakistan tax treaty (2000); China-Poland tax treaty (1988); China-Qatar tax treaty (2001); China-Saudi Arabia tax treaty (2006);

Thirty-two Chinese tax treaties with other Belt and Road countries contain a rather limited wording of Article 8, reproducing the first and last paragraphs of Article 8 of the OECD Model[76] (of them, the tax treaty with Bangladesh covers only profits from the operation of aircraft; one more tax treaty – that with Iran – uses only the first paragraph of the OECD Model). Thus, all actual treaties in question omit inland waterways (which China has with only a little number of countries), and a majority of them ignore the place of effective management aboard a ship (which may be explained by reference to the residency principle).

4.2 Taxation of the Leasing of Vessels, Vehicles and Containers

Each Model differs in its treatment of income from the leasing of vehicles, containers and related equipment. The Commentary on the OECD Model treats leasing on a bareboat charter basis and operations with containers under Article 7 ('Business profits'), unless these are ancillary activities. The Commentary on the UN Model effectively covers this under Article 8 ('Shipping, inland waterways transport and air transport').

Most of the reviewed tax treaties provide no guidance on this issue. However, at least four tax treaties explicitly state that the profit from the operation of vessels and vehicles in international traffic includes that from rental on a bareboat basis and from the use, maintenance or rental of containers (including related equipment for the transport of containers).[77]

4.3 Land Traffic

At the same time, part of the Belt and Road goes on land (*see* the maps in Figures 11.2 and 11.3). Therefore, at least ten Chinese tax treaties, reflecting past experience of the respective parts of the Belt and Road, refer to land transport.[78] However, some of them

---

China-Serbia tax treaty (1997); China-Slovenia tax treaty (1995); China-United Arab Emirates tax treaty (1993); China-Yugoslavia (Bosnia and Herzegovina) tax treaty (1988).
76. Albania-China tax treaty (2004); Armenia-China tax treaty (1996); Azerbaijan-China tax treaty (2005); Bahrain-China tax treaty (2002); Bangladesh-China tax treaty (1996); Belarus-China tax treaty (1995); Brunei-China tax treaty (2004); China-Croatia tax treaty (1995); China-Egypt tax treaty (1997); China-Estonia tax treaty (1998); China-Georgia tax treaty (2005); China-Indonesia tax treaty (2001); China-Israel tax treaty (1995); China-Kazakhstan tax treaty (2001); China-Kyrgyzstan tax treaty (2002); China-Latvia tax treaty (1996); China-Lithuania tax treaty (1996); China-Malaysia tax treaty (1985); China-Mauritius tax treaty (1994); China-Moldova tax treaty (2000); China-Oman tax treaty (2002); China-Philippines tax treaty (1999); China-Romania tax treaty (2016); China-Russia tax treaty (2014); China-Sri Lanka tax treaty (2003); China-Syria tax treaty (2010); China-Tajikistan tax treaty (2008); China-Turkey tax treaty (1995); China-Turkmenistan tax treaty (2009); China-Ukraine tax treaty (1995); China-Uzbekistan tax treaty (1996); China-Vietnam tax treaty (1995).
77. China-India tax treaty (1994); China-Singapore tax treaty (2007); China-Tajikistan tax treaty (2008); China-Ukraine tax treaty (1995).
78. China-Kazakhstan tax treaty (2001); China-Kyrgyzstan tax treaty (2002); China-Laos tax treaty (1999); China-Latvia tax treaty (1996) (railway only); China-Mongolia tax treaty (1991);

use the term 'road vehicles'.[79] Whether the concept of such 'road vehicles' includes railroad vehicles, along with automobiles, is sometimes unclear. For example, the texts of the Chinese tax treaties with Kazakhstan and Kyrgyzstan in English use the term 'road vehicle', while in Russian and the respective national languages they refer to 'land vehicles'. However, in ambiguous cases, the English text prevails.

Table 11.1 summarizes the provisions of selected tax treaties between Belt and Road countries that are located along BRI transportation corridors. While these treaties are apparently OECD-based, many of them cover land transport, as well as specifically provide for the treatment of income from leasing vehicles, containers and related equipment.

This effectively means that the income from the operation of trains launched by China Railway Express Co., currently running between China and EU countries, is taxable in China. This is despite the fact that Chinese tax treaties with some EU countries (e.g., Germany, Poland, Spain) do not cover rail transport; in this case, Article 7 ('Business profits') may replace Article 8, as China Railway Express Co. does not necessarily create a permanent establishment in the respective European countries that are only train destinations.

If the Belt and Road countries would like to raise fiscal revenues from BRI transportation, the obvious answer is to engage their resident companies in the respective transportation).

China-Romania tax treaty (2016); China-Tajikistan tax treaty (2008); China-Turkey tax treaty (1995); China-Turkmenistan tax treaty (2009); China-Uzbekistan tax treaty (2009).
79. China-Kazakhstan tax treaty (2001); China-Kyrgyzstan tax treaty (2002); China-Turkmenistan tax treaty (2009); China-Uzbekistan tax treaty (2009).

Chapter 11: Tax Treaties Between the Belt and Road Countries

Figure 11.2   Existing and Planned Railroad Connections Through Central Asia and the Middle East

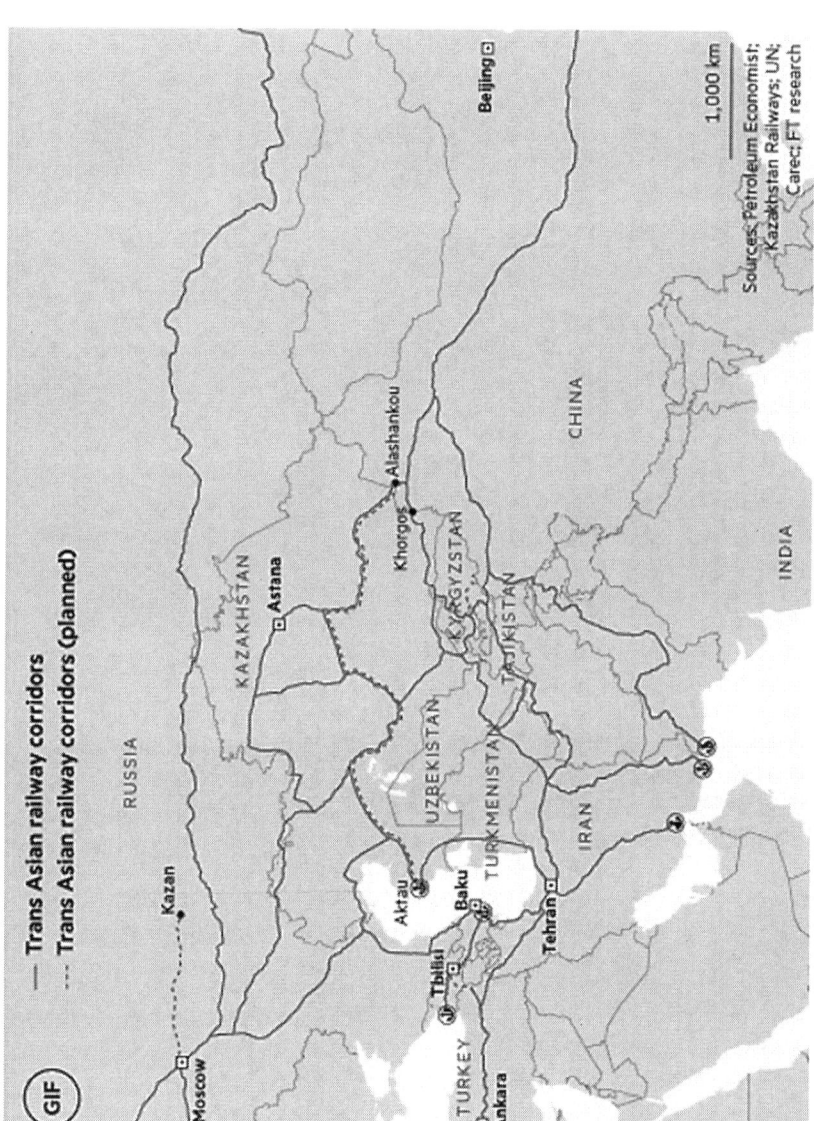

Source: Financial Times.[80]

---

80. J. Kynge, *How the Silk Road Plans Will Be Financed*, Financial Times (9 May 2016), https://www.ft.com/content/e83ced94-0bd8-11e6-9456-444ab5211a2f (accessed 12 Feb. 2018).

Figure 11.3 Railroad Connection from China to Selected European Destinations

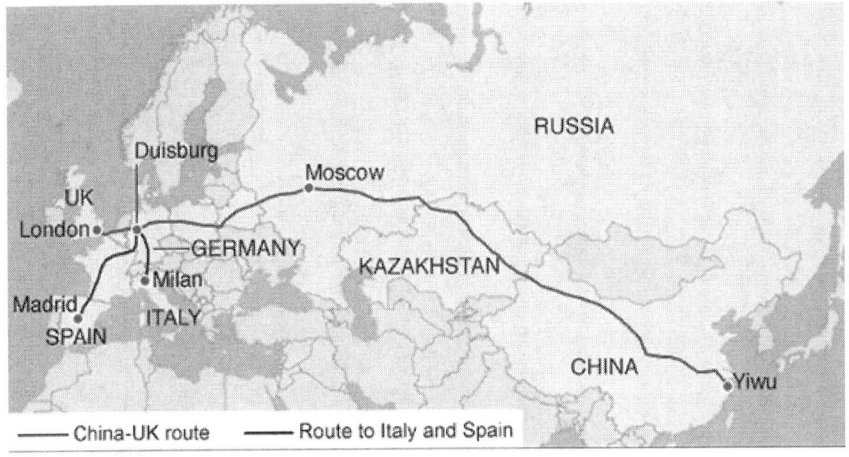

Source: BBC.[81]

Table 11.1 Features of Selected Tax Treaties, Applicable to Taxation of Transportation

Tax Treaty	Types of Transport Covered	Taxation of Leasing of Vehicles, Containers and Related Equipment	Pooling, JV or Operating Agency
Azerbaijan-Kazakhstan (1996)	Sea vessels, aircraft	Residence-based (if ancillary activity)	Yes
Azerbaijan-Russia (1997)	Sea and river vessels, aircraft, automobile and railroad transport	Residence-based	Yes
Belarus-China (1995)	Sea vessels, aircraft	Not specified	Yes
Belarus-Kazakhstan (1997)	Sea and river vessels, aircraft, automobile and railroad transport	Residence-based	Yes
Belarus-Poland (1992)	Sea and river vessels, aircraft, land transport	Residence-based	Yes

---

81. BBC, *supra* n. 7.

Chapter 11: Tax Treaties Between the Belt and Road Countries

Tax Treaty	Types of Transport Covered	Taxation of Leasing of Vehicles, Containers and Related Equipment	Pooling, JV or Operating Agency
Belarus-Russia (1995)	Sea and river vessels, aircraft, automobile and railroad transport	Residence-based	Yes
China-Kazakhstan (2001)	Sea vessels, aircraft, land transport	Not specified	Yes
China-Kyrgyzstan (2002)	Sea vessels, aircraft, land transport	Not specified	Yes
China-Russia (1994)	Any type of transport	Not specified	Yes
China-Tajikistan (2008)	Aircraft, land transport	Residence-based	Yes
Iran-Kazakhstan (1996)	Sea and river vessels, aircraft, automobile and railroad transport	Not specified	Not specified
Iran-Russia (1998)	Sea and river vessels, aircraft, automobile and railroad transport	Not specified	Not specified
Iran-Turkey (2002)	Ships, aircraft, land transport	Not specified	Not specified
Kazakhstan-Kyrgyzstan (1997)	Sea vessels, aircraft, automobile and railroad transport	Residence-based	Yes
Kazakhstan-Russia (1996)	Sea and river vessels, aircraft, automobile and railroad transport	Residence-based	Yes
Kazakhstan-Tajikistan (1999)	Sea vessels, aircraft, automobile and railroad transport	Residence-based (if ancillary activity)	Yes
Kazakhstan-Turkey (1995)	Sea vessels, aircraft, land transport	Residence-based	Yes
Kazakhstan-Uzbekistan (1996)	Sea and river vessels, aircraft, automobile and railroad transport	Residence-based	Yes

Tax Treaty	Types of Transport Covered	Taxation of Leasing of Vehicles, Containers and Related Equipment	Pooling, JV or Operating Agency
Russia-Turkey (1997)	Sea vessels, aircraft, road transport	Residence-based (only for sea vessels and aircraft)	Yes

4.4 Further Modifications Found in Article 8 of Chinese Treaties with Belt and Road Countries

While the wording of Article 8 in a majority of Chinese tax treaties with other Belt and Road countries is rather standardized, some of them contain additional provisions.

Four actual tax treaties provide for limited taxing rights of the source state. Those with Indonesia, Malaysia and Sri Lanka reduce the tax on profits from the operation of ships by 50% (as does the Russia-Turkey tax treaty). The tax treaty with the Philippines limits the withholding tax rate to 1.5% of gross revenue; a 1999 Protocol to it further provides for application by both parties of the lower rate or exemption if the Philippines provides for such in any other tax treaty (however, there is no corresponding obligation for China, should it conclude tax treaty with a similar reduction or exemption).

Two additional tax treaties, those with India and Singapore, extend the scope of Article 8 to the interest on funds 'directly connected with the operation of ships or aircraft in international traffic'.

Three more tax treaties, those with Oman, Qatar and the United Arab Emirates, also apply to the share of profit of Gulf Air derived from China, corresponding to share of the Sultanate of Oman, State of Qatar or the United Arab Emirates in its capital. The same remains true for the State of Qatar and United Arab Shipping Company.

Unlike other analysed treaties, the Russia-Turkey tax treaty provides for taxation of profits from the operation of aircraft and road vehicles only at operator's place of residence.

5 DIVIDENDS: ARTICLE 10 OF THE OECD AND UN MODELS

5.1 General Taxing Rights

Article 10(1) of the OECD Model, reproduced by the UN Model, allows the state where the recipient of dividends is a resident, to tax the dividends received. Article 10(2) of both Models further grants a limited right to tax the dividends to the source state and sets limits on such taxation. The OECD Model limits the applicable income tax withheld at source to 5% of the gross amount for dividends paid out to a company, which is a beneficial owner, resides in another contracting state and holds directly at least 25% of the capital of the company paying out the dividends; in other cases of beneficial ownership, a rate of 15% applies. The UN Model agrees with this approach but does

Chapter 11: Tax Treaties Between the Belt and Road Countries

not suggest withholding tax rates (although the Commentary on the UN Model mentions the 'traditional' ranges of rates of 5% to 15% for direct investment dividends and 15% to 25% for portfolio dividends). The UN Model also stipulates the lower threshold of 10% of direct participation to qualify for the application of a lower tax rate (again while not suggesting the actual withholding tax rate).

The majority of Chinese tax treaties limit the taxation at source to the 10% rate, provided that the dividend recipient is the beneficial owner thereof.[82] At least twelve Chinese treaties with Belt and Road countries additionally include a 5% tax rate on dividends if the recipient directly holds at least 25% of the shares in the company that pays out the dividends.[83] The threshold provisions may contain additional conditions for reduced tax rates, such as the amount of investment in capital[84] or the duration of the holding.[85] The tax treaty with Georgia provides for a conditional 0% rate if the beneficial owner holds at least 50% of the capital and invested more than EUR 2 million.

Additional Chinese tax treaties provide for lower standard withholding tax rates on dividends paid out to a beneficial owner, limiting the source state tax rate to 8%,[86] 7%,[87] 5%[88] or 3%.[89] The tax treaty with Malaysia exempts the dividends paid out by a Malaysian company to a Chinese resident from taxation at source. The tax treaty with the Philippines specifies a 10% rate for dividends if a beneficial owner holds directly at least 10% of the capital and a 15% rate for other cases of beneficial ownership.

Several tax treaties provide for a branch profits tax – a tax on the net profit of a permanent establishment in a host state.[90] Apparently, this clause is found in tax treaties with countries that apply such a tax.

---

82. Albania-China tax treaty (2004); Azerbaijan-China tax treaty (2005); Bangladesh-China tax treaty (1996); Belarus-China tax treaty (1995); Bulgaria-China tax treaty (1989); China-Georgia tax treaty (2005); China-Hungary tax treaty (1992); China-India tax treaty (1994); China-Indonesia tax treaty (2001); China-Iran tax treaty (2002); China-Israel tax treaty (1995); China-Kazakhstan tax treaty (2001); China-Kyrgyzstan tax treaty (2002); China-Malaysia tax treaty (1985) (if paid by Chinese resident); China-Pakistan tax treaty (2000); China-Poland tax treaty (1988); China-Qatar tax treaty (2001); China-Sri Lanka tax treaty (2003); China-Turkey tax treaty (1995); China-Uzbekistan tax treaty (1996); China-Vietnam tax treaty (1995); China-Yugoslavia (Bosnia and Herzegovina) tax treaty (1988).
83. Armenia-China tax treaty (1996); China-Czech Republic tax treaty (2009); China-Estonia tax treaty (1998); China-Latvia tax treaty (1996); China-Lithuania tax treaty (1996); China-Moldova tax treaty (2000); China-Russia tax treaty (2014); China-Singapore tax treaty (2007); China-Syria tax treaty (2010); China-Tajikistan tax treaty (2008); China-Turkmenistan tax treaty (2009); China-Ukraine tax treaty (1995).
84. Article 10(2)(b) China-Georgia tax treaty (2005) (10% and over EUR 100,000); Article 10(2)(a) China-Russia tax treaty (2014) (25% and equivalent of EUR 80,000).
85. Article 10(2)(a) Belgium-China tax treaty (2009) (at least 12 consecutive months).
86. China-Egypt tax treaty (1997).
87. China-United Arab Emirates tax treaty (1993).
88. Bahrain-China tax treaty (2002); Brunei-China tax treaty (2004); China-Croatia tax treaty (1995); China-Kuwait tax treaty (1989); China-Laos tax treaty (1999); China-Macedonia tax treaty (1997); China-Mauritius tax treaty (1994); China-Mongolia tax treaty (1991); China-Oman tax treaty (2002); China-Saudi Arabia tax treaty (2006); China-Serbia tax treaty (1997); China-Slovenia tax treaty (1995).
89. China-Romania tax treaty (2016).
90. For example., Article 10(6) China-Kazakhstan tax treaty (2001) (rate limited to 5%); Article 10(5) China-Indonesia tax treaty (2001) (rate limited to 10%).

On the one hand, all reviewed tax treaties allow the states receiving the investments to secure tax revenue; on the other hand, such tax revenue is restricted by the withholding tax rate, which may be lower than that established under domestic law. At the same time, host countries may choose to exempt dividends under their domestic law. Kazakhstan is an example of this approach, exempting dividends from shares paid to non-residents in two cases: if shares are quoted on the national stock exchange or if shares of company not involved in the mineral extraction industry are owned for at least three consecutive years.

5.2 Definition of Dividends

Both Models provide the same definition of dividends, using as a last resort the reference to the laws of the state where the company distributing the dividends is a resident, and this is effectively reproduced in all reviewed tax treaties. This last-resort provision allows those countries that have adopted Islamic finance instruments and normally treat the respective income as dividends, to use the same treatment at the international level (even while the tax treaties normally do not explicitly cover the income from Islamic finance instruments).

An issue may arise with regard to income derived from tax transparent entities, e.g., from participation in certain forms of non-incorporated partnerships or consortia. In Belt and Road countries, these are popular business arrangements in the mineral extraction industry and exist in some infrastructure projects. The reviewed tax treaties do not specifically cover such type of income, leaving the treatment to domestic law and mutual agreement procedures.

5.3 PE Provision

Article 10(4) generally provides that Article 10(1) and (2) does not apply to certain dividends if the recipient has a PE in the source state and the holding in respect of which the dividends paid belongs to this PE (the so-called PE provision). In this case, Article 7 of the OECD Model will be applicable, taking precedence over Article 10. Article 10(4) of the OECD Model generally is reproduced by the UN Model, albeit with one modification. Whereas the UN Model explicitly mentions a fixed base as well as a PE, the OECD Model refers only to a PE. Furthermore, this limitation applies under the OECD Model only if the holding in respect of which the dividend is paid is effectively connected with the PE. Thus, it limits the scope of Article 10(1) and (2), which is consistent with this rule, as it provides that if the holding is effectively connected with the PE or fixed base in the source state, the source state will not have to limit its taxing rights to the respective interest income.

All reviewed tax treaties follow Article 10(4) of the UN Model, which includes the wording on the fixed base of independent personal services.

5.4 Further Modifications Found in Article 10 of Chinese Treaties with Belt and Road Countries

Three Chinese tax treaties with other Belt and Road countries include an anti-treaty-shopping provision, usually as the last paragraph of the article.[91] It denies the application of Article 10 to those situations where the main purpose of the arrangement is to take advantage of tax treaty provisions. However, there is no further specification as to what constitutes 'tak(ing) advantage of this Article by means of that creation or assignment' – reduction of tax liabilities or profit shifting (along with reduced tax liability).

A unique provision in the Chinese tax treaties with Kuwait and the United Arab Emirates is the exclusive taxing right in the hands of the recipient (and full exemption in the source state) if the dividend recipient is a national government, any of its institutions, any entity wholly owned by the government or a resident company where the government own at least 20%. A similar provision is found in the tax treaty with Romania, which applies if the dividend recipient is a national government, a governing body of political subdivision or a company owned more than 50% by those.

A 1999 Protocol to the tax treaty with the Philippines obliges the Philippines to grant a lower rate or exemption from income tax on dividends if they provide for such lower rate or exemption in any other tax treaty (however, there is no mirroring of this for China).

5.5 Non-Tax BRI Treaties

Another investment opportunity, currently somewhat hindered by political developments and economic decline, is the common trade zone of the Eurasian Economic Union (EAEU) of Armenia, Belarus, Kazakhstan, Kyrgyzstan and Russia, based on the EAEU Treaty of 2014. Its major benefits are a relatively free flow of locally produced goods, uniform requirements for trade across EAEU customs borders and relaxed regulations for internal migration. However, as EAEU Member States did not harmonize corporate taxation to any extent, the tax burden on profit of MNEs differs across these countries – and so do the taxation of dividends and the respective benefits under tax treaties. For example, Russia does not tax income of non-resident companies from rendering of services to its residents, while other EAEU Member States do. Therefore, non-residents in those four countries benefit from the 'Business income' article of tax treaties. Armenia and Kazakhstan exempt dividends domestically, subject to certain ownership criteria; therefore, tax treaties may provide more benefits for dividends from subsidiaries in the three remaining countries.

Some projects are protected under non-tax treaties and applicable domestic law, such as the Agreement on the China-Belarus Industrial Park. In Belarus, Decree 326, adopted within the framework of this agreement, exempts residents of the Park from

---

91. Article 10(8) China-Romania tax treaty (2016); Article 10(6) China-Russia tax treaty (2014); Article 10(6) China-Singapore tax treaty (2007).

corporate profits tax, real estate tax and land tax for ten years from the date of their registration as Park residents; provides for a 50% reduction of liabilities for the same taxes for ten additional years; and establishes a 0% rate on dividends and similar income for five years from the year when gross profit first arose.[92]

6 INTEREST: ARTICLE 11 OF THE OECD AND UN MODELS

6.1 General Taxing Rights

Under Article 11(1) of the OECD Model (reproduced by the UN Model), the residence state of the recipient of interest income has the right to tax this income. However, if the 'beneficial owner of the interest is a resident of the other Contracting State', under Article 11(2), the source state has only a restricted right to tax, limited to a certain rate. Whereas the OECD Model provides that the restricted tax in the source state 'shall not exceed 10% of the gross amount of the interest', the UN Model leaves this rate to the contracting parties to decide in their treaty negotiations.

Article 11(1) was adopted in all but two Chinese tax treaties with Belt and Road countries. The treaty with Bahrain refers not only to interest but also to 'income from debt-claims'.[93] The treaty with Russia (as amended through 2015) even grants the resident state the exclusive right to tax interest income.[94]

The exact wording of Article 11 (2) was adopted by some Belt and Road countries, limiting the source state right to tax to 3%,[95] 7.5%,[96] 8%[97] or 10%[98] of the gross amount of the interest. However, the majority of Chinese treaties with Belt and Road countries include an alternative wording based on the pre-September 1995 version, which uses the wording 'if the recipient is the beneficial owner of the dividends'. According to the Commentary on the OECD Model, the rationale for the change of wording is to clarify that the limitation to tax in the source state is not available when an intermediary is interposed, unless the beneficial owner is a resident of the other contracting state.[99] However, the majority of Chinese treaties with Belt and Road countries include the older wording, as well as the limitation of the source state tax rate to 5%,[100] 7%,[101] or 10%.[102]

---

92. BY: Presidential Decree 326 of 30 June 2014 on activities of Chinese-Belarusian Industrial Park 'Great Stone Industrial Park'.
93. Article 11(1) Bahrain-China tax treaty (2002).
94. Article 11(1) China-Russia tax treaty (2014).
95. China-Romania tax treaty (2016).
96. China-Czech Republic tax treaty (2009).
97. China-Tajikistan tax treaty (2008).
98. Azerbaijan-China tax treaty (2005); China-Georgia tax treaty (2005); China-Indonesia tax treaty (2001); China-Turkmenistan tax treaty (2009).
99. *OECD Model: Commentary on Article 11(2)* para. 11 (2014).
100. China-Kuwait tax treaty (1989); China-Laos tax treaty (1999).
101. China-Israel tax treaty (1995); China-Singapore tax treaty (2007); China-United Arab Emirates tax treaty (1993).
102. Albania-China tax treaty (2004); Armenia-China tax treaty (1996); Bahrain-China tax treaty (2002); Bangladesh-China tax treaty (1996); Belarus-China tax treaty (1995); Brunei-China tax treaty (2004); Bulgaria-China tax treaty (1989); China-Croatia tax treaty (1995);

6.2 Definition of Interest

Article 11(3) of the OECD Model (reproduced by the UN Model) defines the term 'interest'. This definition includes income from debt claims of every kind, in particular income from government securities and income from bonds or debentures, including premiums and prizes attaching to such securities. However, penalty charges for late payment are explicitly excluded from the definition in the OECD and UN Models.

All but three[103] Chinese treaties with Belt and Road countries include the exact wording of the OECD and UN Models.

6.3 PE Provision

Both the OECD and UN Models effectively reproduce the PE provision in respect of interest (adjusting respectively the wording on dividends and holding). The UN Model, however, additionally adopts a limited force of attraction rule in its Article 7(1)(c), which also attributes to the PE those business profit of business activities carried on in the source state of the same or similar kind as those effected through a PE.[104] Thus, it limits the scope of Article 11(1) and (2), which is consistent with this rule, as it allows that if the debt claim is effectively connected with the PE or fixed base or with business activities in the source state of the same or similar kind as those effected through the permanent establishment, the source state will not have to limit its taxing rights to the respective interest income.

None of the Chinese treaties with Belt and Road countries contains the limited force of attraction rule. However, all but one[105] mention in addition to the PE, the fixed base for independent personal services.

6.4 Determining the Source

Article 11(5) of the OECD Model specifies that interest is deemed to be from sources in the residence country of the payer. The wording encapsulates the principle that the source state of the interest is the state in which the payer of the interest is resident. An

---

China-Czechoslovakia (Slovakia) tax treaty (1987); China-Egypt tax treaty (1997); China-Estonia tax treaty (1998); China-Hungary tax treaty (1992); China-India tax treaty (1994); China-Iran tax treaty (2002); China-Kazakhstan tax treaty (2001); China-Kyrgyzstan tax treaty (2002); China-Latvia tax treaty (1996); China-Lithuania tax treaty (1996); China-Malaysia tax treaty (1985); China-Macedonia tax treaty (1997); China-Moldova tax treaty (2000); China-Mongolia tax treaty (1991); China-Nepal tax treaty (2001); China-Oman tax treaty (2002); China-Pakistan tax treaty (2000); China-Philippines tax treaty (1999); China-Poland tax treaty (1988); China-Qatar tax treaty (2001); China-Saudi Arabia tax treaty (2006); China-Serbia tax treaty (1997); China-Singapore tax treaty (2007); China-Slovenia tax treaty (1995); China-Sri Lanka tax treaty (2003); China-Syria tax treaty (2010); China-Turkey tax treaty (1995); China-Ukraine tax treaty (1995); China-Uzbekistan tax treaty (1996); China-Vietnam tax treaty (1995); China-Yugoslavia (Bosnia and Herzegovina) tax treaty (1988).
103. China-Indonesia tax treaty (2001); China-Malaysia tax treaty (1985); China-Turkey tax treaty (1995).
104. *UN Model: Commentary on Article 11(3)* para. 20 (2011).
105. China-Czech Republic tax treaty (2009).

exception to this general principle applies if the reason for the loan has an obvious economic link with the PE in the other contracting state. The UN Model has a slight modification, as it also refers to a fixed base as well as a PE. In this case, the interest will be deemed to arise in the contracting state in which the PE (or in the case of the UN Model – including the fixed base) is situated.

Article 11(5) of the OECD Model is included in two[106] Chinese tax treaties with Belt and Road countries. China's amended tax treaty with Russia does not include such a provision.[107] All other Chinese treaties with Belt and Road countries include, in addition to the residency of the payer as the nexus for determining the source state, also if the payer is the state itself, or a local authority.[108]

6.5 Arm's Length Interest Rate

Finally, Article 11(6), the last paragraph of Article 11 of the OECD Model (reproduced by the UN Model), has the purpose of restricting the application of Article 11 in cases where, by reason of a special relationship between the payer and the beneficial owner or between both of them and some other person, the amount of the interest paid exceeds the amount which would have been agreed upon by the payer and the beneficial owner had they agreed on an amount of interest at arm's length. This provision gives the source state the right to tax the excess portion of such interest payments, i.e., exceeding the arm's length amount, under its laws.

This wording has been adopted in all Chinese tax treaties with Belt and Road countries.

---

106. China-Czech Republic tax treaty (2009); China-Romania tax treaty (2016).
107. Article 5 China-Russia tax treaty (2014).
108. Albania-China tax treaty (2004); Armenia-China tax treaty (1996); Azerbaijan-China tax treaty (2005); Bahrain-China tax treaty (2002); Bangladesh-China tax treaty (1996); Belarus-China tax treaty (1995); Brunei-China tax treaty (2004); Bulgaria-China tax treaty (1989); China-Croatia tax treaty (1995); China-Czechoslovakia (Slovakia) tax treaty (1987); China-Egypt tax treaty (1997); China-Estonia tax treaty (1998); China-Georgia tax treaty (2005); China-Hungary tax treaty (1992); China-India tax treaty (1994); China-Indonesia tax treaty (2001); China-Iran tax treaty (2002); China-Israel tax treaty (1995); China-Kazakhstan tax treaty (2001); China-Kuwait tax treaty (1989); China-Kyrgyzstan tax treaty (2002); China-Laos tax treaty (1999); China-Latvia tax treaty (1996); China-Lithuania tax treaty (1996); China-Macedonia tax treaty (1997); China-Malaysia tax treaty (1985); China-Moldova tax treaty (2000); China-Mongolia tax treaty (1991); China-Nepal tax treaty (2001); China-Oman tax treaty (2002); China-Pakistan tax treaty (2000); China-Philippines tax treaty (1999); China-Poland tax treaty (1988); China-Qatar tax treaty (2001); China-Saudi Arabia tax treaty (2006); China-Serbia tax treaty (1997); China-Singapore tax treaty (2007); China-Slovenia tax treaty (1995); China-Sri Lanka tax treaty (2003); China-Syria tax treaty (2010); China-Tajikistan tax treaty (2008); China-Turkey tax treaty (1995); China-Turkmenistan tax treaty (2009); China-Ukraine tax treaty (1995); China-United Arab Emirates tax treaty (1993); China-Uzbekistan tax treaty (1996); China-Vietnam tax treaty (1995); China-Yugoslavia (Bosnia and Herzegovina) tax treaty (1988).

6.6 Further Modifications Found in Article 11 of Chinese Treaties with Belt and Road Countries

Except for three treaties,[109] all other Chinese with Belt and Road countries contain additional paragraphs to the interest article that are not derived from either the OECD or UN Model. Two-thirds of all Chinese treaties with Belt and Road countries[110] have included a provision stipulating that interest arising in a contracting state and derived by the government of the other contracting state, a local authority or the Central Bank thereof or any financial institution wholly owned by the government of that other state, is to be exempt from tax in the first-mentioned state. Other treaties include a detailed definition on what constitutes a government, local authority or central bank.[111] Still other Chinese treaties, such as that with Kuwait, include a broader provision, applying the special rule for interest withholding tax to: '(...) a company which is resident of the other Contracting State whose shares are at least 20% owned directly or indirectly by the Government of that other Contracting State'.

Additionally, two Chinese treaties include anti-avoidance rules in their interest article, stipulating that the article will not apply if it was the main purpose of any person concerned with the creation or assignment of the debt-claim in respect of which the interest is paid, to take advantage of this article by means of that creation or assignment.[112] Some Chinese treaties include further exemptions, including that with Malaysia. Accordingly, interest to which a resident of China is beneficially entitled is exempt from Malaysian tax if the loan or other indebtedness in respect of which the interest is paid is an approved loan as defined in section 2(1) of the Income Tax Act, 1967 of Malaysia.[113]

---

109. Bosnia and Herzegovina-China tax treaty (1988); China-Israel tax treaty (1995); China-Slovenia tax treaty (1995).
110. Albania-China tax treaty (2004); Armenia-China tax treaty (1996); Azerbaijan-China tax treaty (2005); Bahrain-China tax treaty (2002); Bangladesh-China tax treaty (1996); Belarus-China tax treaty (1995); Bulgaria-China tax treaty (1989); China-Croatia tax treaty (1995); China-Czechoslovakia (Slovakia) tax treaty (1987); China-Egypt tax treaty (1997); China-Estonia tax treaty (1998); China-Georgia tax treaty (2005); China-Hungary tax treaty (1992); China-India tax treaty (1994); China-Iran tax treaty (2002); China-Kazakhstan tax treaty (2001); China-Kyrgyzstan tax treaty (2002); China-Latvia tax treaty (1996); China-Lithuania tax treaty (1996); China-Macedonia tax treaty (1997); China-Moldova tax treaty (2000); China-Mongolia tax treaty (1991); China-Nepal tax treaty (2001); China-Philippines tax treaty (1999); China-Poland tax treaty (1988); China-Qatar tax treaty (2001); China-Saudi Arabia tax treaty (2006); China-Serbia tax treaty (1997); China-Sri Lanka tax treaty (2003); China-Syria tax treaty (2010); China-Tajikistan tax treaty (2008); China-Ukraine tax treaty (1995); China-Uzbekistan tax treaty (1996).
111. Azerbaijan-China tax treaty (2005); Brunei-China tax treaty (2004); China-Czech Republic tax treaty (2009); China-Kuwait tax treaty (1989); China-Laos tax treaty (1999); China-Malaysia tax treaty (1985); China-Oman tax treaty (2002); China-Pakistan tax treaty (2000); China-Singapore tax treaty (2007); China-Turkey tax treaty (1995); China-Turkmenistan tax treaty (2009); China-United Arab Emirates tax treaty (1993); China-Vietnam tax treaty (1995).
112. China-Singapore tax treaty (2007); China-Russia tax treaty (2014).
113. Article 11(3) China-Malaysia tax treaty (1985).

7 ROYALTIES: ARTICLE 12 OF THE OECD AND UN MODELS

7.1 General Taxing Rights

Unlike the earlier examples of dividends and interest, the OECD and UN Models allocate taxing rights in respect of royalties differently.

Under Article 12(1) of the OECD Model, the residence state of the recipient of royalties has the exclusive right to tax this income only if such recipient is a beneficial owner of the royalties. The Commentary on OECD Model further explains this as follows: 'the State of source is not obliged to give up taxing rights over royalty income merely because that income was paid directly to a resident of a State with which the State of source had concluded a convention'. At the same time, if the recipient is not a beneficial owner, its residence state is not entitled to tax the received royalties under this provision, which restricts both the possibility of double taxation and opportunities for treaty shopping.

However, Article 12(1) of the UN Model allows the residence state of the immediate recipient of the royalties (whether the beneficial owner or not) to tax this income, but Article 12(2) grants to the source state a restricted right to tax it, if the 'beneficial owner of the royalties is a resident of the other Contracting State'. As in previous articles, the UN Model leaves the determination of the maximum tax rate to the contracting parties to decide in their treaty negotiations. In this case, treaty benefits are limited so that only the beneficial owner may enjoy the lower tax rate, while other categories of recipients will be subject to domestic tax rules in the source state.

Chinese tax treaties with Belt and Road countries fall into two categories based on the personal scope of the recipient of royalties. The majority of them follow Article 12(1) of the UN Model and cover the immediate recipient of royalties, while two[114] follow Article 12(1) of the OECD Model and cover only the beneficial owner of royalties residing in the other contracting state.

The majority of the Chinese tax treaties with Belt and Road countries stipulate a maximum tax rate of 10% at source to be enjoyed by the beneficial owner.[115] However,

---

114. China-Russia tax treaty (2014); China-Tajikistan tax treaty (2008).
115. Albania-China tax treaty (2004); Armenia-China tax treaty (1996); Azerbaijan-China tax treaty (2005); Bahrain-China tax treaty (2002); Bangladesh-China tax treaty (1996); Belarus-China tax treaty (1995); Brunei-China tax treaty (2004); Bulgaria-China tax treaty (1989); China-Croatia tax treaty (1995); China-Czech Republic tax treaty (2009); China-Estonia tax treaty (1998); China-Hungary tax treaty (1992); China-India tax treaty (1994); China-Indonesia tax treaty (2001); China-Iran tax treaty (2002); China-Israel tax treaty (1995); China-Kazakhstan tax treaty (2001); China-Kuwait tax treaty (1989); China-Kyrgyzstan tax treaty (2002); China-Laos tax treaty (1999) (if royalties paid by Chinese resident); China-Latvia tax treaty (1996); China-Lithuania tax treaty (1996); China-Macedonia tax treaty (1997); China-Malaysia tax treaty (1985); China-Mauritius tax treaty (1994); China-Moldova tax treaty (2000); China-Mongolia tax treaty (1991); China-Oman tax treaty (2002); China-Philippines tax treaty (1999); China-Poland tax treaty (1988); China-Qatar tax treaty (2001); China-Saudi Arabia tax treaty (2006); China-Serbia tax treaty (1997); China-Singapore tax treaty (2007); China-Slovenia tax treaty (1995); China-Sri Lanka tax treaty (2003); China-Syria tax treaty (2010); China-Turkey tax treaty (1995); China-Turkmenistan tax treaty (2009); China-Ukraine tax treaty (1995); China-Uzbekistan tax treaty (1996); China-United Arab Emirates tax treaty (1993); China-Vietnam tax treaty (1995); China-Yugoslavia (Bosnia and Herzegovina) tax treaty (1988).

some tax treaties provide for different rates, limiting the source state right to tax to 3%,[116] 5%,[117] 6%,[118] 7%,[119] 8%,[120] 12.5%[121] or 15%.[122] At least three tax treaties provide for a reduced tax base for 'equipment royalty' by 30%[123] and 40%[124] (thus reducing the effective tax rate to 7% and 6% of the gross amount, respectively). The tax treaty with Malaysia exempts the royalties derived by a resident of China in respect of certain film hire duties.

Considering the fact that China tends to engage in infrastructure and other projects in other Belt and Road countries rather than other way round, this allocation of taxing right to source states seem to work towards financial interests of these other countries. However, the tax treaties among other Belt and Road countries are also mostly based on the UN Model, with a maximum tax rate of 10% at source – which suggests that the UN Model is an effective standard in the region. The use of tax rates in tax treaties among Belt and Road countries lower than 10% is rare (e.g., 5% in the Iran-Russia tax treaty).

7.2 Mutual Agreement on Application

Article 12(2) of the UN Model also provides for a mutual agreement of the competent authorities on application of the tax rate limitation for beneficial owners. However, this provision is found in only eleven Chinese tax treaties with Belt and Road countries.[125]

7.3 Definition of Royalties

The definition of royalties in Article 12(2) of the OECD Model includes only consideration for the use of, or the right to use, intellectual property (citing a variety of examples), while Article 12(3) of the UN Model also includes in the definition those payments 'for the use of, or right to use, industrial, commercial or scientific equipment'.

A majority of Chinese tax treaties with Belt and Road countries quote the wording of the UN Model; however, there are three examples excluding the use of equipment

---

116. China-Romania tax treaty (2016).
117. China-Ethiopia tax treaty (2009); China-Georgia tax treaty (2005); China-Laos tax treaty (1999) (if royalties paid by Laos resident).
118. China-Russia tax treaty (2014).
119. Bulgaria-China tax treaty (1989) (only for use of, or right to use the equipment); China-Latvia tax treaty (1996) (draft version); China-Romania tax treaty (2016).
120. China-Egypt tax treaty (1997); China-Tajikistan tax treaty (2008).
121. China-Pakistan tax treaty (2000).
122. China-Malaysia tax treaty (1985); China-Philippines tax treaty (1999) (only for use of copyright of literary or artistic work).
123. China-Israel tax treaty (1995); China-Poland tax treaty (1988).
124. China-Germany tax treaty (1985).
125. Albania-China tax treaty (2004); Brunei-China tax treaty (2004); China-Georgia tax treaty (2005); China-Kazakhstan tax treaty (2001); China-Kyrgyzstan tax treaty (2002); China-Moldova tax treaty (2000); China-Oman tax treaty (2002); China-Saudi Arabia tax treaty (2006); China-Syria tax treaty (2010); China-Tajikistan tax treaty (2008), China-Turkmenistan tax treaty (2009).

from the definition[126] and two examples of extending the same treatment to technical services.[127] An argument justifying the coverage of the use of equipment in Chinese tax treaties with other Belt and Road countries may be the extensive use of imported equipment in construction projects in situations where the other country often lacks the necessary local equipment.

7.4 PE Provision

Both Models effectively reproduce the PE provision in respect of royalties (adjusting respectively the wording on dividends and holding or interest and debt claim). The UN Model, in addition, explicitly covers those royalties effectively connected with the fixed base of independent professional services and royalties falling under the limited force of attraction rule under Article 7(1)(c), contrary to the example of the OECD Model (thus maintaining consistency with Article 11(3)).

None of the Chinese treaties with other Belt and Road countries introduces the limited force of attraction rule in the case of royalties. However, all but one[128] mentions, in addition to the PE, the fixed base for independent personal services.

7.5 Determining the Source

The UN Model includes Article 12(5), defining the source of royalties – a paragraph which is absent in OECD Model. This UN Model provision specifies that the source of royalties corresponds with the residence of payer, the existence of a PE or fixed base in a contracting state. The wording is almost identical to Article 11(5) of the OECD Model, with the exception of the type of income and fixed base provision.

Article 12(5) of the UN Model is included in all fifty reviewed Chinese tax treaties with Belt and Road countries. Some treaties specify the national government and governing bodies of political subdivisions, along with residents, as possible sources of royalties – a provision absent in the UN Model.[129]

---

126. China-Georgia tax treaty (2005); China-Tajikistan tax treaty (2008); China-Turkmenistan tax treaty (2009).
127. China-India tax treaty (1994); China-Pakistan tax treaty (2000).
128. China-Czech Republic tax treaty (2009).
129. Albania-China tax treaty (2004); Armenia-China tax treaty (1996); Azerbaijan-China tax treaty (2005); Bahrain-China tax treaty (2002); Bangladesh-China tax treaty (1996); Belarus-China tax treaty (1995); Bosnia and Herzegovina-China tax treaty (1988); Brunei-China tax treaty (2004); Bulgaria-China tax treaty (1989); China-Croatia tax treaty (1995); China-Estonia tax treaty (1998); China-Georgia tax treaty (2005); China-Hungary tax treaty (1992); China-India tax treaty (1994); China-Indonesia tax treaty (2001); China-Iran tax treaty (2002); China-Israel tax treaty (1995); China-Kazakhstan tax treaty (2001); China-Kuwait tax treaty (1989); China-Kyrgyzstan tax treaty (2002); China-Laos tax treaty (1999); China-Latvia tax treaty (1996); China-Lithuania tax treaty (1996); China-Macedonia tax treaty (1997); China-Malaysia tax treaty (1985); China-Mauritius tax treaty (1994); China-Moldova tax treaty (2000); China-Mongolia tax treaty (1991); China-Oman tax treaty (2002); China-Pakistan tax treaty (2000); China-Philippines tax treaty (1999); China-Poland tax treaty (1988); China-Qatar tax treaty (2001); China-Saudi Arabia tax treaty (2006); China-Serbia tax treaty (1997); China-Slovenia tax treaty (1995); China-Sri Lanka tax treaty (2003); China-Syria tax treaty (2010); China-

7.6 Arm's Length Royalties Rate

Last paragraphs of the respective articles considering royalties, Article 12(4) of the OECD Model and Article 12(6) of the UN Model (both containing the same wording), virtually reproduce Article 11(6) of both Models with the same intention of imposing a limitation on benefits. This wording was fully adopted in all fifty analysed Chinese tax treaties with Belt and Road countries.

7.7 Further Modifications Found in Article 12 of Chinese Treaties with Belt and Road Countries

Three Chinese tax treaties with Belt and Road countries include an anti-treaty-shopping provision, usually as the last paragraph of the article.[130] This provision denies the application of Article 12 in situations where the main purpose of the arrangement is to take advantage of tax treaty provisions. However, there is no further specification as to what constitutes 'tak(ing) advantage of this Article by means of that creation or assignment' – reduction of tax liabilities or profit shifting (along with reduced tax liability).

Similar provisions also exist in some tax treaties between other Belt and Road countries.[131]

8 CAPITAL GAINS: ARTICLE 13 OF THE OECD AND UN MODELS

8.1 General Taxing Rights

Article 13(1) of both the OECD and UN Models allows the state where the immovable property is located, to tax the gains from the alienation thereof by a resident of the other contracting state. Both Models also agree on the scope of term 'immovable property', defined in Article 6(2) thereof, which generally refers to the domestic law of both contracting states; explicitly includes agricultural livestock and certain rights pertaining to land, immovable property and natural resources; and explicitly excludes ships, boats and aircraft.

The Chinese tax treaties with Belt and Road countries reproduce the same wording and allow taxation of capital gains in the source state.

Turkey tax treaty (1995); China-Ukraine tax treaty (1995); China-United Arab Emirates tax treaty (1993); China-Uzbekistan tax treaty (1996); China-Vietnam tax treaty (1995).
130. Article 12(7) China-Romania tax treaty (2016); Article 12(7) China-Russia tax treaty (2014); Article 12(7) China-Singapore tax treaty (2007).
131. Azerbaijan-Kazakhstan tax treaty (1996); Belarus-Kazakhstan tax treaty (1997); Kazakhstan-Kyrgyzstan tax treaty (1997); Kazakhstan-Russia tax treaty (1996); Kazakhstan-Romania tax treaty (1998); Kazakhstan-Tajikistan tax treaty (1999); Kazakhstan-Uzbekistan tax treaty (1996).

8.2 Taxing the Alienation of PE Property

Article 13(2) of both the OECD and UN Models allows the state where the PE of an enterprise of the other contracting state is located, to tax gains from the alienation of such PE or its movable property. The UN Model extends this provision to cover the fixed base for the fixed base of independent professional services. The Chinese tax treaties with Belt and Road countries use the wording of the UN Model (except the treaty with Poland, which omits this provision altogether).

8.3 Taxing the Alienation of Vessels and Vehicles

Article 13(3) of the OECD Model (reproduced by the UN Model) attributes exclusive taxing rights in respect of capital gains from the alienation of ships, aircraft and certain movable property, engaged in international traffic and inland waterways, to the state where the place of effective management of the respective enterprise is situated.

The Chinese tax treaties with Belt and Road countries differ from the text of the Models in two regards: they usually exclude the provisions on inland waterways (which reflects the absence of these between China and the vast majority of Belt and Road countries) and usually refer to the residence of the operator of ships and aircraft. Thirteen of these tax treaties, however, allocate the taxing rights in respect of capital gains from the alienation of transportation vehicles based on the place of effective management or head office.[132] Eight tax treaties extend this paragraph to cover 'road vehicles'.[133] Whether this concept of 'road vehicles' includes railroad vehicles, along with the automobiles, is sometimes unclear. The text of the Chinese tax treaties with Kazakhstan and Kyrgyzstan in English use the term 'road vehicle', while in Russian and the respective national languages they refer to 'land vehicles'. However, in ambiguous cases, the English text prevails.

8.4 Taxing the Alienation of Shares

Article 13(4) of the OECD Model allows taxation of capital gain from the alienation of shares deriving 50% or more of their value from immovable property located in a contracting state, by that state. Article 13(4) of the UN Model has a broader material scope, also covering capital gain from the alienation of an interest in a partnership, trust or estate, narrowed down by personal scope: it applies only to those enterprises, which: (a) are engaged in the management of immovable property and (b) own

---

132. Bahrain-China tax treaty (2002); Bulgaria-China tax treaty (1989); China-Czech Republic tax treaty (2009); China-Hungary tax treaty (1992); China-Kuwait tax treaty (1989); China-Laos tax treaty (1999); China-Macedonia tax treaty (1997); China-Mongolia tax treaty (1991); China-Pakistan tax treaty (2000); China-Saudi Arabia tax treaty (2006); China-Serbia tax treaty (1997); China-Slovenia tax treaty (1995); China-Yugoslavia (Bosnia and Herzegovina) tax treaty (1988).
133. China-Kazakhstan tax treaty (2001); China-Kyrgyzstan tax treaty (2002); China-Laos tax treaty (1999); China-Mongolia tax treaty (1991); China-Tajikistan tax treaty (2008); China-Turkey tax treaty (1995); China-Turkmenistan tax treaty (2009); China-Uzbekistan tax treaty (1996).

Chapter 11: Tax Treaties Between the Belt and Road Countries

predominantly immovable property (or, as the UN Model puts it, immovable property must constitute at least 50% of total assets).

In this context, Chinese tax treaties with other Belt and Road countries fall into the following groups:

- those omitting Article 13(4) entirely;[134]
- those reproducing the first sentence of Article 13(4) of the UN Model;[135]
- those narrowing the first sentence of Article 13(4) of the UN Model to shares only;[136]
- those copying Article 13(4) of the OECD Model;[137] and
- those extending Article 13(4) of the OECD Model to any alienation of shares.[138]

The UN Model contains a unique Article 13(5), allowing the source state to tax capital gains on shares if the alienator residing in the other contracting state held, directly or indirectly, a certain percentage of the capital of the company the shares of which have been sold. The actual percentage is subject to negotiation by the contracting states. The idea behind this provision is to allow the source state to tax the capital gains from a substantial participation irrespective of the place of the transaction. Some Chinese tax treaties with Belt and Road countries omit this paragraph.[139] Other tax treaties include Article 13(5) loosely based on the same provision of the UN Model, which allows the source state to tax the capital gains on shares not meeting the above 'immovable property' criterion in the case of 'alienation of shares (...) representing a

---

134. Armenia-China tax treaty (1996); Bangladesh-China tax treaty (1996); Belarus-China tax treaty (1995); Brunei-China tax treaty (2004); China-Georgia tax treaty (2005); China-Kuwait tax treaty (1989); China-Poland tax treaty (1988); China-Slovenia tax treaty (1995); China-Syria tax treaty (2010); China-Yugoslavia (Bosnia and Herzegovina) tax treaty (1988).
135. Albania-China tax treaty (2004); China-Malaysia tax treaty (1985).
136. Azerbaijan-China tax treaty (2005); China-Kazakhstan tax treaty (2001); China-Kyrgyzstan tax treaty (2002); China-Moldova tax treaty (2000); China-Mongolia tax treaty (1991); China-Russia tax treaty (1994) (to be replaced); China-Ukraine tax treaty (1995); China-Uzbekistan tax treaty (1996).
137. China-Estonia tax treaty (1998) (under Protocol 2014); China-Romania tax treaty (2016) (excluding shares trading on a stock exchange); China-Russia tax treaty (2014) (not effective yet); China-Singapore tax treaty (2007); China-Tajikistan tax treaty (2008); China-Turkmenistan tax treaty (2009).
138. China-Czech Republic tax treaty (2009).
139. Albania-China tax treaty (2004); Armenia-China tax treaty (1996); Azerbaijan-China tax treaty (2005); Bangladesh-China tax treaty (1996); Belarus-China tax treaty (1995); Brunei-China tax treaty (2004); Bulgaria-China tax treaty (1989); China-Czech Republic tax treaty (2009); China-Estonia tax treaty (1998); China-Georgia tax treaty (2005); China-Hungary tax treaty (1992); China-India tax treaty (1994); China-Indonesia tax treaty (2001); China-Iran tax treaty (2002); China-Israel tax treaty (1995); China-Kazakhstan tax treaty (2001); China-Kuwait tax treaty (1989); China-Latvia tax treaty (1996); China-Lithuania tax treaty (1996); China-Malaysia tax treaty (1985); China-Poland tax treaty (1988); China-Philippines tax treaty (1999); China-Romania tax treaty (2016); China-Russia tax treaty (2014); China-Serbia tax treaty (1997); China-Slovenia tax treaty (1995); China-Syria tax treaty (2010); China-Tajikistan tax treaty (2008); China-Turkey tax treaty (1995); China-Turkmenistan tax treaty (2009); China-United Arab Emirates tax treaty (1993); China-Yugoslavia (Bosnia and Herzegovina) tax treaty (1988).

participation of at least 25% in a company'.[140] However, the wording is unclear as to whether this is to apply to an alienation of at least 25% of the shares (if considered verbatim) or to the alienation of shares where the alienator held at least 25% of the shares (if considered following the UN Model).

8.5 Taxing Rights in Other Cases

The final paragraph of Article 13 under both Models allocates the exclusive right to tax to the resident state of the alienator. Chinese tax treaties with Belt and Road countries (except Poland) have retained it intact (save for the references to the above paragraphs, which differ in their number).

9 INCOME FROM EMPLOYMENT: ARTICLE 15 OF THE OECD AND UN MODELS

9.1 Article 15 of the OECD and UN Models

Article 15 of the OECD Model establishes rules for the taxation of income from employment. Under Article 15(1), such income is taxable in the state where the employment is actually exercised. Article 15(2) is the exception to the general rule, providing that income from employment is taxable in the residence state of the employee. Three conditions must be fulfilled, namely: employment in the other state is limited to 183 days; the employer paying the remuneration is not a resident of the state in which the employment is exercised; and the remuneration is not borne by a permanent establishment of the employer in the state where the employment is actually exercised. Article 15(3) applies to the remuneration of crews of ships or aircraft operated in international traffic, which income is taxable in the contracting state where the place of effective management of the enterprise concerned is situated.

9.2 Article 15(1) and (2) of Chinese Tax Treaties

No Chinese treaty with a Belt and Road country contains an exception to the general rule as can be found in Article 15(1). Furthermore, all such Chinese treaties contain a provision modelled after Article 15(2), with none of the treaties deviating from the 183-day period. However, as many Chinese treaties are not in line with the current

---

140. Bahrain-China tax treaty (2002); China-Croatia tax treaty (1995); China-Egypt tax treaty (1997); China-Kyrgyzstan tax treaty (2002); China-Laos tax treaty (1999); China-Macedonia tax treaty (1997); China-Mauritius tax treaty (1994) (Protocol of 2006; subject to holding for 12 consecutive months before alienation); China-Moldova tax treaty (2000); China-Mongolia tax treaty (1991); China-Oman tax treaty (2002); China-Pakistan tax treaty (2000); China-Qatar tax treaty (2001); China-Saudi Arabia tax treaty (2006); China-Singapore tax treaty (2007) (subject to holding for 12 consecutive months before alienation); China-Sri Lanka tax treaty (2003); China-Ukraine tax treaty (1995); China-Uzbekistan tax treaty (1996); China-Vietnam tax treaty (1995).

version of the OECD Model, under many of them, the 183-day period must be computed within one calendar year or within one fiscal year concerned. This wording offers leeway for tax avoidance.[141] Moreover, the condition that the remuneration not be borne by a permanent establishment that the employer might have in the working-state also includes any fixed base of the employer. This is due to the fact that the former Article 14 of the OECD Model, dealing with independent personal services, used the wording 'fixed base' as a synonym for permanent establishment. As there are no differences between the two terms,[142] the inclusion of the phrase 'fixed base' does not make any difference to the current version of the OECD Model. The Chinese treaty with the Czech Republic defines how the term 'employer' is to be understood.

9.3 Article 15(3) of Chinese Tax Treaties with Belt and Road Countries

Regarding Article 15(3), only a few Chinese treaties allocate the taxing right to the state where the place of effective management of the enterprise operating the ship or the aircraft is located.[143] Certain treaties refer to the place of the head office of the enterprise[144] or refer to both (place of head office and/or effective management).[145] The latter practice might lead to difficulties in determining which state would exactly be entitled to tax the remuneration of crews of ships or aircraft. Nevertheless, the majority of Chinese treaties simply allocate the taxing right to the residence state of the enterprise operating the ship without reference to the place of effective management.[146] The Chinese tax treaty with Serbia allocates the taxing right exclusively to the residence state of the employee.[147] Similarly, the treaty with Pakistan stipulates that only the contracting state of which the employee is a national may tax remuneration derived by employees of an airline or shipping company of a contracting state stationed in the other contracting state. The treaty with Iran does not use the phrase 'remuneration

---

141. *OECD Model: Commentary on Article 15* para. 4 (2014).
142. *OECD Model: Commentary on Article 5* para. 1.1 (2014).
143. For example China-Czech Republic tax treaty (2009); China-Pakistan tax treaty (2000); China-Poland tax treaty (1988); China-Yugoslavia (Bosnia and Herzegovina) tax treaty (1988).
144. *See* e.g., Bulgaria-China tax treaty (1989); China-Laos tax treaty (1999); China-Macedonia tax treaty (1997); China-Mongolia tax treaty (1991); China-United Arab Emirates tax treaty (1993); China-Slovenia tax treaty (1995).
145. *See* e.g., China-Nepal tax treaty (2001) (referring to both the place of head office or of effective management); China-Kuwait tax treaty (1989) (referring to 'the place of head office (effective management) of the enterprise'); China-Saudi Arabia tax treaty (2006) (referring to both the place of head office and the place of effective management); China-Hungary tax treaty (1992) (referring to both the place of head office and the place of effective management); China-Czechoslovakia tax treaty (1987) (referring to 'the place of head office (i.e., effective management) of the enterprise').
146. It is unclear as to how the wording included in the China-Bahrain tax treaty (2002) should be understood ('shall be taxable only in the Contracting State where the place of the enterprise is situated').
147. Article 15(3) China-Serbia tax treaty (1997) ('Notwithstanding the preceding provisions of this Article, remuneration derived by a resident of a Contracting State shall be taxable in that State if the remuneration is paid in respect of:

    (a) [...]; (b) an employment exercised aboard a ship or aircraft operated in international traffic'.).

derived in respect of' but refers to 'remuneration paid by an enterprise of a Contracting State in respect of an employment exercised aboard a ship or an aircraft'. This wording hints that a very strict interpretation applies as to who pays the remuneration.

In principle, Article 15(3) applies only to income from employment exercised aboard a ship or aircraft operated in international traffic, or aboard a boat engaged in inland waterway transport. Certain treaties, however, also include road vehicles in this list.[148] From the perspective of the BRI, such an inclusion will be extremely helpful for international truck drivers, as practical problems can arise given their mobility and the cross-border nature of their activities. This means that it might be extremely difficult to apply the 183-day rule to truck drivers, and as a consequence their salaries could be taxable in several states. The inclusion of international road transport in Article 15(3) is thus welcomed in the interests of simplification.

Further particularities are found in the Chinese treaty with Bosnia and Herzegovina, Article 15 of which contains an additional paragraph modelled after Article 19(1) and (3) of the OECD Model.[149] The treaty with Serbia is the only one that additionally includes a provision for employment exercised at a construction site. Accordingly, remuneration paid for employment exercised for a period of up to twelve months[150] is taxable in the residence state of the employee.

10 DIRECTORS' FEES: ARTICLE 16 OF THE OECD AND UN MODELS

Article 16 deals with remuneration received by an individual or a legal person in the capacity as a member of a board of directors of a company. The taxing right is allocated to the residence state of the company. All Chinese tax treaties contain a provision that is modelled after Article 16 of the OECD Model. Only a few Chinese treaties contain deviations. In some countries, certain companies might have bodies with a similar function to the board of directors. Accordingly, some Chinese tax treaties also include other similar bodies of a company in addition to the board of directors.[151] Another deviation is that some treaties are based on the UN Model, and thus they include a second paragraph under Article 16.[152] The tax treaty with Bosnia and Herzegovina explicitly uses the names of the contracting states instead of referring abstractly to residence state and other state.

---

148. See e.g., China-Kazakhstan tax treaty (2001); China-Kyrgyzstan tax treaty (2002); China-Laos tax treaty (1999); China-Romania tax treaty (2016); China-Tajikistan tax treaty (2008); China-Turkmenistan tax treaty (2009); China-Uzbekistan tax treaty (1996).
149. Article 15(3) & (4) China-Yugoslavia (Bosnia and Herzegovina) tax treaty (1988).
150. During this twelve-month period, the construction site or similar project does not constitute a permanent establishment.
151. See e.g., Albania-China tax treaty (2004); China-Czech Republic tax treaty (2009); China-Estonia tax treaty (1998); China-Hungary tax treaty (1992); China-Indonesia tax treaty (2001); China-Latvia tax treaty (1996); China-Lithuania tax treaty (1996).
152. See e.g., Cambodia-China tax treaty (2016); China-Kuwait tax treaty (1989); China-Thailand tax treaty (1986).

11 METHOD ARTICLES: ARTICLE 23 OF THE OECD AND UN MODELS

11.1 Article 23A and 23B of the OECD and UN Models

Article 23A and 23B of the OECD and UN Models set forth rules on the elimination of double taxation, after allocation rights have been determined. The OECD and UN articles on the elimination of double taxation correspond in most regards to each other. However, Article 23A of the UN Model does not contain a corresponding provision similar to Article 23A(4) of the OECD Model. Furthermore, Article 23A of the OECD Model is also applicable to royalties, which is not the case for Article 23A of the UN Model, as Article 23A(2) of the UN Model merely provides that the source state will allow a deduction from the tax on income derived from Articles 10 and 11 of the UN Model. The wording of Article 23B of the OECD and UN Models basically correspond. Article 23B of the UN Model contains only a few differences in wording, vis-à-vis the corresponding provision in the OECD Model.[153] However, these changes do not change the meaning of the provision.

11.2 Application of the Method Articles in China

China decided to include an article providing for the application of the credit method in almost all of its tax treaties with Belt and Road countries. The application of the exemption method may be found only in the tax treaty with Bosnia and Herzegovina.[154] The text of the article on the credit method in Chinese tax treaties is mainly drafted on the basis of Article 23B of the OECD and UN Models.[155] However, the wording of the article on the credit method in Chinese tax treaties deviates from Article 23B of the OECD and UN Models.

China may grant a credit for the amount of taxes payable on the income derived by Chinese residents in the source state. However, the amount of the credit for taxes on income payable derived in the source state may not exceed the amount of Chinese tax imposed on the Chinese resident, computed in accordance with Chinese tax law and regulations.[156] The requirement to grant a credit for taxes on income 'payable' constitutes a deviation from Article 23B of the OECD and UN Models, as under Article

---

153. Article 23B (1) *UN Model* (2011) ('[...] the first mentioned State shall allow as a deduction from the tax on the income of that resident an amount equal to the income tax paid in that other State; b and as a deduction from the tax on the capital of that resident, an amount equal to the capital tax paid in that other State. Such deduction in either case shall not, however, exceed that part of the income tax or capital tax, as computed before the deduction is given, which is attributable, as the case may be, to the income or the capital which may be taxed in that other State'.); Article 23B(2) *UN Model* (2011) ('Where, in accordance with any provision of the this Convention, income [...]'.).
154. Exemption method with Bosnia and Herzegovina. Article 23A China-Yugoslavia (Bosnia and Herzegovina) tax treaty (1988).
155. C. Wei, *China*, in *The Impact of the OECD and UN Model Conventions on Bilateral Tax Treaties*, at 261, 285 (M. Lang, P. Pistone, J. Schuch & C. Staringer eds., Cambridge 2012).
156. In all treaties concluded with Belt and Road countries applying the credit method, the treaty partners use the term 'payable'.

23B of the OECD and UN Models the residence state must allow 'as a deduction from the tax on the income of that resident an amount equal to the income tax *paid* in that other State'.[157] The deviation of the wording from Article 23B of the OECD and UN Models leads to a result where China may credit an amount of tax that has been 'hypothetically' paid in the source state. Therefore, an actual payment made by the taxpayer in the source state is not required to grant a credit for the amount of taxes payable in the source state. However, China grants a credit only for foreign taxes actually paid by the Chinese resident under its domestic law.[158] Tax treaties have a higher legal status than Chinese domestic law.[159] Therefore, China would be obliged to grant a credit for taxes *payable* on the income, but not actually *paid* in the source state.

An obligation to grant a credit for taxes payable and not actually paid can also be derived by means of interpretation through the application of Article 33 of the Vienna Convention on the Law of Treaties (VCLT). Article 33(1) of the VCLT states that where 'a treaty has been authenticated in two or more languages, the text is equally authoritative in each language, unless the treaty provides or the parties agree that, in case of divergence, a particular text shall prevail'. China has established English and Chinese as authentic languages in all of its tax treaties with Belt and Road countries. Almost all tax treaties with the Belt and Road countries specify the English version of the tax treaty as the prevailing version in case of interpretational divergences.[160] As a result, more emphasis is to be placed on the word 'payable' in the English version of the tax treaty in question, than to the corresponding expression in the Chinese version of the text, even where the Chinese version of the treaty might include the phrase 'tax paid'. This applies to Chinese tax treaties which provide that the English text of the treaty is to prevail in cases of interpretational divergences. If the tax treaty does not provide for the prevalence of one specific language version in cases of interpretational divergences, all authentic languages must be taken into account to ascertain the intention of the contracting states.[161] Therefore, if the Chinese version of a tax treaty provides that taxes 'paid' in the source state are to be credited against the Chinese tax imposed on the Chinese resident, but the English version provides for the application of the credit method on taxes 'payable', Articles 31 and 32 of the VCLT must be taken into account in order to ascertain the intention of the contracting states as regards the application of the credit method to either 'taxes paid' or 'taxes payable' in the source state.

---

157. Article 23B (1) *UN Model* (2011); Article 23B (1)(a) *OECD Model* (emphasis added).
158. CN: Article 23 Enterprise Income Tax Law (EITL); CN: Article 7 Individual Income Tax Law (IITL).
159. *See* J. Li, *International Taxation in China: A Contextualized Analysis*, at 102–103 (IBFD 2016).
160. All treaties with Belt and Road countries except China-Cambodia tax treaty (2016); China-Pakistan tax treaty (2000); China-Philippines tax treaty (1999); China-Singapore tax treaty (2007).
161. Article 33(1) & (3) *Vienna Convention on the Law of Treaties* (1969).

11.3 Taxes Payable under Chinese Tax Treaties

Several tax treaties specify what types of income must be included under the scope of the definition of 'tax on that income payable'. In this regard, Chinese tax treaties often provide that the amount of tax which would have been paid in the source state if the tax had not been exempted or reduced in conformity with the special incentive laws assigned for promoting economic development in the source state, are also to be included in the tax base of the source state in order to credit the amount on taxes payable in China.[162] In this regard, some tax treaty provisions on this so-called tax sparing credit[163] specify a validity period for the application of the tax sparing, which is ten years starting from the day when the tax treaty entered into force, with the possibility to extend the validity period by mutual agreement.[164] The tax treaty with Pakistan also provides that other incentive measures which may be introduced in Pakistan's national law after the date of signature of the tax treaty, are to be actually seen as 'tax paid' in Pakistan.[165]

In addition to the inclusion of provisions on a tax sparing credit, certain Chinese tax treaties with Belt and Road countries also include a specific percentage of the gross amount of dividends, interest and royalties, creditable in China.[166] The gross amount must also be deemed to be 'tax payable' under the specific tax treaties.

11.4 Indirect Tax Credit

Direct tax credits refer to a credit granted to the taxpayer by the residence state for foreign taxes paid. In contrast to a direct foreign tax credit, an indirect foreign tax credit refers to a credit granted to a resident taxpayer for taxes paid by a different person, such as a foreign company owned by the taxpayer. China has included provisions on the indirect foreign tax credit in a couple of its treaties with Belt and Road countries,

---

162. Brunei-China tax treaty (2004); Cambodia-China tax treaty (2016); China-Kuwait tax treaty (1989); China-Oman tax treaty (2002); China-Pakistan tax treaty (2000); China-Thailand tax treaty (1986); China-Vietnam tax treaty (1995); China-Sri Lanka tax treaty (2003), Article 24(3) China-Macedonia tax treaty (1997) ('For the purposes of this Article, the term 'tax payable' shall be deemed to include the amount of tax which would have been paid if the tax had not been exempted or reduced in accordance with the relevant incentives designed to promote economic development in the domestic laws or connected regulations of either Contracting State'.).
163. *See* G. Santos, *Interpretative Treaty Override, Breach of Confidence and the Gradual Erosion of the Importance of Tax Treaties*, 69 Bull. Intl. Taxn. 1, at 17, 18 et seq. (2015).
164. Brunei-China tax treaty (2004); Cambodia-China tax treaty (2016); China-Sri Lanka tax treaty (2003).
165. *See* Article 24(2)(b)(ii) China-Pakistan tax treaty (2000) ('any other similar special incentive measures designed to promote economic development in the Islamic Republic of Pakistan which may be introduced in the laws of the Islamic Republic of Pakistan after the date of signature of this Agreement, and which may be agreed upon by the competent authorities of the Contracting States'.).
166. Article 23(3) China-Vietnam tax treaty (1995): 10% of the gross amount; Article 24(3) China-Pakistan tax treaty (2000): 10% of the gross amount (interest), 15% of the gross amount (dividends, royalties, technical services).

establishing a threshold of either 10%[167] or 20%[168] ownership in a company that is a resident of the source state, in order to grant a credit to a Chinese resident in China for taxes paid by a foreign company on dividends.

---

167. Bangladesh-China tax treaty (1996); Belarus-China tax treaty (1995); Bulgaria-China tax treaty (1989); Cambodia-China tax treaty (2016); China-Croatia tax treaty (1996); China-Czechoslovakia (Slovakia) tax treaty (1987); China-Estonia tax treaty (1998); China-Hungary tax treaty (1992); China-India tax treaty (1994); China-Indonesia tax treaty (2001); China-Israel tax treaty (1995); China-Kuwait tax treaty (1989); China-Malaysia tax treaty (1985); China-Pakistan tax treaty (2000); China-Latvia tax treaty (1996); China-Lithuania tax treaty (1996); China-Mongolia tax treaty (1991); China-Poland tax treaty (1988); China-Singapore tax treaty (2007); China-Slovenia tax treaty (1995); China-Syria tax treaty (2010); China-Thailand tax treaty (1986); China-United Arab Emirates tax treaty (1993); China-Ukraine tax treaty (1995); China-Vietnam tax treaty (1995).
168. China-Czech Republic tax treaty (2009); China-Russia tax treaty (2014); China-Tajikistan tax treaty (2008); China-Turkmenistan tax treaty (2009).

Chapter 11: Tax Treaties Between the Belt and Road Countries

Table 11.2 Features of Selected Tax Treaties; Sorted by their Date of Signature

State	Date of Signature	Residency (Article 4(3) OECD/UN Model) – Tiebreaker – Persons Other than Individuals	Permanent Establishment (Article 5(3)(a) OECD/UN Model) -Construction Site Threshold	Dividends (Article 10(2) OECD/UN Model) – Withholding Threshold	Interest (Article 11(2) OECD/UN Model) – Withholding Threshold	Royalties (Article 12 UN Model) – Withholding Threshold
Malaysia	23.11.1985	Modified Version: place of effective management of its business in one of the contracting states and the place of head office of its business in the other contracting state	Article 5(3)(a) OECD/UN Model	taxation at source: 10%	taxation at source: 10%	taxation at source: 10%; 5% if royalties are paid by Laos residents; 15% for the use of copyright of literary or artistic work
Poland	07.06.1988	Modified Version: place of effective management of its business in one of the contracting states and the place of head office of its business in the other contracting state	Article 5(3)(a) OECD/UN Model	taxation at source: 10%	taxation at source: 10%	taxation at source: 10%

239

State	Date of Signature	Residency (Article 4(3) OECD/UN Model) – Tiebreaker – Persons Other than Individuals	Permanent Establishment (Article 5(3)(a) OECD/UN Model) -Construction Site Threshold	Dividends (Article 10(2) OECD/UN Model) – Withholding Threshold	Interest (Article 11(2) OECD/UN Model) – Withholding Threshold	Royalties (Article 12 UN Model) – Withholding Threshold
Bosnia and Herzegovina	02.12.1988	Modified Version: place of effective management of its business in one of the contracting states and the place of head office of its business in the other contracting state	6 months	taxation at source: 10%	taxation at source: 10%	taxation at source: 10%
Bulgaria	06.11.1989	place of head office	Article 5(3)(a) OECD/UN Model	taxation at source: 10%	taxation at source: 10%	taxation at source: 10%; 7% for the use of, or right to use the equipment
Pakistan	15.11.1989	Modified Version: place of effective management of its business in one of the contracting states and the place of head office of its business in the other contracting state	Article 5(3)(a) OECD/UN Model	taxation at source: 10%	taxation at source: 10%	taxation at source: 12.5%
Kuwait	25.12.1989	Article 4(3) OECD/UN Model	Article 5(3)(a) OECD/UN Model	taxation at source: 5%	taxation at source: 5%	taxation at source: 10%

State	Date of Signature	Residency (Article 4(3) OECD/UN Model) – Tiebreaker – Persons Other than Individuals	Permanent Establishment (Article 5(3)(a) OECD/UN Model) -Construction Site Threshold	Dividends (Article 10(2) OECD/UN Model) – Withholding Threshold	Interest (Article 11(2) OECD/UN Model) – Withholding Threshold	Royalties (Article 12 UN Model) – Withholding Threshold
Mongolia	26.08.1991	place of head office	18 months	taxation at source: 5%	taxation at source: 10%	taxation at source: 10%
Hungary	17.06.1992	Modified Version: place of effective management of its business in one of the contracting states and the place of head office of its business in the other contracting state	12 months	taxation at source: 10%	taxation at source: 10%	taxation at source: 10%
The United Arab Emirates	01.07.1993	place of head office	24 months	limiting the source country tax rate to 7%	taxation at source: 7%	taxation at source: 10%
India	18.07.1994	place of head office	183 days	taxation at source: 10%	taxation at source: 10%	taxation at source: 10%
Croatia	09.01.1995	place of head office	12 months	taxation at source: 5%	taxation at source: 10%	taxation at source: 10%
Belarus	17.01.1995	mutual agreement procedure	18 months	taxation at source: 10%	taxation at source: 10%	taxation at source: 10%
Slovenia	13.02.1995	place of head office	12 months	taxation at source: 5%	taxation at source: 10%	taxation at source: 10%

State	Date of Signature	Residency (Article 4(3) OECD/UN Model) – Tiebreaker – Persons Other than Individuals	Permanent Establishment (Article 5(3)(a) OECD/UN Model) -Construction Site Threshold	Dividends (Article 10(2) OECD/UN Model) – Withholding Threshold	Interest (Article 11(2) OECD/UN Model) – Withholding Threshold	Royalties (Article 12 UN Model) – Withholding Threshold
Israel	08.04.1995	place of head office	12 months	taxation at source: 10%	taxation at source: 7%	taxation at source: 10%
Vietnam	17.05.1995	mutual agreement procedure	Article 5(3)(a) OECD/UN Model	taxation at source: 10%	taxation at source: 10%	taxation at source: 10%
Turkey	23.05.1995	place of head office	12 months	taxation at source: 10%	taxation at source: 10%	taxation at source: 10%
Ukraine	04.12.1995	mutual agreement procedure	18 months	taxation at source: 10%; 5%, if the recipient is a company (other than a partnership) directly holding at least 25% of the shares in the company, which pays out the dividends	taxation at source: 10%	taxation at source: 10%

Chapter 11: Tax Treaties Between the Belt and Road Countries

State	Date of Signature	Residency (Article 4(3) OECD/UN Model) – Tiebreaker – Persons Other than Individuals	Permanent Establishment (Article 5(3)(a) OECD/UN Model) -Construction Site Threshold	Dividends (Article 10(2) OECD/UN Model) – Withholding Threshold	Interest (Article 11(2) OECD/UN Model) – Withholding Threshold	Royalties (Article 12 UN Model) – Withholding Threshold
Armenia	05.05.1996	mutual agreement procedure	12 months	taxation at source: 10%; 5%, if the recipient is a company (other than a partnership) directly holding at least 25% of the shares in the company, which pays out the dividends	taxation at source: 10%	taxation at source: 10%
Lithuania	03.06.1996	mutual agreement procedure	12 months	taxation at source: 10%; 5%, if the recipient is a company (other than a partnership) directly holding at least 25% of the shares in the company, which pays out the dividends	taxation at source: 10%	taxation at source: 10%

State	Date of Signature	Residency (Article 4(3) OECD/UN Model) – Tiebreaker – Persons Other than Individuals	Permanent Establishment (Article 5(3)(a) OECD/UN Model) -Construction Site Threshold	Dividends (Article 10(2) OECD/UN Model) – Withholding Threshold	Interest (Article 11(2) OECD/UN Model) – Withholding Threshold	Royalties (Article 12 UN Model) – Withholding Threshold
Latvia	07.06.1996	mutual agreement procedure	12 months	taxation at source: 10%; 5%, if the recipient is a company (other than a partnership) directly holding at least 25% of the shares in the company, which pays out the dividends	taxation at source: 10%	taxation at source: 10%
Uzbekistan	03.07.1996	mutual agreement procedure	12 months	taxation at source: 10%	taxation at source: 10%	taxation at source: 10%
Bangladesh	12.09.1996	Modified Version: place of effective management of its business in one of the contracting states and the place of head office of its business in the other contracting state	Article 5(3)(a) OECD/UN Model	taxation at source: 10%	taxation at source: 10%	taxation at source: 10%

Chapter 11: Tax Treaties Between the Belt and Road Countries

State	Date of Signature	Residency (Article 4(3) OECD/UN Model) – Tiebreaker – Persons Other than Individuals	Permanent Establishment (Article 5(3)(a) OECD/UN Model) –Construction Site Threshold	Dividends (Article 10(2) OECD/UN Model) – Withholding Threshold	Interest (Article 11(2) OECD/UN Model) – Withholding Threshold	Royalties (Article 12 UN Model) – Withholding Threshold
Serbia (Yugoslavia)	01.03.1997	Modified Version: place of effective management of its business in one of the contracting states and the place of head office of its business in the other contracting state	12 months	taxation at source: 5%	taxation at source: 10%	taxation at source: 10%
Macedonia	09.06.1997	place of head office	12 months	taxation at source: 5%	taxation at source: 10%	taxation at source: 10%
Egypt	13.08.1997	Modified Version: place of effective management of its business in one of the contracting states and the place of head office of its business in the other contracting state	12 months if within 24-month period	taxation at source: 8%	taxation at source: 10%	taxation at source: 8%

245

State	Date of Signature	Residency (Article 4(3) OECD/UN Model) – Tiebreaker – Persons Other than Individuals	Permanent Establishment (Article 5(3)(a) OECD/UN Model) -Construction Site Threshold	Dividends (Article 10(2) OECD/UN Model) – Withholding Threshold	Interest (Article 11(2) OECD/UN Model) – Withholding Threshold	Royalties (Article 12 UN Model) – Withholding Threshold
Estonia	12.05.1998	mutual agreement procedure	12 months	taxation at source: 10%; 5%, if the recipient is a company (other than a partnership) directly holding at least 25% of the shares in the company, which pays out the dividends	taxation at source: 10%	taxation at source: 10%
Laos	25.01.1999	place of head office	12 months	taxation at source: 5%	taxation at source: 5%	taxation at source: 10%; 5% (if royalties are paid by Laos residents)

Chapter 11: Tax Treaties Between the Belt and Road Countries

State	Date of Signature	Residency (Article 4(3) OECD/UN Model) – Tiebreaker – Persons Other than Individuals	Permanent Establishment (Article 5(3)(a) OECD/UN Model) -Construction Site Threshold	Dividends (Article 10(2) OECD/UN Model) – Withholding Threshold	Interest (Article 11(2) OECD/UN Model) – Withholding Threshold	Royalties (Article 12 UN Model) – Withholding Threshold
Philippines	18.11.1999	mutual agreement procedure	Article 5(3)(a) OECD/UN Model	taxation at source: 15%; 10%, if the recipient is a company directly holding at least 10% of the shares in the company, which pays out the dividends	taxation at source: 10%	taxation at source: 10%; 15% for the use of copyright of literary or artistic work
Moldova	07.06.2000	mutual agreement procedure	12 months	taxation at source: 10%; 5%, if the recipient is a company (other than a partnership) directly holding at least 25% of the shares in the company, which pays out the dividends	taxation at source: 10%	taxation at source: 10%
Qatar	02.04.2001	place of head office	9 months	taxation at source: 10%	taxation at source: 10%	taxation at source: 10%

State	Date of Signature	Residency (Article 4(3) OECD/UN Model) – Tiebreaker – Persons Other than Individuals	Permanent Establishment (Article 5(3)(a) OECD/UN Model) – Construction Site Threshold	Dividends (Article 10(2) OECD/UN Model) – Withholding Threshold	Interest (Article 11(2) OECD/UN Model) – Withholding Threshold	Royalties (Article 12 UN Model) – Withholding Threshold
Kazakhstan	12.09.2001	mutual agreement procedure	12 months	taxation at source: 10%	taxation at source: 10%	taxation at source: 10%
Indonesia	07.11.2001	mutual agreement procedure	6 months	taxation at source: 10%	taxation at source: 10%	taxation at source: 10%
Oman	25.03.2002	mutual agreement procedure	9 months	taxation at source: 5%	taxation at source: 10%	taxation at source: 10%
Iran	20.04.2002	place of head office	12 months	taxation at source: 10%	taxation at source: 10%	taxation at source: 10%
Bahrain	16.05.2002	mutual agreement procedure	12 months	taxation at source: 5%	taxation at source: 10%	taxation at source: 10%
Kyrgyzstan	24.06.2002	mutual agreement procedure	12 months	taxation at source: 10%	taxation at source: 10%	taxation at source: 10%
Sri Lanka	11.08.2003	mutual agreement procedure	183 days if within 12-month period	taxation at source: 10%	taxation at source: 10%	taxation at source: 10%
Albania	13.09.2004	mutual agreement procedure	9 months	taxation at source: 10%	taxation at source: 10%	taxation at source: 10%

State	Date of Signature	Residency (Article 4(3) OECD/UN Model) – Tiebreaker – Persons Other than Individuals	Permanent Establishment (Article 5(3)(a) OECD/UN Model) -Construction Site Threshold	Dividends (Article 10(2) OECD/UN Model) – Withholding Threshold	Interest (Article 11(2) OECD/UN Model) – Withholding Threshold	Royalties (Article 12 UN Model) – Withholding Threshold
Brunei	21.09.2004	mutual agreement procedure	Article 5(3)(a) OECD/UN Model	taxation at source: 5%	taxation at source: 10%	taxation at source: 10%
Azerbaijan	17.03.2005	Article 4(3) OECD/UN Model	12 months	taxation at source: 10%;	taxation at source: 10%	taxation at source: 10%
Georgia	22.06.2005	place of head office	6 months	taxation at source: 10%; 0%, if the beneficial owner is a company which holds directly or indirectly at least 50% of the capital of the company paying the dividends and has invested more	taxation at source: 10%	taxation at source: 5%

State	Date of Signature	Residency (Article 4(3) OECD/UN Model) – Tiebreaker – Persons Other than Individuals	Permanent Establishment (Article 5(3)(a) OECD/UN Model) -Construction Site Threshold	Dividends (Article 10(2) OECD/UN Model) – Withholding Threshold	Interest (Article 11(2) OECD/UN Model) – Withholding Threshold	Royalties (Article 12 UN Model) – Withholding Threshold
				than 2 million Euro in the capital of the company paying the dividends; 5%, if the beneficial owner is a company which holds directly or indirectly at least 10% of the capital of the company paying the dividends and has invested more than 100,000 Euro in the capital of the company paying the dividends		

State	Date of Signature	Residency (Article 4(3) OECD/UN Model) – Tiebreaker – Persons Other than Individuals	Permanent Establishment (Article 5(3)(a) OECD/UN Model) -Construction Site Threshold	Dividends (Article 10(2) OECD/UN Model) – Withholding Threshold	Interest (Article 11(2) OECD/UN Model) – Withholding Threshold	Royalties (Article 12 UN Model) – Withholding Threshold
Saudi Arabia	23.01.2006	Article 4(3) OECD/UN Model	Article 5(3)(a) OECD/UN Model	taxation at source: 5%	taxation at source: 10%	taxation at source: 10%
Singapore	11.06.2007	mutual agreement procedure	Article 5(3)(a) OECD/UN Model	taxation at source: 10%; 5%, if the recipient is a company (other than a partnership) directly holding at least 25% of the shares in the company, which pays out the dividends	taxation at source: 7%	taxation at source: 10%

State	Date of Signature	Residency (Article 4(3) OECD/UN Model) – Tiebreaker – Persons Other than Individuals	Permanent Establishment (Article 5(3)(a) OECD/UN Model) -Construction Site Threshold	Dividends (Article 10(2) OECD/UN Model) – Withholding Threshold	Interest (Article 11(2) OECD/UN Model) – Withholding Threshold	Royalties (Article 12 UN Model) – Withholding Threshold
Czech	28.08.2009	Article 4(3) OECD/UN Model	12 months	taxation at source: 10%; 5%, if the recipient is a company (other than a partnership) directly holding at least 25% of the shares in the company, which pays out the dividends	taxation at source: 7.5%	taxation at source: 10%
Russia	13.10.2014	Article 4(3) OECD/UN Model	18 months	taxation at source: 10%; 5%, if the recipient is a company (other than a partnership) directly holding at least 25% of the shares in the company, which	taxation at source: 5%	taxation at source: 6%

State	Date of Signature	Residency (Article 4(3) OECD/UN Model) – Tiebreaker – Persons Other than Individuals	Permanent Establishment (Article 5(3)(a) OECD/UN Model) -Construction Site Threshold	Dividends (Article 10(2) OECD/UN Model) – Withholding Threshold	Interest (Article 11(2) OECD/UN Model) – Withholding Threshold	Royalties (Article 12 UN Model) – Withholding Threshold
Romania	04.06.2016	Article 4(3) OECD/UN Model	12 months	pays out the dividends and this holding amounts to at least 80,000 Euros or its equivalent in any other currency taxation at source: 3%	taxation at source: 3%	taxation at source: 3%

12 CONCLUSION

The rationale of tax treaties is to relieve a taxpayer in either country of its liability to pay some or all of the tax due in both countries on the same income or capital. Tax treaties generally create increased certainty and set limits on the taxation of cross-border investments by allocating taxing rights between foreign direct investment recipient countries and the residence country of the investor. The allocation of taxing rights includes a specification of maximum withholding tax rates on interest, dividends, royalties and other payments from source states – generally below the rates otherwise applicable under domestic law. Tax treaties are also responsible for mitigating double taxation by 'harmonizing tax definitions, defining taxable bases, assigning taxing jurisdictions, and indicating the mechanisms to be sued to remove double taxation when it arises'.[169] Accordingly, having a broad and functioning treaty network among Belt and Road countries is a way to smooth out tax friction along the Road. However, for more predictable results, having more harmonized treaties – with standardization of certain key provision – could reduce the level of complexity in engaging in cross-border business along the Belt and Road. Ideally Belt and Road countries could create a BRI Model Tax Treaty, which should be drafted through dialogue between all Belt and Road countries, e.g., through the inauguration of a BRI tax treaty forum. One could also explore a process for a simplified multilateral instrument, which would enable a rapid updating of existing treaties.

To begin the debate, the authors provide some suggestions here. However, they first start with tax treaty design questions that need to be decided by China with the Belt and Road countries as a first step.

12.1 Tax Treaty Design Questions

Generally, tax treaties tend to shift taxing powers from the source state to the residence state – which might not be that problematic if two treaty partners are involved with largely symmetrical investment patterns.[170] However, when two countries have an asymmetrical investment position – as is quite likely in the relationship between China and Belt and Road countries, this shift in taxing powers could bring about a significant loss of tax base for various Belt and Road countries.[171] Under the BRI, the Belt and Road countries will mainly consist of net capital importing countries, with the capital streaming predominantly from China into the economy of the other Belt and Road countries, and capital income flowing back to China. Thus, the shift in taxing powers

---

169. P.L. Baker, *An Analysis of Double Tax Treaties and their Effect on Foreign Direct Investment*, 21 Intl. J. Econ. of Bus. 3, at 341, 344 (2014).
170. J. Braun & M. Zagler, *The True Art of the Tax Deal: Evidence on Aid Flows and Bilateral Double Tax Agreements*, Discussion Paper 17–011, Zentrum für Europäische Wirtschaftsforschung GmbH, available at http://ftp.zew.de/pub/zew-docs/dp/dp17011.pdf (accessed 12 Feb. 2018).
171. T. Rixen & P. Schwarz, *Bargaining Over the Avoidance of Double Taxation: Evidence from German Tax Treaties*, Finanzarchiv/Public Finance Analysis, available at http://dx.doi.org/10.2139/ssrn.2502529 (accessed 12 Feb. 2018).

from the source state to the residence country induced by a tax treaty could potentially bring about the disadvantage of tax revenue foregone from reduced withholding tax rates, in addition to the expense of treaty negotiation and administration.[172]

To neutralize these effects, a tax treaty must bring about sufficient gains from increased foreign direct investment to offset any tax revenue losses. What China together with Belt and Road countries could additionally address is a specific tax treaty policy with Belt and Road countries. There might be agreement that when entering into negotiations with Belt and Road countries, the asymmetric relationship should be borne in mind and the treaty should be aligned with the development objective of the region – which presupposes sufficient tax revenues generated in all participating countries.

12.2 Suggestions

The authors' analysis has shown that the majority of provisions in Chinese tax treaties with Belt and Road countries follow the provisions of the OECD or UN Model. However, the multiple deviations from the Models, along with different tax rates and limited anti-treaty-shopping provisions, create a potential for tax competition among countries and tax abuse by taxpayers.

Therefore, to begin the debate, the authors provide some suggestions for possible improvements to level the playing field in the BRI territory in the area of tax treaties, namely: harmonization of the construction PE timeframe, including the deemed PE for insurance undertakings; deciding on a common approach regarding the treatment of oil and gas pipelines; and a common approach to curtailing treaty shopping.

12.3 Harmonization of Construction PE Timeframe

While the majority of PE criteria are compatible, the timeframe for the creation of a construction PE varies from 183 days to 24 months – meaning that a project with the same characteristics could constitute a PE in one Belt and Road country (and entail tax and compliance issues), but not in another (and create a reduced tax burden for the company). This situation is worsened by the inclusion (or not) of certain activities in the definition of a construction PE, such as assembly or supervision of the construction project.

One can generally conclude that the majority of Chinese tax treaties with Belt and Road countries follow the UN Model with regard to activities falling within the scope of a construction PE. However, the time threshold – especially in newer treaties (*see* Table 11.2) – tends to include longer time periods of twelve months. Considering that many Belt and Road countries need the development of infrastructure and Chinese companies are performing such projects, construction companies would probably benefit

---

172. *See* e.g., M. Keen & P. Mullins, *Principles and Practice of International Taxation for the Extractive Industries*, in *International Taxation and the Extractive Industries* (P. Daniel, M. Keen, A. Swistak & V. Thuronyi eds., Routledge 2017).

from a longer timeframe for triggering a PE. However, this could mean reduced revenue potential for host countries (except those applying a branch profits tax), so the exact mechanism should be subject to discussion.

12.4 Inclusion of Deemed PE for Insurance Undertakings

Only seven Chinese tax treaties with Belt and Road countries currently include the deemed PE provision for insurance undertakings. However, because a common way to reallocate functions and risks within a multinational group is through insurance structures – known as captive insurance arrangements, the authors believe that a wider coverage of such provision would be beneficial for Belt and Road countries. Captive insurance refers to a special affiliate – generally located in a low-tax jurisdiction – that internally insures risks of various group companies.[173] While this practice may have valid business reasons, such a structure is often used by multinationals to shift profits through tax-deductible insurance premiums to captive insurance companies. This profit shifting practise is also addressed in the OECD/G20 BEPS Project.[174]

Accordingly, the authors believe that a simple measure to attribute deductible insurance premiums back to the tax base of the payer country would be to include this provision, as stipulated in Article 5(6) of the UN Model. This would trigger a PE where a non-resident enterprise collects insurance premiums or insures risk in the source state, unless such activities are conducted by an independent agent. Furthermore, the provision does not require the activities to occur through a fixed place of business in the source state or for any minimum period of time. It is sufficient that the collection of premiums take place in the source state or if the risks that are insured are located therein.[175]

Thus, including such a provision in Chinese tax treaties with Belt and Road countries could limit the profit shifting exposure. However, as the treaty provision cannot impose tax where the income is not subject to tax under domestic law, there needs to be a corresponding domestic tax law establishing the right to tax the relevant income derived from insurance premiums before this measure could be effective.

---

173. For details on captive insurance structures, *see* R. Palan, R. Murphy & C. Chavagneux, *How Globalization Really Works*, at 95–97 (Cornell U. Press 2010).
174. For a summary of measures against captives under the BEPS Project, *see* e.g., EY Global Tax Alert, *Publication of Final OECD BEPS Reports: Implications for Captive Insurers* (12 Oct. 2015), available at http://www.ey.com/Publication/vwLUAssets/Publication_of_final_OECD_BEPS _reports_Implications_for_captive_insurers/$FILE/2015G_CM5850_Publication%20of%20fin al%20OECD%20BEPS%20reports%20-%20Implications%20for%20captive%20insurers.pdf (accessed 12 Feb. 2018).
175. B.J. Arnold, *Taxation of Income from Services*, in *United Nations Handbook on Selected Issues in Protecting the Tax Base of Developing Countries*, at 66–67 (A. Trepelkov, H. Tonino & D. Halka eds., UN 2015).

12.5 Treatment of Oil and Gas Transportation by Pipeline

As existing and planned cross-border oil and gas pipelines are one of the major business projects connecting Belt and Road countries, agreeing on a common approach for the characterization and taxation of pipelines will avoid uncertainties, double taxation and double non-taxation, and will also help to limit tax disputes and administrative burdens for taxpayers and tax administrations. A pipeline is technically a transport facility, and its operation by an oil and gas extraction company residing in another country could be characterized as a preparatory or auxiliary activity not leading to a PE, and income from its operation could be treated as income from immovable property or other income. These multiple potential characterization options have the potential to lead to multiple taxation outcomes.

In practice, these issues are often mitigated by establishing a special local company – the operator of the pipeline. For more certainty in cases where the operation of a pipeline constitutes one of a company's activities, Belt and Road countries could agree that transportation of oil and gas in a cross-border pipeline always constitutes a core business activity of an oil and gas company, and thus satisfies all tests related to the basic fixed place of business PE rule.

In a second step, this would still require an agreement on guidelines regarding the allocation of income from cross-border pipelines – an endeavour complex in nature, as the attribution of assets, risks and free capital, as well as the recognition of dealings, seems to be a difficult task when it comes to technically complex assets, with a cross-border, onshore and offshore character. However, in the long run, agreeing on a treatment and allocation rules a priori would boost certainty and limit tax disputes.

12.6 Special Provision on Interest Income

The special provision limiting source state withholding tax when the recipient of the interest income is a financial institution connected to the government of the other state is of high relevancy for the BRI. Infrastructure investments are generally highly geared and much of the debt funding will be provided via public and private financiers. Thus, having a more harmonized and broader clause incorporated in the treaties, which in turn would make the funding of infrastructure projects more attractive (also for the private sector), would be advisable if the desire is to promote such investments.

12.7 A Common Approach to Anti-Treaty Shopping

The authors' final suggestion is based on three Chinese tax treaties which include anti-treaty-shopping provisions in the articles on dividends, interest and royalties, and involves limiting the number of tax treaties covering beneficial owners rather than immediate recipients of such income. There will be opportunities for aggressive tax avoidance as long as tax treaties with Belt and Road countries provide for tax rates for such types of income ranging from 3% to 15%. A more widespread prevalence of anti-treaty-shopping mechanisms (whether in the form of a limitation on benefits, beneficial owner provision or other mechanisms) could secure the tax revenue of the countries in question, as well as create a more fair tax environment.

CHAPTER 12
VAT Challenges in the Belt and Road Initiative

Yuliya Shved & Karoline Spies

1   VAT as a 'Good Tax'
    1.1   The Character and Importance of VAT
    1.2   Neutrality
    1.3   Implementing the Destination Principle
2   The Belt and Road Initiative and VAT
    2.1   VAT in the Belt and Road Countries
    2.2   VAT Transactions in the Belt and Road Initiative
    2.3   VAT Challenges in the Belt and Road Initiative and Solutions Thereto
        2.3.1   *Double Taxation (or Non-Taxation)*
        2.3.2   *Lack of Dispute Resolution Mechanism*
        2.3.3   *Disproportional Documentary Requirements*
        2.3.4   *Irrecoverable Input VAT*
3   Existing Harmonization: The EAEU Treaty
    3.1   Historical Background
    3.2   The EAEU and VAT
    3.3   Scope
    3.4   Supply of Goods
        3.4.1   *Place of Taxation*
        3.4.2   *Export of Goods*
        3.4.3   *Import of Goods*
        3.4.4   *Practice*
    3.5   Supply of Services and Works
        3.5.1   *Place of Taxation*
        3.5.2   *Documentary Requirements*

3.5.3 *Practice*
3.6 **Conclusion**
4   **A Comprehensive Multilateral Treaty for VAT? Or Mere Soft Law Instruments?**

1 VAT AS A 'GOOD TAX'

1.1 The Character and Importance of VAT

The significance of VAT on a global basis is steadily increasing. In the last three decades, there has been a global move towards the introduction of consumption taxes. Currently, already more than 160 countries worldwide levy a VAT.[1] Apart from the new introduction of VAT, many states have also taken measures to increase their already existing indirect taxes in the past years by increasing rates or narrowing the scope of exemptions.[2] VAT raised approximately one-fifth of total tax revenues in the OECD and worldwide in 2016 – the all-time high.[3] The reasons for this rise of VAT are manifold:[4] From an economic perspective, VAT is seen as a neutral tax and less detrimental to economic growth than income taxes. From an administrative perspective, VAT is relatively easy to manage, as the collection of the tax is mainly outsourced to businesses. In addition to these policy benefits, VAT also has a comparatively high capacity to raise tax revenue which may be, indeed, the major driver for its popularity. As the states, due to the policy challenges caused by the economic and financial crisis, have a need to maintain and/or achieve fiscal sustainability without harming economic growth, VAT seems to be the logical choice. Due to increasing cross-border trade and the increasing popularity of VAT, the causes of double taxation will increase in the (near) future.

VAT is defined as a broad-based indirect tax on consumption.[5] The most significant characteristics of a VAT are: taxation of final consumption, the neutrality principle, the destination principle and the indirect-collection method.[6] The overarching purpose of a VAT is the taxation of final consumption of goods and services by private households. Based on this purpose, VAT should be neutral on businesses. This basic principle of neutrality is recognized by tax policymakers[7] and the

---

1. According to a study by the OECD (OECD, *Consumption Tax Trends 2016: VAT/GST and Excise Rates, Trends and Policy Issues*, 181 (OECD Publishing 2016)), 166 countries operated a VAT as of 1 Jan. 2016; including all OECD Member Countries and major economies (except the US).
2. OECD, *Consumption Tax Trends 2016*, supra n. 1, at 11; European Commission, *Tax Reforms in EU Member States 2014: Tax Policy Challenges for Economic Growth and Fiscal Sustainability*, at 17 (2014).
3. OECD, *Consumption Tax Trends 2016*, supra n. 1, at 14, 16.
4. *Ibid.*, at 19.
5. OECD, *International VAT/GST Guidelines*, Chapter I, para. 1.2 (OECD Publishing 2017); B. Terra & J. Kajus, *Introduction to European VAT (Recast)*, section 7.2 (IBFD online, last reviewed on 1 Jan. 2017); T. Ecker, *A VAT/GST Model Convention*, 92 (IBFD, 2013).
6. OECD, *Consumption Tax Trends 2016*, supra n. 1, at 19–33; OECD, *International VAT/GST Guidelines*, supra n. 5, paras. 1.1 to 1.15.
7. OECD, *Consumption Tax Trends 2016*, supra n. 1, at 20–21.

OECD.[8] Based on the neutrality principle, VAT law should not influence business decisions and not discriminate between businesses in similar situations.[9] The neutrality principle is also tremendously linked to the right of equal treatment guaranteed by the constitutional law of many jurisdictions.[10] A further consequence of the taxation of final consumption is the destination principle,[11] under which supplies that take place in a cross-border setting are to be taxed within the jurisdiction where consumption takes place, regardless of the location of the supplier.[12] To guarantee the destination principle, exports are zero-rated or made VAT free, meaning that exports are exempt from VAT (invoice without VAT) with the right to input VAT deduction on connected input costs, or the tax incurred on exported goods or services (if any) is to be refunded.[13] Currently, there is widespread consensus at the OECD level that the destination principle is preferable to the origin principle from both a theoretical and practical standpoint.[14]

Although VAT should be borne by private households, VAT – being an indirect tax – is collected in stages by businesses. In order to guarantee neutrality, businesses have a right to deduct VAT paid to other businesses (invoice-credit method), provided that the goods and services are used to carry out taxable transactions.[15] Thus, VAT should – as a rule – not be a cost element for businesses.[16] Moreover, as under VAT law businesses act as tax collectors without being remunerated for it, VAT law should be interpreted and drafted carefully in order to keep the compliance costs for businesses at a proportional level.[17]

So far, there is neither an international legal framework[18] nor – compared to income tax – a great number of publications dealing with international VAT issues. However, uncoordinated application of VAT systems raises risks of double- and non-taxation. The OECD has only recently begun to devote more attention to the VAT area. In 2012 a Global Forum on VAT was established: a platform for a worldwide

---

8. OECD, *International VAT/GST Guidelines*, supra n. 5, at Chapter 2.
9. *Ibid.*, Guidelines 2.1 and 2.2. For the EU, *see* e.g., UK: ECJ, 10 Nov. 2011, Joined Cases C-259/10 & C-260/10, *The Rank Group*, ECLI:EU:C:2011:719, para. 41.
10. *See* e.g., UK: ECJ, 10 Apr. 2008, Case C-309/06, *Marks & Spencer plc v. Commissioners of Customs & Excise*, ECLI:EU:C:2008:211, para. 49; SK: ECJ, 26 Oct. 2017, Case C-534/16, *Finančné riaditel'stvo Slovenskej republiky v. BB construct s.r.o.*, ECLI:EU:C:2017:820, para. 29.
11. OECD, *Consumption Tax Trends 2016*, supra n. 1, at 24–25.
12. *Ibid.*, at 24–32.
13. *Ibid.*, at 24.
14. OECD, *International VAT/GST Guidelines*, supra n. 5, paras. 1.8 et seq. & Guideline 3.1; OECD, *Consumption Tax Trends 2016*, supra n. 1, at 24–25.
15. OECD, *Consumption Tax Trends 2016*, supra n. 1, at 20. Only a minor number of countries seems to use the subtraction method (e.g., Japan).
16. However, under the EU VAT Directive 2006/112/EC – similar to the legal basis in many other states – not every entrepreneur is entitled to a full deduction of input VAT. The most prominent example of exempt transactions that do not generate a right to deduct input VAT are financial services (Articles 131–137 of the EU VAT Directive). For companies conducting such business, input VAT is a cost element.
17. This is in particular highlighted in German literature. *See* e.g., H. Stadie, *In dubio pro fisco – BFH verneint Ist-Besteuerung für Freiberufler-GmbH*, 2 Umsatzsteuer-Rundschau, at 45, 48–55 (2011)).
18. *But compare* the proposed text for a VAT/GST Model Convention developed by Ecker, *supra* n. 5.

dialogue on the design and operation of VAT.[19] After discussions with several stakeholders, in April 2014 the OECD published the International VAT/GST Guidelines summarizing general principles for national VAT regimes and proposing solutions for certain international issues. Although these Guidelines have a soft law character only, it is presumed that they will gain increasing importance in the future, as they have already been endorsed by approximately 100 jurisdictions/international organizations. In September 2016, the OECD Council adopted the Guidelines as a Recommendation which gives them the status as the 'first OECD legal instrument in the area of VAT' and the 'first internationally agreed framework for the application of VAT to cross-border trade'.[20] The Recommendation is addressed to OECD member countries and non-members that have adhered to it.

Of course, neither the OECD International VAT/GST Guidelines nor any other international legal instrument forces states to introduce a VAT. This is still the free policy decision of each state. However, if a policy decision is made in favour of a VAT, the character and aim of a VAT and its guiding principles should always be kept in mind.

1.2 Neutrality

The OECD International VAT/GST Guidelines include basic principles that any domestic VAT system should follow. Based on the neutrality principle, the Guidelines in particular highlight the following guiding principles for the design of a VAT system (Chapter 1):

- the burden of VAT should not lie on businesses. To ensure this principle, suppliers should be entitled to full input VAT deduction at each stage. Exceptions to this rule should be clear and explicit within the legislation and should be justified by valid administrative/tax policy arguments;[21]
- businesses in similar situations carrying out similar transactions should be treated equally, in particular with respect to the level of taxation;[22]
- VAT rules should not influence business decisions. In particular, they should not induce business to adopt a specific legal structure (subsidiary/branch);[23]
- foreign businesses should not incur irrecoverable VAT. States can choose from different means to achieve this result;[24] and
- necessary administrative requirements for foreign businesses should be proportional.[25]

---

19. The First Global Forum on VAT took place in Paris, France on 7-8 Nov. 2012.
20. OECD, *International VAT/GST Guidelines*, supra n. 5, at 4.
21. *Ibid.*, paras. 2.3-2.5.
22. *Ibid.*, Guideline 2.2.
23. *Ibid.*, Guideline 2.3.
24. *Ibid.*, Guidelines 2.4 & 2.5, paras. 2.15-2.18.
25. OECD, *International VAT/GST Guidelines*, supra n. 5, Guideline 2.6.

1.3 Implementing the Destination Principle

The Guidelines particularly focus on the implementation of the destination principle for the supply of services and include place-of-taxation rules for B2B (Chapter 2) and B2C services (Chapter 3). The Guidelines seek to ensure that the place-of-taxation rules are applied consistently by promoting an internationally accepted standard with a view to minimizing uncertainty, revenue risks and compliance costs. To achieve this aim, the Guidelines identify common objectives, but need not be literally incorporated.[26] So far, the Guidelines do not include rules for the cross-border supply of goods. However, internationally recognized principles can also be found in the periodical report on Consumption Tax Trends published by the OECD.[27]

The supply of 'goods' – commonly understood as 'tangible property' – should be taxed in the jurisdiction where the goods are located at the time of the transaction. Cross-border VAT on goods commonly is closely linked to customs. When a transaction involves the movement of goods to another jurisdiction, the exported goods are generally 'free of VAT' (zero-rated) in the origin state and are also freed of any input VAT costs via credit or refund. In order to guarantee taxation at the place of destination, the goods are subject to VAT in the state of destination at the same time as customs duties. Deduction of this import VAT should be possible in the same way as input tax deduction on domestic supplies. For simplification reasons, many states apply exemptions for the import of low-value goods and the import of goods in the personal luggage of final customers.[28]

A 'service' is commonly negatively defined as any supply other than the supply of tangible property, and also includes intangibles. Some jurisdiction, however, deal with intangibles as a separate third category (*see* section 3.5 on the Treaty on the Eurasian Economic Union (EAEU)).[29] Most jurisdictions distinguish between B2B and B2C supplies, as both categories follow a different understanding of 'consumption' and also require different means of tax collection. The OECD International VAT/GST Guidelines also follow this differentiation.[30]

In principle, services should be taxed in the jurisdiction of actual use (B2B) or consumption (B2C). However, as VAT needs to be charged before the time of actual use or consumption, there is a need for feasible proxies to achieve legal certainty.[31] Under the general rule, B2B services including the supply of intangibles are to be taxed in the jurisdiction where the business customer is located. The location of the customer is to be located by reference to the business agreement.[32] If the business customer is a legal entity with establishments in different jurisdictions ('multiple location entity'), the taxing right accrues to the jurisdiction where the establishment using the service is

---

26. *Ibid.*, para. 3.4.
27. OECD, *Consumption Tax Trends 2016*, supra n. 1, at 26–28.
28. *Ibid.*, at 26.
29. *Ibid.*, at 28.
30. OECD, *International VAT/GST Guidelines*, supra n. 5, para. 3.5.
31. *Ibid.*, para. 3.6.
32. *Ibid.*, Guidelines 3.2 & 3.3.

located.³³ Of utmost importance to ensure neutrality in international trade is that the supplier is allowed to make the supply free of VAT in its jurisdiction, but still retains the right to full input VAT credit on inputs related to making such international supplies, equally to domestic supplies.³⁴

With respect to B2C services, the Guidelines suggest that the place of taxation primarily rests with the place of usual residence of the final customer.³⁵ The Guidelines propose one major exception for B2C services: in the case of on-the-spot supplies where supplier and customer are present at the same place at the same time (e.g., restaurant services, beauty and cultural services), the taxing right should accrue to the jurisdiction of actual supply.³⁶

In addition to these general rules for B2B and B2C services, the OECD Guidelines also acknowledge that some jurisdictions might want to implement more specific rules for certain services. In this respect, the Guidelines highlight that such special rules are to be used only if the reference to the customer's location or the place of actual supply does not lead to an appropriate result when considering neutrality, efficiency, certainty, simplicity, effectiveness and fairness.³⁷ One example where such special rules might be justified are services and intangibles directly connected with immovable property which may be more accurately taxed in the jurisdiction where the immovable property is located.³⁸ This principle is has already been implemented by many jurisdictions.³⁹ Moreover, special rules may also be legitimate for the international transport of persons and other services connected with movable property.⁴⁰

2 THE BELT AND ROAD INITIATIVE AND VAT

2.1 VAT in the Belt and Road Countries

The VAT systems in the countries that are part of the Belt and Road Initiative are very diverse. Russia and China seem to have comprehensive VAT systems. China is currently undergoing a reform of its VAT system and will ultimately have a modern VAT system. Moreover, also many other countries, such as Armenia, Azerbaijan, Belarus, Georgia, Kyrgyzstan, Moldova, Pakistan, Philippines, Singapore, Tajikistan, Turkmenistan and Uzbekistan, have a VAT system in place.⁴¹ Rates, exemptions, paying obligations, registration and documentation requirements, and procedural rules

---

33. *Ibid.*, Guideline 3.4.
34. *Ibid.*, para. 3.10.
35. *Ibid.*, Guideline 3.6.
36. *Ibid.*, Guideline 3.5.
37. *Ibid.*, Guideline 3.7, paras. 3.155–3163.
38. *Ibid.*, Guideline 3.8, paras. 3.170–3.179.
39. For example., Article 47 EU VAT Directive.
40. OECD, *International VAT/GST Guidelines*, supra n. 5, paras. 3.167 and 3.180.
41. OECD, *Consumption Tax Trends 2016*, supra n. 1, at 181 (Annex A). Verified by the IBFD database and Ernst & Young, *2017 Worldwide VAT, GST and Sales Tax Guide*, available at http://www.ey.com/gl/en/services/tax/worldwide-vat--gst-and-sales-tax-guide---rates (accessed 22 Nov. 2017).

are different in every country.[42] Also, the tax policy developments vary from country to country. For example, Kazakhstan had a plan to scrap its VAT regime in favour of a simplified sales tax system (as of 2016). However, this plan was withdrawn in December 2016. Of course, it is still each country's free policy decision whether to introduce a VAT at all. Many countries that are part of the Belt and Road Initiative are underdeveloped, and their development and growth depend to a large extent on tax revenue. Thus, the overall aim for the countries that are part of the Belt and Road Initiative should be to achieve an accurate balance between securing revenue, on the one hand and simplifying the procedures for businesses, on the other.

VAT on cross-border trade is partly also regulated by bilateral and multilateral treaties, especially the Treaty on the Eurasian Customs Union (*see* section 3.). However, not all countries that are part of the Belt and Road Initiative are parties to such treaties (especially China). Their territorial scope is rather limited.

2.2 VAT Transactions in the Belt and Road Initiative

The Belt and Road Initiative will involve in particular the following transactions: building of infrastructure (e.g., roads, rails); the passing through of goods along these roads; and exploiting extractive industries. For VAT purposes, it is important to bear in mind that these undertakings will primarily consist of B2B transactions (not B2C transactions). Based on the logic of a VAT system, these B2B transactions should not result in any VAT costs for businesses. Moreover, as businesses act as (unpaid) tax collectors for the state, compliance rules should be simple. However, the development and growth of many countries that are part of the Belt and Road Initiative depend to a large extent on tax revenue. An appropriate balance between these two (partly conflicting) objectives of ensuring simplicity and generating revenues is needed.

2.3 VAT Challenges in the Belt and Road Initiative and Solutions Thereto

The Belt and Road Initiative may involve a number of VAT issues triggered by non-harmonized domestic VAT rules, the lack of a comprehensive knowledge of VAT systems and the lack of qualified staff and human resources within tax administrations. There are four main obstacles to cross-border transactions in the Belt and Road Initiative in the area of VAT, namely double taxation or non-taxation, dispute resolution, documentary-requirements, and irrecoverable input VAT. These will be discussed separately below.

---

42. For example the standard rates differ in every country, and some countries also provide reduced rates. Examples of standard rates: Armenia 20%, Azerbaijan 18%, Belarus 20%, China 17%, Georgia 18%, Kazakhstan 12%, Moldova 20%, Philippines 12%, Russia 18%, Ukraine 20%, Uzbekistan 20%. For details, *see* OECD, *Consumption Tax Trends 2016*, *supra* n. 1, at 181 (Annex A).

2.3.1 Double Taxation (or Non-Taxation)

As the domestic VAT systems are not exhaustively harmonized, two or more states may levy VAT on the same supply of goods or services, leading to double taxation. Even if states – following the OECD International VAT/GST Guidelines – agree in principle to implement the destination principle, they may use different proxies to define the place of consumption, and may have also a different understanding of the basic principles in detail, for example when determining whether a supply concerns a good, a service or an intangible. Double taxation in VAT involves overlapping jurisdictions based on the domestic law of at least two states and is triggered if at least two states tax the same supply.[43] As VAT is an indirect tax and focuses on transactions rather than persons, juridical double taxation in VAT, in contrast to direct tax law, does not require a tax burden on the same taxpayer, but may also involve two different taxpayers (supplier and buyer).[44] Similarly, non-harmonized VAT rules can also lead to non-taxation if both states allocate the taxing right to the other state. Non-taxation has distortive effects on the competition and economy and is equally to be prevented. The instruments to prevent double taxation and non-taxation are the so-called place-of-taxation rules, which should allocate the taxing right on one supply to one jurisdiction only, by establishing common proxies for the place of consumption. The OECD International VAT/GST Guidelines include place-of-taxation rules for services which could serve as guidance for countries that are part of the Belt and Road Initiative.[45]

However, if one looks at the place-of-taxation rules in the OECD International VAT/GST Guidelines and established international practice, double taxation may not be the most critical problem in the Belt and Road project, at least at first glance. It is common ground that the cross-border supply and transfer of goods should lead to taxation only in the importation state. The state of origin should zero-rate or exempt the supply. Also, the EAEU Treaty follows this principle (*see* section 3.4.2.). Moreover, it is also common ground that the place of taxation for infrastructure projects should rest with the state where the infrastructure (immovable property) is located.[46] The EAEU Treaty also stipulates this principle (*see* section 3.5.1.). Technical or advisory services should be taxed at the place of establishment of the customer.[47] The EAEU Treaty also seems to follow this principle (*see* section 3.5.1.). Thus, for most transactions, no double taxation or non-taxation should occur if the states follow the destination principle and the international standard as laid down in the OECD VAT/GST Guidelines.

Conflicts and double taxation may, however, still occur for some supplies. For example, when identifying the place of taxation for technical or advisory services, states may disagree as to whether the customer has a permanent establishment in a state and whether the services were provided to that establishment or the head office. There is no common definition of the term '(permanent) establishment' for VAT

---

43. Ecker, *supra* n. 5, at 535 et seq.
44. For example AT: ECJ, 11 Sep. 2003, Case C-155/01, *Cookies World Vertriebsgesellschaft mbH iL v. Finanzlandesdirektion für Tirol*, ECLI:EU:C:2003:449.
45. *See supra* section 1.3.
46. OECD, *International VAT/GST Guidelines*, *supra* n. 5, Guideline 3.8.
47. *Ibid.*, Guideline 3.2.

Chapter 12: VAT Challenges in the "Belt-Road" Initiative

purposes which is, however, frequently used as a proxy under domestic place-of-taxation rules for services. As yet, the OECD VAT/GST Guidelines also do not give a detailed definition. Only in a footnote is it stated that an establishment 'comprises a fixed place of business with a sufficient level of infrastructure in terms of people, systems and assets to be able to receive and/or make supplies. Registration for VAT purposes by itself does not constitute an establishment'.[48] This description is rather vague, and issues of consistency or divergence with the definition in Article 5 of the OECD Model Convention (OECD Model) – which includes much more detail, including negative and positive examples and timing requirements – may arise.[49]

Furthermore, states can also disagree as to whether services are linked closely to an immovable property and, thus, fall within the special place-of-taxation rule or the general B2B rule. The OECD VAT/GST Guidelines call for a 'very close, clear and obvious link or association with the immovable property', and provide an indicative list of such services, including the sale and leasing of real estate, construction, and maintaining services provided to the immovable property.[50] Still, in particular for intellectual services (e.g., advisory, architectural) the connection to immovable property might be highly disputed.

Moreover, and even more significantly, to achieve neutrality and to avoid a double burden of VAT, it is not sufficient that the state of origin (in the case of the supply of goods) or the state of residence of the supplier (in the case of the cross-border supply of services) exempts the supply. Additionally, an accurate implementation of the neutrality and destination principles also requires that the state of origin or state of residence of the supplier grant an input VAT deduction for input costs necessary for making the supply, based on the same principles as applicable for domestic supplies.[51] Denying an input VAT credit for costs connected to the export of goods or services leads to a double burden of VAT, contradicts the neutrality principle and will tremendously distort competition. Some domestic VAT systems in Belt and Road countries still seem to deny an input VAT credit for the export of services or impose very strict requirements.[52]

2.3.2 Lack of Dispute Resolution Mechanism

If there is a dispute between states or between a non-resident taxpayer and tax administrations, there is no international legal framework to rely on and to resolve the dispute. One might discuss the applicability of dispute resolution or arbitration rules under international treaties not specifically targeted at VAT (e.g., income tax treaties,

---

48. *Ibid.*, at footnote 24.
49. On a systematic comparison of the concept of a permanent establishment as defined in Article 5 of the OECD Model and the concept of a fixed establishment as used in the EU VAT Directive, see K. Spies, *Permanent Establishment versus Fixed Establishment: The Same or Different?*, 71 Bull. Intl. Taxn. 12 (2017).
50. OECD, *International VAT/GST Guidelines*, *supra* n. 5, para. 3.173.
51. *See also* OECD, *Consumption Tax Trends 2016*, *supra* n. 1, at 26; OECD, *International VAT/GST Guidelines*, *supra* n. 5, para. 3.10.
52. *See* section 3.5.

investment treaties, WTO law). However, these treaties may provide only very limited help. Most critically, dispute resolution for double taxation issues requires a legal basis to rely on and, thus, a binding bilateral or multilateral VAT treaty with place-of-taxation rules in the first place. As long as there is no such bilateral or multilateral treaty in place, dispute resolution for double taxation issues seems not feasible. The OECD VAT/GST Guidelines as a mere soft law instrument are not sufficient in this regard. Moreover, only China and Russia have a comprehensive tax treaty network for direct tax matters. Thus, the mutual agreement procedure in Article 25 of the OECD Model – even if it could be applied to VAT – cannot be relied on in most cases. Moreover, WTO rules, bilateral investment treaties and free trade agreements may cover only very severe obstacles (expropriation) and are not targeted at double taxation.

2.3.3 Disproportional Documentary Requirements

Even if states follow the destination principle and apply similar place-of-taxation rules and proxies, they still also might impose different and very burdensome documentary requirements in order to benefit from zero-rating, input VAT refund or other benefits. For example, the EAEU Treaty permits the contracting states to require the exporting supplier to provide a payment confirmation of VAT by the buyer in the importing state within strict time limits in order to be eligible for zero-rating (*see* section 3.4.2.). Such evidence rules and burden of proof could be in conflict with the neutrality and non-discrimination principle.

2.3.4 Irrecoverable Input VAT

Irrecoverable input VAT may in particular arise in two main scenarios: (i) the state of residence of the supplier providing services to foreign business customers ('exporting' state) disallows input VAT deduction for costs connected to the 'exported' services and (ii) non-resident businesses buy goods or services that are subject to VAT in a state different from their residence state and this state makes the input VAT refund subject to strict condition (e.g., taxable output supplies). Both categories have in common that some countries still seem to use VAT as a means to obtain revenue also in B2B transactions – which indicates that these countries do not fully understand the logic of a VAT system.

The first category was already discussed in section 2.3.1. This scenario may appear, for example, in the states that are party to the EAEU Treaty (*see* section 3.5.). Neutrality in international trade can be achieved only if the 'exporting' state permits input VAT deduction for such scenarios on an equal level to domestic supplies.

The second category can arise in even more countries. It seems that many countries do not allow for input VAT refund for non-residents or make input VAT refund subject to several conditions. In these situations, VAT becomes a cost element for businesses which might hinder investments. Such scenarios of input VAT costs might in particular occur when setting up infrastructure projects by non-resident businesses, as the place of taxation of such supplies rests with the jurisdiction where the immovable property is located. Moreover, also the import or the pass-through of goods could trigger similar issues. The lack of presence of the taxable persons raises risks of tax evasion and avoidance. Thus, many states make input VAT refund for non-residents subject to strict requirements. Various restrictions can be identified: tax registration; special audits and inspections; the limitation of refund to VAT payable on taxable supplies; a carry-forward for excess of input VAT only (with a statute of limitations) or a *de minimis* threshold. Another problem could be that the conditions are not even clearly specified in the legislation. Moreover, even if the refund is ultimately granted, refund procedures (including special audits) might take a very long time, which in turn leads to high cash-flow costs for businesses.

The overall aim for the countries that are part of the Belt and Road Initiative should be to achieve an accurate balance between securing revenue on the one hand, and simplifying the procedures for businesses on the other. From a general perspective, it is also important to promote awareness of the character of a VAT, namely that VAT is not a means for revenue generating in B2B transactions, but only in B2C transactions.

Especially with respect to the second category, there are two means by which states can limit the burdens for non-residents business and prevent irrecoverable input VAT:[53]

- *prevent taxation*. One option is to prevent taxation of the supply in the first place. Preventing taxation for B2B transactions avoids the problem of refund procedures, as it solves the problem one level earlier. However, this approach would have to be accompanied by anti-abuse and fraud measures which ensure that only (eligible) businesses profit from the exemption regime. This approach could include different means, such as an exemption for specific industries/transactions, purchase exemption certificates for business, zero-rating or tax-free zones;
- *simplify input VAT refund*. A second option would be to simplify the refund regime and call for only vital (proportional) conditions. Such a system should be accessible via an online portal and be explained by easily available manuals in English. The conditions for input VAT refund and the administrative procedure should be as simple as possible. For pass-through goods, an exemption is a better option than a burdensome and time-consuming refund procedure. The OECD VAT/GST Guidelines list the possibility of a *de minimis* threshold and the requirement of local registration as proportional requirements.

Both approaches carry different pros and cons (*see* Figure 12.1). Most of all, preventing taxation seems to be more favourable for the business customer, as he does not suffer any cash-flow disadvantage. It is also easier to administer than a refund procedure. However, this approach would entail the need for anti-abuse and anti-fraud measures. For example, for pass-through goods, a tracking system would be necessary to make sure that only those goods profit from the exemption which really pass through

---

53. *See also* OECD, *International VAT/GST Guidelines*, *supra* n. 5, paras. 2.56–2.59.

the country. Also when applying zero-rating for supply of goods or services connected with infrastructure projects, it would be necessary to implement control systems to check whether the receiving persons are indeed using the goods/services for business purposes. This approach could also include burdensome documentary requirements on the side of the supplier, as he will need to verify the status of its customer. Moreover, tax-free zones with a (too) broad scope (including, for example, income taxes and wage taxes) – although easier to administer than exemptions or zero-rating – may lead to large disproportionate losses in tax revenue.

The approach of a simplified VAT refund system is more favourable for states, as they will benefit from a cash-flow advantage. It also reduces the compliance burden of the supplier, as it shifts the responsibilities to the customer. However, the business customer is at a liquidity and compliance disadvantage.

A third option would be to implement a mix of both measures (prevention for some supplies/industries and simplification for others).

Figure 12.1   Overview: Pros and Cons of the Two Options

	Prevent taxation	Simplified VAT refund
+	• No money inflow and outflow • Business friendly, since there is no need to claim VAT back	• Less compliance burden on the supplier • Cash-flow advantage for states
−	− Definition of exempt transactions/tax-free zone crucial − Overly broad scope may lead to disproportionate losses in revenue − Necessity of anti-fraud and anti-abuse measures − Supplier must verify status and location of the customer	− Adequate balance difficult: requirements might be disproportionate − Money flow may trigger risks of fraud and evasion − Compliance costs and cash-flow disadvantage for customer

3   EXISTING HARMONIZATION: THE EAEU TREATY

3.1   Historical Background

Here, a brief overview is provided on the process of harmonization and existing system with respect to VAT between Member States of the Eurasian Economic Union (EAEU) involved in the Belt and Road Initiative.

Armenia, Azerbaijan, Belarus, Kazakhstan, Kyrgyzstan, Moldova, Russia, Tajikistan and Uzbekistan are Member States of the Commonwealth of Independent States

Chapter 12: VAT Challenges in the "Belt-Road" Initiative

(CIS).[54] Initially, VAT on cross-border trade between CIS Member States was based on the origin principle,[55] which was replaced by the destination principle at the beginning of the 2000s.

By signing the Treaty on the Establishment of the Economic Union in Moscow on 24 September 1993,[56] the CIS Member States agreed to promote economic integration in phases. The following four consecutive phases were chosen as the most appropriate:[57]

(1) establishment of an intergovernmental (multilateral) free trade area;
(2) a customs union;
(3) a common market of goods, services, capital and labour; and
(4) a currency (monetary) union.

Moving towards the consistent implementation of the provisions of the Treaty, on 15 April 1994 the CIS Member States signed the Agreement on Establishment of the Free Trade Zone.[58] The Agreement itself did not include any provisions regarding VAT in a cross-border context, and was later supplemented by a Protocol, signed on 2 April 1999. Under Article 17 of this Protocol, the CIS Member States 'do not levy any indirect taxes (VAT and excise taxes) on goods (works, services) which were exported from the customs territory of one member state to the customs territory of the other member state'.[59] This provision, in fact, already obliged the CIS Member States to apply a zero rate of VAT on exports of goods (works, services) or tax exemption, if there was no zero rating in the domestic law of the particular Member State. During 1999–2003, the Protocol entered into force for Tajikistan (24 November 1999), Uzbekistan (24 November 1999), Belarus (24 November 1999), Moldova (13 December 1999), Ukraine (15 December 1999), Armenia (22 January 2000), Kazakhstan (27 January 2000), Kyrgyzstan (01 February 2000), Azerbaijan (12 July 2000) and Georgia (21 January 2003).

Moreover, some CIS countries also concluded a number of bilateral and multilateral treaties on indirect taxes, as a rule, with the other CIS Member States.[60] These treaties more or less followed the same structure and aimed at the implementation of the destination principle for the cross-border supply of goods (works, services). For instance, in 2000, Russia concluded tax treaties with Kazakhstan, Armenia, and

---

54. Turkmenistan and Ukraine are associate states to the CIS. Moreover, Georgia was part of the CIS until August 2009.
55. Schenk Alan, Thuronyi Victor, Cui Wei, *Value Added Tax. A Comparative Approach.* 195 (Cambridge University Press, 2015).
56. Договор о создании Экономического союза [Электронный ресурс]: [заключен в г. Москве, 24.09.1993 г.] // ConsultantPlus. Russia / Closed JSC 'ConsultantPlus'. – Moscow, 2017.
57. Короткова, К.Е. Формы интеграционного взаимодействия стран постсоветсткого пространства / К.Е. Короткова // Вест. Волгогр. гос. ун-та. Сер. 4, Ист. 2013. – № 2 (24). – С. 147 – 155.
58. О создании зоны свободной торговли: Соглашение стран СНГ от 15.04.1994 Г. // ConsultantPlus. Russia / Closed JSC 'ConsultantPlus'. – Moscow, 2017.
59. Authors' translation.
60. T. Ecker & E. Variychuk, *VAT Treaties: The Russian Federation*, 2 World J. VAT/GST Tax 2, at 81 (2013).

Azerbaijan.[61] In 2001, agreements were signed by Russia with Uzbekistan and Moldova.[62] Belarus signed bilateral agreements with Ukraine (11 December 1998), Moldova (28 June 1999), Kazakhstan (1 September 1999), Tajikistan (14 June 2000), Armenia (20 March 2001), Azerbaijan (6 April 2002), Turkmenistan (15 July 2002) and the Russian Federation (1 January 2005).[63] Thus, step by step, the CIS countries implemented the destination principle with the aim of providing neutrality of VAT in international trade.[64]

In 2004, Belarus and Russia signed the Agreement on the Principles of Indirect Taxes[65],[66] which served as a basis for a subsequent multilateral Agreement on the Principles of Indirect Taxes signed by Belarus, Kazakhstan and Russia in 2008.[67],[68]

---

61. Соглашение между Правительством Российской Федерации и Правительством Республики Казахстан о принципах взимания косвенных налогов во взаимной торговле [Электронный ресурс]: [совершено в г. Астане 09.10.2000 г.]; Соглашение между Правительством Российской Федерации и Правительством Армении о принципах взимания косвенных налогов во взаимной торговле [Электронный ресурс]: [совершено в г. Москве 20.10.2000 г.]: в ред. от 25.09.2007; Соглашение между Правительством Российской Федерации и Правительством Азербайджанской Республики о принципах взимания косвенных налогов во взаимной торговле [Электронный ресурс]: [совершено в г. Баку 29.11.2000 г.] // ConsultantPlus. Russia / Closed JSC 'ConsultantPlus'. – Moscow, 2017.

62. Соглашение между Правительством Российской Федерации и Правительством Республики Узбекистан о принципах взимания косвенных налогов во взаимной торговле [Электронный ресурс]: [совершено в г. Минске 04.05.2001 г.]; Соглашение между Правительством Российской Федерации и Правительством Республики Молдова о принципах взимания косвенных налогов во взаимной торговле [Электронный ресурс]: [совершено в г. Кишинэу 29.05.2001 г.]: в ред. от 18.07.2007 г. // ConsultantPlus. Russia / Closed JSC 'ConsultantPlus'. – Moscow, 2017.

63. Соглашение между правительством Республики Беларусь и кабинетом министров Украины о принципах взимания косвенных налогов при экспорте и импорте товаров (работ, услуг) [Электронный ресурс]: [совершено в г. Минске 11.12.1998 г.]; Соглашение между правительством Республики Беларусь и правительством Республики Молдова о принципах взимания косвенных налогов при экспорте и импорте товаров (работ) [Электронный ресурс]: [совершено в г. Минске 11.02.1999 г.] Республики Таджикистан о принципах взимания косвенных налогов при экспорте и импорте товаров (работ) [Электронный ресурс]: [совершено в г. Минске 14 дек. 1999 г.]; Соглашение между правительством Республики Беларусь и правительством Республики Казахстан о принципах взимания косвенных налогов при экспорте и импорте товаров (работ) [Электронный ресурс]: [совершено в г. Минске 02.02.1999 г.]; Соглашение между правительством Республики Беларусь и правительством Республики Армении о принципах взимания косвенных налогов при экспорте и импорте товаров (работ) [Электронный ресурс]: [совершено в г. Ереване 31.10.2000 г.]; Соглашение между правительством Республики Беларусь и правительством Туркменистана о принципах взимания косвенных налогов при экспорте и импорте товаров (работ, услуг) [Электронный ресурс]: [совершено в г. Ашхабаде 17.05.2002 г.]; Соглашение между правительством Республики Беларусь и правительством Азербайджанской Республики о принципах взимания косвенных налогов при экспорте и импорте товаров (работ, услуг) [Электронный ресурс]: [совершено в г. Баку 09.08.2001 г.]; Соглашение между правительством Республики Беларусь и правительством Российской Федерации о принципах взимания косвенных налогов при экспорте и импорте товаров, выполнении работ, оказании услуг [Электронный ресурс]: [совершено в г. Астане 15.09.2004 г.] // ConsultantPlus: Belarus. / 'JurSpectre' LTD, National Centre of Legal Information. – Minsk, 2017.

64. M. Janušková, *The Principle of Neutrality: VAT and Direct Taxes*, in *Global Trends in VAT/GST and Direct Taxes*, at 161 (S. Pfeiffer & M. Ursprung-Steindl eds., Linde 2015).

65. Authors' translation.

66. Соглашение между Правительством Российской Федерации и Правительством Республики Беларусь О принципах взимания косвенных налогов при экспорте и импорте товаров, выполнении работ, оказании услуг (вместе с Положением о порядке взимания косвенных налогов и механизме контроля за их уплатой при перемещении товаров между Российской Федерацией и Республикой Беларусь) [Электронный ресурс]: [15.09.2004]: с изм. от 23.03.2007// ConsultantPlus. Russia / Closed JSC 'ConsultantPlus'. – Moscow, 2017.

67. Authors' translation.

68. Соглашение между Правительством Российской Федерации, Правительством Республики Беларусь и Правительством Республики Казахстан О принципах взимания косвенных налогов при экспорте и импорте товаров, выполнении работ, оказании услуг в Таможенном союзе [Электронный ресурс]: [25.01.2008]: в ред. от 11.12.2009 // ConsultantPlus. Russia / Closed JSC 'ConsultantPlus'. – Moscow, 2017.

Both mentioned agreements were a milestone for the further harmonization of VAT rules and set a pattern for the current system of the EAEU.

3.2 The EAEU and VAT

On 29 May 2014, the existing multilateral agreement on indirect taxes was replaced by the Treaty on the EAEU[69,70] (the EAEU Treaty) which was initially signed only by Belarus, Kazakhstan and Russia, while Armenia and Kyrgyzstan joined the Treaty on 10 October 2014 and 23 December 2014, respectively. Appendix 18 of the Treaty, namely the Protocol on the Procedure of Indirect Taxes Collection and the Mechanism of Control over their Payment in Export and Import of Goods, Works, Services[71,72] (the Protocol), regulates VAT issues for cross-border transactions.

As a result, the VAT law within the EAEU consists of two levels that can be designated as a supranational (integration) level and a national level.[73] The integration level is represented by the EAEU Treaty, while the national level includes domestic VAT laws of the Member States. Articles 71 and 72 of the Treaty are of utmost importance for VAT, and set the destination and non-discrimination principles of indirect taxation. The Protocol (Appendix 18 to the Treaty) itself contains key provisions for the area of VAT, in particular:

– definitions of the terms used;
– rules for indirect taxes on exports of goods;
– rules for indirect taxes on imports of goods; and
– rules for indirect taxes on the performance of works and rendering of services.

The Treaty does *not* include any rules on the requirements for input VAT refund.

3.3 Scope

The substantial scope of the EAEU Treaty is limited to the supply of 'goods', 'works' and 'services'. Under Article 3 of the Protocol, a supply of goods covers the supply of 'movable or immovable property, vehicles, and all types of energy'.[74,75] Article 2 of the Protocol defines 'work' as an activity the results of which have material form and can be supplied in order to satisfy the needs of legal and (or) physical persons; a 'service' is an activity, the results of which do not have material form, supplied and consumed

---

69. Authors' translation.
70. Договор о Евразийском экономическом союзе [Электронный ресурс]: [подписан в г. Астане 29.05.2014]: в ред. оГ 08.05.2015 Г. // ConsultantPlus. Russia / Closed JSC 'ConsultantPlus'. – Moscow, 2017.
71. Authors' translation.
72. Authors' translation.
73. *See* Баразгова, Л.К. Правовое регулирование взимания косвенных налогов в экспортно-импортных операциях: дис. ... канд. юрид. наук: 12.00.14 / Баразгова Л. К – М., 2010. – 188 с.
74. Authors' translation.
75. Договор о Евразийском экономическом союзе [Электронный ресурс]: [подписан в г. Астане 29.05.2014]: в ред 08.05.2015 Г. // ConsultantPlus. Russia / Closed JSC 'ConsultantPlus'. – Moscow, 2017.

in the process of this activity. Moreover, the term 'services' also includes the transfer and granting of patents, licenses, trademarks, copyrights and other rights.

It is presumed that supplies of goods or services (works) to third countries (export) are not covered by the EAEU Treaty and left to the discretion of the Member States. The EAEU Treaty also does not distinguish between B2B and B2C supplies, so the same rules seem to be applicable to both types of supplies.

3.4 Supply of Goods

3.4.1 Place of Taxation

Under Article 71(1) of the EAEU Treaty, the Member States must apply the destination principle to the cross-border supply of goods within the Union. This rule is specified in the Protocol, under which the place of taxation for the cross-border supply of goods is the state where the goods were imported. The goods are taxed by the tax authorities that registered the taxpayer. Based on these rules, exports must be zero-rated and imports must be taxed at the same rates as domestic supplies. In general, the EAEU Treaty (Protocol) does not affect the domestic place-of-supply rules which are to be identified by domestic law. However, as the exporting Member State must apply zero-rating for the export to another Member State, the exporting state is not the place of taxation, even if it is the place of supply under domestic law.[76]

3.4.2 Export of Goods

Zero-rating (and subsequent VAT deduction) is mandatory only for cross-border supplies of goods from one Member State to another and must be backed with sufficient documents, in accordance with the provisions of the Protocol and domestic laws of the exporting Member State. Under Article 4 of the Protocol, the following documents must be submitted together with the tax declaration in order to confirm the right to zero-rating:

- agreements (contracts) concluded with the taxpayer of the other Member State or with a taxpayer of the state which is not the EAEU Member State by virtue of which the export is being conducted;
- a bank statement confirming the actual export receipts on the exporter's account, unless otherwise stipulated by the law of the Member State. If the agreement (contract) provides a cash payment and such payment is allowed by the law of the exporting Member State, the taxpayer must provide a copy of the bank statement confirming that the taxpayer transferred the received amounts to its bank account and copies of incoming cash orders confirming the actual receipt of the receipts from the buyer, unless otherwise stipulated by the domestic law of the exporting Member State;

---

76. Ecker & Variychuk, *supra* n. 60, at 81, 87.

- a (paper or electronic) statement (confirmation) of the import of goods and VAT payment, along with a confirmation note from the tax authority of the importing Member State confirming the VAT payment (exemption or other method of the fulfilment of tax obligations);
- transport (consignment) and (or) other documents as per the law of the Member State confirming the movement of goods from the territory of one Member State to the territory of the other Member State. These documents are not required if it is allowed by domestic law; and
- other documents stipulated by the domestic law of the exporting Member State.

The statement of the import of goods and VAT payment is a compulsory document in order to qualify for zero-rating, while all other documents must be submitted only if it is required by the domestic law of the Member State.

The exporter must submit the documents to its tax (not customs) authorities within 180 calendar days from the date of shipment. If the exporter fails to provide the documents, it must pay VAT before expiration of the 180-day period which allows it to retain the right to the deduction (offset) of the input tax. Otherwise, the tax authorities are entitled to collect the tax, penalties and enforce other penal measures in accordance with the domestic law of the exporting Member State. If the taxpayer provides the documents after expiration of the 180-day period, the paid VAT is deducted (set off), refunded in accordance with the law of the exporting Member State.

If the statement (confirmation) of the import of goods and VAT payment is not submitted, the tax authority may (but is not obliged to) accept zero-rating and deduction (offset) if there is an electronic confirmation from the tax authority of the importing Member State that the importer paid the full amount of the tax (or is exempted from the payment).

3.4.3 Import of Goods

Under the EAEU Treaty, imports are to be taxed at the same rates as domestic supplies. The Treaty also stipulates three scenarios in which the import of goods is not to be subject to VAT:

- if under domestic law the supply is not taxable (exempted from taxation) in a purely domestic situation;
- if the goods are bought by individuals not for business purposes; and
- if the goods are supplied within one legal entity. However, domestic law may oblige a taxpayer to notify the tax authorities about the importation/exportation of such goods.

The import VAT is to be paid by the legal owner of the goods in the importing Member State or, if it is allowed by domestic law, by a commissionaire, agent or representative involved in the transaction. The same rule applies if goods are supplied under the contract between the taxpayers of two Member States but from the territory of a third Member State, as well as under the contract between a taxpayer of the Member State and a taxpayer of a non-member state but imported from the territory of a Member State.

If a taxpayer of one Member State purchases goods that have been imported by the taxpayer of the other Member State but VAT has not been paid yet, it is to be paid by the legal owner of the goods in the importing Member State or, if it is provided by domestic law, by a commissionaire, agent or representative of the importer of goods (if the goods will be sold through them). The same rule is applicable if goods were imported by the commissionaire, agent or representative who is a taxpayer of the importing Member State.

The tax is collected by the tax (not customs) authorities. The taxpayer must pay VAT not later than the twentieth day of the month following the month of registration of the imported goods. In case of non-payment, incomplete payment or missing the terms of the payment, as well as in the case of failure to submit tax returns, not complying with the terms for their submission or in case of inconsistency between data in the importer's tax declarations and the data received from the tax authorities of the exporting Member State, the tax authorities are entitled to collect the tax and penalties, as well as apply other liability measures under law of the importing Member State.

Similar to the provisions on export, the Protocol contains detailed documentation requirements regarding import. Under Article 20 of the Protocol, together with the tax declaration, the importer must submit to the tax authorities the following documents:

- a statement (confirmation) of the import of goods and VAT payment on paper (in four copies) and in electronic form, or a statement (confirmation) in electronic form with an electronic (electronic-digital) signature;
- a bank statement confirming the VAT payment on imported goods, or another document confirming the fulfilment of tax obligations, if it is stipulated under the domestic law of the Member State. If the tax authorities take a decision on the tax offset against any excess tax paid in the past, the bank statement (a copy) is not required;
- transport (consignment) and/or other documents under the law of the Member State confirming the movement of goods from the territory of one Member State to the territory of the other Member State. These documents are not required if their issuance is not stipulated by domestic law;
- an invoice issued in accordance with the laws of the Member State, if it is required by domestic laws. If an invoice is not required or the goods are supplied by a taxpayer from a non-Member State, the taxpayer may submit any document provided by the supplier in order to confirm the value of the imported goods;
- import agreements (contracts) under which the supply is undertaken;
- agreements (contracts) of the commission, assignment or agency agreement (contract), if any; and
- if goods are imported from a third state or a taxpayer of a third state involved, the import agreements (contracts) together with an information message from

the supplier are required. The information message must include the following information about the taxpayer of a third Member State and the agreement (contract) between this taxpayer and the supplier: number identifying the person as a taxpayer of a Member State; full name of the taxpayer (organization or individual entrepreneur) of the Member State; the location (residence) of the taxpayer of the Member State; number and date of the contract (contract); and number and date of the specification. If the taxpayer acts as a commissionaire, agent or representative, the above-mentioned information regarding the legal owner of the goods is also required. If the import agreements (contracts) contain the essential data, the information message is not required.

All of the above-mentioned documents (except that mentioned in the first bullet point, i.e., the statement (confirmation)) may be provided either in electronic form or in hard copies duly verified in accordance with domestic law. The tax authorities must check the documents within ten working days. After the inspection, they must either confirm the tax payment (exemption or other method of fulfilment of tax obligations) or provide a justified denial. In case of confirmation, one copy of the statement (on paper) is left with the tax authorities while the other three are to be returned to the taxpayer with the note of the tax authority as a confirmation of the VAT payment (exemption or other method of fulfilment of tax obligations). Subsequently, the taxpayer must send the two copies of the statement with the confirmation note to the supplier. If the statement is in electronic form, the tax authorities will provide the answer to the taxpayer in the same form.

Tax authorities of the importing Member State also send information about the VAT payment to the tax authorities of the exporting Member State.

3.4.4 Practice

As follows from the EAEU Treaty, in order to benefit from zero-rating, the supplier depends on the buyer's ability to pay in due time both for the goods and VAT. After this, the buyer needs to obtain a confirmation note on the statement about the VAT payment from its tax authorities and send this document to the supplier. Only upon receiving the statement with the confirmation note, the supplier may submit the required documents to its tax authorities and benefit from zero-rating.

If the buyer pays VAT but fails to send the required documents to the supplier, the latter will not be able to claim its right to zero-rating. The tax authority of the exporting Member State may, but is not obliged to, allow application of a zero rate if there is an electronic confirmation from the tax authority of the importing Member State about the full payment of the tax by the buyer or other fulfilment of tax obligations.

If the buyer fails to pay VAT to the importing Member State, the supplier is forced to pay the full amount of VAT to its state. Then, in order to recover the paid VAT, the supplier may sue the buyer based on the civil law. However, this leads to additional litigation expenses and is subject to execution of the decision. During all this time, the amounts paid to the government as VAT, as well as amounts spent on legal proceedings, will cause financial hardship for the supplier.

As was mentioned, the pattern of the current VAT rules is based on the Agreement on the Principles of Indirect Taxes signed by Belarus and Russia in 2004.[77] At that time, the system carried high risks for suppliers and relatively high transaction costs for businesses, and increased compliance costs and expenses for tax administrations. These conclusions were confirmed by the economic data of the Ministry of Statistics and Analysis of the Republic of Belarus.[78] However, since then, the core of the system, especially as concerns documentation requirements, has stayed comparatively the same.

Initially, many suppliers and buyers simply refused to conclude low-value contracts, as the transaction cost of such contracts were too high. However, step by step, in order to reduce the possible losses that could be caused by the existing legal regulations, business developed several approaches. For example, a supplier might require a buyer to transfer the full payment for the goods (including VAT) to the supplier's bank account and later, if the buyer fulfils its obligations, either refunds the money (paid for VAT purposes) or credits it as advanced payment for future supplies. However, it is no wonder that the supplier can also delay the refund – which creates additional losses for the buyer.

The parties can also include in the contract the obligation to provide copies of the statement with the confirmation note of the tax authority of the importing Member State within the required period of time and liability for the delay. This situation is widespread in the judicial practice.[79] When considering such disputes, the courts proceed from their civil-law nature and treat the delay caused by the buyer, as a violation of the contract. If the amount of the liability is not fixed in the contract, the courts treat the VAT paid by the supplier to its tax authorities as a damage caused by the buyer which must be compensated. However, any court decision is subject to further execution in the territory of the importing Member State – something that also requires extra time, effort and additional expense.

It could also happen that the buyer sends a fake statement in order to confirm the VAT payment. In the case of inconsistency between the data in the supplier's tax declarations and the data received from the tax authorities of the importing Member State, the supplier will have to pay VAT and penalties, and bear other responsibilities under the law of the exporting Member State. As the practice overview of the Supreme

---

77. *Supra* n. 65.
78. German economic group in Belarus, http://research.by (accessed 15 Apr. 2017).
79. Обзор практики применения хозяйственными судами норм международных конвенций, соглашений, договоров и правовой помощи, участницей которых выступает Республика Беларусь, и норм иностранного права: Обзор Высшего Хоз. Суда Респ. Беларусь, 26 дек. 2007 Г., № 04-08/255; Decision of the International Arbitration Court at the Belarusian Chamber of Commerce and Industry, 30 May 2006, № 546/61-05; Decision of the Economic Court of Gomel Region, 23 July 2007 Г., № 214-7/2007; 23 July 2007, № 215-7/2007); 09 August 2007 Г., № 284-3/2007; 4 September 2007, № 182-14/2007/7/14 [Электронный ресурс] // ConsultantPlus: Belarus. / 'JurSpectre' LTD, National Centre of Legal Information. – Minsk, 2017.

Commercial Court of Belarus[80] shows, legal action is the only way for the supplier to cover losses caused by the buyer.

3.5 Supply of Services and Works

3.5.1 *Place of Taxation*

The last part of the Protocol deals with the taxation of the supply of works and services. The tax is to be paid in the Member State the territory of which is recognized as the place of supply of services (works). Similar to the OECD VAT/GST Guidelines and the EU VAT Directive, Article 29 of the Protocol contains several different place-of-taxation rules for various services and works. Under Article 29, services or works are considered to be supplied and, therefore, taxed within the territory of the Member State of the EAEU when:

(1) services (works) are related directly to immovable property situated in this Member State;
(2) services (works) are related directly to movable property or transport vehicles situated in this Member State;
(3) services in the field of culture, art, education, physical culture, tourism, recreation and sport are provided within the territory of this Member State;
(4) a taxpayer of this Member State purchases:
   - consulting, legal, accounting, auditing, engineering, advertising, design or marketing services, information processing services, as well as research, developmental and experimental-technological (technological) works;
   - work, services to develop programs for computers and databases (software and information products of computer technology), their adaptation and modification, and the maintenance of such programs and databases;
   - services for personnel provision if the staff works at the buyer's place of business;
   - transfer, granting or assignment of patents, licenses, other documents certifying the rights to industrial property protected by the state, trademarks, trade names, service marks, copyright, related rights or other similar rights;
   - renting, leasing and providing for use on another legal basis of movable property, with the exception of renting, leasing and provision for use on another legal basis of vehicles; and

---

80. Обзор практики применения хозяйственными судами норм международных конв енций и соглашений, участницей которых выступает Республика Беларусь, и норм иностранного права [Электронный ресурс]: Обзор Высшего Хоз. Суда Респ. Беларусь, 10 авг. 2007 г., № 04-08/160/2 // ConsultantPlus: Belarus. / 'JurSpectre' LTD, National Centre of Legal Information. – Minsk, 2017.

- rendering of services by a person who, on his or her behalf but for the main participant of the contract or on behalf of the main participant of the contract, attracts another person for the performance of works or services mentioned in this provision;
(5) services or works are provided by a taxpayer of this Member State, unless otherwise stipulated in the above-mentioned rules.

In the Protocol, the place of taxation regarding the supply of the last two categories of services (works) are interrelated with the meaning of the term 'a taxpayer of this Member State'. Under Article 1 of the Protocol, a taxpayer is 'a payer of taxes, fees and charges of the Member States'.[81] No other details or guidance is specified, and, thus, is left to the discretion of the Member States.

As a result of these place-of-taxation rules, the Member State where the place-of-taxation is located, is permitted to tax. However, in contrast to the supply of goods, zero-rating is compulsory only for the export of works on processing of customer-supplied raw materials (toll manufacturing contract), while taxation of other services (works) is not fixed in the Protocol. This leads to the presumption that Member States are free to choose how to tax the export of works and services (*see also* section 3.5.3).

The last-mentioned, fifth rule still follows the origin principle, rather than the destination principle. This may raise issues of double taxation or non-taxation if other Belt and Road countries have implemented the destination principle for such services or works. However, as the first four rules already cover a very broad range of services and works, the substantive scope of the fifth rule seems very limited. Also, issues of double or non-taxation due to this rule might, thus, be limited to minor cases.

3.5.2 *Documentary Requirements*

The place of taxation of services (works) can be confirmed by the following documents:

- agreement (contract) for performance of works or provision of services, concluded by taxpayers of the Member States;
- documents confirming the fact of performance of works or rendering of services; and
- other documents provided for by the law of the Member States.

If a taxpayer supplies several types of services (works) and some of them are auxiliary in relation to others, the place of their supply (taxation) is the place of supply of the main services (works).

There are also special provisions in the Protocol regarding the supply of works on processing of customer-supplied raw materials (toll manufacturing contract) which were imported to the territory of one Member State from the territory of another Member State with an intention of subsequent export of processed products to the

---

81. Authors' translation.

territory of that state. In order to confirm the right to zero-rating the supplier must submit, together with the tax declaration, the following documents (copies) on paper:

- a contract concluded between taxpayers of the Member States;
- documents confirming the fact of work performance;
- documents confirming the export (import) of produced goods;
- a statement (on paper in the original or in copy at the discretion of the tax authorities of the Member States) or a list of statements (on paper or in electronic form with an electronic (electronic-digital) signature of the taxpayer). In the case of export of the products to third countries, a statement (list of statements) is not provided to the tax authority;
- a customs declaration confirming the export of products to the third countries; and
- other documents stipulated by the law of the Member States.

The documents (except of a statement or a list of statements) may be submitted electronically in accordance with the law of the Member States. The format of these documents is determined by the tax authorities of the Member States or other regulatory legal acts of the Member States.

The statement (a list of statements) is a compulsory document to be submitted in order to benefit from zero-rating, while all other documents must be provided only if required by domestic law.

3.5.3 *Practice*

When implementing the place-of-taxation rules in their domestic law, the Member States seem to have a different understanding of the meaning and scope of the provisions. In particular, as the provisions on services and works – in contrast to the rules on goods – do not include any rules for the residence state of the supplier ('exporting' state), some Member States seem to be of the opinion that they are free to set up their rules for such export supplies of services. For the supply of goods, the Protocol clearly stipulates that the state of origin must zero-rate the supply which includes the right to input VAT deduction for costs connected to the export. For the supply of services and works, the Protocol does not include rules for the exporting Member State.

Based on this systematic difference, some states seem to deny the input VAT deduction for costs connected to 'exported' exempt supplies of services and works.[82]

---

82. *See* e.g., Article 93 Tax Code of the Republic of Belarus / Налоговый кодекс Республики Беларусь (Особенная часть) [Электронный ресурс]: кодекс Респ. Беларусь, 29 дек. 2009 г., № 71-3: принят Палатой представителей 11 декабря 2009 г.: одобр. Советом Респ. 18 декабря 2009 г.: в ред. Закона Республики Беларусь от 18.10.2016 г. № 432-3 // ConsultantPlus: Belarus. / 'JurSpectre' LTD, National Centre of Legal Information. – Minsk, 2017.; Article 164 Tax Code of the Russian Federation / Налоговый кодекс Российской Федерации (часть вторая) [Электронный ресурс]: 05 авг. 2000 г. № 117-ФЗ: принят Гос. Думой 19 июля 2000 г.: одобр. Советом Федерации 26 июля 2000 г.: в ред. Фед. закона от 30.10.2017 N 304-ФЗ // ConsultantPlus: Russia / Closed JSC 'ConsultantPlus'. – Moscow, 2017.

This could lead to a double burden of VAT, and is in conflict with the tax neutrality and destination principle. Therefore, although the EAEU Treaty and its Protocol aims at harmonization and simplification, they have raised a number of problems in practice and, thus, do not comprehensively and systematically implement the destination and neutrality principle.

3.6 Conclusion

The Treaty contains harmonizing elements, especially by implementing the destination principle and concerning documentation requirements. However, the requirements in the Treaty create a disproportionate burden on businesses and impede the free movement of goods and services in the region. In the Treaty, the Member States put the protection of the public interest as the main priority. The supplier is responsible for the actions of the buyer, whereas the interests of states are totally protected: if the required documents are absent, the supplier pays the tax to the treasury of the exporting Member States and, respectively, the buyer is also responsible for the tax payment in the importing Member State. Moreover, the provisions on the supply of services and works are not comprehensive and raise interpretation problems – which could lead to irrecoverable input VAT and a double burden of VAT.

4 A COMPREHENSIVE MULTILATERAL TREATY FOR VAT? OR MERE SOFT LAW INSTRUMENTS?

The optimal solution to tackle all VAT challenges efficiently is the agreement of a multilateral treaty between all countries along the Belt and Road Initiative. Some of the challenges, in particular double taxation, are already addressed by the EAEU Treaty. However, as the EAEU Treaty and its Protocol are limited to very few countries and focus on place-of-taxation rules only, they cannot effectively solve the problems identified. However, it could be the starting point for a more comprehensive approach.

Such a comprehensive multilateral treaty should include basic guiding rules on the neutrality principle in order to prevent discrimination and guarantee input VAT deduction for businesses, place-of-taxation rules in order to prevent and resolve cases of double taxation (by relying on the OECD VAT/GST Guidelines), rules on dispute resolution (and arbitration), rules that limit documentation requirements to be eligible for zero-rating, and a minimum standard on input VAT refund for non-resident businesses.

The binding place-of-taxation rules in order to prevent double taxation could be based on the OECD International VAT/GST Guidelines and/or the existing rules in the EAEU which are all very similar. These allocation rules should be supplemented by a provision on dispute resolution giving the taxpayer the possibility to initiate a mutual agreement procedure (or even an arbitration) if a double taxation case has not been resolved within a reasonable period. The setting up of binding place-of-taxation rules is, however, not sufficient to prevent all VAT obstacles in countries that are part of the Belt and Road Initiative. Most countries agree that infrastructure projects are taxable in the country where the infrastructure is built. Thus, due to this common understanding, there should not (as a rule) be many double taxation problems. Moreover, place-of-taxation rules do not help to simplify compliance burdens and input VAT refund. Thus, in addition to the place-of-taxation rules, the multilateral treaty should also include limitations on documentary requirements to benefit from zero-rating and rules to guarantee input VAT refund for non-resident businesses.

As laid down in section 2.3.4., the problem with regard to input VAT refund, especially for non-residents, could be solved by (at least) two (alternative) solutions: preventing taxation for B2B transactions (e.g., tax-free zones, zero rating) or allowing for input VAT refund in a simplified refund procedure. Each alternative has its pros and cons. In order to meet the needs of different states, the multilateral treaty could set only a binding objective and leave flexibility for the countries regarding how to achieve the result. More specifically, the countries could agree on the objective that B2B transactions generated by the Belt and Road Initiative should not lead to VAT costs for the (non-resident) businesses involved. The states would be free to decide if they would like to achieve this result by setting up a tax-free zone, specific VAT exemptions or zero-rating, or by relying on a (simplified) refund procedure. This solution would take into account the diversity of the countries involved and leave them discretionary power. In those countries which insist on a refund procedure, it seems to be necessary to promote awareness that VAT is not a means for revenue generating in B2B transactions (but for consumption only). If countries would like to gain revenue from the infrastructure projects, they could still levy a fee or rely on the income and wage taxes connected to the projects.

If an agreement on a comprehensive multilateral treaty is not feasible or achievable in the short- or even long-term, a strong promotion of the already existing OECD VAT/GST Guidelines and their detailed explanation on the neutrality and destination principles could also be a very efficient tool to foster harmonization. Soft law instruments have proven to be a successful instrument for agreeing on a common understanding in the direct tax law area (*see*, in particular, the recent and ongoing OECD/G20 BEPS project) and, may also lead to staged integration, fostering the possibility of an agreement on hard law (bilateral or multilateral treaty) in the future.

CHAPTER 13
Asia: Global Tax Policy Post-BEPS and the Perils of the Silk Road

Romero J.S. Tavares & Jeffrey Owens[*]

1   Putting Asia and BEPS in Perspective
       1.1   Investment Climate
       1.2   Consequences of BEPS Measures
2   Navigating Asia Through BEPS Minimum Standards and Recommendations
       2.1   Policy Choices Underlying Joint Enforcement of BEPS Actions: Digital Economy Ring-Fencing Versus Permanent Establishment and Transfer Pricing Reforms
            2.1.1   A New Nexus in the Form of a Significant Economic Presence
            2.1.2   A Withholding Tax on Certain Types of Digital Transactions
            2.1.3   An 'Equalization Levy'
       2.2   The Effectiveness of New Standards for Interest Deductibility and Hybrid Mismatches
3   Equity Considerations
4   Conclusion

---

[*] The views expressed in this article are solely those of the authors. The authors acknowledge the support of the FondszurFörderung der wissenschaftlichenForschung (Austrian Science Fund).

1 PUTTING ASIA AND BEPS IN PERSPECTIVE

1.1 Investment Climate

The resilience and promise of Asian economies remains remarkable. The riches of the East have for ages fascinated the Western world and yet a new, two-way Silk Road has emerged over the last few decades and is now solidly paved and expanding,[1] fostering global trade and investment flows into the twenty-first century. Developing Asia is not only the world's leading destination of Foreign Direct Investment (FDI) but also the world's leading investor.[2] East and West are no longer distinguishable along oversimplified terms, as the lines have blurred between capital exporters and importers, and between developed and emerging economies.[3]

Nations in both hemispheres seek to attract FDI and fiercely compete for capital inflows and labour. Eastern and Western multinational enterprises (MNEs) not only compete with one another on their home turfs but also in emerging and developing markets across the globe.[4]

Asian growth is therefore fuelled by flows of FDI, which fostered the insertion of Asian firms in highly sophisticated global value chains (GVCs),[5] often managed by

---

1. *See* United Nations Conference on Trade and Development (UNCTAD), World Investment Report 2015, *Reforming International Investment Governance*, United Nations (Geneva, 2015) (UNCTAD WIR 2015), pp. 2-12, 40-51, 71-77. China's unfolding 'One Belt, One Road' (or 'Silk Road Economic Belt') Strategy launched in 2013 by President Xi Jinping and approved in 2015, along with its '21st Century Maritime Silk Road' Initiative and other regional infrastructure development projects, seek not only to foster regional integration, regional investment and regional trade throughout Asia (including Eurasia), but also to further enable the *global expansion* of Asian developing economies, and to consolidate their emergence as world-leading economic powers. *See also* EY, *Riding the Silk Road: China sees outbound investment boom – Outlook for China's outward foreign direct investment* (Mar. 2015), available at http://www.ey.com/Publication/vwLUAssets/ey-china-outbound-investment-report-en/$FILE/ey-china-outbound-investment-report-en.pdf.
2. *See* UNCTAD WIR 2015, *supra* n. 1. Developing Asia became the world's largest investor in 2014, as multinational enterprises (MNEs) across the region increased their investments abroad by 29% to reach a staggering USD 432 billion (out of USD 468 billion invested by MNEs from all developing economies). The term 'Developing Asia' used in this study includes China, but excludes Japan and South Korea, which are considered in this analysis to be developed nations.
3. *See* R.J.S. Tavares & J. Owens, *Human Capital in Value Creation and Post-BEPS Tax Policy: An Outlook*, 69 Bull. Intl. Taxn. 10, p. 591 (2015), Journals IBFD.
4. Chinese firms, for instance, are increasingly successful in their bid for opportunities in extractive industries, infrastructure, energy and even financial services, not only in developing economies in Africa or within Asia but worldwide; whereas Indian firms have increased their investments in Sub-Saharan Africa in diverse sectors. *See* UNCTAD WIR 2015, *supra* n. 1, p. 13, International Monetary Fund, *World Economic and Financial Surveys, Regional Economic Outlook, Sub-Saharan Africa – Navigating Headwinds* (2015) *and* S.C. Radelet, *Emerging Africa: how seventeen countries are leading the way*, Center for Global Development, Brookings Institution Press (2010).
5. *See* OECD, WTO and UNCTAD Report prepared for submission to the G20 Trade Leaders' Summit in St Petersburg, September 2013, *Implications of Global Value Chains for Trade, Investment, Development and Jobs* (2013) (the OECD/WTO/UNCTAD GVC Report (2013)), OECD, *Interconnected Economies: Benefiting from Global Value Chains* (2013) (the OECD GVC Report 2013), OECD, WTO and World Bank Group Report prepared for submission to the G20 Trade Ministers Meeting in Sydney, 19 Jul. 2014, *Global Value Chains: Challenges, Opportunities, and Implications for Policy* (2014) (the OECD/WTO/WB GVC Report (2014)) *and* OECD and World Bank Group Report prepared for submission to G20 Trade Ministers Meeting Istanbul, 6 Oct. 2015,

MNEs from developed countries (most notably the United States), and which have placed Asia at the epicentre[6] of a global surge of international trade of goods and services. A delicate balance, therefore, has been struck between the benefits to Asia from connecting with the world's developed economies through MNEs and their GVCs, and the benefits to the world's developed economies from accessing Asian markets. This interdependence cannot be overlooked, particularly by Asian tax administrations, and requires great understanding and coordination.

1.2 Consequences of BEPS Measures

This interdependency and the emergence of BRICS has influenced the G20 Mandate to redesign what came to be perceived as a broken international tax system, with BRICS on an equal footing with OECD members. In the now ubiquitous Base Erosion and Profit Shifting (BEPS) Project,[7] a new standard of international tax coordination has emerged. And yet, instead of ending MNE tax avoidance, the OECD and the G20 have agreed to a 'new normal' for tax competition with new ground rules for corporate tax avoidance.[8]

The new impetus to international cooperation achieved through the Global Forum on Transparency and Exchange of Information for Tax Purposes,[9] which crystallized in the accession of ninety-six countries to the Multilateral Convention on Automatic Exchange of Information (MCAEOI), was a remarkable achievement. A similarly impressive result was the January 2016 accession of no less than thirty-one countries to the Multilateral Competent Authority Agreement (MCAA),[10] which enables the automatic exchange of country-by-country reports (CbCR), following Action

---

Inclusive Global Value Chains: Policy options in trade and complementary areas for GVC Integration by small and medium enterprises and low-income developing countries (2015).

6. *See* OECD/WTO/UNCTAD GVC Report (2013) p. 5, OECD/WTO/WB GVC Report (2014), p. 13, *United States Census Bureau News* (5 May 2015) *and* WTO, International Trade Statistics, *Trade in Global Value Chains* (2014).
7. *See* OECD, *Addressing Base Erosion and Profit Shifting*, OECD Publishing (February, 2013) available at http://www.oecd.org/tax/addressing-base-erosion-and-profit-shifting-978926419 2744-en.htm, *Action Plan on Base Erosion and Profit Shifting*, OECD Publishing (May, 2013), available at http://www.oecd.org/tax/action-plan-on-base-erosion-and-profit-shifting-978926 4202719-en.htm *and* J. Owens, *BEPS: Looking Back; Looking Forward*, Journal of the State Administration of Taxation of the People's Republic of China (forthcoming, 2016).
8. *See* Tavares & Owens, *supra* n. 3 *and* R.J.S. Tavares & B.N. Bogenschneider, *The New de minimus Anti-Abuse Rule in the Parent Subsidiary Directive: Validating EU Tax Competition and Corporate Tax Avoidance?* 43 Intertax, Issue 8/9 (2015), pp. 484-494.
9. *See* OECD Press Release, *Global Forum on tax transparency pushes forward international co-operation against tax evasion* (30 Oct. 2015) available at http://www.oecd.org/newsroom/global-forum-on-tax-transparency-pushes-forward-international-co-operation-against-tax-evasion.htm.
10. *See* OECD Press Release, *A boost to transparency in international tax matters: thirty-one countries sign tax co-operation agreement to enable automatic sharing of country by country information* (27 Jan. 2016) available at http://www.oecd.org/newsroom/a-boost-to-transparency-in-international-tax-matters-31-countries-sign-tax-co-operation-agreement.htm.

13 of the BEPS Project.[11] Unprecedented transparency concerning the footprint of large MNEs and their GVCs, through the exchange of CbCR (authorized not only by domestic laws but also under the MCAA), is one of the main outcomes of the BEPS Project. Tax administrations throughout the world are now asking what to do with all this information and data.[12] Whether the global sharing of such information will alter the international allocation of taxing rights between residence and source countries, however, remains highly uncertain.

The reform of substantive rules to curb tax avoidance through BEPS (the 'anti-BEPS' rules) has not yet altered the broader issue of residence versus source country taxing rights. In the area of transfer pricing, in particular, the final BEPS report[13] appears to have fallen short of the expectations raised by many commentators[14] and by countries,[15] such as China[16] and India,[17] and the United States was quick to take the broader residence versus source debate off the agenda.

Formulary apportionment approaches are openly supported in the country report from China[18] and are implied in the approaches supported by Brazil and India.[19] China and India, in particular, joined the BEPS Project with rather clear positions on the

11. See OECD, *Transfer Pricing Documentation and Country-by-Country Reporting, Action 13 – 2015 Final Report*, OECD/G20 Base Erosion and Profit Shifting Project, OECD Publishing (Oct. 2015), available at http://dx.doi.org/10.1787/9789264241480-en *and* Owens, *supra* n. 7.
12. See J. Owens, *Tax Policy in the 21st Century: New Concepts for Old Problems*, Eur. U. Inst., Issue 2013/05 – Global Governance Program, Robert Schuman Ctr Advanced Stud. (2013) *and* J. Owens, *The Role of Tax Administrators in the Current Political Climate*, 67 Bull Intl. Taxn. 3 (2013), Journals IBFD.
13. OECD, *Aligning Transfer Pricing Outcomes with Value Creation, Actions 8–10 – 2015 Final Reports*, OECD/G20 Base Erosion and Profit Shifting Project, OECD Publishing, Paris (Oct. 2015) available at http://dx.doi.org/10.1787/9789264241244-en.
14. See Y. Brauner, *BEPS: An Interim Evaluation*, 6 World Tax Journal. 1 (2014), Journals IBFD, M.C. Durst, *Limitations of the BEPS Reforms: Looking Beyond Corporate Taxation for Revenue Gains*, International Centre for Tax and Development (ICTD), Working Paper 40 (September, 2015), available at www.ictd.ac *and* Tavares & Owens, *supra* n. 3, pp. 590–595. For academic studies of more revolutionary transfer pricing reforms or the adoption of global formulary apportionment, *see, for example*, R. Avi-Yonah, *The Rise and Fall of Arm's Length: a study in the Evolution of United States International Taxation*, 15 Va. Tax Rev. 89 (1995), Y. Brauner, *Value in the Eye of the Beholder: The Valuation of Intangibles for Transfer Pricing Purposes*, 28 Va. Tax Rev. 79 (2008) *and* J. Clifton Fleming, R. Peroni & S. Shay, *Formulary Apportionment in the U.S. International Income Tax System: Putting Lipstick on a Pig?*, 36 Mich. J. Intl L. 1 (2015).
15. See Tavares & Owens, *supra* n. 3, p. 592.
16. See J. Yuesheng, *Value Creation Theory of the BEPS Report and China's Reasonable Share in Global Value Allocation*, 22 Intl. Transfer Pricing J. 4, pp. 223–229 (2015), Journals IBFD, Owens, *supra* n. 7 *and* J. Li, *China and BEPS: From Norm-Taker to Norm-Shaker*, 69 Bull. Intl. Taxn. 6 and 7, pp. 355–370 (2015), Journals IBFD.
17. See P. Prakash, *Emerging Transfer Pricing and International Tax Issues*, 20 Intl. Transfer Pricing J. 6, pp. 374–378 (2013), Journals IBFD, S. Gill, *Intangibles and TransferPricing: The Perils Faced by Multinationals in India*, 18 Intl. Transfer Pricing J. 1, pp. 47–56 (2011) Journals IBFD *and* S. Wagh, *Transfer Pricing Aspects of MarketingIntangibles: An Indian Perspective*, 69 Bull. Intl. Taxn. 9, pp. 520–530 (2015), Journals IBFD.
18. See United Nations Department of Social and Economic Affairs, *United Nations Practical Manual on Transfer Pricing for Developing Countries*, United Nations (2013), available at http://www.un.org/esa/ffd/documents/UN_Manual_TransferPricing.pdf (the UN TP Manual), pp. 374–388.
19. *Ibid.*, at pp. 358–374 and pp. 388–409.

perceived weaknesses of the functionally separate legal entity approach, as currently practiced under the arm's length principle (ALP) of Article 9 of the OECD Model Tax Convention on Income and on Capital,[20] and as interpreted in the OECD Transfer Pricing Guidelines.[21]

The UN Transfer Pricing Manual[22] does not discard the ALP, but it can be mistaken for an instrument that advocates in favour of such country practices, beyond seemingly implicit support. Specific country practices, which do not conform to the OECD TP Guidelines, are included to illustrate the approach of these countries in their interpretation (or criticism) of the OECD TP Guidelines and the ALP, in language drafted by the representatives of such countries.[23]

Although global formulary apportionment is rejected by the OECD,[24] which also discourages the use of 'safe harbours' (which are inconsistent with the ALP),[25] it allows the use of 'other methods', which satisfy the ALP.[26] The OECD recognizes that safe harbours can be useful for administrative efficiency, but continues to reject methods that would be inconsistent with the ALP.

As such, if the core of transfer pricing rules remains unchanged under the ALP, what are countries to do with the abundant information and CbCRs, which they will receive? Will the granular information on GVCs of MNEs reveal BEPS risks and lead to legally grounded assessments, which could not have occurred in the past? Or will the scrutiny of massive MNE data[27] simply reveal the complex (and still legitimate) operation of the ALP of transfer pricing under the functionally separate legal entity approach?

New minimum standards to achieve greater coherence[28] in domestic anti-abuse rules and greater substance to diminish harmful tax competition[29] were presented in

---

20. OECD, *Model Tax Convention on Income and on Capital*, OECD (22 Jul. 2010), Models IBFD (the OECD Model Convention).
21. OECD *Transfer Pricing Guidelines for Multinational Enterprises and Tax Administrations*, OECD (2010), International Organizations' Documentation IBFD (the OECD TP Guidelines).
22. United Nations Department of Social and Economic Affairs, *United Nations Practical Manual on Transfer Pricing for Developing Countries*, United Nations (2013), available at http://www.un.org/esa/ffd/documents/UN_Manual_TransferPricing.pdf.
23. Tavares & Owens *supra* n. 3, p. 593, note that '[s]uch an approximation to global formulary apportionment in the context of the OECD/G20 BEPS project may be regarded as a compromise and may be labelled using euphemisms, i.e., a 'more flexible approach to the arm's length principle', but such language and approximation could, indeed, represent a rather perilous deviation.'
24. OECD TP Guidelines, *supra* n. 21, pp. 37–41.
25. *Supra* n. 21, pp. 159–167.
26. *Ibid.*, p. 61.
27. See Durst, *supra* n. 14, p. 14.
28. See OECD, *Neutralising the Effects of Hybrid Mismatch Arrangements, Action 2 – 2015 Final Report, OECD/G20 Base Erosion and Profit Shifting Project*, OECD Publishing (October 2015) available at http://dx.doi.org/10.1787/9789264241138-en *and* OECD, *Limiting Base Erosion Involving Interest Deductions and Other Financial Payments, Action 4 – 2015 Final Report, OECD/G20 Base Erosion and Profit Shifting Project*, OECD Publishing (October 2015) available at http://dx.doi.org/10.1787/9789264241176-en.
29. See OECD, *Countering Harmful Tax Practices More Effectively, Taking into Account Transparency and Substance, Action 5 – 2015 Final Report, OECD/G20 Base Erosion and Profit Shifting Project*, OECD Publishing (October 2015) available at http://dx.doi.org/10.1787/9789264241190-en. In

the anti-BEPS rules, while old standards which aim to curb the improper use of tax treaties were relaunched, although countries had greater freedom in terms of unilateral adoption and interpretation.[30] In effect, tax competition would be accepted for transparent jurisdictions through the adoption of BEPS minimum standards, such as implementation of the modified nexus rule and phasing out of 'IP box' regimes. Moreover, many BEPS Actions materialized into the softer forms of 'recommendations' and 'best practices' reports, which will allow countries to remain engaged in fierce, albeit transparent, tax competition, which will drive down nominal corporate tax rates.

Coherence of international tax rules would be enhanced through the implementation of new domestic laws seeking to neutralize hybrid mismatches under BEPS Action 2, and seeking to limit excessive interest regarding interest deductibility under BEPS Action 4. Quite notoriously, however, no minimum 'coherence' standards were agreed to in respect of anti-deferral or Controlled Foreign Company (CFC) rules under BEPS Action 3, and only a report on best practices was presented in the final report.[31]

Therein lie some of the new perils which are expected to surface along the Silk Road. Some of the potential pitfalls that can emerge in Asia post-BEPS pertain to the risk of uncoordinated and unilateral *over-implementation* of what may be interpreted as anti-BEPS measures, particularly in the area of transfer pricing and tax treaty entitlement. The inadvertent enforcement of anti-avoidance or anti-abuse theories, which were experimented with in the discussion drafts (and in academia) leading to the final BEPS reports, may overburden tax administrations throughout Asia, and cause a tsunami of litigation with highly uncertain prospects. This may be a risky venture for tax administrations to embark upon. Going 'beyond arm's length'[32] and seeking to adopt unilaterally formulary apportionment results through interpretation of anti-BEPS language or policies is a danger that could hurt economies in Asia.

The adoption of such unilateral action would not only have highly uncertain revenue results (given the complex nature of the factual and legal problems which would be at stake), but, irrespective of the outcome of the protracted litigation that would ensue, uncoordinated enforcement or unilateral aggressiveness and litigation in the area of transfer pricing would be detrimental to the operation of GVCs in Asia by the

---

addition to reinforcing transparency standards, a new modified nexus rule was created under Action 5, which ostensibly seeks to achieve coherence, and yet represents a substance requirement.

30. *See* R.J.S. Tavares, *The 'Active Trade or Business' Exception of the Limitation on Benefits Clause* in *Base Erosion and Profit Shifting: The Proposals to Revise the OECD Model Convention* (M. Lang et al. eds, Linde Verlag 2016), OECD, *Preventing the Granting of Treaty Benefits in Inappropriate Circumstances, Action 6 – 2015 Final Report, OECD/G20 Base Erosion and Profit Shifting Project*, OECD Publishing (October 2015) available at http://dx.doi.org/10.1787/9789264241695-en, OECD, *Preventing the Artificial Avoidance of Permanent Establishment Status, Action 7 – 2015 Final Report, OECD/G20 Base Erosion and Profit Shifting Project*, OECD Publishing (Oct. 2015) available at http://dx.doi.org/10.1787/9789264241220-en, M. Lang, *BEPS Action 6: Introducing an Antiabuse Rule in Tax Treaties*, Tax Notes Intl. p. 655 (19 May 2014) and as WU International Taxation Research Paper No. 2014-09, available at http://ssrn.com/abstract=2500827 *and* Owens, *supra* n. 7.
31. *See* OECD, *Designing Effective Controlled Foreign Company Rules, Action 3 – 2015 Final Report, OECD/G20 Base Erosion and Profit Shifting Project*, OECD Publishing (Oct. 2015) available at http://dx.doi.org/10.1787/9789264241152-en.
32. *See* Tavares & Owens, *supra* n. 3, p. 592.

United States and European MNEs. This could trigger potential distortions through disaggregation or fragmentation of such value chains,[33] potentially dampening inward FDI and knowledge-based capital[34] (KBC) transfers into Asia. Further, such an uncoordinated stance could inspire similarly unilateral and aggressive postures in other developing and emerging nations wherein Asia is itself an investor, not to mention triggering adverse responses in the developed world. Harmful tax competition may become the new normal.

Since the G20 Summit in November 2015, countries have entered into the second phase of the G20/OECD Project, which comprises both the implementation of reforms already agreed to, as well as the continuing debate and negotiation of sensitive issues on which consensus could not be reached. China remains at the forefront of this debate as it takes over the G20 Presidency. On 10 October 2015, its State Tax Administration (SAT) issued all BEPS reports in Mandarin, while announcing BEPS implementation plans to be carried out in advance of China's hosting the G20 and the Forum on Tax Administration in 2016.[35] Further, on 17 September 2015, China issued new transfer pricing guidelines[36] to implement the anti-BEPS, which measures it understands to be pertinent.

Quite strikingly, China is now also adopting an innovative 'other method',[37] the 'Value Contribution Apportionment Method' (VCAM), under which 'MNE profits are to be allocated across the value chain based on analysis of how value creating contributions have been made to group profits, with reference being made to assets, costs, sales and employees.'[38] While BEPS Actions 8-10 indicate Development, Enhancement, Maintenance, Protection and Exploitation (DEMPE) as the standard to assess value creation pertaining to intangibles, as substantive activities that would allow the recognition of intangible ownership and control over risk, China is adopting a broader view on intangibles by setting out a 'DEMPEP' approach, which adds 'promotion' to the definition of activities which entitle returns on intangibles.[39] By adding 'promotion' to the DEMPE standard, China reinforces its view that market-specific advantages or

---

33. *Ibid.*, pp. 598–599 *and* S.I. Langbein, *U.S. Transfer Pricing and the Outsourcing Problem*, Tax Notes Intl, pp. 1065–1092 (2005).
34. *See* OECD GVC Report (2013), *supra* n. 5, p. 209, OECD, *Human Capital Investment – An International Comparison* (OECD 1998), *The Well-Being of Nations – The Role of Human and Social Capital* (OECD 2001), *Human Capital* (OECD 2007), *Supporting Investment in Knowledge Capital, Growth and Innovation* (OECD 2013) and World Economic Forum, *The Human Capital Report* (2013).
35. C. Xing, W. Zhang, L. Li & C. Turley, *China at the forefront of global BEPS implementation*, in *China – Looking Ahead*, 5th ed., International Tax Review, available at http://www.internationaltaxreview.com/IssueArticle/3511704/Archive/China-at-the-forefront-of-global-BEPS-implementation.html.
36. C. Chi, J. Kondos, S. Liu & K. Liao, *China's new transfer pricing guidelines and BEPS*, in *China – Looking Ahead*, 5th ed., International Tax Review, available at http://www.internationaltaxreview.com/IssueArticle/3511707/Archive/Chinas-new-transfer-pricing-guidelines-and-BEPS.html. Not surprisingly, the positions contained in the guidelines are consistent with the views expressed by J. Yuesheng, *supra* n. 16. *See also* Li, *supra* n. 16.
37. *See* OECD TP Guidelines, *supra* n. 21, p. 61, allowing the use of 'other methods that satisfy the arm's length principle'.
38. C. Chi, J. Kondos, S. Liu & K. Liao, *supra* n. 36.
39. *See* the OECD final transfer pricing report, *supra* n. 13.

market premium could rise to the level of a unique and valuable intangible (in addition to framing comparability analyses), which is a controversial stance.

China is also expanding the interpretation of Location Specific Advantages (LSAs), which would reinforce its pre-BEPS view on comparability, particularly with respect to market premium and lead to ever-increasing use of the profit split method (PSM) post-BEPS, as well as the use of the new VCAM.

Both methods could be used when the Chinese authorities ascertain that local intangibles or LSAs would justify disregarding otherwise comparable transactions or enterprises from third countries, and if LSAs and market premium rise to the level of unique and valuable intangibles, a substantial portion of global profits from value chains operated by MNEs would be allocated to China.

Combating tax avoidance and abusive practices is a goal that must be pursued multilaterally if we are to avoid erecting non-tariff barriers which would harm global trade. The multilateral effort of the G20 and the OECD, with the support of the United Nations,[40] is the appropriate path to achieve this goal. A similar multilateral taskforce has not emerged to coherently enable FDI,[41] and each nation governs its own investment climate. Having an efficient state that ensures the welfare of its constituents while allowing the functioning of a competitive and transparent tax system (and an attractive investment climate) may be the unilateral policy chosen by countries that can afford it. Similarly, adopting measures to foster productivity gains in a particular country, or to promote inward and outward investment, which benefits a certain country or region (such as building infrastructure in Developing Asia along the New Silk Road[42] or attracting automotive FDI through 'Make in India')[43] are national policy priorities, which are promoted unilaterally. It would be a mistake for the same Asian countries to reverse these priorities and to cannibalize their strategic initiatives to embark on a unilateral anti-BEPS crusade, while relying on multilateralism to achieve country-specific productivity gains and while depending upon foreign investment to enable local development strategies. If Asian countries keep this framework in perspective post-BEPS (i.e., fighting abuse through multilateral action and simultaneously fostering investment through unilateral action), the implementation of anti-BEPS measures would have positive revenue effects without overwhelming tax administrations and taxpayers in Asia. That approach would allow blossoming Asian economies to continue on their path of enrichment and growth.

---

40. The United Nations Financing for Development Office, Committee of Experts on International Cooperation in Tax Matters, is an important force in this multilateral effort. Actions in particular through the Sub-Committee on Article 9 (Transfer Pricing) and the Sub-Committee on Base Erosion and Profit Shifting for Developing Countries can bridge the dialogue between the G20, the OECD and developing nations, and are therefore critically important.
41. See UNCTAD WIR-2015, *supra* n. 1, 'Chapter V. International Tax and Investment Policy Coherence'.
42. See *supra* n. 1.
43. Whilst infrastructure is drawing substantial investments along the Silk Road, manufacturing continues to be an engine of Asian growth. Fostering manufacturing in general, and the automotive industry in particular, is critical for India, for example, and a core element of the 'Make in India' strategy launched by Prime Minister Modi in September, 2014: *see* http://www.makeinindia.com/.

This study revisits some of the main features of the final BEPS deliverables and discusses policy choices, which are particularly relevant to Asia. All countries in Asia have multiple policy choices concerning the adoption of alternative anti-BEPS minimum standards, and in the consideration and interpretation of recommendations and best practices. Ideally, they should continue to follow a coordinated path and adopt a multilateral stance to address the BEPS problem, to protect the competitiveness and robustness of Asian economies, while at the same time protecting their revenue base.

2 NAVIGATING ASIA THROUGH BEPS MINIMUM STANDARDS AND RECOMMENDATIONS

2.1 Policy Choices Underlying Joint Enforcement of BEPS Actions: Digital Economy Ring-Fencing Versus Permanent Establishment and Transfer Pricing Reforms

In the BEPS Action 1 reports,[44] the OECD acknowledges, first and foremost, that the so-called 'digital economy' is not a sector that can be 'ring-fenced' from the rest of the economy for tax purposes, as nowadays the digital economy is the economy itself. In the knowledge economy, 'the wealth of companies lie[s] very much in what they know rather than the physical products they produce'[45] and, as such, all MNEs create value and function through digital technologies. The tax policy challenges associated with the mobility of capital and intangible asset ownership, which are notoriously exacerbated in certain high-technology firms, can also be observed in many (if not all) other economic sectors and industries. The lengthy Action 1 reports compile descriptive analyses produced by OECD staff on different aspects of the digital economy, as well as excerpts from business and economics literature concerning, for example, the impact of information and communication technologies (ICT) on the economy as a whole, and in particular on the operation of GVCs. In addition, the reports also give key illustrations and examples (which were provided by industry) showing how pervasive this so-called digital economy is, and how embedded KBC and ICT-driven intangibles are, in every valuable product or service and function of international business.

The reports emphasize that such advancements in productivity through ICT and KBC are indeed favourable to global economic growth, and hence should not be discouraged. Nonetheless, they also emphasize that these characteristics of the global economy demonstrate the inadequacy of current international tax standards and laws, and hence all actions of the BEPS project, dealing with the entire economy, without ring-fencing, would be justified. Therefore, a multilateral solution has been designed comprising all actions of the BEPS Project as a whole.

---

44. *See* OECD, *Addressing the Tax Challenges of the Digital Economy, Action 1 – 2015 Final Report*, OECD/G20 Base Erosion and Profit Shifting Project, OECD Publishing (October 2015), available at http://dx.doi.org/10.1787/9789264241046-en, OECD, *Addressing the Tax Challenges of the Digital Economy*, OECD/G20 Base Erosion and Profit Shifting Project, OECD Publishing (2014) http://dx.doi.org/10.1787/9789264218789-en (the Action 1 reports) and Owens, *supra* n. 7.
45. Owens, *supra* n. 12(*Tax Policy in the 21st Century: New Concepts for Old Problems*), p. 3.

However, in setting forth tax policy proposals under Action 1 the reports appear to be somewhat contradictory. Again, the primary conclusion from Action 1 is that all other actions of the Project should be sufficient to tackle the BEPS concerns, which are highlighted or exacerbated in the high-technology sectors and which are more commonly referred to as exponents of the digital economy, i.e., e-commerce – in particular business-to-consumer (B2C) – and Internet- and cloud-based enterprises, search engines, etc. The Action 1 reports confirm that such concerns or issues exist and will become evermore prevalent in all other sectors of the economy (e.g., manufacturing, infrastructure, life sciences, financial services, and even extractives), given the impact of ICT and KBC on all GVCs. This primary conclusion builds upon the supposedly overriding assumption that no ring-fencing is feasible (or to use the terms of the report, 'difficult, if not impossible').[46] As part of this primary conclusion, reference was made in particular to Action 7 on Permanent Establishments (PEs).[47] The proposed modifications to the list of exceptions to the definition of a PE (viz. 'preparatory and auxiliary' activities), and what is referred to as 'artificial arrangements', which would no longer avoid PE characterization (e.g., in-country fragmentation of PEs that carry on a unitary business, and agency PEs through local negotiation of material elements of a contract), are at the core of the new standards proposed by the OECD to tackle the perceived problem.

Some detailed nuances concerning the definition of such PE terms to be included in the new Article 5 of the OECD Model Convention, as well as in the OECD Commentary, remain rather controversial. Nevertheless, reference is also made in the Action 1 reports to the BEPS Actions 8, 9 and 10 findings on transfer pricing, emphasizing that legal ownership alone (of an intangible asset or of capital, for example) should no longer justify *all* return accruing to the legal owner, while in several discussions it is implied that ownership would not justify *any* entrepreneurial or residual return, which would potentially represent an abandonment of the ALP, and a radical reallocation of taxing rights away from residence, capital exporting countries.[48] A potentially disproportionate 'force of attraction' of tangible assets and routine (low-risk) functions, and of customer location (i.e., the market) and assembled workforce, could result in disproportionate allocation of taxing rights to such newly ascertained PEs.

China, for example, tends to view the exploitation of its consumer market through a Chinese PE as representative of an intangible asset which is unique and valuable to an entire global firm, and, therefore, often objects to the comparability of third-country (firm or transactions) data in transfer pricing studies, while pursuing the

---

46. *See* OECD Action 1 final report, *supra* n. 44, p. 11.
47. *Ibid.*, p. 12 *and* OECD Action 7 final report, *supra* n. 30.
48. This issue is clearly evidenced in the debate over Cost Contribution Agreements. For instance, the disregard of capital contributions (or the exclusion of returns for entrepreneurial risk taking) was evident in the *Public Discussion Draft of the OECD/G20 BEPS Project, BEPS Action 8: Revisions to Chapter VIII of the Transfer Pricing Guidelines on Cost Contribution Arrangements (CCAs)* (OECD 2015), an approach which is incorporated under the transfer pricing reports of Actions 8, 9 and 10 (albeit softened through the adoption of the 'DEMPE' approach), but also under Action 5: *see* Tavares & Owens, *supra* n. 3, p. 592.

application of profit split approaches with indicators geared towards 'market intangibles'.[49] This stance can be viewed as an approximation to global formulary apportionment with predominance of the sales factor.[50]

The Indian position on 'location savings' and supply-side advantages, on the other hand, can recapture synergetic gains associated with an assembled workforce[51] and require increased profit markups under one-sided transfer pricing methods, or even view the activities of skilled labour based in India as indicative of unique and valuable contributions justifying the use of a global profit split. India's view on the definition of intangible assets and contributions by local labour is quite sophisticated,[52] but rather controversial,[53] and only through bilateral or multilateral coordination could these views be reconciled and actionable without triggering double taxation or leading to other distortionary results.[54]

The tax burden in countries with a substantial consumer market or with a substantial workforce can increase if the Chinese or Indian approaches are fully adopted. This may be perceived as an adequate policy response to the BEPS concerns raised by the digital economy. Double taxation might ensue if these adjustments are effected unilaterally, while other countries continue to conform to the OECD TP Guidelines. Other jurisdictions might follow China and India, which could shift taxing rights away not only from the United States or Europe, but from other Asian countries which serve as regional supply chain hubs or treasury centres for global MNEs and/or are also capital exporters (such as Hong Kong, Singapore, the Republic of Korea and Japan).

It should be noted, however, that the primary 'no ring-fencing' conclusion of Action 1 is not absolute; it is dependent upon the redrafting of changes to the OECD Model Convention concerning PEs and anti-abuse provisions, and on the effective amendment of more than 3,000 existing bilateral tax treaties, which would occur if the Multilateral Instrument of Action 15[55] (an instrument which is very much in the interest of Asian countries) is successfully negotiated, crafted and executed. And it may be dependent upon the outcome of the ongoing debate concerning the application of the profit split method under BEPS Action 10 – a debate that is far from over and which extends into 2016[56] and possibly beyond.

---

49. *See* Yuesheng, *supra* n. 16, Li, *supra* n. 16*and* ns. 35–37.
50. *See* Durst, *supra* n. 14, *citing* Avi-Yonah, *supra* n. 14, *and* Tavares & Owens, *supra* n. 3.
51. *See* A. Panse, *Workforce in Place: Is It an Intangible to Pay For?*, 21 Intl. Transfer Pricing J. 3, pp. 147–153 (2014), Journals IBFD.
52. *See* M. A. Kane, *Labour Rents, Arm's Length Transfer Pricing and Intangibles: Still Searching for a Solution to the BEPS*, 69 Bull. Intl. Taxn. 6 and 7 (2015), pp. 371–374, Journals IBFD *and* Tavares & Owens, *supra* n. 3.
53. *See* Prakash, *supra* n. 17.
54. *See* UN TP Manual, *supra* n. 22.
55. *See* OECD, *Developing a Multilateral Instrument to Modify Bilateral Tax Treaties, Action 15 – 2015 Final Report*, OECD/G20 Base Erosion and Profit Shifting Project, OECD Publishing (October 2015) available at http://dx.doi.org/10.1787/9789264241688-en *and* J. Owens & N. Bravo, *BEPS implementation: the role of a multilateral instrument*, International Tax Review, 27 Oct. 2015, available at http://www.internationaltaxreview.com/Article/3500941/BEPS-implementation-The-role-of-a-multilateral-instrument.html.
56. *See* OECD, *supra* n. 13, p. 11.

Contrary to the expectations of some countries and commentators at the onset of Project BEPS,[57] the final BEPS reports do not change Article 9 of the OECD Model Convention; therefore, the ALP is to remain enshrined in the law of treaties. As such, in the area of transfer pricing, the BEPS Project will lead to amendments to the OECD TP Guidelines, which is the main guidance for implementing the ALP crystallized in Article 9. Still, the OECD TP Guidelines will undergo significant amendments, some of which could lead to a more flexible interpretation of the ALP,[58] particularly in the context of the profit split method. The OECD TP Guidelines are, to a great extent, followed by domestic transfer pricing laws throughout the world; hence, such domestic laws should change as a result of whatever multilateral consensus is reached through the ongoing debate following the 2016 'conclusion' of the BEPS Project.

There is a danger that domestic laws will be amended incoherently and selectively to reflect the unilateral interpretation of needed anti-BEPS transfer pricing measures, ranging from a reinterpretation of Article 9 and the ALP to the definition of intangible assets and the application of profit splits. That scenario may occur in countries which have expected[59] a more 'revolutionary' approach to the ALP and is evidenced in the anti-BEPS reforms currently being implemented in China.[60]

In other words, the ostensive conclusions from Action 1 on the digital economy (i.e., no ring-fencing and no special rules) from the viewpoint of source countries are actually conditioned upon a satisfactory extension of the PE standard and of source country taxing rights under the ALP. Whether the multilateral measures will be deemed satisfactory will be ascertained unilaterally by each country (irrespective of the potential pressure exerted through peer reviews); hence, it is quite possible that (particularly for digital economy-related situations, or for IP-rich MNEs operating vertically integrated GVCs) country-specific interpretations and potential deviations, and incoherent application of PE rules and of the ALP might increasingly arise. In the absence of effective dispute resolution mechanisms (i.e., a mutual agreement procedure (MAP) with binding arbitration) under Action 14,[61] this is a prospect that could act as a very real brake on cross-border activities.

Contrary to the OECD's emphasis on multilateral coordination, the Action 1 reports take a perilous turn, which may turn into a slippery slope. They clearly state that other 'options', which are contrary to the 'no ring-fencing' approach, are admissible and 'could' be adopted unilaterally.[62] These are three options that were

---

57. See supra n. 14.
58. See supra n. 15.
59. See Owens, supra n. 7.
60. Supra ns. 16, 35, 36 and 38.
61. OECD, *Making Dispute Resolution Mechanisms More Effective, Action 14 – 2015 Final Report*, OECD/G20 Base Erosion and Profit Shifting Project, OECD Publishing (Oct. 2015) available at http://dx.doi.org/10.1787/9789264241633-en. See also M. Lang & J. Owens, *International Arbitration in Tax Matters* (IBFD 2016); in particular, J. Owens & L. Turcan, *Proposal for New Institutional Framework for Mandatory Dispute Resolution*, and J. Kollmann, *The new OECD Proposal to Making Dispute Resolution more Effective: BEPS Action 14: A Comparison between the December 2014 Draft and the Final 5 Oct. 2015 Recommendations*.
62. See OECD Action 1 final report, supra n. 44, p. 13.

discarded during the BEPS Project due to a lack of consensus concerning their reasonableness and appropriateness, as follows:

2.1.1 A New Nexus in the Form of a Significant Economic Presence

This option (commonly referred to as a 'digital PE rule') extends the effects of PE characterization to Internet-based transactions according to volume of data transfers or web accesses across borders, number of consumers or users, or licensees within a territory, etc. Again, if this new nexus rule goes beyond the PE definition arising from tax treaties, it remains to be seen whether the income attribution rules would conform to the OECD TP Guidelines or to the ALP, or whether some method of formulary apportionment would be adopted unilaterally.

2.1.2 A Withholding Tax on Certain Types of Digital Transactions

A withholding tax (WHT) may contradict treaty obligations to the extent that it extrapolates the taxation of business profits under Article 7, or if inconsistent with current withholding tax limitations under Article 12 (not to mention a potential conflict with other obligations arising from trade or investment agreements, or even from local constitutional laws).

2.1.3 An 'Equalization Levy'

Such a levy (which is similar to the United Kingdom's diverted profits tax[63] and has inspired similar measures in other countries, such as Australia[64]) may be interpreted as a non-income tax imposed on corporate transactions to the extent that it taxes transactions wherein no income is produced within the country imposing the tax, and which can therefore equate to a non-tariff barrier to international trade. The United Kingdom, nonetheless, views its diverted profits tax as a tool consistent with the ALP and as an enforcement weapon against transfer pricing abuse (or as a statutory

---

63. See HMRC, *Guidance on the Diverted Profits Tax* (30 Nov. 2015), available at https://www.gov.uk/government/uploads/system/uploads/attachment_data/file/480318/Diverted_Profits_Tax.pdf. The United Kingdom levy may be implemented with increased assertions of PEs and resorting to attribution rules. This would occur either within the meaning of the ALP (in the context of treaties where the Authorized OECD Approach to the Attribution of Profits to PEs is used) or, potentially, through apportionment standards established under domestic United Kingdom law. *See OECD Model: Commentary on Article 7 Concerning the Taxation of Business Profits*, paras. 6–9 (2010).
64. *See* Australian Government, The Treasury, Media Release, *UK and Australia agree to collaborate on multinational tax*, available at http://jbh.ministers.treasury.gov.au/media-release/030-2015/.

mechanism needed to address fact patterns where the United Kingdom interpretation of the ALP would be better served through this alternative levy, instead of through the mechanics of the OECD TP Guidelines).

The use of any such tax policy options, if not coherent with the ALP, could represent the creation of a new corporate tax burden on the underlying factors (e.g., sales, assets and/or workforce), as opposed to a tax on corporate income.[65] In fact, it can represent a non-tariff barrier to trade in the form of corporate taxation and could be subject to challenge through the WTO. Whether the incidence of such tax would ultimately burden corporate profits, or whether it would predominantly affect consumers in Asia, is rather uncertain.[66] Yet countries in Asia should be wary of the potential dampening effect of such measures on local production and consumption, which is crucial to sustainable economic growth in the region.

In addressing 'broader tax challenges raised by the digital economy', the Action 1 reports turn again to B2C e-commerce concerns as illustrative of issues concerning market competition and consumption-based taxation. The OECD work in this respect – parallel with that of the EU – brings forth a sensible recommendation concerning consumption-based taxation, directly applicable to value added taxes (VAT) and goods and services tax (GST). The OECD and the EU concluded that, by adopting a destination-based VAT/GST,[67] a more equitable and proportionate application of VAT/GST should result, and should facilitate a more efficient allocation of resources. As emphasized by the OECD, it should also diminish BEPS concerns.

It is curious that the adoption of WHT or diverted profits tax, dissociated from corporate income and from transfer pricing (or as a surrogate for sales-based formulary apportionment), can in essence represent an increase in destination-based taxation, while VAT/GST shifts in the same direction. Consumers in destination markets may end up footing the BEPS bill, i.e., the taxing rights of countries that are large consumer markets of imported goods (e.g., North American countries, European countries, Japan, China and India) and/or large suppliers of labour to GVCs (particularly China and India) would increase vis-à-vis countries that are significant exporters of capital in key sectors of the digital economy (e.g., the United States) or significant net exporters of goods (e.g., Germany and Brazil). The lesser the content and value of intangibles embedded in such exports of goods, the more exporting countries will lose revenue relative to destination markets. In this scenario, the treasuries of countries which are exporters of commodities and which rely on significant extractive industries and natural resources (e.g., Brazil, African countries and Developing Asia countries) are likely to lose the most in relative terms. This is partly why the BEPS debate, no matter what the outcome, may be perceived as alien (or even contrary) to the interests of many developing countries. In addition to the inherent complexity and uncertain outcome of OECD transfer pricing enforcement, which could drain administrative

---

65. *See* Tavares & Owens, *supra* n. 3, p. 595 *and* K. Clausing, *Lessons for International Tax Reform from the US State Experience under Formulary Apportionment*, International Centre for Tax and Development, Research Report 2 (Mar. 2014), available at www.ictd.ac. < http://www.law.nyu.edu/sites/default/files/upload_documents/Kimberly%20Clausing.pdf >.
66. *See* Tavares & Owens, *supra* n. 65.
67. *See* OECD, Action 1 Final Report, *supra* n. 44, p. 94.

Chapter 13: Global Tax Policy Post-BEPS and the Perils of the Silk Road

resources in developing countries, the revenue prospects related to anti-BEPS measures for such countries, which are not massive consumer markets or are not significant suppliers of skilled labour to GVCs, is close to nihil.[68]

The Action 1 reports also note that CFC rules are to be reinforced under Action 3, in order to tackle in residence states potentially untaxed highly mobile, passive or residual income related to the digital content of goods and services. Changes to CFC legislation would be, by definition, effected under domestic laws. However, the Action 3 final report does not impose minimum standards; instead, it provides a compilation of best practices, which can be useful to foster the debate and the development standards in some capital exporting countries (e.g., the inception of stricter notions of tainted or passive income under existing regimes, refinement of 'switch over' rules, or the creation of CFC legislation in countries that do not have it).[69] Nonetheless, the United States debate concerning the offshore profits of United States MNEs and United States tax deferral, which partly fuelled the political climate that sparked the BEPS Project, is quite advanced in relation to what is contained in the OECD report on best CFC practices.[70] As such, the OECD work on CFC best practices is unlikely to influence or alter the course of the United States tax policy debate. However, while the foreign profits of United States MNEs remain subject to United States tax deferral and to a low effective rate of non-United States tax, source countries in Asia and throughout the world will remain tempted to claim taxing rights over such income (through reinterpretations of the ALP, WHT, or the inception and enforcement of a diverted profits tax).[71] Unilateral anti-BEPS actions may prompt the United States to take retaliatory action.[72]

It is, therefore, clear that while the assumption of 'no ring-fencing' appears to be quite sensible and is ostensibly adopted in the primary conclusion that no 'special rules' are required, the prospect of such special rules being adopted unilaterally with the blessing of the OECD represents more than a 'minimum standard'. It is in fact a negotiating 'condition' (or a threat mainly affecting United States interests) for a more significant reform of transfer pricing standards (and of inter-nation allocation of taxing rights), which are still unfolding with the implementation of BEPS Actions 7–10.

In order to preserve FDI and KBC flows into Asia, and to avoid an undue shift of the corporate tax burden to Asian consumers and workers, it would be advisable for all

---

68. Durst, for example, *supra* n. 14, suggests such developing nations, particularly those with substantial extractive industries, devote administrative resources and efforts to the creation and enforcement of excise taxes, instead of devoting administrative resources to anti-BEPS activities.
69. Owens, *supra* n. 7, notes that reforms of CFC rules have been occurring since 2014.
70. For an overview of issues and limitations of the United States anti-deferral rules, *see* J. Clifton Fleming, R. Peroni & S. Shay, *Worse than Exemption*, 59 Emory L. J. 79 (2009) *and* J. Clifton Fleming, R. Peroni & S. Shay, *Getting Serious About Curtailing Deferral of U.S. Tax on Foreign Source Income*, 52 SMU L. Rev. 455 (1999).
71. *See* R.J.S. Tavares, B. Bogenschneider & M. Pankiv, *The Intersection of EU State Aid and United States Tax Deferral: A Spectacle of Fireworks, Smoke and Mirrors*, 19(3) Florida Tax Review (2016), pp. 121–188.
72. *See* United States Senate, Finance Committee Press Release, *Finance Committee Members Push for Fairness in EU State Aid Investigations – In Letter to Treasury Secretary, Senators Warn of Potential Adverse Impact on American Firms* (5 Jan. 2016) *and* Tavares, Bogenschneider & Pankiv, *supra* n. 71.

Asian countries to refrain from adopting unilateral anti-BEPS measures. Developing special rules to single out Internet companies or B2C transactions, or other specific transaction types or sectors, would disproportionately burden such companies, sectors and transactions (and possibly Asian consumers), while not addressing overarching BEPS concerns, which would still affect multiple industries. Adopting an aggressive unilateral stance on the existence of PEs would overwhelm local tax administrations without a material increase in revenues if transfer pricing standards remain unchanged, whereas adopting a broader, more sophisticated interpretation of the ALP through coordinated action may be a better way to secure revenues.

Coordinated action – be it multilateral or bilateral – such as the recent endeavour by the United States and India to foster the use of bilateral Advance Pricing Agreements (APAs),[73] and by India and Germany to enhance bilateral cooperation and information exchange,[74] is the only recommendable path forward. Indeed, APAs have been widely used in Japan, and are increasingly used in China and in other countries throughout Asia. Joint audits of GVCs would also be a good practice to combat BEPS. Finally, reinforced MAPs (with binding arbitration) would be required to properly allocate taxing rights and to avoid double taxation, even within Asia. Japan seems to be leading the way in this respect and has reconsidered its historical aversion to MAP arbitration, as it has joined the 'coalition of the willing' and will therefore endeavour to implement a MAP arbitration clause in the Action 15 Multilateral Instrument. And yet only the active engagement of other leading Asian economies, such as China and India, would enable widespread adoption of MAP arbitration.[75]

2.2 The Effectiveness of New Standards for Interest Deductibility and Hybrid Mismatches

The OECD work on interest deductibility under Action 4[76] achieved a broad consensus and sets forth recommendations for reforms of domestic laws. The concern that significant base erosion and profit shifting exists through intra-group interest payments[77] is further addressed through the minimum standards proposed under Action

---

73. See United States Internal Revenue Service (IRS) Rev. Proc. 2015–41, 2015–35 IRB 263 and Press Release, *IRS to Begin Accepting Bilateral Advance Pricing Agreement Requests for India on February 16* (1 Feb. 2016), available at https://www.irs.gov/uac/Newsroom/IRS-to-Begin-Accepting-Bilateral-Advance-Pricing-Agreement-Requests-for-India-on-February-16.
74. See Government of India, Ministry of Finance, Press Release, *India and Germany to Continue to Exchange Tax Related Information Spontaneously on the Basis of the Existing Agreements; Both Countries Agreed to Explore Other Possibilities of Enhancing Exchange of Information; They Agreed to Resume Negotiations on Partial Revision of the DTAA Between the two Countries with a View to Bring the Provisions Relating to Exchange of Information to International Standards*, available at http://pib.nic.in/newsite/PrintRelease.aspx?relid=126415.
75. See J. Owens, L. Turcan, J. Kollmann, A. Majdanska & S. Sabnis, *What Can the Tax Community Learn from Dispute Resolution Procedures in Non-Tax Agreements?*, 69 Bull. Intl. Taxn. 10, pp. 577–589 (2015), Journals IBFD and J. Kollmann, P. Koch, A. Majdanska & L. Turcan, *Arbitration in International Tax Matters*, Tax Notes Intl (30 Mar. 2015), pp.1189–1195.
76. See OECD, *supra* n. 28.
77. The type of 'base erosion' that should be targeted by anti-BEPS measures is that which results from abusive 'profit shifting', i.e., that which can be related to abusive schemes involving hybrid

2[78] on hybrid mismatches and Action 5[79] on harmful tax practices. However, the recommended limitations on interest deductibility and the minimum standards applicable to hybrid mismatches can be quite distortionary, as they could adversely affect FDI in manufacturing and infrastructure sectors, or they will become rather innocuous if enforcement practices are created without corresponding revenue gains. Hence, the detailed design and implementation of such rules, particularly in Developing Asia, should be carefully considered.

The cost of capital of enterprises can vary considerably from country to country, and across different sectors of the same MNE, which are exposed to varying levels of risk. The same MNE can operate diverse businesses, or diverse functions, in different countries, each resembling separate firms. Each business segment of an MNE, in each country and/or within each value chain it operates nationally, regionally or globally, can have a unique determination of its appropriate level of indebtedness. A global MNE reporting entity would, therefore, simply consolidate and compile an average figure of indebtedness, at an average interest cost, neither of which should necessarily be taken as a legitimate benchmark for a given country's interest limitation.

In setting forth a general statutory limitation for related-party debt through an interest deductibility ceiling at a pre-set percentage of earnings (or through benchmarks of global third-party indebtedness or interest expense), the particular functions and risks of the relevant enterprise operating in a given country would be disregarded. This can lead to distortions. Either an excessive limit would be set and serve as an incentive for excessive related-party indebtedness, or an insufficient limitation would serve as a disincentive to FDI (and an incentive to the financial sector).

Indebtedness limitations on related-party loans tying intra-group debt to global benchmarks of third-party debt would curb highly artificial capital structures and limit the potential abuse of thin capitalization rules. But for some ventures the limitation could be irrational and the anti-base erosion measure rather innocuous – an irrational limitation could cause the substitution of related-party debt with loans from financial institutions to fund infrastructure or manufacturing projects in Developing Asia. This would boost the financial sector where spreads would be earned at the expense of productive investment elsewhere, thus dampening FDI in Asia. Interest deductions would not decrease and hence the measure would cause no revenue increase for countries in Asia which need FDI to fund their infrastructure projects and manufacturing industries. This could harm India and the rest of Developing Asia disproportionately, while it would enrich financial institutions in centres that are active in the East, such as Hong Kong and London.

A general statutory limitation suggested under Action 4 would not dampen FDI (and perhaps even encourage it) only if it takes the form of an optional safe harbour.

---

mismatches, transfer mispricing or harmful tax practices. Base erosion in and of itself is a broader, separate phenomenon, which can have multiple causes and which can be addressed by separate policies. Interest deductibility in scenarios that do not involve profit shifting, therefore, is a base erosion consideration which is should not be equated with abuse or considered in haste, or as an integral part of the implementation of anti-BEPS measures.

78. *See* OECD, *supra* n. 28.
79. *See* OECD, *supra* n. 29.

Such a safe harbour approach could be adopted for ease of administration (as compared to a complex transfer pricing analysis of interest deductibility considering both indebtedness levels and interest rates); however, embedding such a safe harbour option in a statutorily fixed ceiling could encourage unnecessary indebtedness.

It should be noted that the ability to repatriate cash steadily, even from loss-making entities (which would not otherwise have such repatriation capacity),[80] can induce FDI in capital-intensive sectors and green field projects in Asia, such as infrastructure and automotive.[81] Such FDI would not be particularly deterred by the WHT normally applicable to such interest flows. Nonetheless, in source countries with relatively low sovereign risk, compared to the country of residence, and in source countries that impose no WHT on interest, there could be undue base erosion effects through interest deductibility.[82] This potential base erosion effect from interest deductibility in arrangements between nations with equivalent sovereign risk does not necessarily represent 'profit shifting'.

In the absence of hybrid mismatches and of intermediary countries which engage in harmful tax practices by artificially[83] channelling what is referred to as 'stateless income',[84] no profit shifting should be deemed to occur. Hence, adopting anti-BEPS measures affecting indebtedness that does not raise BEPS concerns would be irrational, over-implementation actions, which could dampen FDI in sectors that are instrumental to sustainable economic growth of Asia. In this sense, Action 4 would have to be viewed as redundant and unnecessary in the context of curbing BEPS, if it is expected that Actions 2 and 5 will be effective.[85]

Nevertheless, the Action 4 recommendations endeavour to develop common international standards for thin capitalization rules and for common debt limitations or interest limitations as a separate matter, aside from targeting abusive or artificial arrangements, which lead to stateless income via profit shifting (which should have been the main purpose of the BEPS Project). And they fuel a debate concerning whether any such interest deductibility limitation rules should be based on some pro-rated or formulary allocation of an MNE's overall debt, perhaps even beyond the ALP. Limitations that disregard the economic functions of particular enterprises and the true indebtedness required in capital-intensive projects could force MNEs to incur greater third-party indebtedness, i.e., borrowing more from unrelated financial

---

80. Capital-intensive projects would tend to account for losses in early years arising from depreciation of property, for example, which would limit the repatriation capacity of capital-intensive firms that are financed with equity. Indebtedness is often significant in optimum, arm's length capital structures for such projects. Arm's length interest accruals, however, may surpass formulary interest barriers, causing a distortion.
81. *See supra* n. 43.
82. Related-party indebtedness tends to be a more relevant tax-motivated arrangement in transactions involving developed countries, and is often viewed as leading to abuse in the EU: *see* Tavares &Bogenschneider, *supra* n. 8.
83. Not all intermediary FDI hubs are artificial: *see* Tavares & Owens, *supra* n. 3, p. 593 *citing* UNCTAD WIR 2015, *supra.* n. 1, pp. 188–190.
84. *See* E. Kleinbard, *Stateless Income*, 11 Fl. Tax Rev. 9 (2011).
85. Arguably, even Action 3 (Strengthening CFC Rules) would be more appropriate to address BEPS through interest deductibility, rather than separately addressing interest deductibility in and of itself.

institutions in multiple countries. This would potentially cause an artificial increase in the overall interest expense of MNEs and increased profits in the financial sector, reducing the efficiency and the profitability of capital-intensive, non-financial sectors. These measures could, therefore, adversely affect FDI in manufacturing and infrastructure in Asia. That possibility calls for coherent policies concerning international taxation and foreign investment.

As to the proposal of the BEPS Project to address hybrid mismatches, widespread consensus was reached and crystallized into minimum standards. The construct of the so-called 'linking rule'[86] is circular and thus tautological; it rigorously solves the problem of double non-taxation as a matter of 'juridical incidence' (which is a subject-to-tax standard). As such, the new legal construct was celebrated as a victory over BEPS. The new construct, however, does not address double non-taxation as a matter of 'effective incidence', as it does not govern the tax rates applicable to sovereign states. This is particularly visible in the cases of deduction and non-inclusion of income.[87]

Hence, from a practical perspective, the rule can be rather innocuous. If a deduction is granted in a source country without a corresponding inclusion in the recipient country, a hybrid mismatch is deemed to exist and, thus, through the application of the linking rule, the source country is primarily allowed to deny such deduction. Secondarily, if the source country does not deny the deduction, the recipient country would selectively tax the income in question in order to eliminate the hybrid mismatch, i.e., the recipient country would apply the 'defensive rule'. Nonetheless, if the recipient country treats the income as taxable at the onset, while the source country treats it as deductible, no hybrid mismatch would be deemed to occur – and the linking rule would not operate. Ergo, if the income is subject to tax at the recipient country at an effective rate of tax, which is a small fraction of the effective rate of tax of the source country, the arbitrage of sovereign tax rates would have the equivalent effect of double non-taxation. Countries that function as treasury centres and hubs for transit FDI, and which would often not tax certain types of dividend and interest income, would thus neutralize the hybrid mismatch rule by adopting a low rate of tax which would be generally applicable to such inflows.

As such, for Asian countries that serve as financial centres, subjecting investment income to a low rate of corporate income tax would avoid the application of the hybrid mismatch rule, and preserve their financial sectors. Whereas for Asian source countries which attract inward FDI in the form of intercompany debt, to devote substantial resources to the enforcement of the Action 2 hybrid mismatch rules (through the exchange of information seeking to ascertain whether to reverse corporate tax deductions for payments made to countries that serve as financial centres does not appear to be fruitful. Instead, the maintenance of moderate rates of WHT in Developing Asia, negotiated in bilateral tax treaties, should suffice to counter BEPS concerns without jeopardizing FDI and economic growth.

---

86. Under the linking rule, deductible payments should correspond to taxable income, and vice versa: see OECD, *supra* n. 28.
87. See OECD, *supra* n. 28.

3 EQUITY CONSIDERATIONS

As discussed above, the incidence of a corporate tax disproportionately biased by perceived market intangibles in China or by human capital-driven location savings in India, or elsewhere in Developing Asia, could ultimately lead to an increase in consumer prices and reduction of the consumer market, or otherwise to a deflation of workers' income, adversely affecting market sizes and domestic savings. All of such effects could harm economic growth in Developing Asia. And yet these equity effects have not been the subject of much discussion in the BEPS debate. Similarly, incoherent applications of transfer pricing standards, or unilateral interpretations of the ALP, could cause the fragmentation of GVCs throughout Asia, and a shift of ownership of facilities away from United States or EU MNEs, which are rich in terms of KBC, via outsourcing to third-party contractors, which do not own, or function in possession of, the same level of intangibles. The potential reduction in sharing and deployment of foreign-owned KBC in Asia could adversely affect productivity and income of Asian workers, and ultimately lead to a reduction of growth.

All of these economic effects have welfare considerations. Sustaining productivity gains through the continuing insertion of Developing Asia in GVCs operated by developed country MNEs is absolutely critical to sustain the levels of economic growth that are required to reduce social inequalities in Asia. Given its population, demographics, and persistent inequalities, inward FDI by KBC-rich MNEs, and the full insertion of Asia in the global knowledge economy are essential to Developing Asia.

Nonetheless, risking a shift of the corporate tax incidence post-BEPS to Asian consumers and to Asian workers would have a perverse inequality effect of its own. The whole point of the BEPS Project, when it started, was to ensure large corporations would pay their fair share of taxes. However, the ultimate corporate tax burden of large corporations is shared by people: capital owners, workers and consumers. Anti-BEPS measures, which tend to shift the corporate tax burden to capital owners, would reduce social inequalities, whereas measures that shift the tax burden to consumers and workers would widen the gap.

A partial adoption of anti-BEPS rules may encourage opportunistic behaviour by certain countries to continue, and more countries may embark upon a beggar-my-neighbour quest to intermediate global flows of capital and trade, attracting disproportionate revenues and employment at the expense of other countries: the infamous race to the bottom, which would leave governments facing budget deficits with no option but to deepen austerity measures and to increase personal, social security, and consumption-based taxes. Although the ultimate incidence of such non-corporate taxes would also be dictated by relative elasticities of capital versus labour and consumption in each country, it is highly probable that capital owners would be the least affected.

Reinforcing CFC rules, on the other hand, would tend to shift the tax bill to capital owners. Strengthening transfer pricing rules multilaterally, to reallocate income away from artificially interposed tax havens, and to approximate such income to source countries, would redistribute the anti-BEPS burden globally. Conversely, unilateral and incoherent national policies on transfer pricing would tend not to redistribute the tax burden globally, but would instead disproportionately affect the countries that take unilateral or uncoordinated action. Countries that take such action would most likely attract a considerable share of their intended anti-BEPS tax burden to the production factors situated within their borders; that is, instead of foreign capital owners, the burden could be carried primarily by local labour and local consumers.

Therefore, all countries, and in particular Developing Asia, should continue to develop transfer pricing standards multilaterally and coherently. Asia should continue to exert influence, including at the United Nations, to enhance the interpretation of the ALP embedded in the OECD TP Guidelines, particularly in the area of intangibles and the application of the profit split method, and not venture into unilateral approximations to formulary apportionment standards (irrespective of the potential merits of a global shift to an alternative method or formula). In parallel, country interpretations of the ALP should be made transparent and could be enforced in transactions that do not involve treaty partners. To the extent unilateral interpretations expand or contradict notions contained in the OECD TP Guidelines, such notions should not be enforced unilaterally but through bilateral APAs (which are essential where treaty partners are involved), or even agreed to as general standards under bilateral treaty protocols concerning Article 9.

4 CONCLUSION

Asia has trailed a glorious path. Inward FDI and the insertion of Asian economies in GVCs operated by United States and EU MNEs have been critical to sustain productivity gains, particularly in Developing Asia, and have been instrumental to the emergence of China and India as global economic powers. Post-BEPS tax policies in Asia must not jeopardize that trajectory.

Expanded PE rules and broadened interpretations of the ALP should be used for Asian countries to negotiate more sophisticated bilateral or multilateral APAs. The new anti-BEPS weapons should not be wielded unilaterally. Aggressive, unilateral action would overburden tax administrations with PE assessments, which would not yield considerable taxable income and would therefore be inefficient and ineffective. Adopting unilateral and incoherent transfer pricing positions would have damaging and distortionary effects for Asian economies, and cause massive litigation of highly uncertain prospects.

China's post-BEPS transfer pricing regulations and approach to LSAs and intangibles (with its new DEMPEP standard) and its innovative VCAM – irrespective of their technical merits – are worrying, as these new definitions and methods are unilateral and could, therefore, trigger double taxation. The profit split method (or China's VCAM) should not be applied unilaterally while other methods are systematically disregarded. And where the profit split method is applicable – be it due to LSAs or other comparability factors – the relative value of unique contributions should be ascertained bilaterally or multilaterally, through coordination, in order to prevent double taxation or the fragmentation of GVCs, which would be detrimental to the country's welfare and to the world.

In this sense, APAs will be increasingly instrumental for tax administrations to promote a more sophisticated interpretation of the ALP in a coordinated fashion, and without creating multiple instances of double taxation and protracted tax controversy; most importantly, without adversely affecting FDI and the operation of GVCs in Developing Asia. Similarly, the implementation and enforcement of new interest limitations or WHT should be balanced with the need to attract FDI for capital-intensive infrastructure and manufacturing projects, which are strategic for Developing Asia. Infrastructure investments for the New Silk Road and *Make in India*, among other initiatives, demand such coherence.

The world post-BEPS invites Asia to use international coordination to its best advantage. India is setting an example in its new endeavour to promote APAs with the United States and to cooperate closer with Germany. Cooperative compliance programmes should be launched as a means to foster APA programmes and joint risk monitoring activities throughout the region, and to reduce controversy. Joint audits of GVCs would further ensure APAs remain relevant over time, and the unprecedented access to information resulting from the remarkable work of the Global Forum on Transparency and Exchange of Information for Tax Purposes and from the successful operation of the MCAEOI and MCAA should ensure abusive transactions will no longer be feasible. Differences in interpretation will arise concerning treaty entitlement or abuse, PE recognition and transfer pricing, and such differences would be best solved bilaterally or multilaterally, through MAP arbitration, so as to preserve coherence.

Instead of taking uncoordinated positions, which threaten the investment climate and the welfare of consumers and workers in Developing Asia, Asian countries should implement anti-BEPS measures in coordination with other nations, and reflecting the investment priorities, which are strategic for Asia. This would sustain inward FDI flows and the continuing insertion of Asian countries in GVCs, which enable their access to KBC, and further sustain outward Asian investments, which flourish throughout the world.

CHAPTER 14
Creating a Positive Tax Climate for Complex Multijurisdictional Investment Projects

Jonathan Leigh Pemberton & Alicja Majdanska

1 Introduction
2 Cooperative Compliance as a Way to Improve Tax Compliance and Business Confidence Domestically
    2.1 The Concept of Cooperative Compliance
    2.2 Essential Features of Cooperative Compliance
3 Multilateral Cooperative Compliance: From Domestic Relationship to Cross-Border Cooperation
4 A Potential of Multilateral Cooperative Compliance for the OBOR Initiative
5 JITSIC as a Model?
6 Conclusion

1 INTRODUCTION

Over the last decade, China experienced unprecedented growth of inward and outward foreign direct investment. Within a bit less than ten years (2006–2015), China's outward and inward foreign direct investment grew by six times, while during 2014 alone China's overseas merger and acquisition values increased by 74%.[1] This was

---

1. J.P. Owens, *Tax Compliance Risk for Chinese Outbound Investment*, 2016 ECUPL International Tax Dialogue: – A New Campaign for Chinese Tax Reform: The Chinese Outbound Investment (9 May 2016).

driven by a concerted plan initiated by the Chinese government called the 'Go Global' Strategy on Outward Foreign Direct Investment.[2]

As a continuation of this strategy, a multibillion dollar project, focused mainly on transport, was instituted that spans Central Asia, namely the One Belt, One Road (OBOR) initiative.[3] The aim of this initiative is to build a new Silk Road linking Asia, Africa and Europe. The landmark programme will require the investment of billions of dollars in infrastructure projects, including railways, ports and power grids. Bearing in mind that investment projects will, in most cases, cover several countries, there is a significant risk of double taxation and other tax disputes over how to allocate profits along the value chain. A tax component could become a significant cost driver in the OBOR initiative unless some steps are taken to mitigate these tax risks.

At the domestic level, cooperative compliance is an initiative that tax administrations employ to both improve tax certainty and minimize tax risks. In an international context, such as the OBOR initiative, multilateral cooperative compliance may be a way to mitigate the risk that tax disputes impede the progress of the project. Multilateral cooperative compliance was recommended as an innovative multilateral approach to fostering tax certainty in the 2017 OECD/IMF report for the G20 Finance Ministers.[4] This report responded to a request from the G20 Leaders at their summit in Hangzhou, China in September 2016 to work on issues of tax certainty.

This chapter discusses the potential of a multilateral cooperative compliance programme to improve tax certainty and contribute to the success of the OBOR initiative. It highlights the benefits that both tax administrations and multinationals (MNEs) participating in the OBOR initiative could derive from building multilateral relationships based upon the concept of cooperative compliance.

The chapter begins with a brief explanation of the concept of cooperative compliance as this is the foundation for multilateral cooperative compliance. First, the authors present the benefits that it promises to deliver to both tax administrations and taxpayers, followed by an explanation of how a multilateral cooperative compliance programme would build on the concept of cooperative compliance and also how it would differ from other tools that tax administrations may want to use to improve compliance and enhance tax certainty. They highlight the potential benefits of a multilateral cooperative compliance programme specifically in the context of the OBOR initiative. Finally, the authors look at some existing forums for international cooperation among tax administrations.

---

2. 'The development of China's policy to encourage outward investment from 1979 to the official announcement of the "go global" strategy in 2000 .... Since then the "go global" policy has been strengthened and further elaborated'. For more, see K. Davies, *China Investment Policy: An Update*, OECD Working Papers on International Investment, at 1 (2013), available at https://www.oecd.org/china/WP-2013_1.pdf (accessed 10 Jun. 2017).
3. See e.g., R. Wang & C. Zhu, *Annual Report on the Development of the Indian Ocean Region (2015): 21st Century Maritime Silk Road* (Springer 2016); T. Hancock, *China Encircles the World with One Belt, One Road Strategy*, Financial Times (4 May 2017).
4. IMF/OECD, *Tax Certainty: IMF/OECD Report for the G20 Finance Ministers*, at 34 (Mar. 2017), available at https://www.oecd.org/tax/tax-policy/tax-certainty-report-oecd-imf-report-g20-finance-ministers-march-2017.pdf (accessed 10 Jun. 2017).

2 COOPERATIVE COMPLIANCE AS A WAY TO IMPROVE TAX COMPLIANCE AND BUSINESS CONFIDENCE DOMESTICALLY

2.1 The Concept of Cooperative Compliance

The concept of cooperative compliance emerged first at the national level in 2005, when it was introduced under the name 'horizontal monitoring' in the Netherlands. It gained wider recognition internationally in 2008 when the OECD Forum on Tax Administration promoted it in its report *Study into the Role of Tax Intermediaries*.[5] This 2008 report devoted a section to the notion, which it described as an 'enhanced relationship' between the taxpayer and tax administration. Later, in 2013 the OECD published a fuller discussion[6] of the thinking behind the idea and adopted the term 'cooperative compliance'. In part, this was to avoid any suggestion that participating taxpayers could obtain 'enhanced' benefits that are not available to all.

Cooperative compliance represents a shift from a retrospective and primarily repressive control, to a cooperative relationship between tax administration and taxpayers that is much more likely to involve a discussion of tax treatment in real-time or even prospectively. It is intended to deliver quality compliance, which means payment of taxes due on time in an effective and efficient manner. At the heart of the concept is a simple exchange of transparency for certainty. The taxpayer undertakes to be wholly transparent about the tax positions that it has taken in its return and the transactions that are likely to give rise to a tax risk. The taxpayer does not limit this disclosure to the information required by the administrative provisions of tax law and does not seek to invoke legal privilege to prevent access to documents that could be relevant to the determination of a tax liability. In return, the tax administration agrees to offer the taxpayer early certainty about the tax treatment of the taxpayer's business transactions. Experience shows that this is often easiest to achieve if the discussion takes place as close as possible to the time when those transactions take place, which is why the cooperative model often encourages the parties to discuss issues before a tax return is even filed, or, in certain circumstances, before a transaction takes place.

Clearly, trust between the taxpayer and tax administration is central to the effective operation of the cooperative compliance model, but the OECD's 2013 report emphasizes that this trust must be justified. In particular, the tax administration needs to be satisfied that the transparency and disclosure by the taxpayer is underpinned by a system of control that ensures that the disclosure is complete and accurate. The core features of the concept include: justified or demonstrable trust; transparency; cooperation; collaboration; voluntary disclosure; timely advice on significant positions; and early legal certainty. The cooperative compliance model works on the basis that if a taxpayer is voluntarily and fully transparent, and able to show 'how it does that', the tax administration should provide early tax certainty and do so in advance, where appropriate.

---

5. OECD, *Study into the Role of Tax Intermediaries* (OECD Publishing 2008).
6. OECD, *Cooperative Compliance: A Framework – From Enhanced Relationship to Cooperative Compliance* (OECD Publishing 2013).

The cooperative compliance model offers a win-win situation for both taxpayers and the tax authorities. The taxpayer receives early certainty and overall should incur reduced compliance costs, while the tax administration benefits from a more efficient use of limited resources. Establishing the relationship may require some initial investment by both the taxpayer and the tax administration, but over time it will reduce the costs incurred by both. By discussing and resolving cases earlier, it is possible to avoid abortive enquiries and costly and time-consuming litigation, while directing the resources saved to higher-risk cases. Moreover, both parties could benefit from certain reputational gains: taxpayers engaging in the cooperative compliance model demonstrate their willingness to pay their fair share of tax and the tax administration demonstrates a willingness to engage constructively with a key segment of its taxpayer population. This might explain why the cooperative compliance model has been adopted in one form or another in almost thirty jurisdictions worldwide.

2.2 Essential Features of Cooperative Compliance

There is no prescribed method for implementation of cooperative compliance, which is understandable, given the diversity of tax environments from one country to the next. However, the OECD has codified essential features that each programme aiming to be called 'cooperative compliance' should have. The original 2008 OECD report indicated seven essential features of the cooperative compliance model, and the 2013 report confirmed their validity. Five of them concern the tax administration, while two deal with the taxpayer's approach to its tax obligations. Tax administrations need to demonstrate commercial awareness, impartiality, proportionality, openness and responsiveness.

Commercial awareness on the part of a tax administration means that it should have a good understanding of the commercial drivers that are behind transactions and activities undertaken by taxpayers. Tax administrations need to understand the broader context of an activity or transaction and respond in a way that minimizes avoidable and potentially costly disputes and uncertainty. To these ends, tax administrations in many countries have established special units to deal with particular groups of taxpayers, for example taxpayers active in specific sectors (such as banking or mining) or of a certain size. Tax administrations in the region adopting this model include China, Kyrgyzstan and Tajikistan. While countries adopt a variety of criteria to define their large taxpayer population, this type of organizational model certainly encourages specialization by key administration staff. This improves their understanding of particular industries, specific businesses and the tax risks they may pose.

The second feature that should characterize the actions of the tax administration is impartiality. Tax administrations are required to approach the task of issue resolution with a high level of consistency and objectivity. They should maintain a professional and critical attitude towards the large businesses they deal with and the information they obtain in the course of their dealings with such businesses. Failure to maintain impartiality will have a damaging effect on overall confidence in the tax administration and will undermine trust. To address this risk, the governance process that the tax administration uses to ensure that its decisions are soundly made should be transparent, even if the decisions themselves remain confidential. To ensure transparency about the decision making process, and the consistency and fairness of the decisions themselves, the 2013 OECD report distinguished six principles that should be observed in the governance of cooperative programmes, namely: integrity rules and core values; standard working programmes and operating systems; the involvement of a second (or even more) pair(s) of eyes in the decision making process; training programmes and programmes of regular contact between experts involved; rotation systems; and review and monitoring systems.

The actions of the tax administration also need to be proportionate. This aspect of cooperative compliance extends to the choices that the tax administration makes in allocating resources and deciding which taxpayers, or which tax issues, to prioritize. For instance in 2016,[7] China introduced the credit rating of business taxpayers' behaviour regarding tax payments, and the methods and criteria for arriving at the ratings.[8] Business taxpayers deemed to have a low risk level and high compliance awareness will be guided and advised by the tax administration in respect of compliance with special tax adjustment rules. Business taxpayers with a high-risk level run the risk of being audited and receiving special tax adjustments without prior guidance or warning. The introduction of the risk-based tax administration cycle affects the way that Chinese tax authorities deploy their resources and their relations with taxpayers. In China, the credit rating programme was supported by the introduction of a digital reporting obligation for selected business groups (the so-called Thousand Groups Project).[9] The data collected in this programme will not only help the SAT predict tax collection, but also will optimize the deployment of SAT resources.

The last two aspects that should characterize the behaviour of a tax administration within the cooperative compliance relationship are openness and responsiveness. Both attributes are likely to help establish a constructive relationship with taxpayers and make it much easier to address tax issues with the taxpayer in real-time. Real-time working is the most effective way to achieve early certainty which benefits both parties and is very valuable commercially. In the Netherlands, part of the process of establishing a cooperative compliance relationship involves addressing and resolving any existing legacy of open tax issues. In Singapore, there is a platform for large corporate

---

7. In fact, the tax credit rating system has been progressively developed in China through a range of SAT circulars. These include SAT Announcement 40 (2014), SAT Announcement 48 (2015) and SAT Announcement 85 (2015), with further guidance in SAT Public Consultation Draft Circular on Special Tax Adjustments (2015).
8. KPMG, *China Looking Ahead*, Intl. Tax Rev., at 48, available at https://home.kpmg.com/cn/en/home/insights/2016/12/china-looking-ahead-itr-201601.html (accessed 6 Jun. 2017). The tax credit rating system has been progressively developed through a range of SAT circulars. These include SAT Announcement 40 (2014), SAT Announcement 48 (2015) and SAT Announcement 85 (2015), with further guidance in SAT Public Consultation Draft Circular on Special Tax Adjustments (2015).
9. PWC, China Requests More Data from Large Businesses under the 'Thousand Groups Project', available at https://www.pwc.com/gx/en/tax/newsletters/tax-policy-bulletin/assets/pwc-china-requests-data-from-businesses-in-thousand-groups-project.pdf (accessed 3 Jun. 2017).

taxpayers where they can discuss significant current events that have tax impacts with the tax administration so as to reduce downstream difficulties in assessments and objections.

Under the cooperative compliance model, taxpayers are required to provide disclosure and transparency. Disclosure requires the taxpayer to provide the tax administration with all the information that it needs to make fully informed risk assessment of the tax issues arising from a tax return, including any specific transactions or positions that raise questions which are particularly uncertain, difficult or controversial from the perspective of the tax administration. Transparency refers to the framework within which these individual acts of disclosure take place. There has been some discussion as to whether disclosure of a taxpayer's tax position should be structured as mandatory or voluntary, but most cooperative compliance relationships are entered into voluntarily.[10]

The more pressing practical question concerns how the taxpayer is to demonstrate that trust in its disclosures is justified. The practical response is that the taxpayer should have in place a robust process for managing, controlling and monitoring the correctness of reported tax positions. In other words, the taxpayer should have an internal control system that enables it to validate the outputs it provides to the tax administration. This system is known as the tax control framework.[11] It is the cornerstone of cooperative compliance, as it justifies trust between taxpayers and tax authorities. The two-pronged approach (tax control framework and the willingness to disclose positions voluntarily) has been fully integrated, for example, into the Australian framework. In Australia, within the Annual Compliance Arrangements with Large Corporate Taxpayers programme, which is the ATO's cooperative compliance regime, two requirements must be met. First, the large business must have a sound tax risk management process and second, demonstrate a willingness to operate in an open and transparent relationship by making full and true disclosure of a major tax risks in a real time environment.[12]

Cooperative compliance enhances the efficiency and effectiveness of the overall compliance strategy and the audit programme by encouraging an approach based on tax risk management. If the tax administration can rely on a taxpayer's disclosures, it can allocate its resources to other taxpayers that are not transparent and pose greater risk.

The concept of cooperative compliance is not new to the SAT. The SAT has already initiated the tax compliance agreement programme.[13] The aim of this programme is to leverage the sound internal control through the tax risk management systems of the enterprises participating in the programme in order to minimize the

---

10. OECD, *Cooperative Compliance*, supra n. 6, at 33.
11. For more on a tax control framework, *see* OECD, *Cooperative Compliance*, supra n. 6.
12. For more details, *see*: Australian Taxation Office, *Annual Compliance Arrangements with Large Corporate Taxpayers*, The Auditor-General ANAO Report No.5 2014–15 Performance Audit, http://www.anao.gov.au/~/media/Files/Audit%20Reports/2014%202015/Report%205/AuditReport_2014-2015_5.pdf (accessed 20 Sep. 2015).
13. KPMG, *supra* n. 8, at 48.

need for inspection of taxpayers' tax reporting and compliance.[14] Along with the programme, the SAT issued the Guidelines on Tax Risk Management in Large Enterprises to guide large enterprises in their tax risk management.[15] However, like any other programme that has some features of cooperative compliance, it can be applied only domestically.

3 MULTILATERAL COOPERATIVE COMPLIANCE: FROM DOMESTIC RELATIONSHIP TO CROSS-BORDER COOPERATION

The concept of multilateral cooperative compliance further develops the cooperative compliance model that involves a bilateral relationship between a tax administration and a large business taxpayer, into a multilateral relationship that can involve a large business taxpayer and two or more tax administrations. The underlying principles of the cooperative compliance model remain the same.

In 2013, there was some initial experience of multilateral cooperative compliance. The 2013 OECD Report states that such a relationship was established by the Dutch and UK tax administrations.[16] The cooperation covered a variety of different legal and tax questions. The collaboration has resulted in rapid information sharing, quick resolution of issues and the prevention of unnecessary and prolonged disputes.

Multilateral cooperative compliance shares some common features with other compliance tools. For instance, there are similarities with multilateral advanced pricing agreements. However, advanced pricing agreements are concerned only with transfer pricing. The scope of multilateral cooperative compliance is not limited to one type of tax issue; it covers all tax risks that arise in a particular case. It can also cover more than one tax.

Recently the idea of multilateral cooperative compliance was brought on board in a pilot programme developed by the OECD under the name International Compliance Assurance Program (ICAP).[17] Currently ICAP involves tax administrations from eight jurisdictions[18]. Within ICAP tax administrations conduct tax risk assessment of largest business taxpayers on the basis of their country-by-country reports and additional documents requested in the pilot programme. So far the scope of ICAP is limited to transfer pricing and permanent establishment risks.[19]

Some features of multilateral cooperative compliance can be found in other compliance initiatives. It can be seen similar to a mutual agreement procedure (MAP).

---

14. *See*: http://www.chinatax.gov.cn/eng/n2367721/c2390301/content.html (accessed 10 Jun. 2017).
15. CN: Notice of the State Administration of Taxation on Issuing the Guidelines on Tax Risk Management of Large Enterprises (for Trial Implementation), available at http://www.law infochina.com/Display.aspx?lib=law&Cgid=117050 (accessed 19 May 2017).
16. OECD, *Cooperative Compliance*, supra n. 6, at 34.
17. More information about the pilot programme available in: OECD, *International Compliance Assurance Programme Pilot Handbook*, (OECD Publishing 2018).
18. Australia, Canada, Italy, Japan, the Netherlands, Spain, the United Kingdom and the United States.
19. Some comments on the ICAP: A. Majdanska & J. Leigh-Pemberton, *The OECD's International Compliance Assurance Programme*, TPI – Transfer Pricing International 3&4 (2018).

Both instruments operate in cross-border cases. However, by comparison to a multilateral cooperative compliance programme, the scope of a MAP is limited. A MAP takes place only in the context of disputes concerning tax treaties and involves a negotiation between just two governments in which the taxpayer is not directly involved. This means that a MAP does not cover disputes over indirect taxes, such as VAT. Moreover, a MAP is initiated to resolve a specific case and is initiated post-factum and post-tax return, so that it does not deliver the early certainty that is a feature of cooperative compliance. Furthermore, cooperative compliance aims to ensure ongoing tax certainty. This means tax certainty with respect to any tax arrangement that a taxpayer might have. It is not expected to settle only one issue, but provides an ongoing framework for cooperation between the tax administration and a taxpayer.

Joint audits have some similarities with multilateral cooperative compliance. In a joint audit, two or more tax administrations work together to examine an issue or transaction of one or more related taxable persons with cross-border business activities.[20] This provides an opportunity for a taxpayer to make a presentation and share information with the countries in a single process.[21] The potential benefits of joint audits were articulated in the 2010 OECD study entitled *Joint Audit Report*.[22] Specifically, they should enable quicker issue resolution, more streamlined fact finding and more effective compliance. They are expected to shorten examination processes and reduce costs, both for tax administrations and for taxpayers. Joint audits are aimed at achieving similar goals to multilateral cooperative compliance. However, they are based on the idea of a comprehensive tax audit. This means that they are usually set up to examine a specific issue or a specific transaction.

By contrast, multilateral cooperative compliance aims to establish an ongoing relationship. In addition, as opposed to the idea of a tax audit, multilateral cooperative compliance relies on an audit of the tax control framework to provide assurance; and only specific issues that raise particular doubts as to the correct tax treatment should be subject to a detailed investigation. In this way, multilateral cooperative compliance should be more efficient than a joint audit because its scope is limited to well-targeted issues. Thus, although the two instruments are very similar, there are some significant differences between joint audits and multilateral cooperative compliance.

4 A POTENTIAL OF MULTILATERAL COOPERATIVE COMPLIANCE FOR THE OBOR INITIATIVE

In response to the OBOR initiative, the SAT introduced a series of different programmes. It expanded the Chinese treaty network to cover all countries participating in the OBOR initiative. As a result, in 2015, tax treaties were renewed or signed with Cambodia, India, Italy, Pakistan, Romania, Russia and Spain. Extensive research was

---

20. I.J.J. Burgers & D. Criclivaia, *Joint Tax Audits: Which Countries May Benefit Most?*, 8 World Tax J. 3, at 306 (2016).
21. *Ibid.*, at 309.
22. OECD, Ctr. for Tax Policy & Admin., *Joint Audit Report: Sixth Meeting of the OECD Forum on Tax Administration*, 15–16 Sept. 2010, Istanbul Communiqué (September 2010).

carried out with regard to tax systems of different jurisdictions, including OBOR countries. In terms of tax administration, assistance was provided to domestic enterprises to resolve tax-related disputes with OBOR countries by means of a MAP. In addition, tax service is now available through various channels, including official websites and telephone inquiries. None of these steps, however, addresses any potentially contentious tax issues in advance, nor provides early tax certainty to participants in the OBOR initiative. Multilateral cooperative compliance could be a way to do this and to avoid long and costly tax disputes that may emerge once the OBOR initiative unfolds.

Multilateral cooperative compliance, in common with domestic cooperative compliance programmes, encourages MNEs to be transparent on a voluntary basis. Not only is this valuable in terms of the taxation of those MNEs in the cooperative compliance programme, but it also helps tax administrations to acquire valuable data and commercial insights. In the context of cross-border project like the OBOR initiative, this could significantly reduce tax costs of handling the tax assessment of taxpayers that operate cross-border. In particular, it should make it much easier to determine which activities in a business generate value and how profits should be allocated between states. Most of the investments in the OBOR initiative will involve operations in more than one country. This will entail reviewing businesses' value chain, how tax risks are managed and what drives customer and shareholder value.

The know-how acquired through multilateral cooperative compliance will positively inform the assessment and determination of the tax liabilities of other taxpayers. Tax administrations will acquire information and commercial awareness that will help them to detect, understand and address the tax risks posed by other taxpayers that are not part of the programme. In addition, they may obtain an appreciation of the tax risks associated with a certain type of transaction, business or an entire industry. This appreciation could be crucial in auditing and assessing the tax positions of other taxpayers.

In return for the transparency from MNEs participating in cooperative compliance relationship, the tax administration provides earlier tax certainty. In general, the tax administration will be better placed to provide a business with the certainty that it needs to make key commercial decisions. In the context of the OBOR initiative, it could help to prevent cases of double taxation or even double non-taxation. In the long run, this kind of relationship should give rise to fewer protracted disputes, which normally involve significant costs. This is particularly relevant to the multibillion investments in multiple jurisdictions that are expected under the OBOR initiative. The OBOR initiative could result in many cross-border tax disputes. If a dispute arises under a tax treaty, a MAP is usually invoked to resolve the case. However, as noted, a MAP is usually invoked only when a dispute has already arisen and there are concerns as to the capacity to handle MAP disputes in a timely manner in some countries.[23] Some investments could be put at risk by tax disputes. To ensure smooth realization of the OBOR initiative, the OBOR countries may want to consider how to ensure dispute

---

23. J. Kollman et al., *Arbitration in International Tax Matters*, 77 Tax Notes Intl. 13, at 1189–95 (2015).

minimization. Multilateral cooperative compliance could be an answer. It provides a platform for an open discussion of tax positions. It should reduce the risk of incorrect tax assessments and the need to pursue legal remedies. Even if a dispute does arise and needs to be settled by the courts, it is much more likely to be limited to the correct interpretation of the law, as the facts should already have been agreed.

Cooperation between tax administrations and taxpayers in assessing the correct tax liability helps both sides to establish mutual trust. From the perspective of the tax administration, it constitutes trust in the full openness of the taxpayer and that that the taxpayer will disclose all relevant facts and issues. From the perspective of the taxpayer, this means that it will not be surprised by an unexplained change in interpretation of the law; additional or unexpected tax charges; or burdensome audits. This is especially critical in the context of multijurisdictional projects, such as the OBOR initiative, where each country follows its own tax policy and strategy. This could make a multijurisdictional investment difficult to manage. Multilateral cooperative compliance offers a means to resolve potential difficulties in advance, creating a positive climate for OBOR investment.

5 JITSIC AS A MODEL?

Given the benefits of multilateral cooperative compliance, the next question is what is necessary to make it work. Specifically, the issue is whether countries before entering into multilateral initiative on cooperative compliance are obliged to introduce cooperative compliance programme at the domestic level. It would be beneficial for all parties to multilateral cooperative compliance, if tax administrations involved were to have had experience in this type of cooperation. However, the lack of a domestic initiative should not exclude any country from joining multilateral cooperative compliance. Interesting inspiration can be drawn from the Joint International Tax Shelter Information Centre (JITSIC).

The Joint International Taskforce on Shared Intelligence and Collaboration, formerly the Joint International Tax Shelter Information & Collaboration (JITSIC), reformulated in 2014 and again in 2016, provides an example of a forum for tax administrations to cooperate and collaborate.[24] Its roots are in the JITSIC established in 2004 by the tax administrations of Australia, Canada, the United Kingdom and the United States, and later joined by China, France, Germany, Japan and Korea (Rep.). It aimed at supplementing their ongoing work in identifying and curbing tax avoidance and shelters and those that promote and invest in them. The basis for cooperation was a memorandum of understanding signed by participating tax administrations.[25] Delegates from each of the countries exchanged information in real time on abusive tax schemes, their promoters and investors, consistent with the provisions of bilateral tax treaties. The countries were sharing their best practices on risk assessment and other

---

24. For more on the JITSIC, see http://www.oecd.org/tax/forum-on-tax-administration/jitsic/ (accessed 30 May 2017).
25. *Joint International Tax Shelter Information Centre, Memorandum of Understanding*, available at https://www.irs.gov/pub/irs-utl/jitsic-finalmou.pdf (accessed 1 June 2017).

key areas of interest and increasing the transparency of cross-border transactions in order to create a level playing field for taxpayers that voluntary comply with their tax obligations.

The new format of the forum highlights the need for collaboration and cooperation. It is aimed at providing better possibilities for tax administrations to exchange information and undertake collaborative casework. It is noteworthy that advances in international collaboration that have resulted from JITSIC and related developments are among the drivers behind the ICAP referred to earlier.

A similar model could be put forward for a multilateral cooperative compliance programme for the OBOR initiative. The design of a multilateral cooperative compliance programme could start with the establishment of a platform for OBOR countries where tax administrations could share their experiences. A taxpayer approaching this type of body would be able to discuss a case with all OBOR countries at once. Any potential contentious issues could be resolved at a very early stage in the investment.

6 CONCLUSION

There is a Chinese saying, 'If you want to develop, build a road.' In order to achieve true development, it is necessary to build not only roads but also channels for communication between taxpayers and tax administrations. An environment of legal certainty, trust and mutual understanding plays a crucial role in enhancing better tax compliance, which in turn generates increased tax revenue. Tax revenue, in turn, is the key to providing public benefits that support strong and durable growth.

The concept of cooperative compliance offers a promise of building a road of communication between the tax administration and large business taxpayers. It enhances tax certainty – a key for foreign direct investment. It minimizes compliance costs, both for the tax administration and the taxpayer, by preventing lengthy disputes. The values it promotes are valuable not only domestically. Given that large business taxpayers operate cross-border, the question is how to ensure that the same benefits can be obtained internationally.

The authors suggest multilateral cooperative compliance as a potential solution and a way to provide a positive tax climate for complex international projects such as the OBOR initiative. Without proper solutions, tax issues could derail the OBOR initiative.

Multilateral cooperative compliance could help to minimize conflicts between tax administrations and businesses by establishing a relationship based on transparency and justified trust. At the same time, it should ensure that countries involved in the OBOR initiative secure their fair share of the tax revenue that will be generated by the project.

Index

A

Accounting Directive, 186
Acquisition, 89, 91, 179, 182, 307
Administrative assistance, 56, 158
Advanced pricing agreements (APA), 13, 15, 18, 28, 172, 187–191, 194, 195, 300, 305, 306
Afghanistan, 28, 41, 42, 44, 62, 85, 91, 106, 110, 150, 151, 153, 157, 158, 164
Africa, 3, 30, 57, 308
Albania, 26, 41, 60, 86, 106, 173, 180, 183, 201, 248
Allocation of the taxing right, 56, 254, 288, 294, 299
Anglo-American legal system, 42, 46
Anti-abuse rule, 63, 64, 269, 289, 290, 295
  general, 63, 64
  specific, 63, 64
Anti-avoidance
  clause, 43
  legislation, 43
  provisions, 43, 46
  rules, 11, 170, 225
Arbitration, 9, 21, 267, 282, 296, 300, 306
Arm's length principle (ALP), 36, 171, 172, 174, 182, 185, 188, 190, 192, 193, 289, 294, 296–300, 302, 304, 305, 306
Armenia, 26, 41, 45, 86, 106, 151, 152, 154, 159, 160, 170, 173, 180, 182, 201, 221, 243, 264, 270–273
Artificial arrangements, 294, 302
Asian Development Bank, 127, 128, 171
Asian Highway Network, 142
Asian Infrastructure Investment Bank (AIIB), 4, 117
Audit, 7, 18, 173–175, 178, 182, 185, 188–190, 193, 194, 269, 279, 300, 306, 311, 312, 314–316
Australia, 31–33, 297, 312, 316
Azerbaijan, 26, 41, 59, 60, 86, 106, 110, 142, 145, 146, 150, 151, 154, 155, 157, 158, 164, 170, 173, 180, 182, 201, 207, 249, 264, 270–272

B

Bahrain, 26, 41, 43, 45, 60, 86, 106, 170, 173, 180, 183, 201, 222, 248
Bangladesh, 26, 41, 43, 60, 85, 106, 180, 183, 201, 213, 244
Base erosion profit shifting BEPS
  Action 1, 293, 294
  Action 2, 290
  Action 3, 290, 299
  Action 4, 290, 301, 302
  Action 5
    Action 5 Final Report, 191
  Action 6, 63–68
    Final report, 65
  Action 8, 294
  Action 10, 295

Index

Action 13
   Action 13 Final Report, 185–187
   Action 14, 17, 296
   Action 14 Final Report, 190
   Action 15, 295, 300
   anti-BEPS rules, 288, 290, 304
   neo-BEPS, 35–35,
   post – BEPS, 63, 180, 285–306
Basic Multilateral Agreement on International Transport for Development of the Europe-Caucasus-Asia Corridor, 154
Belarus, 25, 26, 41, 60, 86, 106, 145, 151, 152, 159, 173, 174, 180, 182, 201, 221, 241, 264, 270–273, 278, 279
Belt and Road Initiative, 3–47, 84–87, 90–102, 105–113, 259–283
Beneficial owner, 25, 45, 60–62, 218, 219, 222, 224, 226, 227, 249, 250, 257, 258
Benefit test, 176, 177
Best practices, 5, 8, 10, 17, 152, 166, 190, 290, 293, 299, 316
Bhutan, 28, 41, 43, 44, 62, 85, 106, 108, 110
Bilateral, 10–12, 18, 44–46, 110–111, 161–162
Bilateral Investment Treaties (BIT), 18, 268
Black Sea, 145
Blockchain technology, 17
Bosnia and Herzegovina, 27, 41, 46, 59, 60, 73, 86, 106, 180, 201, 234, 235, 240
Brazil, 288, 298
BRI Model Tax Treaty, 11, 254
BRI Tax Academy, 12, 13, 17, 18
BRI Tax Forum, 4
BRICS, 287
Brunei, 25, 27, 41, 45, 46, 59, 60, 85, 106, 170, 173, 180, 183, 201, 249

Bulgaria, 26, 27, 41, 45, 46, 50, 60, 86, 106, 142, 154, 180, 183, 201, 240
Burden
   administrative burden, 11, 15, 142, 167, 193, 257
   tax burden, 33, 42, 46, 58, 59, 67, 80, 91–102, 116–118, 188, 221, 255, 266, 295, 298, 299, 304, 305
Business model, 7, 92, 172
Business-to-business (B2B), 263–265, 267–269, 274, 283
Business-to-consumer (B2C), 263–265, 269, 274, 294, 298, 300

C

Cambodia, 27, 41, 51–53, 73, 85, 87, 106, 110, 314
Canada, 30–33, 316
Capacity Building, 18, 30, 146, 192
Capital flow, 12, 43, 109, 110
Capital gains, 229–232
Capitalization rules, 43, 301, 302
Caspian Sea, 145, 199
Central and Eastern Europe, 40, 43, 57, 86, 106–108
Central Asia, 115–135, 151–152
Central Asia Regional Economic Cooperation (CAREC), 151–152
Central route, 145, 146
Chinese Corporate Income Tax Law, 58
Chinese Unicom Red Chip Company, 69–71
Circular, 92, 303
Civil law, 42, 46, 91, 188, 277, 278
Collaboration, 8, 192, 309, 313, 316, 317
Common law, 91
Commonwealth of Independent States (CIS), 106, 107, 270
Comparable uncontrolled price (CUP) method, 172, 176, 178
Compatibility clauses, 22

Index

Competition, 6, 9, 11, 14, 36–38, 62, 67, 146, 190, 193, 255, 266, 267, 287, 289–291, 298
Conduit arrangement, 64
Consistency, 5, 12, 16, 18, 36, 42, 182, 228, 267, 310, 311
Continental law, 91
Contracting state, 25, 45, 58–61, 63, 64, 66, 70, 72–74, 160, 201–205, 209–211, 218, 222, 224–226, 228–234, 236, 239–241, 244, 245, 268
Controlled foreign company (CFC), 290, 299, 304
Convention on International Transport of Goods under Cover of TIR Carnets (TIR Convention), 155–158, 161
Convention on the Contract for the International Carriage of Goods by Road (CMR Convention), 148, 152, 160–161
Cooperative compliance
  cooperative compliance programme, 306, 308, 314–317
  multilateral cooperative compliance, 7–8, 308, 313–317
  tax compliance agreement programme, 312
Cost contribution agreements (CCAs), 13
Cost contribution arrangements (CCA), 12, 180–184
Country-by-country reporting (CbCR), 186, 187, 287–289
Croatia, 25, 41, 45, 60, 86, 106, 173, 180, 182, 201, 241
Cross-border activity, 6, 296
Customs (custom duties), 17, 99, 100, 154, 156, 157, 161, 263
Czech Republic, 41, 45, 50, 59, 85, 86, 106, 110, 180, 182, 201, 233

D

Data, 5, 12, 14, 15, 18, 24, 31, 33, 50–52, 69, 107–109, 117, 120–134, 163, 173–176, 184–189, 192–194, 276–279, 288, 289, 294, 297, 311, 315
Deduction, 79, 183, 235, 236, 261–263, 267, 268, 274, 275, 281, 282, 301, 303
Demand, 29, 36, 77, 189, 306
Derivative benefits, 64
Destination principle, 9, 10, 260, 261, 263–264, 266–268, 271, 272, 274, 280, 282, 283
Developing countries, 8, 10, 12, 20, 30, 37, 76, 78, 85, 135, 170, 173, 175, 184, 298, 299
Development, Enhancement, Maintenance, Protection and Exploitation (DEMPE), 14, 179, 180, 192, 291, 305
Development Bank of China, 59, 71–74
Digital economy, 62, 293–300
Diplomatic protection, 76–79
Disclosure
  voluntary disclosure, 8, 309
Dispute resolution, 9, 10, 16–18, 21, 79, 265, 267–268, 282, 296
Dividends, 25, 27, 45, 58–60, 62, 67–71, 89, 90, 92, 95, 96, 99, 101, 218–223, 226, 228, 237–254, 257, 303
Documentation requirements, 15, 182, 193, 264, 276, 278, 282
Domestic law, 13, 58, 59, 62, 63, 68, 69, 71, 72, 74–76, 78, 157, 167, 180, 201, 220, 221, 229, 236, 254, 256, 266, 271, 274–277, 281, 288, 290, 296, 299, 300
Double taxation, 5, 9, 16, 19, 21, 22, 24, 28, 44, 56, 58, 65, 66, 77, 79, 80, 89, 110–112, 170, 191, 192, 195, 201, 202, 226, 235, 254, 257, 260, 266–268, 280, 282, 283, 295, 300, 305, 306, 308, 315

E

East Asia, 40, 57, 91, 95
East Timor, 28, 41, 44, 62, 85, 106, 108-110
e-commerce, 294, 298
Economic Belt, 40, 43, 47, 106, 107, 138-140
Economic Cooperation Organization (ECO), 157-158
Economic Cooperation Organization Transit Transport Framework Agreement, 157-158
Economic output, 108, 109
Economic ownership, 179
Economic union, 151, 152, 159-160, 221, 263, 270, 271
Egypt, 25, 27, 41, 42, 45, 61, 86, 88, 90, 106, 107, 180, 183, 201, 207, 245
Emerging countries, 8, 10, 12, 20
Emerging markets, 30-32, 38, 286
Employment income, 58
Enhanced relationship, 309
Equalization levy, 297-300
Estonia, 26, 41, 45, 50, 59, 85, 86, 89, 106, 180, 182, 201, 246
EU Code of Conduct on Transfer Pricing Documentation, 184
Eurasian Economic Union (EAEU), 152, 159-160, 221, 263, 266, 268, 270-282
Euro zone, 91
European Commission, 36
European Union (EU), 138, 139, 145, 154, 162, 167
Exchange of information, 13, 36, 112, 185-187, 300, 303
Excises, 17, 18
Exemption rules, 77
Expenditure, 116, 118-127, 129-135
Export, 274-275

F

Favourable treatment, 65
Final Report, 47, 63, 65, 66, 68, 178, 179, 185-187, 190, 191, 290, 299
Financial Crisis, 33, 36, 37, 86, 120, 122, 126, 260
Financial institutions, 11, 59, 72, 73, 225, 257, 301
Fiscal Crisis, 36-37
Fiscal revenue, 116, 119-122, 124, 126, 127, 129-135, 214
Fiscal security, 36
Fixed place of business, 205-208, 256, 257, 267
Foreign direct investment (FDI), 4-7, 11, 15, 22, 49-53, 68, 84-88, 109, 110, 199, 254, 255, 286, 291, 292, 299, 301-308, 317
France, 31-33, 129, 316
Free trade zones, 15

G

G20, 19, 21, 32, 33, 36, 47, 62-69, 80, 111, 174, 179, 187, 256, 283, 287, 291, 292, 308
Georgia, 26, 41, 45, 57, 61, 86, 106, 107, 110, 142, 145, 146, 150, 154, 155, 158, 164, 173, 174, 180, 182, 201, 207, 219, 249, 264, 271
Germany, 31-33, 96, 97, 201, 214, 298, 300, 306, 316
Global economy, 33, 37, 91, 293
Global Forum on Transparency and Exchange of Information for Tax Purposes, 287, 306
Global Forum on VAT, 261
Globalization, 35-38, 85
GNI, 108, 110

Going Global, 28, 29, 37, 42, 58-60, 62, 66, 68-78, 80, 83-103, 112
Goods and services
 intra-group services, 13, 175-178, 181, 182
Governance, 35, 37, 310, 311
Government Budget Deficit, 31
Government-owned financial institution, 59
Gross domestic product (GDP), 5, 30-33, 50, 108-110, 117, 121, 123, 125-127, 130-135, 199

H

Harmful tax competition, 6, 190, 289, 291
Harmonisation, 155
Home country, 60
Hong Kong, 24, 56, 69, 70, 88-90, 93, 95, 101, 102, 199, 295, 301
Horizontal monitoring, 309
Huaxin Cement Limited Company, 71-74
Hungary, 12, 26, 41, 42, 60, 86, 88, 90, 95-98, 106, 109, 178, 180, 182, 201, 241
Hybrid mismatches, 290, 300-303

I

Identification, 41, 44, 70
Imbalance of payment, 36
Implementation, 3, 6, 11, 13, 17, 21, 42, 46, 47, 56, 63, 66, 68, 78, 79, 80, 92, 111-113, 116, 147, 158, 162, 170, 171, 184, 186, 187, 188, 191, 263, 267, 271, 290-292, 299, 301, 302, 306, 310
Import, 9, 17, 59, 99, 100, 109, 138, 152, 160, 163-165, 199, 263, 269, 273-277, 281
Incentives, 6, 15-16, 18, 64, 112, 183, 188, 194, 237, 301

Inclusive Framework, 67, 185, 187
Independent personal services, 58, 220, 223, 228, 233
India, 26, 27, 32, 33, 41, 42, 46, 50, 60, 80, 85, 88-91, 99-102, 106-108, 110, 146, 153, 175, 180, 183, 199, 201, 206, 208, 218, 241, 288, 292, 295, 298, 300, 301, 304-306, 314
Indirect-collection method, 260
Indonesia, 12, 25, 26, 41, 43, 51-53, 56, 59, 60, 80, 85, 87, 88, 90, 106, 108, 178, 180, 182, 201, 218, 248
Infrastructure, 4, 10, 11, 18, 37, 49, 57, 116, 117, 138-140, 147, 148, 151, 152, 154, 156, 158, 162, 167, 171, 199, 220, 227, 255, 257, 265-268, 270, 282, 283, 292, 294, 301-303, 306, 308
Innovation, 4, 119
Intangible assets, 36, 98-102, 293-296
Intangible properties, 12, 171, 178-180
Intangibles, 13, 14, 171, 179, 180, 183, 192, 193, 263, 264, 291-293, 295, 298, 304, 305
Inter-connectivity, 3
Interest beneficiary, 72
International Court of Justice, 77
International Law Commission, 77
International market, 66, 67, 154
International organizations, 4, 14, 139, 142-152, 165, 191, 192, 262
International Road Transport Union (IRU), 143-146, 156
Interpretation, 5, 9, 29, 77, 169, 188, 190, 234, 236, 282, 289, 290, 292, 293, 296, 298-300, 304-306, 316
Intra-group services, 13, 175-178, 181, 182
Intra-group transactions, 178
Investment, 49-53, 84-90, 95-102, 109, 286-287, 307-317

Index

Investment treaties, 9, 18, 267, 268
Invoice-credit method, 261
IP box regimes, 290
IP protection, 14, 193
Iran, 26, 41–43, 60, 86, 87, 106, 107, 129, 139, 142, 145, 146, 150, 153–155, 157, 158, 164, 173, 180, 183, 201, 213, 233, 248
Iraq, 28, 41, 44, 62, 86, 91, 106, 110
Islamic legal system (Islamic law system), 42, 46, 91
Israel, 26, 41, 43, 45, 50, 59, 60, 73, 85, 86, 106, 180, 183, 201, 242

J

Japan, 24, 31–33, 56, 295, 298, 300, 316
The Joint International Taskforce on Shared Intelligence and Collaboration, 316
Joint International Tax Shelter Information Centre (JITSIC), 316–317
Jordan, 28, 41, 42, 44, 62, 86, 106, 110
Jurisdiction, 9, 12, 13, 15, 19, 24, 40, 46, 56, 62, 70, 79, 80, 92, 93, 95–98, 101, 173, 175, 179, 180, 188, 190–195, 254, 256, 261–264, 266, 268, 290, 295, 307–317

K

Kazakhstan, 67, 116, 120–121
Kuwait, 25–27, 41, 45, 46, 57, 59, 60, 73, 86, 106, 109, 129, 170, 180, 183, 201, 202, 210, 221, 225, 240
Kyrgyzstan, 117–118, 124–126

L

Laos, 25, 41, 45, 51–53, 56, 59, 60, 87, 91, 106, 173, 201, 239, 246
Latin America, 31, 32

Latvia, 26, 41, 45, 50, 59, 61, 85, 86, 89, 106, 180, 182, 201, 244
Lebanon, 28, 41, 42, 44, 62, 86, 106, 110
Legal framework, 9, 14, 142, 154, 193, 261, 267
Legal privilege, 7, 309
Legislation, 5–7, 12–14, 43, 77, 147, 186, 262, 269, 299
Limitation on benefits (LOB), 62–65, 68, 182, 229, 258
Lithuania, 26, 41, 45, 86, 106, 180, 182, 201, 243
Local file, 184–185
Location savings, 12, 14, 173–175, 192, 295, 304
Location Specific Advantages (LSAs), 292, 305

M

Macao, 24, 56
Macedonia, 25, 27, 41, 45, 46, 57, 60, 86, 106, 180, 183, 201, 245
Malaysia, 25–27, 41, 43, 45, 46, 51, 52, 59–62, 85, 87–90, 106, 180, 182, 199, 201, 218, 219, 225, 227, 239
Maldives, 28, 41, 44, 62, 85, 106, 108, 110
Manufacturing activities, 12, 14, 170–175, 192
Maritime Silk Road, 40, 43, 47, 106, 107, 138
Master file, 184
Measures for the Implementation of Tax Treaty Negotiation Procedures, 79
Mediation, 6, 16
Member States, 146, 147, 148, 153, 154, 157–160, 186, 221, 270, 271, 274, 280–282
Minimum standard, 17, 21, 22, 63, 64, 185, 191, 282, 289, 290, 293–303

Index

Moldova, 26, 41, 45, 50, 86, 106, 154, 170, 173, 180, 182, 201, 247, 264, 270–272
Monetary policy, 91
Mongolia, 25, 40–42, 45, 50, 60, 85, 91, 106, 107, 151, 153, 173, 183, 201, 241
Montenegro, 25, 41, 45, 46, 57, 60, 86, 106, 180, 183, 201
Most-favoured-nation treatment, 68
Multilateral Competent Authority Agreement (MCAA), 186, 287
Multilateral Competent Authority Agreement on the Exchange of Country-by-Country Reports (Multilateral CAA), 185
Multilateral Convention on Automatic Exchange of Information (MCAEOI), 287, 306
Multilateral Convention on Mutual Assistance in Tax Matters, 187
Multinational enterprises (MNEs), 5, 14, 28, 44, 80, 170, 171, 173, 175, 179, 181, 192, 199, 221, 286–289, 291–293, 295, 296, 299, 302–305, 308, 315
Mutual agreement procedure (MAP), 28, 71, 188, 204, 220, 241–244, 246–249, 251, 268, 282, 296, 313
Myanmar, 41, 43, 44, 91, 106, 109, 110

N

National Development Bank of China, 59, 71, 72, 74
Nepal, 25–27, 41, 43, 45, 60, 61, 85, 106, 173, 180
Neutrality, 9, 260, 261, 262, 264, 267, 268, 272, 282, 283
Neutrality principle, 260–262, 267, 282
New Eurasian Land Transport Initiative (NELTI), 143, 146, 156
New Silk Road, 138–149, 292, 306, 308
Nexus, 224, 290, 297

Non-discrimination, 79, 268, 273
Non-taxation, 9, 21, 63, 191, 257, 261, 265–267, 280, 303, 315
Northern route, 145

O

OECD Transfer Pricing Guidelines for Multinational Enterprises and Tax Administrations (OECD TP Guidelines), 12, 13, 170
Oman, 25, 27, 41, 42, 45, 46, 59, 60, 86, 106, 180, 183, 201, 218, 248
One-Belt-One-Road (OBOR), 29, 169–195, 308, 314–317
Operating profit, 58
Organization for Economic Co-Operation and Development (OECD)
  OECD Income and Capital Model Convention and Commentary (OECD Model Commentary), 64, 65
  OECD International VAT/GST Guidelines, 9, 262, 263, 266, 282
  OECD Model, 11, 24, 25, 27, 44, 64, 65, 201–206, 208–213, 218, 220, 222–224, 226–235, 267, 268, 289, 294–296
  OECD's Multilateral Instrument, 10, 11, 19–22, 36, 254, 295, 300
Origin principle, 9, 261, 271, 280
Ownership
  beneficial, 25, 45, 60–62, 218, 219, 222, 224, 226, 227, 249, 250, 257, 258
  full, 73
  main, 73

P

Pakistan, 25–27, 41, 43, 45, 46, 51–53, 59–61, 85, 88–91, 106, 142, 146, 150, 151, 153, 154, 157, 158, 160, 164, 180, 183, 199, 201, 233, 237, 240, 264, 314

Index

Palestine, 28, 41, 42, 44, 62, 86, 106, 108–110
Passive income, 45–46, 95–102, 299
Passive investment income, 58
People's Bank of China, 59
Permanent establishment (PE)
  construction PE, 25, 255–256
  digital PE, 297
  PE thresholds, 11, 205, 210
  service PE, 10, 25
Philippines, 26, 27, 41, 43, 45, 50, 73, 85, 106, 180, 183, 201, 210, 218, 219, 221, 247, 264
Place-of-taxation, 9, 10, 263, 264, 266–268, 279–283
Poland, 26, 41, 45, 60, 61, 86, 88, 90, 96, 106, 182, 201, 214, 216, 230, 232, 239
Population, 47, 107–109, 135, 304, 310
Portugal, 31, 110
Predictability, 5, 16, 194
Preferential treatment, 55–81, 116
Preparatory and auxiliary activities, 294
Principal purpose test (PPT), 62–66, 68
Principles, 6, 7, 9, 10, 22, 36, 37, 46, 57, 64, 65, 68, 73, 77, 92, 96, 111, 113, 119, 127, 138, 156, 161, 171, 172, 174, 176, 182, 185, 188, 190, 192, 193, 213, 223, 224, 234, 260–264, 266–268, 271–274, 278, 280, 282, 283, 289, 311, 313
Private sector, 5, 16, 18, 257
Profit Split Method (PSM), 36, 175, 176, 292, 295, 296, 305
Public finance, 35, 116–119, 130
Public sector, 18

Q

Qatar, 26, 41, 60, 86, 106, 173, 180, 183, 201, 218, 247

Qualified residents, 64

R

Ratification, 19, 21
Refund, 9, 10, 66, 70, 71, 74, 75, 261, 263, 268, 269, 270, 273, 275, 278, 282, 283
Regional Strategic Framework, 147
Registry
  financial, 12, 173
Republic of Korea, 295
Research and development (R&D), 172, 179
Resident, 52, 58–62, 64, 66–70, 72, 73, 75, 78, 79, 92–102, 201–204, 212, 214, 218–223, 225–227, 229, 232, 235–239, 246
Resident company, 60, 94–102, 221
Resources
  natural resources, 17, 44, 87, 205–207, 229, 298
Revenues, 30–32, 120–124, 126, 127, 129–135, 255, 265, 268, 269
Right of taxation, 58, 60
Ring fencing, 293–300
Romania, 26, 27, 41, 45, 60, 61, 73, 86, 89, 106, 154, 180, 182, 201, 207, 221, 253, 314
Route, 3, 4, 17, 18, 79, 84, 138–140, 142, 143, 145–148, 157, 162, 166
Royalties, 25–27, 45–46, 58, 61–62, 68, 69, 74, 75, 90, 98, 100, 101, 112, 182, 192, 226–229, 235, 237, 239–254, 257
Russia, 3, 8, 10, 12, 18, 25, 26, 40, 41, 50, 51, 56, 60, 73, 85, 87–91, 106–108, 110, 128, 131–134, 139, 145, 146, 150, 152–154, 156, 158–160, 164, 174, 180, 182, 199, 201, 218, 221, 222, 224, 252, 264, 268, 270–273, 278, 314

S

Safe harbours, 14, 37, 176–178, 192, 289, 301, 302
Saudi Arabia, 25, 27, 41, 42, 45, 60, 86, 88–91, 106, 110, 180, 183, 201, 251
Secrecy, 12, 173, 176
Serbia, 25, 27, 41, 45, 46, 57, 60, 86, 106, 180, 183, 201, 233, 234, 245
Service and financial transactions, 12
Shanghai Cooperation Organization (SCO), 153–154
Significant economic presence, 297
Silk Road Infrastructure Fund, 4
Silk Route, 84
Simplification, 10, 151, 153, 165, 234, 263, 270, 282
Singapore, 12, 25–28, 41, 44, 45, 50–53, 56, 59, 60, 67, 85, 87–90, 106, 109, 110, 177, 180, 182, 199, 201, 203, 204, 218, 251, 264, 295, 311
Slovakia, 26, 41, 46, 50, 60, 85, 106, 180, 182
Slovenia, 25, 41, 45, 50, 59, 60, 73, 85, 86, 106, 180, 182, 201, 241
South Asia, 40, 41, 43, 44, 53, 57, 85, 106, 107
Southeast Asia, 27, 40, 41, 44, 46, 50, 53, 85, 91, 106, 107
Southern route, 145, 146
Special Economic Zones, 15–16, 18
Sri Lanka, 25–27, 41, 43, 45, 46, 60, 85, 106, 180, 183, 201, 207, 218, 248
Stakeholders, 6, 7, 13, 186, 189, 191, 193, 262
Standardization, 11, 254
State Administration of Taxation (SAT), 4, 24, 28–30, 52, 69, 74, 76, 78, 79, 80, 92, 291, 311–314

Subsidiary, 59, 67, 71, 74, 75, 78, 81, 89, 93, 95–102, 185, 193, 203, 211, 212, 221, 262
Supply, 9, 10, 143, 163, 171, 209, 263, 264, 266, 267, 269, 270, 271, 273, 274–283, 295
Supremacy, 76, 92
Sustainable development, 4
Syria, 26, 41, 42, 45, 57, 59, 86, 106, 108–110, 170, 173, 180, 201

T

Tajikistan, 26, 27, 41, 45, 59, 60, 61, 71, 72, 75, 78–80, 85, 106, 110, 118–119, 126–135, 139, 142, 146, 150, 151, 153, 154, 157–159, 164, 173, 180, 182, 199, 201, 264, 270, 271, 272, 310
Tangible property, 263
Tariffs, 17, 18, 99, 152, 154, 159, 160, 163–166
Tax Administration Law, 58
Tax planning methods, 62
Tax residence certificate, 70, 71
Tax
  abuse, 11, 255
  administration, 5
  assessment, 8, 315, 316
  barriers, 4, 8–18
  base, 15, 37, 47, 62, 63, 170, 227, 237, 254, 256
  benefits, 47, 63, 66–69, 75, 80, 111, 112
  capital, on, 16, 229–231
  certainty, 4–8, 16, 18, 190, 308, 309, 314, 315, 317
  competition, 6, 11, 190, 255, 287, 289–291
  compliance
    compliance costs, 5, 6, 184, 261, 263, 270, 278, 310, 317

Index

consumption tax, 53, 117, 122, 127, 260, 263
control framework, 6, 312, 314
Corporate Income Tax, 39–47, 51, 53, 58, 67, 70, 88–89, 92, 93, 95, 96, 98, 99, 101, 102, 110, 112, 113, 303
cost, 8, 315
discrimination, 56, 79
disputes, 5, 8, 10, 16–17, 28, 56, 69, 76, 77, 78, 79, 80, 89, 91, 111, 112, 257, 308, 315
double taxation, 5, 9, 16, 19, 21, 22, 24, 28, 44, 56, 58, 65, 66, 77, 79, 80, 89, 110–112, 170, 191, 192, 195, 201, 202, 226, 235, 254, 257, 260, 265–268, 280, 282, 283, 295, 300, 305, 306, 308, 315
evasion, 43, 56, 66, 110, 157, 269
exemption, 44, 58, 59, 71–73, 75, 78, 93, 271
expense, 58, 68, 69, 75, 80, 89
havens, 36, 304
incentives, 6, 15–16, 18, 64, 112, 183
income tax, 16, 39–47, 88–89,
indirect taxes, 110, 112, 122, 237–238, 260, 261, 266, 271–273, 278, 314
international taxation, 19, 35–47, 56, 99, 303
investment taxes, 49–53, 88–90, 307–317
liability, 7, 74, 189, 221, 229, 309, 315, 316
national tax, 47, 63, 68, 70, 118
National taxes, 5, 16, 47, 63, 68, 70, 118
place-of-taxation, 9, 10, 263, 264, 266–268, 279–283
planning, 5, 15, 43, 44, 62, 68, 83–103, 192

policy, 5–6, 21, 29, 30, 46, 51–53, 87, 112, 113, 116, 118, 119, 260, 262, 265, 285–306, 316
profit tax, 5, 16, 117
property, on, 16, 122, 127, 230
rate
   nominal rate, 42, 112
   progressive tax rates, 42, 53
   reduced tax rate, 58–61, 219
reform, 35–38, 63, 117, 118, 195
refund, 71, 74, 75
return, 7, 8, 276, 309, 312, 314
revenues, 12, 21, 32, 36, 113, 117, 119, 120, 126, 127, 189, 220, 255, 258, 260, 265, 270, 317
ruling, 36, 80
sparing, 27, 28, 46, 112, 237
status, 65
Tax Agreements, 19, 20
Tax Ombudsman, 16
tax on immovable property, 5, 264, 269
Tax Residency, 28–29, 70–71
tax-free zones, 269, 270, 283
taxpayer, 5–8, 12–15, 17, 18, 28, 29, 62, 64, 69, 70, 75, 76, 116, 173, 174, 177, 178, 184–195, 202, 236, 237, 254, 255, 257, 266, 267, 274–277, 279–282, 292, 308–317,
treaty
   tax treaty entitlement, 290
   treaty network, 10, 12, 13, 19, 22, 24, 57, 111–112, 187, 268, 314
turnover tax, 53
value added tax (VAT), 111, 118, 122, 127, 259–283, 298
   VAT refund, 9, 10, 268–270, 273, 282, 283
withholding tax (WHT), 11, 26–28, 60, 67, 71, 89, 95, 96, 99, 100, 101, 218–220, 225, 254, 255, 257, 297–299, 302, 303, 306

Index

Technical service, 98, 175, 208, 228
Thailand, 25-27, 41, 45, 46, 51-53, 56, 59, 61, 85, 87, 88, 90, 91, 106
Thin capitalization, 43, 301, 302
Threshold, 11, 25, 27, 28, 58, 205-207, 210, 219, 238, 239-253, 255, 269
Tie-breaker, 203-204, 239-253
Trade, 109, 152-162, 165-166
Training, 13, 16, 17, 30, 189, 191, 311
Transactional net margin method (TNMM), 172, 176
Transactions
  business transactions, 7-8, 182, 262, 297, 309
  financial transactions, 4, 12, 14, 171, 175-178, 192
Transfer Pricing Handbook recently released by the World Bank Group (World Bank Handbook), 170, 179, 183, 185
Transfer pricing
  documentation, 13, 15, 171, 184-187, 193, 194
Transparency, 6-, 112, 119, 167, 184, 188, 191, 195, 287, 288, 306, 309, 311, 312, 315, 317
Transport Corridor Europe-Caucasus-Asia (TRACECA), 154-155
Treaty Benefits, 58, 62-71, 77, 78, 81, 226
Treaty on the Eurasian Customs Union, 265
Treaty on the Eurasian Economic Union (EAEU), 221, 263, 266, 268, 270-282
Treaty Shopping, 63-65, 67, 226, 255
Turkey, 26, 32, 33, 41, 42, 45, 50-52, 59, 60, 86, 90, 106, 107, 129, 142, 145, 146, 150, 154, 156-158, 180, 183, 201, 242
Turkmenistan, 119, 129-131

U

Ukraine, 25, 26, 41, 45, 86, 106, 154, 180, 182, 201, 242, 271, 272
UN Economic and Social Commission for Asia and the Pacific (ESCAP), 146-148
UN Economic Commission for Europe (the UN Commission), 148-149
Uncertainty
  economic uncertainty, 4
  tax uncertainty, 5-7, 16, 179, 189, 310
Unfair treatment, 56
Unilateral, 8, 20, 27, 187-191, 290-292, 295-297, 299, 300, 304, 305
United Arab Emirates, 25-27, 41, 42, 45, 59, 60, 86, 106, 170, 173, 180, 183, 201, 208, 218, 221, 241
United Kingdom, 31-33, 91, 201, 297, 298, 316
United States, 31-33, 36, 75, 89, 129, 287, 288, 291, 295, 298, 299, 300, 304-306, 316
United Nation (UN)
  UN Handbook on MAP, 17
  UN Model, 201-253
  UN Transfer Pricing Manual, 13, 289
United Nations Practical Manual on Transfer Pricing for Developing Countries (UN Manual), 170, 179, 184
US Model Convention (US Model), 64
Uzbekistan, 117, 121-123

V

Value chain, 8, 15, 170, 286, 291, 292, 301, 308, 315
Value Contribution Apportionment Method (VCAM), 291, 292, 305
Value creation, 36, 171, 180, 291
Vietnam, 12, 26, 27, 41, 45, 46, 51, 59, 60, 87-90, 106, 175, 178, 180, 183, 201, 209, 242

W

WCO, 17
Western Asia, 107
World Bank, 41, 107, 108, 127, 128, 170, 179, 183, 185
WTO law, 9, 267

Y

Yantai Jerry Petroleum Company (Jerry Company), 74–75
Yemen, 28, 41, 44, 62, 86, 106, 110

Z

Zero-rated (free of VAT), 263
Zero-rating, 10, 268–270, 274–275, 277, 280–283